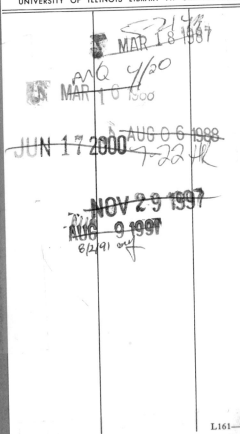

backgrounds and approaches to
Junior High
MUSIC

backgrounds and approaches to

Junior High

MUSIC

Hugo D. Marple

Texas Tech University

WM. C. BROWN COMPANY PUBLISHERS
Dubuque, Iowa

Consulting Editor • **FREDERICK W. WESTPHAL,** California State University, Sacramento

Printed in the United States of America

ISBN 0–697–03411–9

To My Mother

who for thirty-five years
taught, counseled, and encouraged
the young adolescent

Contents

TODAY AND TOMORROW

OVERVIEW AND SUMMARY

Teaching Plans

Preface

This book is written to assist those persons engaged in the teaching of the young adolescent: the prospective teacher, the newly assigned teacher, and the administrator. All of these areas present concerns and challenges which intersect.

For more than fifteen years, while working with student teachers, principals have remarked over and over again: "This young person knows music, no debate on that point. In fact, they may know more than needed. But the question I have would concern their understanding of the junior high school, the unique student it services, and the teacher's role in servicing both. How could they better understand the relationship of the school and its students?"

Teachers assigned to this middle school in our communities need to know more than music. Probably such a statement necessitates greater emphasis at this level than for the elementary or senior high schools.

This book attempts to assist the young teacher in examining the background of the junior high school, the forces which have tended to shape it in various communities, the responses made to it by the music profession, and recent forces and problems confronted by the schools and the teaching of music. Such a task requires analysis and synthesis, both of which may be in less detail than some may wish. Yet, the introduction to these ideas from the point of view of the music teacher becomes the concern of this book.

To those who would consider much of this material of little significance to the musician, let it be said that it has been too often the case that the music teacher student has not understood his role as an educator, has not comprehended his association with the general concepts of education, and has resisted or negated the focus of the school. It should be the conclusion of the reader that music is seriously considered as one of the learning processes rather than an ancillary concern. The teacher should make every attempt to prove this to be so.

Within this text, the administrator will find ways in which music fits into the aims, goals, and patterns of the educational system. Although a music book, it does not deal with the technical matter of music so much as the manner in which music can assist those programs in the middle school as defined by the school faculty or the administration.

How to Use This Book

Primarily, this book may be used as a text for classes which assist the young music teacher in preparing for the middle or junior high school. Procedures for the teaching of music used in various schools are described and examples given. The student may study, rewrite, plan from, or teach from these examples; or he may consider them a stimulus for those of his own devising. The teacher of such a class may use this text as a guide for planning and discussion, and then move into specific teaching devices considered most appropriate to himself and his class.

Or, this book could be used as auxillary reading to provide the student a background and understanding of the link between administrative goals and the role of music. It will also assist the student in understanding the history of the junior high school, and summarize personality characteristics of the students he will be teaching. As such it could be read quickly and used as a reference throughout a course.

This text will be helpful to the young person who has trained to be a teacher of elementary or high school music but whose assignment has been made to the middle school.

The administrator will find assistance in understanding the link between education and the field of music.

To those who have read the text, a special thanks, for they have aided me in thinking more clearly, in writing more understandably, and in including viewpoints which should not have been omitted.

Acknowledgments

Many administrators, teachers, and students indirectly provided direction for this text and to credit all of them would be impossible. However, for particular contributions, acknowledgment should be given:

To the library staff of Texas Tech University, who always assisted eagerly.

To the following students who made suggestions during the formative period: Chelcy Bowles, Brenda Bryant, Margaret Cavenaugh, Janeen Drew, Ellen Field, Bill Gammill, Billie Hill, Janet Jones, Diane Kesey, Al Klaerner, Danny Norris, Kathryn Prater, Clifford Rice, Mary Ann Roberson, Bill Snodgrass, Judy Storm, and Len Teague.

To those who supplied pictures for the text, including Mel Bay, Roger Bintz, Earl Cole, Charles Clark, Diane Clark, David Friend, Harriette Grieser, J. Albert Kindig, Betty Lou Larson, Homer Marple, Sylvia Perry, Wes Phillips, John Schaffer, Vaun Smith, and Tom Seymour.

To junior high teachers who, in a variety of ways, expressed professional concern for the project: Josephine Caruso, Yonkers, New York; Derenda Collins, Flint, Michigan; Louis Barrett, Mesa, Arizona; John Hinton, Tuscaloosa, Alabama; Frederick A. Johnson, Plainville, Connecticut; Sharon King, Shelbina, Missouri; Cornelia Madsen, American Fork, Utah; Sona D. Nocera, Potsdam, New York; Donald Roach, Tampa, Florida; Larry Sheets, Greenfield, Wisconsin; Bobby Siltman, Abilene, Texas; and Rita Znachinski, Richmond, Virginia.

To Carol Bolland and Rubyetta Cain, who read the text and made suggestions.

Introduction

This text was written for classes which are part of the music education requirements of your degree. This means that the purpose of this course is to help you prepare to teach music in the schools. In some ways it could assist you with private teaching as well.

Many of the classes which have preceded this one should form some kind of background for you. Even when you were in high school you were making some kinds of introductory steps for this class. But most particularly is this true of the theory classes, literature classes, applied music classes, and private studio work. This doesn't mean that every small bit of information that you acquired in these classes will be used directly, but, most assuredly, they will be used indirectly.

You have been asked to wait for this class until you are upperclassmen. Two reasons exist for this. First, it is hoped that you are mature enough to complete the work. You probably could have read and understood most of the material when you were younger, but the difference between understanding it superficially and understanding it with a goal of using it as a means of assisting young boys and girls is our real problem. Secondly, this class is placed in your junior or senior year so that you will be closer to the time when you will use the material in student teaching or on the job, and not far removed from your professional goal.

The material a person covers in a music education class often differs from the material of other music classes. For the most part, it emphasizes how to teach and how young people learn. In addition, it begins the process of being involved with people, the process of approaching people, working with them, and helping them understand some of the things you know. Consequently, for some of you this will be a change so great that you will fail in making this transition and will keep trying to make of this class something that it is not.

Secondly, this class is involved with reading the printed page. Some of you need improvement in reading and writing skills, and those who try to improve will find a lifetime benefit.

Thirdly, you will be dealing in organizational concepts that have not earlier been a part of your responsibility. These will seem different, and in some cases you will try to excuse your inability to deal with them by claiming nonrelevance.

Because you are busy people and this is a busy year, some of you will try to take this course but not become a part of it. This means that you will try to talk off the top of your head rather than read the assignments, or sometimes you will skim through the assignments rather than study them. Those who really wish to learn, will have to study the material and processes of the course. Just reading through the assignments and material will not be good enough. If all you do is read the material, you will be an observer and not a member of the class. You may fool the teacher in this process, but you won't fool yourself.

As you will learn, the teacher is a guide through various aspects of the field of music education. The teacher is not a know-it-all, and so together with you, the teacher is exploring and learning also.

Some assistance might be gained from the following points:

Join the Class

Just because you are in attendance doesn't mean that you have become a part of the group. Be sure to plug in when you come into class. Be alert to what is being done and said, and if you are not secure in what is being done, ask questions. Don't hesitate to speak out if you have a question, an illustration of a point, a different point of view. Your teacher welcomes your comments if they are valid and not random statements taking up time, not a repetition of the obvious or what has been stated by others.

Use Your Texts and Handouts

Read the assigned material before you come to class. Don't try to read material after the fact, even though it might fit your schedule better. Mark your material for main points, questions to ask in class, or instances where you disagree with the text or class discussion. Bring all of your material with you to class at all times even though you may not use it every class period. Although you may disagree, remember that what you read has been written by those who have much experience in the field.

The Text Isn't Everything

No one text can state everything and this one should not be your only source. Much is to be gained in reading from library sources. Music students are particularly slow about using the library, even though they are close by all day long. Get in the habit of going to the library, looking for other books on the subject, and spending some time in reading there. This will be a necessity if the books are on reserve. You will get much less from the course if you depend only upon the text and the daily class activities.

Don't Put Off Learning Until Tomorrow

Many of you have learned the processes involved in practicing, performing, and in lecture or theory classes. Because you are working in an area which many times seems subjective, don't pass it off lightly, only to find that when you have reached your student teaching you wish to know those items covered in this class. Learn the material as you proceed. You can assist yourself in this by—

underlining main points in texts and handouts;
outlining lectures and outside reading;
reading assigned material in text and library;
discussing in and out of class with your classmates;
participating in class and out of class as a professional teacher;
imagining you are a teacher in a school this semester.

If you are careful about these learning processes you will find that you will be much better prepared to become a student teacher and take your place in the school systems as a teacher of high quality.

Yesterday
and
Today

1

The Junior High School

The junior high school has been with us through our lifetime, and most of us are a product of the school. Therefore, it seems almost too obvious to mention that a majority of junior high schools includes grades seven, eight, and nine of our educational pattern. In a minority of situations, other grade divisions have been used, and, until recently, these also adopted the junior high label in order to designate their differentiation from upper or lower divisions.

Behind any particular division lies an underlying concept that points to benefits for breaking the educational process at that point. Although seldom verbalized, it is believed that the junior high school should be different in some ways from the elementary school on one hand and the secondary school on the other. Not all of the differences can be unique, yet differences somehow should exist.

Physical differences are most obvious to the junior high school student. In most elementary schools, students still are taught most of the day in a single room, and, with the exception of two or three special areas, the students are taught by a single grade teacher. In the junior high, this pattern is changed. Being older and more mature, boys and girls visit a different room for each of their various subjects.

In the junior high school, instructors teach their specialities rather than one teacher being involved with a large number and variety of subjects. This assists the teachers in the number of preparations necessary and places them in areas for which they are well trained.

In some junior highs, the students are asked to begin making class choices, introducing them to the elective process. Coming down to us from the collegiate curriculum, the elective process has now reached the junior high school for a few selected subjects. Required subjects are still in the majority, but, increasingly, students have choices as to additional courses which round out the school day and the student's schedule.

An emphasis is placed upon independent thinking in the junior high school. Much of the educational material of the elementary school is strictly informative, but with his entrance into the junior high school, the student is asked to make more decisions and begin the independent thinking process.

It is during these years that the student first comes into contact with school extra- or co-curricular organizations. Many of these organizations require of the student some out-of-school time which he must budget into his day, while others tend to introduce the student to weekend social life which is mostly school centered.

If the student is intelligent and near the top of his class in a particular subject, some junior high schools offer him the opportunity of joining an accelerated group. The accelerated group will move faster and more deeply into the subject. As complimentary as this first appears, this will not always produce situations which are the most satisfying. For example, a student in an honors group might earn a grade of HB (Honors B), but if the same student had not been involved with honors class, his grade most certainly would have been an A. The compensation of quality learning versus the grade is indeed a sophisticated decision for young minds.

Cast from the show "Those Were The Days," Parrish Junior High School. Salem, Oregon. Charles Graber, director.

Although the student is involved with educational pursuits which are at the junior high level, he also must be alert to making subject matter choices which could affect the high school or college career. Some parents and a few educational authorities consider it unfortunate that students must begin this early to make educational choices which contain long lasting ramifications.

It is within the confines of this school and this age bracket that the child is first introduced consistently to social pressures from his peer group. Not secure regarding his own judgments, this age finds security within the group; and the group, without too many communicative skills or too much effort, relays to its constituency behavior patterns which are often cruel to many, too childish for a few, and too mature for others. A discussion of the junior high school personality will be found in Chapter 9.

Early School Reorganization

Briefly, let us review some of the reasons for the existence of the junior high school.

At one time, the elementary school was the only pre-college training institution in our country. Students could graduate from the six years of elementary school and move directly into college. Since most colleges existed for the purpose of training clergy, higher education had a limited clientele. As knowledge increased and more generous support for education was available, the elementary school became pressured to concern itself more obviously with training for the business and commercial world. Consequently, one year, and later two years, were added to the elementary school. These were intended to review the material of the first six years and to assure elementary school graduates a working knowledge of those skills used in business.

At the same time, our colleges were broadening their course offerings and requesting more schooling as a prerequisite for entering students. This meant that the elementary school faced a demand on one hand for a greater intellectual emphasis, and on the other, for a more complete schooling which should be more practical, with no attention to college preparation. To satisfy these diverse goals, an upper school—a typically American free educational institution—developed.

Despite the fact that the high school was originated to service better those who did not wish a collegiate education, it was not long before this institution offered a college preparatory course. With such an emphasis, the higher school began to invade what had been the unique bailiwick of the so-called Latin grammar schools and the upper grades of the elementary schools. The resultant confusion caused concerned educators to face reorganization of the educational system.

Some sources credit the beginnings of the reorganization of American education to President Eliot of Harvard and his speech in 1888 before the National Education Association. Although interested in reorganization of the preparatory schools, three of his four main concerns, which follow, were directed to the colleges and the entering student:

1. Modify the college entrance requirements. (These were to be more consistent with public education but specifically to not require Latin, thus opening doors to students not interested in preparing for the ministry.)
2. Urge prospective college students to enroll in college as soon as possible. (This undoubtedly was directed to those who delayed college to take preparatory work in the free high schools or to work on farm or in business after elementary school.)
3. Shorten the college course from four to three years. (It should be noted that originally the bachelor's degree was a three-year program, and had been changed only somewhat earlier to four years.)
4. Persuade the schoolmen of the elementary and secondary schools to better sequence and standardize their courses.

Although voicing a general concern, his speech had only an indirect effect upon the immediate reorganization of the preparatory schools.

But reorganization was in the wind, and citizens as well as professional school personnel were concerned. The Department of Superintendence of the NEA in 1893 appointed a committee of fifteen to study elementary education. This group immediately raised the question of how to divide the elementary and high school years. The majority opinion refuted the then current proposition that the elementary school be shortened to six years, with six years for the high school. The committee feared this would only mean that students would leave the school system all the sooner. Some even recommended a nine-year elementary to offset the custom of eighth-grade termination.

The debate continued as to reorganization. Many meetings were held, many committees were appointed and reported; but continually college entrance requirements spoke loudly on the one hand, while how to teach elementary subjects and what was to be taught were loudly proclaimed on the other. It was around 1910 that most breakthroughs came, and the lower high school was organized in concerned cities of our country.

Muskegon Report

Not all arrangements were as we now organize them. For example, in Muskegon, Michigan, in 1904 Superintendent Joseph Frost wrote:

> The city is now organized with the tenth, eleventh, and twelfth grades grouped in the high school proper; the eighth and ninth in the high school annex; the seventh grades of the entire city congregated in one school for the departmental work; and the first six grades occupying ward buildings. This plan was adopted in order to give the children an opportunity to take work in manual training earlier than the ninth year. The departmental work in the seventh grade is conducted very much as the work in the high school, except that the students are kept under closer supervision, and we are able to give them special instruction along the lines of their interests. The present arrangement is very satisfactory and is a great improvement over the old plan. When it was adopted a large number of people petitioned the board of education to have the old eighth grade system reestablished. They said they would rather have their children have the old-fashioned eighth grade system than a complete high school course. They did not want their children sent to the high school at such an immature age. I felt that the opposition was due entirely to the fact that the parents did not like any system that was different from the one employed when they were in school. We have continued this plan and now I think that the community at large is entirely in sympathy with it. In fact, it keeps the children in school and makes the transition from the grades to the high school easier. It also gradually introduces the student to the freedom of the high school by having the close supervision in the seventh grade and less close when in the eighth and ninth, and greater freedom in the tenth, eleventh, and twelfth. I could cite many instances showing how boys have been kept in school by getting them properly started in their high school work in the eighth year.[1]

1. Frank Forest Bunker, *The Junior High School Movement—Its Beginnings* (Washington: W. F. Roberts Company, 1935), p. 222.

Reform Debate in Minneapolis

Many other systems across the country were following experimentation in the arrangement of the grades. In some cities, the schoolboard and faculty did not desire change but it was pushed as a result of citizens' committees. An example in point is the report which came from civic clubs of Minneapolis, Minnesota, in 1910, requesting that the board of education adopt the six-three-three plan for the city.[2] The superintendent of schools opposed the citizens' plan, and although he won the battle with the the board of education, he eventually lost the war. The reasons of the citizens' group for adopting the six-three-three plan instituting a junior high school were well spelled out in the request. Whenever needed, almost identical advantages for this approach to educational organization are given today.

Music in the Early Junior High School

Before the existence of the junior high school, music had been a part of the elementary school curriculum. Lowell Mason had introduced music into the Boston public schools in 1838 as a subject to be learned along with arithmetic and spelling, so that by the latter decades of the nineteenth century some music in the schools was almost unanimously accepted. Even though trained music teachers were rare, classroom teachers attended institutes and summer workshops to extend their ability in this new area. Some of the teachers learned to sing in church choirs or studied piano as proper preparation for feminine adulthood. Consequently, when the elementary school was extended to include grades seven and eight, music was taught by those classroom teachers, even though it was usually only singing. Daily, or at least three times a week, the upper grades would be expected to learn new songs and to comprehend the theory drills appropriate for these songs.

Educators had high hopes for the new lower high school. Students who would be going to college would have the upper high school to prepare themselves; students planning on terminating their education at the end of the ninth grade to enter the commercial world would be able to use three years for review, learning, and the exploration of areas to assist them in living in an adult society. With a three-year curriculum, students, more than ever before, could explore their individual interests, aptitudes, and capacities. In this school, students were bound not only to the bare essentials dictated by higher learning or the business world, but could be given an opportunity to explore a complete realm of materials to expand their appreciation and their aesthetic selves. Thus, music would of necessity be a valued offering in this new school.

But music should not give only a knowledge of chorus singing, such as found in the old upper grades of the elementary school; it should also teach the major

2. This statement appears at the end of the chapter.

forms of composition, the instruments of the band and orchestra, and the themes of great masterpieces. For some, the child study movement of the early twentieth century and the influence of psychology began to be realized in this new school. For others, the cultural and aesthetic values of the fine arts were needed to offset what could have been an overemphasis on the vocational and utilitarian values in other parts of the curriculum.

With these high ideals in mind, most of the junior high schools in the country, during the second decade of the twentieth century, required music for all three years of the junior high school in a program built to include singing, sight-reading skills, theory, and listening.

In his study of the junior high school, James Glass of the University of Chicago stated that a "majority of the junior high schools surveyed required music throughout the three years of the junior high school, giving a progressively organized and required course in music."[3] Out of a desire on the part of educators to give our future citizens the best we could offer, the general music program developed.

In a 1916 study by Aubrey Douglass,[4] 63 percent of the junior high schools required music in the seventh grade, 13 percent offered additional electives in music for seventh graders, and 24 percent of the seventh grades offered no music; 61 percent of the junior high schools required music in the eighth grade, 22 percent offered some electives in music for eighth graders, while only 17 percent offered no music in that grade; 40 percent of the junior high schools required music in the ninth grades, 40 percent offered electives in music for ninth graders, and 20 percent had no music for this grade.

In 1917 in our country, 791 junior high schools accepted a six-three-three organization. These schools, distributed throughout the United States, included 79 in Massachusetts, 51 in California, 47 in New York, 46 in Indiana, 40 in Iowa, 34 in Ohio, 31 in Utah, 29 in Illinois, 29 in North Dakota, and 25 in Oklahoma; some other states listed relatively few: Wisconsin 17, Texas 10, Tennessee 8, Connecticut 7, Kentucky 7, Maine 6, North Carolina 3, and Arizona 3. Despite this disparity, one can conclude that the junior high school movement was gaining in acceptance and, consequently, required music was gaining general acceptance.[5]

When new buildings were built for this new lower high school, music was not forgotten. For example, the Ben Blewett Junior High School of St. Louis described its facilities as including manual training shops, domestic science workrooms, a

3. James M. Glass, *Curriculum Practices in the Junior High School* (Chicago: University of Chicago Press, 1924), p. 50.

4. Aubrey Augustus Douglass, *The Junior High School* (Bloomington, Illinois: Public School Publishing Company, 1916), pp. 78–87.

5. John Briggs, *The Junior High School* (Boston: Houghton Mifflin Company, 1920), p. 65.

model apartment, a girls' gym, and a large lunchroom in the basement; the first floor contained offices, classrooms, laboratories, study hall, dressmaking rooms, and art rooms; the second floor contained classrooms, commercial rooms, laboratories, and the school library; the third floor contained classrooms, laboratories, music rooms, boys' gymnasium, and an auditorium seating 800. It should be noted that music was given more than one room and that it was located on the same floor as the auditorium.

In addition to the required class in music, electives were common in almost all schools. These electives included ensembles such as orchestra, band, choirs, and glee clubs, as well as special courses in music theory and appreciation.

Thus, the lower high school made an impact upon the educational scene, with a determination to broaden the offerings and effectiveness of education for the masses since it could be the termination of public education for large numbers of students. Where the junior high school existed during these early decades, one could be assured that a genuine attempt was made at giving the student a musical education befitting the goals of the school.

Uniqueness of the Junior High School

Placed between two other individual institutions of learning, the junior high school has the potential of becoming an educational organization with a special function. The adoption of elementary technics on one hand or of high school characteristics on the other often eclipse its potential. We have outgrown the concept that it shall be a terminal school for those interested in the trades or not interested in higher education. In most junior high schools it is not possible to begin the preparation of a vocational skill. Its specific responsibilities toward good citizenship have diminished, and guidance functions are often more obvious in the high school.

In some schools only one unique course exists for the junior high school: a study of vocations. Several subjects become terminal; these include reading (not remedial), spelling, general science, and general music. All students will continue to read and spell under guidance of several teachers, although not considered as formal subjects. Science in other forms will be required. Only music usually offers no required instruction for the student after junior high. Considering this, the music teacher then must ask himself the following question: "What is it that we should teach to the junior high school student which will enable him to take his place in society some seven years later and become an intelligent consumer of the art of music?" When faced honestly, this question helps us comprehend a situation wherein the general music class in the junior high school becomes the last opportunity for large segments of the population to gain some portion of a musical education.

Problems Facing Junior High Music

Several questions immediately come to mind: At what grade should music become elective and no longer compulsory? How long a period per day should music be taught? How many periods per week?

Administrators have wrestled with these questions for years. They have looked to the professional for guidance, but usually the junior high music teacher has been too busy with high school performance groups or elementary educational pursuits to give much assistance. Too often the junior high has had no music teacher except one borrowed from other levels, reminding us that colleges have been lax in specifically training personnel to teach in this most important school. More often than not, the administrators have held the line for music more than the teacher of music.

Since the elementary school also offers required music classes, administrators have looked there for an answer as to how much time should be allotted to music in grades seven, eight, or nine. Noting that music receives approximately 100 minutes per week in the lower school, they have attempted to assign a similar amount to the general music class at the junior high level. Since the junior high operates on periods which are nearly an hour in length, administrators have most often given the music teacher two periods per week for general music.

In considering the requirement question, administrators have usually taken the advice of the local music teachers and have required little or no music unless the local teacher has requested it. In addition, they have altered the requirement when new teachers came into the system. Consequently, no norm exists. At times, music teachers have traded away requirements in general music in order to spend more time with high school or elementary classroom teaching and/or preparation.

Recently administrators have requested that the music teachers of the country seriously address themselves to the problem of general music in the junior high school. Recently more administrators have returned to the position that some general music should be required for each level of the junior high school, with specialized ensembles being offered as electives in addition.

Considerable national attention now points toward upgrading the level of general music teaching in the junior high, including increased interest in some musical education for each year of the school. In order to be successful, teaching method and procedures must be improved and colleges must give consideration to the training of music education majors, with special emphases upon junior high general music.

LEARNING ACTIVITIES

1. As a class project, visit a junior high school.
   a. Discuss with the principal what he considers to be unique in his school as

compared to the elementary and senior high. Within the last few years, what has the junior high school adopted which was once the sole jurisdiction of the high school? Consider not only course offerings but also such items as year books, extra-class offerings, and social events as well.

   b. Discuss with the principal the dropout problem. Consider this problem not only from the standpoint of one school but the entire city; a region of the state; the state. How does the school attempt to cope with this problem?

   c. Discuss the mobility problem with the principal. What percentage of the student body did not attend elementary school in the city? Is this a typical figure for the state? What problems ensue as a result of mobility?

2. Of those reasons given by citizens of Minneapolis in 1910 for the establishment of a junior high school, how many are still valid today? Can you add others?

3. Should junior high schools offer two tracks of learning today? Why? If so, what should be the emphasis of the noncollegiate track? What learnings should be included?

A PLAN FOR THE REARRANGEMENT OF THE PUBLIC SCHOOL SYSTEM OF THE CITY OF MINNEAPOLIS

I. The Plan

A. We recommend that intermediate schools be established comprising the seventh, eighth and ninth grades. This involves—

   a. The housing of these grades together in buildings exclusively devoted to that purpose.

   b. The establishment of such administrative relations between each high school and the intermediate schools in its district as to avoid any hiatus between them, any duplication of work, or any lowering of the standard in such high school subjects as may continue to be offered in the ninth grade.

We would suggest that this end may be most surely attained by making each high school principal the supervisor of the intermediate schools in his district.

B. We further recommend that differentiation begin at the seventh grade, at least to the extent of offering two parallel courses, one containing much handwork and intensive training in practical branches, the other emphasizing preparation for high school.

C. Finally, we recommend that promotion in the intermediate schools be by subjects in place of by grades.

II. The Reasons

In our opinion the foregoing provisions are all equally essential to the success of the plan. The reasons for this conclusion are, in brief, as follows:

1. A thousand pupils drop out of school every year in Minneapolis during or at the end of the eighth grade, and another thousand during or at the end of the ninth grade; that is, before being in high school long enough to accomplish anything

worth while. If this combined army of 2,000 children who now leave school every year in Minneapolis prepared for doing nothing in particular could be given a unified course, under one roof, beginning at the seventh grade, the effect would be—(a) to hold in school through the ninth grade many of those who now leave during or at the end of the eighth grade; and (b) to give them all a far more valuable preparation for practical life than is now possible.

2. At about 12 years of age, which usually marks the beginning of adolescence, children begin to differ markedly in their tastes and capacity; and to attempt longer to teach them all everything offered in these grades, or which may profitably be offered there, is in our opinion a grievous waste of the pupils' time, the teachers' energy, and the people's money.

3. In the face of these growing differences between pupils, to compel them to repeat subjects which they have mastered, merely because they have failed in other subjects in the same grade, is to cultivate apathy and distaste for school.

4. A large percentage of those who leave school during the eighth and ninth years are boys, and it is well known that many of these now lack interest and energy in school work. We believe that such changes as are recommended would tend to hold their interest and increase their energy during these years. However, if interest in school work is once aroused many who would otherwise drop out at the first opportunity are likely to continue through the entire high school course.

5. By concentrating the work of these three grades in relatively few centers, yet so placed as to be within walking distance for children 12 to 15 years of age, it would be possible to provide assembly halls, gymnasiums, and ample facilities for handwork of all kinds. Such rooms and facilities are imperatively needed for children in these grades, yet cannot be provided on an adequate scale for all buildings except at prohibitive cost.

6. By such concentration it would also be possible to equalize classes, avoiding both very large and very small sections. In this way the efficiency of the work could be notably increased.

7. By concentration of these grades it would likewise be possible to have teachers devote themselves to whatever line of work they can do best, thus reducing the pressure on teachers of improving the quality of their work.

8. By separating the larger from the smaller children the problem of discipline would be materially simplified, since the methods suited to one age are not suited to another. In this way the principals would be freed from many needless annoyances and enabled more effectively to supervise the work of teaching.

9. It is impossible, and it would be undesirable if possible, to train boys of 12 to 15 or 16 years of age for definite trades; but it is possible and highly desirable to give them such general training of the hand and eye as shall enable them readily to adapt themselves to the requirements of whatever occupation they finally enter. This we regard as one of the most important ends to be obtained by the provisions of a unified course under one roof for grades 7, 8, and 9.

10. Finally, the plan proposed would in our opinion make for economy as well as efficiency.

If the intermediate schools should render schoolwork not only more effective but also so much more attractive as to hold in school many who now drop out and thus increase the number of children to be educated, we have full confidence that the people of Minneapolis would rejoice in the fact and consider money so spent well spent.

Respectfully submitted,

E. V. Robinson, Chairman

ADDITIONAL READINGS AND BIBLIOGRAPHY

BEATTIE, JOHN W. *Music in the Junior High School.* New York: Silver Burdett Company, 1930. (chaps. 1, 2, 3, & 7)

BILLET, ROY OREN. *Teaching in the Junior and Senior High School.* Dubuque, Iowa: Wm. C. Brown Company Publishers, 1963. (chaps. 1–3)

BRIGGS, JOHN. *The Junior High School.* Boston: Houghton Mifflin Company, 1920. (chaps. 1, 2, 3, 4, & 5)

BUNKER, FRANK FOREST. *The Junior High School Movement—Its Beginnings.* Washington, D. C.: W. F. Roberts, 1935. (chaps. 2, 4, & 5)

DOUGLASS, AUBREY A. *The Junior High School.* Bloomington, Illinois: Public School Publishing Co., 1916.

GLASS, JAMES M. *Curriculum Practices in the Junior High School.* Chicago: University of Chicago Press, 1924. (chaps. 2, 3, & 5)

GRUHN, WILLIAM THEODORE. *The Modern Junior High School.* New York: The Ronald Press Company, 1956. (chaps. 1, 2, 3, 4, & 7)

NOAR, GERTRUDE. *The Junior High School, Today and Tomorrow.* Englewood Cliffs, New Jersey: Prentice-Hall, Inc., 1961. (chap. 1)

VAN TIL, WILLIAM. *Modern Education for the Junior High School Years.* Indianapolis: The Bobbs-Merrill Co., Inc., 1967. (chaps. 1–5).

NOTE: Parenthetical numbers at the end of the bibliographic listings indicate those chapters which appear most pertinent. In some cases, where the book is small or where the complete book seems appropriate, "all" is used to indicate that the entire book could be beneficial. A few listings carry no numbers when that book or reference does not divide easily into chapters or only scattered portions are relevant.

2

General Music

General music is the phrase used most often to define music in the junior high school. This same phrase should be used to describe music in the elementary school, as well, since these programs have similar goals and may have some processes in common. As explained later in this chapter, one cannot comprehend junior high general music satisfactorily without considering the nature of the music program in the elementary school from which the students come.

Definitions

To be definitive about the word *general,* consider that it implies (*a*) what is not particular, or (*b*) that which affects the whole.

(*a*) We should understand *not particular* to mean that the area of music studied is broad and all encompassing, not limited to or emphasizing one or a few areas. All facets of music should be included and equally emphasized.

(*b*) If it *affects the whole,* one assumes this to mean the "whole child," or the whole of the educational system. The term whole child, although earning some abuse in recent years, indicates a concern for the mental, physical, and psychological aspects of any one personality and would indicate that music taught would benefit and/or develop these areas in an obvious manner. If the term *whole* refers to the educational system, then we should expect music to be taught for every child, in every grade, in every room. In no way should general music in the elementary or junior high schools be a restrictive subject for a few talented people.

In another regard, the word *general* points to that which is prevalent among the majority, or is not limited to a special group. Therefore, if general music exists in the elementary school, it in no way should be limited to grades four, five, and six while omitting grades one, two, or three. The same must be true of the junior high: a strict definition of general music would indicate it as being not only for one grade but for the entire school of grades seven, eight, and nine. Elementary and junior high school music, then, become for all students a broad-based subject which includes all aspects of music.[1]

In thinking about general music for the junior high school we should consider not only what we as teachers want to teach in grades seven, eight, and nine, but more importantly, what the child needs in relation to his past musical experiences. To assist in the recognition and understanding of this past and to prepare for our work in general music in the junior high school, one should be cognizant of two considerations of the general school music program: scope or extent and sequence and level.

Scope or Extent

One common approach in defining the scope or extent of general music lists five areas which comprise its base and consequently prescribe a general music program. Without equal emphasis on these areas, the program loses its generalness, tends more toward a restrictive or limited offering, and seriously affects the music program of the junior high school. Although often verbalized in different ways, they are most easily remembered if listed as:

> singing
> rhythm
> music reading
> listening
> creativity

Do not think of these as being in preferential order. All take their turn at being of major importance, which is to say that over a given period of time all become more important, or of lesser importance, and thus equal.

---

1. Music in the junior high schools should not be taught in a specialized manner even though it is often referred to as a "specialized subject." To be more precise, when we are teaching music in the elementary or junior high school we are not solely teaching theory, we are not studying only the works of one composer, nor are we involved just with the music of the baroque or the romantic period. We are doing all of this and much more. To say it in another way, this does not mean that a class is so lacking in content that some theory is not taught in the general music class; that one does not discuss a work of Bach if it is appropriate; or that stylistic periods are not studied if that material needs to be covered for a valid presentation.

It is particularly important for the college student to understand the distinction between general music being not specialized in one sense, while still containing detail. This distinction must be clear since college students become too used to considering public school music classes in terms of the detail and specialization of their own college music subjects and ensembles.

All of these together can equal what we call music appreciation and/or music learning:

> rhythm
> creativity ⎫
> listening ⎬ music appreciation
> singing ⎭ and/or
> music reading music learning

When an elementary music teacher prepares her work for any given grade in the elementary school she is continually cognizant of these musical learnings. She doesn't make these obvious by saying, "Now, boys and girls, today we are going to stress area number two; we are going to emphasize rhythm." Quite the reverse; the use of these areas may be so subtle or so smoothly connected to one another as to be recognizable only to an experienced observer. A good elementary music program will envelop and be defined by these areas, and in the lower grades, all five of them should receive equal emphasis almost every day. In the upper elementary grades and junior high, one might employ them in less even percentages on a given day, to be followed by a reversal at the next class meeting. But all of these should be taught with equality to qualify as general music.

General music class involved in creative activity, Merton Williams Junior High School. Hilton, New York. Marcia Bannister, teacher.

Some music teachers—probably more than is suspected—avoid the teaching of one or more of these areas. They omit them, I suspect, not only because of preference but because of ignorance in knowing what to do or how to make them effective. The principal, the students, and usually the parents, are not aware of these omissions, but in such situations the teacher cheats the children. Such imbalance later affects the junior high music classes.

Sequence and Level

A second consideration which should concern us is sequence and level. As teachers of junior high music we should understand normal pupil development in music to assist us in defining the progress point of our students and their learning needs.

Boys and girls usually do not enter junior high school with equal skills or backgrounds in music. The reasons for this are several, including—

> different music teachers,
> different elementary schools,
> differing interests in music,
> instrumental music experiences for some.

Despite obvious differences leading to immediate concerns or problems, the junior high teacher is expected to teach music to a heterogeneous group of young people. Understanding the sequence of learning in the music program and the most obvious level for this learning will assist the junior high teacher in prescribing music activities which will be attractive and interesting because of a correct learning climate. Many problems of a disciplinary and educational nature are propagated by a failure on the part of the junior high teacher to understand sequence and level.

Sequential learning has been attempted for years. Recently the teaching machine in educational circles and the computer in the business and scientific world have reawakened our interest in sequential learning. These tools impress us with the fact that what we once thought of as satisfactory sequential learning procedures were actually faulty or too loosely connected. Some students learned despite the gaps in the process, but others were not keeping pace because of these omissions.

In the field of junior high music, where unequal skills present more difficulties than in elementary classrooms, the understanding of sequence becomes even more important.

Closely allied with sequence is level, meaning an understanding of the position on the learning scale or a recognition of what has been learned and what remains to be learned considering age, experience, and maturity. Music teachers are prone to conceive of level through their experience with the maturing personality rather than through norms established for particular students in junior high general music. Problems and frustrations surely ensue. Being of major importance, sequence and level will be discussed further in Chapter 3.

An understanding of sequence culminates in a recognition of the skills that could be acquired by a junior high student through six years of good elementary music teaching. Although idealistic for some systems or completely unrealistic in other situations, these understandings act as a goal or determinant of standards for the junior high teacher.

LEARNING ACTIVITIES

1. To assist you in understanding this sequence and the skills which develop, study two or more elementary music series from first through sixth grades, keeping the five areas of development constantly in mind. As you work, make a list of skills to be learned during each grade.
2. What should a sixth grade student bring with him to junior high? Recently, after such a survey, my students prepared the following list of skills which an entering junior high student should have learned through previous study. How does your list compare to this one?

   By the end of the sixth grade, a student should—

   a. recognize major, minor, and pentatonic by sound and understand their technical and musical differences;
   b. recognize the I, IV, and V^7 chords by sound, and be able to spell them in simple keys;
   c. recognize half and complete cadences by sound and appearance;
   d. differentiate between homophonic and polyphonic by sound and appearance;
   e. identify 2/4, 3/4, or compound rhythms by feel, and know what these signatures imply rhythmically;
   f. recognize the most used melodic skips by sight and sound;
   g. understand differences between simple and compound signatures;
   h. identify repetition and contrast in melody, rhythm, and phrases;
   i. know simple forms, and should have had experience in applying these formulae to written and aural music;
   j. be able to read and comprehend even, uneven, or syncopated rhythms;
   k. move rhythmically to express the mood of the music;
   l. know that music is made up of phrases which are alike or different and

that phrases not only combine to make sections which are alike or different, but affect the interpretation of the music;

m. recognize orchestral instruments alone and in combinations;

n. sing simple music in two and three parts by ear or from the printed page;

o. play a dictated melody on the bells or other simple instruments;

p. read common tone patterns and rhythm patterns from a score, understanding how the terms (1) step, (2) skip, (3) repeat apply to the pattern;

q. know the commonly used musical symbols, expressive markings, and musical terms, and be able to demonstrate some voice control aimed at expressive singing;

r. have an introduction to musical styles;

s. have a familiarity with folk dances from a variety of countries;

t. know the conducting patterns of simple meters and be able to use them in classroom experiences;

u. be able to create additional verses to a song, observing the poetic meter, or be capable of creating simple melody to given texts;

v. create instrumental introductions and codas; add a descant to song materials; or create rhythmic accompaniments, using simple instruments;

w. understand the principle of transposition and write some simple examples;

x. have developed an appreciation for music of each historical period and be familiar with a few major composers;

y. experience the singing of more than one language.

This list reminds us how much can be learned in elementary music; how thrilling the results of a good program must be to the children, the teacher and the parents; and how great the challenge is for good junior high school music.

3. Beginning in first grade and continuing on a grade basis through sixth, list the changes evidenced in one area of general music as planned by any one elementary music series.

4. Read through the learning list given above and compare your own personal musical learning at the end of sixth grade to our ideal; or, compare the learning of a younger brother or sister.

5. Examine a number of elementary series music books for grades five and six. With each, consider what the compilers had in mind for the five areas of general music.

6. Although this text deals with music for the junior high, why is the general music program of the elementary school a concern in these beginning chapters?

7. Discuss with a student friend majoring in elementary music how an elementary music program can be balanced in time and in concern.

8. Sing through one sixth-grade music book, remembering that sixth grade is part of the junior high school in many communities. With each song, list the two most obvious learning areas appropriate to the song.

ADDITIONAL READINGS AND BIBLIOGRAPHY

ANDREWS, FRANCES M., and COCKERILE, CLARA E. "General Music Classes in Secondary Schools" in *Your School Music Program*. Englewood Cliffs, New Jersey: Prentice-Hall, Inc., 1959.

HARTSELL, O. M. "Preparing the General Music Teacher" in *Perspectives in Music Education, Source Book III,* edited by Bonnie Kowall. Washington, D. C.: Music Educators National Conference, 1966.

HOFFER, CHARLES R. "The Junior High School General Music Class" in *Teaching Music in the Secondary Schools*. Belmont, California: Wadsworth Publishing Co., Inc., 1969.

ROE, PAUL F. "The General Music Class" in *Choral Music Education*. Englewood Cliffs, New Jersey: Prentice-Hall, Inc., 1970.

SUR, WILLIAM, and SCHULLER, CHARLES. "The General Music Class" in *Music Education for Teenagers*. New York: Harper & Row, Publishers, 1958.

3

Sequence and Level

Sequence and level were defined in the preceding chapter, but they deserve more of our attention than a passing definition. Many unrecognizable problems occur daily in teaching as a result of a poor understanding of these two learning properties.

Level concerns every junior high school teacher since it should be standard procedure in general music to ascertain where each student might be in the learning process for each facet of the music program. If all students came to the junior high school with the same elementary school musical experiences, the problem even then would not be solved. However, elementary musical experiences differ greatly. Although important for the elementary teacher of music, level designation becomes all the more critical in junior high school because it is within this age grouping that all social or educational problems of the preceding years finally make an obvious appearance, many times becoming acute.

Ascertaining level could imply an extensive testing program. However, there are no quick and easy objective tests which will assist the teacher in making equally quick and easy judgments concerning level. Some testing may be beneficial, but it is important that the teacher make daily subjective judgments about his class until such time when he believes with some confidence that he knows the level of the students for those capacities deemed necessary. This is but one reason why the junior high school music program should be planned as well or better than programs at other levels.

Once the appropriate level is ascertained, the teacher then can proceed to plan the musical learning processes which the class needs. With the usual wide variety of levels present in any one general music class, planning would appear to be a most frustrating, if not impossible, task. Teaching appears more simple if the teacher understands level in a narrow and limiting sense, in which one series of skills is purported to be satisfactory for a given grade or subject. The good or experienced teacher will understand level in its breadth along with various related and associative aspects.

One of the related aspects is sequence: the progressive step-by-step process through which material is best taught to a given student or group of students. This correctly implies that the sequence might not remain constant from one class to another, or that the sequence best suited for class procedure might not always be the best sequence for a given individual within the class. The teacher must make certain choices based upon experience, experimentation, knowledge of current level, and/or the personality of the class or person. This is not always the most easily solved educational problem. Even experienced teachers can misjudge a situation. Beginning teachers should understand the sequence process, work with it, and be justifiably concerned when lesson plans fail to define sequential learning procedures properly. Teachers should also recognize that failure to understand level and sequence will lead to daily problems which could mount to the critical point.

In the preceding chapter, a number of musical goals were considered for the student entering junior high music. A majority of the students in a good elementary school music program will attain most of these goals, but realistically speaking, not all students will attain each of them. More often than not, such failure will not be the fault of the student since these goals are not unusually difficult nor unrealistic for the average student in a concerned program. Individual differences will occur, and some students will enter the junior high school general music program below level. With poor sequencing, little or no progress will be made.

The teacher must recognize that any person can be taught at any level, and should be. We often have the mistaken idea that a student in the junior high school should be given junior high school learning situations even if he is not ready for them. Confusing social maturity with learning level is common. If necessary, begin teaching the junior high school student at the first-grade level. The difference in approach will center upon the manner (technic) of the teaching, the speed of the sequencing, and the maturity of material.

Consequently, a good junior high school teacher will know and understand level and sequencing so that he can make use of this in his daily work. Failure to do so, as we have said, will produce numerous problems which could be avoided.

On the following pages of this chapter you will find a level and sequence chart. This kind of chart could prove somewhat controversial. Teachers in the elementary school may consider some of these goals much too simple for the level suggested, while other teachers will consider them too difficult. The goal listed for each grade has been established as a norm for large numbers of students rather than considering any one school system or smaller group.

Use the chart by reading the material from left to right for any one skill. This gives not only level but an outline in sequencing. For example: if a class in junior high school has no musical experience with the term *cadence,* the chart assists you in quickly ascertaining that they are at the third-grade level with this particular concept. Further to the right, this column suggests how to assist the students in learning about, and working with, cadences to bring them to junior high school level.

Listing this idea as a third-grade concept should not deter any teacher from including it as part of a junior high school presentation. Because a concept can begin to be taught as early as third grade does not limit it, since it may be simple in origination and complex at maturity. Do not advise the students of their level, and be sure the material and vocabulary used are appropriate for the junior high school. The speed of the sequencing should depend upon the class, their readiness to comprehend the learning steps, and the materials used to assist in the learning.

LEARNING ACTIVITIES

Many young people in the junior high school are not at the accepted level in their musical learnings. This is true in schools where poor elementary music programs exist, or in schools which service areas of economic or cultural deprivation. Other young people in the junior high school may be only minimally below accepted levels in their musical learnings. The teacher should be familiar with a wide variety of learning levels in order to be prepared to diagnose the sequence of steps to promote efficient additional learning. When this analysis fails, learning usually falters.

1. On pages 24–35 you will find the sequence charts with part of the material missing from the columns for upper grades.
   a. For some items, the skills and concepts have been listed for grades one through four, but the fifth and sixth grade material is missing. Complete the teaching sequence one should use for the fifth and sixth grades. Use the appropriate music texts to assist you. Remember, many contemporary schools place the sixth grade in the adolescent school so that this activity becomes valid for us as teachers of these young people.
   b. For other items, you will discover that material has been included for all but the junior high school. Complete the junior high school columns for all pages, including those which you have just completed for the fifth and sixth grades.

   Satisfactory completion of these charts will assist you in understanding the young person and his musical needs better than most processes except weeks of teaching.

Learning Activities continue on page 35.

LEVEL AND SEQUENCE CHART

Skill and/or Concept	First and Second Grade	Third Grade
RHYTHM		
1. Move rhythmically to express mood of the music.	Simple bodily responses to rhythms.	Beginnings of creativity in movement directed by structure & mood.
2. Understand all simple rhythms.	Introduction of long and short sounds, lines, patterns to distinguish rhythms. Use of rhythm instruments to stress, create, distinguish various rhythms.	Reading, tapping & conducting of simple rhythms from printed material by name of note (quarter & eighth, etc.)
3. Conduct in simple meters with common patterns.	Using bodily movement without pattern to feel rhythm.	Introduction of bodily movement patterns to express rhythmic pulsation.
4. Identify 2/4, 3/4, 4/4 meters & common rhythms; within the context interpret their meaning musically.	Introduction to differentiation in feeling of 2 & 3 pulsations per measure.	Creating rhythms in two and three pulsations per measure. Simple dictation.
5. Identify repetition & contrast in melody, rhythm, and phrases.	Understand repetition and contrast of simple rhythmic patterns; later, similar approach for melody. Phrasing begun in 1st reading to beginnings of understanding form through repetition or change. Use of letters for descriptive purposes.	Further study of melody, rhythm, and phrasing as they relate to simple form. Continue use of letters.
6. Know and use compound signatures.	Compound signatures used in rote singing as two pulsation songs.	Identifying compound meter by ear and feel.

Fourth Grade	**Fifth and Sixth Grade**	**Junior High School**
Continue to move creatively with mood, rhythm, or form of music. Be able to follow simple directions for group activity.	Be able to follow complicated directions (national or historic dances) for group action and use motion as part of creative group responses.	
Reading, tapping & conducting of rhythms including quarters, eighths, halves, whole and dotted quarters.	Introduction to reading of compound rhythms and dotted eighth & sixteenth combinations.	
All simple patterns used by students as a means of assisting with musical understanding, rhythmic reading.	Continued use as before. Conducting of peers in original compositions & during singing.	
Reading & writing (creating) rhythms in these meters. Continued dictation.	Daily use of these meters in creative, rhythmic, reading, and singing activities.	
Introduction to repetition & contrast in standard forms.		
Introduction to reading of compound meters.		

Skill and/or Concept	*First and Second Grade*	*Third Grade*
RHYTHM (cont'd)		
7. Introduction to syncopation.	Rote singing of syncopation.	Rote singing of syncopation.
SINGING		
1. Sing & know a large number of appropriate songs of many types (patriotic, folk, rote, reading, etc.)	Introduction of rote materials appropriate to grade. 100% rote)	Review & introduction of rote & reading materials appropriate to grade (70–75% rote—25–30% reading)
2. Effectively use & develop range according to maturity.	Low treble voice, usually accompanied by possible narrow range. 1st grade: small B to C^2; 2nd grade voice should elevate and become more flexible. c^1 to d^2.	Range developing average c^1 to f^2.
3. Phrase and interpret song material.	Introduced to phrase through physical movement and breath points while singing. Introduce tempo and dynamics.	Recognize simple 2- or 3-part form. Continue to be expressive through dynamics and tempo.
4. Recognize and sing most melodic intervals. A concern for intonation.	Most diatonic intervals sung by rote, with emphasis upon seconds and thirds. Intervals shown by hand levels or pitch pictures.	Easy reading of simple scale and diatonic intervals. Rote singing on all diatonic intervals.
5. Sing multiple parts by ear and from notes.		
6. Differentiate between, recognize, & participate in homophonic & polyphonic music.	Introduction to rhythmic instrument accompaniment in contrasting rhythm to vocal line.	Contrast between unison and parts, unaccompanied and accompanied: vocal line vs. instrumental accompaniment (ostinatos and descants)

Fourth Grade	**Fifth and Sixth Grade**	**Junior High School**
Syncopation sung by rote and rhythmic reading.		
Review & introduction of rote & reading materials appropriate to grade. Introduction of rounds (40–60% rote—40–60% reading)		
Range average: c^1 to g^2.	Greatest range potential of elementary years. Small B^b to A^2 possible.	
Sing with adequate breath support. Stress contour of phrase.	Stress expressive singing in unison & parts, and how form affects interpretation.	
Singing chromatic changes leading to simple modulations or melodic alterations.	Understanding simple intervals by name & sound. Singing of any interval in melodic context. Stress correct intonation in part work.	
Introduction to rounds & canons.	Singing of 2-part songs. Introduction to 3-part singing in 6th grade. Creating an extra harmony part.	
Contrast between unison and parts, unaccompanied and accompanied: introduction to rounds.	Introduction to fugal or contrapuntal concepts. Simple part singing including descants, ostinatos, rounds, & canons.	

Skill and/or Concept	*First and Second Grade*	*Third Grade*
MUSIC READING		
1. Read notation from a score.	Introduction to letter and line notation in 1st grade. Introduction to standard notation in 2nd grade. Introduction to tonal patterns in 2nd grade.	Simple reading of rhythms & pitch. Continued use of tonal patterns.
2. Recognize commonly used musical symbols, expressive markings, & musical terms.	Introduction to basic music symbols in 2nd grade, such as lines & spaces, clef & signature, etc.	Introduction to additional symbols, including some expressive markings.
3. Read simple rhythms; understand meter signatures.	Introduction of longs & shorts to distinguish rhythms. Use of rhythm instruments to stress rhythm. Introduction to standard notation.	Reading of simple rhythms from printed material. Use of notation for creative work.
4. Read and play a melody on bells or other simple instrument; an accompaniment on autoharp.	Create rhythmic and melodic phrases on bells or simple rhythm instruments.	Simple reading of melodies & rhythms on bells.
5. Recognition of simple chords.		Harmony changes introduced as an aural concept in relation to autoharp.
6. Differentiate between homophonic and polyphonic.		Understand unison, parts, accompaniment, & simple score.
7. Identify repetition & contrast in melody, rhythm, & phrases.	Begin with simple rhythmic patterns in 1st grade; melody added in the 2nd. Phrasing begun in 1st, with the beginnings of understanding form through repetition or change.	Relate printed page to aural concepts previously heard.

Fourth Grade	**Fifth and Sixth Grade**	**Junior High School**

Continued reading at more advanced level; single-line score only.

Using all simple musical terms & expression symbols in performance & discussion of creative work.

Reading of rhythms using rhythmic syllables, involving quarters, eighths, halves, whole & dotted quarters.

Introduction to playing autoharp. Continue with more difficult melodies on bells. Introduction to recorder.

Spelling of chords introduced after playing on autoharp.

Introduction to fugal or contrapuntal concepts through simple part singing.

Introduction to repetition and contrast through written form.

Simple part singing reviewed. Additional reading of simple & contrapuntal music. Introduction to 3-part music.

Introduction of phrase rhythm and its formal aspects as a part of music reading.

Skill and/or Concept	*First and Second Grade*	*Third Grade*
MUSIC READING (cont'd)		
8. Recognize rounds, canons, aba, aabb, variations, & other forms.	Simple aba forms of 3 and/or 4 lines discussed & used in 2nd grade.	Continued use of letter names to distinguish simple forms.
9. Recognize major & minor scales and scalar concepts; relate to key signatures.	Begin hearing difference in major & minor sound, through rote song material.	Sing major scale from ladder or hand position. Sing various major tonal patterns.
LISTENING		
1. Recognize orchestral instruments singly and in combinations.	Begin to study tone color of all instruments. Hear high and low qualities.	Continued study of tone color of all instruments. Recognize and name by color & expressive ability.
2. Have a familiarity with folk music and folk dances of a variety of countries.	Folk songs as a part of listening material; sung as a part of rote song learning.	Folk music of several countries as an introduction to cultural ideas & social-science coordination.
3. Be familiar with a variety of composers & representative compositions.	Introduction to a few standard composers as related to appropriate literature for listening.	Further introduction to standard composers of well-known literature as appropriate to singing or listening material.
4. Have a growing knowledge of musical styles & large & small forms.	Introduction to simple forms. Ex: march, lullaby; phrases, same or different.	Introduction to styles of simple compositions. Ex: waltz, minuet, simple 3-part forms

Fourth Grade	**Fifth and Sixth Grade**	**Junior High School**
Introduction to round & canon through rote singing & reading.	Further use of round & canon. Use of larger aba & aabb forms. Introduction of variation form. Creative forms with instruments.	
Hear difference between major & minor song material & tonal patterns. Write major scales & use signatures.	Learn difference in major & minor scale construction. Learn difference by triadic study. Continued use of minor material. Recognize by sight.	
Introduction to families & color of instruments in combination.		
Continued use of folk music of many countries in song & recorded material and as an introduction to simple folk dances.		
Further study of standard composers & literature as appropriate to singing or listening material.		
Introduction to some larger forms & well-known compositions which exemplify them. Ex: suites & incidental music.		

Skill and/or Concept	*First and Second Grade*	*Third Grade*
LISTENING (cont'd)		
5. Hear accompaniments as well as melodic lines; recognize homophonic & polyphonic structures.	Aware of multiple sounds; identify simple characteristics of melody.	Aware of chord accompaniment and major or minor tonality. Emphasis upon tonal patterns.
6. Understand rhythm as a basis for melodic & harmonic movement.	Even & uneven rhythm. Hear rhythm of melody & pulsations. Aware of 2 & 3 feel.	Expand hearing of rhythmic relationships. Use rhythmic patterns as a basis for rhythm vocabulary.
CREATIVITY		
1. Move rhythmically to express mood of the music.	Simple bodily responses to simple rhythms. Introduction to creative rhythmic movement.	Creative movement based on mood & form of music.
2. Create rhythmic accompaniments on percussion or background instruments.	Choose appropriate percussive color accompaniment to selected song material where appropriate. Sensitive to a number of rhythmic patterns & use them in a creative manner.	Understand the role of simple rhythms & rhythmic patterns in repetitive accompaniments or backgrounds.
3. Play a melody on bells or other simple melodic instruments.	Create rhythmic & melodic patterns on bells. Contrast skip & step interval relationships.	Create simple melodies & rhythmic phrases on bells. Phrase structure emphasized as an understanding of form.

Fourth Grade	**Fifth and Sixth Grade**	**Junior High School**
Contrast between unison & parts, unaccompanied & accompanied; aware of type of accompaniment and simple chordal backgrounds. Recognize scale & chordal sequence in melodic line.	Introduction to fugal or contrapuntal concepts. Simple part singing; recognize common intervals & how compositions use them in song & recorded material.	
Expand rhythm complexities. Hear rhythm of phrase & form.	Hear phrase rhythm along with rhythm patterns as a part of form & expression.	
Continue to move creatively with mood of music. Be able to create simple movement in cooperation with others.	Be able to follow more complicated musical compositions in group movement response. Musical form receives greater attention as a guide.	
Begin to notate created rhythmic accompaniments to known melodies. Use autoharp. Use duple & simple meters.	Create multi-line rhythmic accompaniments to known melodies with correct notation & instrumentation. Use syncopation as well as most common patterns in simple & duple meters.	
Continue with more musical melodies on bells. Introduction to creative melodic phrases on recorder. Introduction to chord-line melodies.		

Skill and/or Concept	First and Second Grade	Third Grade
CREATIVITY (cont'd)		
4. Create musical phrases or compositions; use language as a creative tool.	Create original rhythmic phrases in terms of long and short sounds & symbols. Sing original 3- or 4-note cadences & answers to questions.	Create own melody for poem supplied by teacher. Text guides musical characteristics used.
5. Create descants or original harmony for melodic lines.	Create & evaluate simultaneous sounds and rhythms.	Create ostinati for songs.

Seventh-grade general music class, Wise Junior High School. Albion, New York. Earl S. Cole, instructor.

Fourth Grade	**Fifth and Sixth Grade**	**Junior High School**
Continue with creation of original tunes for verses or poems. Write original verses for songs.		
Choose harmony for known songs by creating an autoharp accompaniment.		

LEARNING ACTIVITIES continued

2. Pages 36–47 contain the completed chart. Compare the statements on these pages with those pages which you have completed for question 1.
3. Rethink your own musical background as you entered junior high school. On the completed chart, note where you were in the learning process of each skill or concept.
   a. After you have completed the chart and in order to assist you with efficient learning, review the chart pages to consider how a teacher would have to teach you.
   b. Compare your notes with other students of your class and discuss the teaching problems you may have discovered.
4. a. Compare two sixth-grade elementary music series texts. Do you notice differences of goals in any of the learnings found on the completed chart?
   b. Compare two seventh-grade, junior high music texts. What particular emphasis do you find for each? How do they differ? How are they similar in educational focus?
   c. Of the books compared in parts a. and b. of this question, which would you prefer for a sixth grade in an adolescent school? Which would you prefer for a seventh grade whose musical learnings are obviously below level? For a seventh grade whose learnings are almost at level?

LEVEL AND SEQUENCE CHART

Skill and/or Concept	First and Second Grade	Third Grade
RHYTHM		
1. Move rhythmically to express mood of the music.	Simple bodily responses to rhythms.	Beginnings of creativity in movement directed by structure & mood.
2. Understand all simple rhythms.	Introduction of long and short sounds, lines, patterns to distinguish rhythms. Use of rhythm instruments to stress, create, distinguish various rhythms.	Reading, tapping & conducting of simple rhythms from printed material by name of note (quarter & eighth, etc.)
3. Conduct in simple meters with common patterns.	Using bodily movement without pattern to feel rhythm.	Introduction of bodily movement patterns to express rhythmic pulsation.
4. Identify 2/4, 3/4, 4/4 meters & common rhythms; within the context interpret their meaning musically.	Introduction to differentiation in feeling of 2 & 3 pulsations per measure.	Creating rhythms in two and three pulsations per measure. Simple dictation.
5. Identify repetition & contrast in melody, rhythm, and phrases.	Understand repetition and contrast of simple rhythmic patterns; later, similar approach for melody. Phrasing begun in 1st reading to beginnings of understanding form through repetition or change. Use of letters for descriptive purposes.	Further study of melody, rhythm, and phrasing as they relate to simple form. Continue use of letters.
6. Know and use compound signatures.	Compound signatures used in rote singing as two pulsation songs.	Identifying compound meter by ear and feel.

Fourth Grade	**Fifth and Sixth Grade**	**Junior High School**
Continue to move creatively with mood, rhythm, or form of music. Be able to follow simple directions for group activity.	Be able to follow complicated directions (national or historic dances) for group action and use motion as part of creative group responses.	Be able to evaluate the mood of music, in terms of individual or group movement; follow complicated directions for group action and image group motion as part of creative group responses—to interpret form, rhythm, or aesthetic qualities of music.
Reading, tapping & conducting of rhythms including quarters, eighths, halves, whole and dotted quarters.	Introduction to reading of compound rhythms and dotted eighth & sixteenth combinations.	Further rhythmic reading to strengthen understanding of combinations of simple rhythms, and perfect rhythmic reading skills.
All simple patterns used by students as a means of assisting with musical understanding, rhythmic reading.	Continued use as before. Conducting of peers in original compositions & during singing.	Conduct peers, with an emphasis not only upon patterns but with some indication that the aesthetic style is understood.
Reading & writing (creating) rhythms in these meters. Continued dictation.	Daily use of these meters, in creative, rhythmic, reading, and singing activities.	Continued use of these meters as called for by materials. Study of alternating simple signatures and polyrhythmic ideas.
Introduction to repetition & contrast in standard forms.	Introduction of phrase rhythm and its formal aspects.	Study of standard compositions in regard to melodic repetition, rhythmic uses, and phrase units as a part of form and function as well as a part of aesthetic unity.
Introduction to reading of compound meters.	Study of rhythmic reading of compound meters.	Further use of compound meter in contrast with simple meters. Better understanding through listening, creative work, and rhythmic reading.

Skill and/or Concept	*First and Second Grade*	*Third Grade*
RHYTHM (cont'd)		
7. Introduction to syncopation.	Rote singing of syncopation.	Rote singing of syncopation.
SINGING		
1. Sing & know a large number of appropriate songs of many types (patriotic, folk, rote, reading, etc.)	Introduction of rote materials appropriate to grade. 100% rote)	Review & introduction of rote & reading materials appropriate to grade (70–75% rote—25–30% reading)
2. Effectively use & develop range according to maturity.	Low treble voice, usually accompanied by possible narrow range. 1st grade: small B to C²; 2nd grade voice should elevate and become more flexible. c¹ to d².	Range developing average c¹ to f².
3. Phrase and interpret song material.	Introduced to phrase through physical movement and breath points while singing. Introduce tempo and dynamics.	Recognize simple 2- or 3-part form. Continue to be expressive through dynamics and tempo.
4. Recognize and sing most melodic intervals. A concern for intonation.	Most diatonic intervals sung by rote, with emphasis upon seconds and thirds. Intervals shown by hand levels or pitch pictures.	Easy reading of simple scale and diatonic intervals. Rote singing on all diatonic intervals.
5. Sing multiple parts by ear and from notes.		
6. Differentiate between, recognize, & participate in homophonic & polyphonic music.	Introduction to rhythmic instrument accompaniment in contrasting rhythm to vocal line.	Contrast between unison and parts, unaccompanied and accompanied: vocal line vs. instrumental accompaniment (ostinatos and descants)

Fourth Grade	**Fifth and Sixth Grade**	**Junior High School**
Syncopation sung by rote and rhythmic reading.	Further rhythmic reading, study of syncopation.	Further use of syncopation as a rhythmic device but also as an historic and aesthetic one.
Review & introduction of rote & reading materials appropriate to grade. Introduction of rounds (40–60% rote—40–60% reading)	Review & introduction of rote and reading materials appropriate to grade. Introduction to part singing (5th: 40% rote, 60% reading; 6th: 20% rote, 80% reading)	Introduction of materials appropriate to maturity, interest, and skill in three & four parts. (5–10% rote—90–95% reading)
Range average: c^1 to g^2.	Greatest range potential of elementary years. Small B^b to A^2 possible.	Explain and correctly use the changing adolescent singing voice.
Sing with adequate breath support. Stress contour of phrase.	Stress expressive singing in unison & parts, and how form affects interpretation.	Show relation of unity, variety, rhythmic, melodic, and harmonic form to interpretation.
Singing chromatic changes leading to simple modulations or melodic alterations.	Understanding simple intervals by name & sound. Singing of any interval in melodic context. Stress correct intonation in part work.	Understanding the intervalic relationship of standard intervals, with a concern for intonation and chords.
Introduction to rounds & canons.	Singing of 2-part songs. Introduction to 3-part singing in 6th grade. Creating an extra harmony part.	Continue singing of 3 parts and introduction to 4-part singing. Continue creating harmony parts. Introduction to F-clef for all students. Creating harmony in parts simultaneously.
Contrast between unison and parts, unaccompanied and accompanied: introduction to rounds.	Introduction to fugal or contrapuntal concepts. Simple part singing including descants, ostinatos, rounds, & canons.	Polyphonic structure studied. Some polyphonic singing. Ready for polyphonic listening.

Skill and/or Concept	*First and Second Grade*	*Third Grade*
MUSIC READING		
1. Read notation from a score.	Introduction to letter and line notation in 1st grade. Introduction to standard notation in 2nd grade. Introduction to tonal patterns in 2nd grade.	Simple reading of rhythms & pitch. Continued use of tonal patterns.
2. Recognize commonly used musical symbols, expressive markings, & musical terms.	Introduction to basic music symbols in 2nd grade, such as lines & spaces, clef & signature, etc.	Introduction to additional symbols, including some expressive markings.
3. Read simple rhythms; understand meter signatures.	Introduction of longs & shorts to distinguish rhythms. Use of rhythm instruments to stress rhythm. Introduction to standard notation.	Reading of simple rhythms from printed material. Use of notation for creative work.
4. Read and play a melody on bells or other simple instrument; an accompaniment on autoharp.	Create rhythmic and melodic phrases on bells or simple rhythm instruments.	Simple reading of melodies & rhythms on bells.
5. Recognition of simple chords.		Harmony changes introduced as an aural concept in relation to autoharp.
6. Differentiate between homophonic and polyphonic.		Understand unison, parts, accompaniment, & simple score.
7. Identify repetition & contrast in melody, rhythm, & phrases.	Begin with simple rhythmic patterns in 1st grade; melody added in the 2nd. Phrasing begun in 1st, with the beginnings of understanding form through repetition or change.	Relate printed page to aural concepts previously heard.

Fourth Grade	**Fifth and Sixth Grade**	**Junior High School**
Continued reading at more advanced level; single-line score only.	Continued reading of more complicated rhythm, pitch & 2- & 3-part music. G clef only.	Continued reading of rhythms, melodic lines, & part music leading to adult score. Introduction of F-clef.
Using all simple musical terms & expression symbols in performance & discussion of creative work.	Use of all symbols as needed. More musical terms as needed.	Review of usual musical terms. Use in creative assignments.
Reading of rhythms using rhythmic syllables, involving quarters, eighths, halves, whole & dotted quarters.	Introduction of compound rhythms & the dotted eighth & sixteenth. Less common signatures introduced.	Further rhythmic reading to strengthen understanding and perfect common rhythm skills. Some irregular uses of rhythm.
Introduction to playing autoharp. Continue with more difficult melodies on bells. Introduction to recorder.	Continue use of autoharp. Continue use of recorder and bells through reading of music & creatively.	Use melodic instruments not only as a learning device for fundamentals, but as an expression of musical & artistic values. Read instrumental and percussion notation and simple scores. Guitar introduced.
Spelling of chords introduced after playing on autoharp.	I, IV, V^7 sequence introduced by creating written accompaniment with these chords. Read simple chords in block form.	Needs aural emphasis, through singing & recorded material. Read simple chords for guitar, piano, autoharp, or write for accompaniments.
Introduction to fugal or contrapuntal concepts through simple part singing.	Simple part singing reviewed. Additional reading of simple & contrapuntal music. Introduction to 3-part music.	Polyphonic structure studied. Some polyphonic singing. Ready for polyphonic listening.
Introduction to repetition and contrast through written form.	Introduction of phrase rhythm and its formal aspects as a part of music reading.	Study of standard compositions in regard to melodic repetition, rhythmic uses, & phrase units as a part of form & function; also a part of aesthetic unity.

Skill and/or Concept	**First and Second Grade**	**Third Grade**
MUSIC READING (cont'd)		
8. Recognize rounds, canons, aba, aabb, variations, & other forms.	Simple aba forms of 3 and/or 4 lines discussed & used in 2nd grade.	Continued use of letter names to distinguish simple forms.
9. Recognize major & minor scales and scalar concepts; relate to key signatures.	Begin hearing difference in major & minor sound, through rote song material.	Sing major scale from ladder or hand position. Sing various major tonal patterns.
LISTENING		
1. Recognize orchestral instruments singly and in combinations.	Begin to study tone color of all instruments. Hear high and low qualities.	Continued study of tone color of all instruments. Recognize and name by color & expressive ability.
2. Have a familiarity with folk music and folk dances of a variety of countries.	Folk songs as a part of listening material; sung as a part of rote song learning.	Folk music of several countries as an introduction to cultural ideas & social-science coordination.
3. Be familiar with a variety of composers & representative compositions.	Introduction to a few standard composers as related to appropriate literature for listening.	Further introduction to standard composers of well-known literature as appropriate to singing or listening material.
4. Have a growing knowledge of musical styles & large & small forms.	Introduction to simple forms. Ex: march, lullaby; phrases, same or different.	Introduction to styles of simple compositions. Ex: waltz, minuet, simple 3-part forms

Fourth Grade	**Fifth and Sixth Grade**	**Junior High School**
Introduction to round & canon through rote singing & reading.	Further use of round & canon. Use of larger aba & aabb forms. Introduction of variation form. Creative forms with instruments.	Further use and explanation of all forms as they apply to standard literatures as well as intermediate material.
Hear difference between major & minor song material & tonal patterns. Write major scales & use signatures.	Learn difference in major & minor scale construction. Learn difference by triadic study. Continued use of minor material. Recognize by sight.	Recognize major, minor, and pentatonic differences readily by aural and visual means; write & spell common scales easily. Consider aesthetic implications of scalar material.
Introduction to families & color of instruments in combination.	Introduction to the playing of instruments which provide intimate understanding of color of single instruments.	Emphasis upon instruments in groups & recognizing those which are performing at any given moment in combination; their expressive qualities stressed. Ethnic and regional instruments explored and studied.
Continued use of folk music of many countries in song & recorded material and as an introduction to simple folk dances.	Continued folk dance material & folk songs, particularly as they assist in the understanding of social studies in these grades.	Continued use of folk material particularly with an understanding of the role and history of folk music generally. Stress upon contemporary folk interests.
Further study of standard composers & literature as appropriate to singing or listening material.	Study of composers in relation to form & style; some emphasis upon biography & the geographic area from which they came.	Beginnings of detailed study of appropriate composers, with more emphasis upon style in relation to period than to biography.
Introduction to some larger forms & well-known compositions which exemplify them. Ex: suites & incidental music.	Introduction to styles using historical terms & references to denote differences. Introduction to rondo & variations.	Continued use of mature style & form concepts as witnessed in standard compositions. Contemporary forms contrasted to historical ones.

Skill and/or Concept	First and Second Grade	Third Grade
LISTENING (cont'd)		
5. Hear accompaniments as well as melodic lines; recognize homophonic & polyphonic structures.	Aware of multiple sounds; identify simple characteristics of melody.	Aware of chord accompaniment and major or minor tonality. Emphasis upon tonal patterns.
6. Understand rhythm as a basis for melodic & harmonic movement.	Even & uneven rhythm. Hear rhythm of melody & pulsations. Aware of 2 & 3 feel.	Expand hearing of rhythmic relationships. Use rhythmic patterns as a basis for rhythm vocabulary.
CREATIVITY		
1. Move rhythmically to express mood of the music.	Simple bodily responses to simple rhythms. Introduction to creative rhythmic movement.	Creative movement based on mood & form of music.
2. Create rhythmic accompaniments on percussion or background instruments.	Choose appropriate percussive color accompaniment to selected song material where appropriate. Sensitive to a number of rhythmic patterns & use them in a creative manner.	Understand the role of simple rhythms & rhythmic patterns in repetitive accompaniments or backgrounds.
3. Play a melody on bells or other simple melodic instruments.	Create rhythmic & melodic patterns on bells. Contrast skip & step interval relationships.	Create simple melodies & rhythmic phrases on bells. Phrase structure emphasized as an understanding of form.

Fourth Grade	**Fifth and Sixth Grade**	**Junior High School**
Contrast between unison & parts, unaccompanied & accompanied; aware of type of accompaniment and simple chordal backgrounds. Recognize scale & chordal sequence in melodic line.	Introduction to fugal or contrapuntal concepts. Simple part singing; recognize common intervals & how compositions use them in song & recorded material.	Polyphonic structure studied. Some polyphonic singing. Ready for polyphonic listening. Recognize chordal qualities in backgrounds. Study aesthetic organization of melodic line in relation to accompaniment.
Expand rhythm complexities. Hear rhythm of phrase & form.	Hear phrase rhythm along with rhythm patterns as a part of form & expression.	Hear & recognize polyrhythms. Hear rhythm as an aesthetic element.
Continue to move creatively with mood of music. Be able to create simple movement in cooperation with others.	Be able to follow more complicated musical compositions in group movement response. Musical form receives greater attention as a guide.	Be able to aesthetically evaluate rhythmic mood & movement of music. Understand appropriate movement & verbalize creative movement possibilities for complex musical forms.
Begin to notate created rhythmic accompaniments to known melodies. Use autoharp. Use duple & simple meters.	Create multi-line rhythmic accompaniments to known melodies with correct notation & instrumentation. Use syncopation as well as most common patterns in simple & duple meters.	Continue creative activities involving a wide range of accompanying instruments including percussion, guitar, piano, autoharp, & voice.
Continue with more musical melodies on bells. Introduction to creative melodic phrases on recorder. Introduction to chord-line melodies.	Continue use of recorder & bells as creative tools for accompaniments and melodies. Use in connection with beginning experiences on any orchestral instrument.	Stress expression of musical & artistic values in creative work. Improvisation on a variety of melodic instruments with accompaniment.

Rhythm

Learning 1: The average seventh-grade student becomes more self-conscious of personal movement because of his irregular growth patterns. Those students who feel self-sufficient with their body or who have little self-consciousness will be able to make additional use of the body to aid in the learning of music. The learning is more of a synthesis of previous ideas than an introduction of new ones.

Learning 2: A review to maintain skill in rhythmic reading sets the learning in order to secure a self-sufficient understanding.

Learning 3: A review of skills, with an emphasis upon developing some aesthetic depth to the meaning of conducting with simple patterns.

Learning 4: A review of common meters; in addition, a study of the rearrangement of pulsations as an exploration into twentieth century music.

Learning 5: A greater emphasis upon the listening and understanding of standard compositions than is possible in previous grades, it concerns the understanding of macro as well as micro rhythms.

Learning 6: A review aimed toward smoother performance and broader understanding; although more difficult than simple meters, compound rhythms are within the musical abilities of most adolescents.

Learning 7: Going beyond the uses of syncopation commonly found in the material of earlier grades, this exploration can make use of the seventh-grade series texts which include some of this material, but additional experiences should be gained through discussion, observation, and listening to music of several periods.

Rhythm Summary

Because of the maturity of the student, a greater emphasis should be placed upon the aesthetic aspects of music. For some students the body may be used to interpret music and assist with aesthetic and formal understandings. However, for the majority of students this will not be feasible. Most of the learnings in Rhythm are of a review nature, with some additional breadth to assist comprehension and/or later use. Two new goals predominate: a broader realization of the function of form through its rhythmic components of macro and micro rhythms; and a more complete knowledge of syncopation, not only as a trait of the popular idioms of the past century, but as a historic musical device.

Singing

Learning 1: The student explores new uses of singing skills built throughout previous grades, and material appropriate for his maturity level will attract his interest. Although the popular songs of the day have a great appeal, other material should be used to introduce the student to as wide a musical understanding and aesthetic base as possible. These could well include barbershop materials of earlier years, show tunes, choruses from operettas or operas, and choral standards from previous centuries. The skills required for singing three or four parts will tend to limit the choices for a given group.

Learning 2: The early adolescent years should be used to explore the maturing young voice, not only for the boy who will have the majority of the problems, but also for the girl who needs to realize that her additional fullness of sound is not a limitation of range. With this change comes accommodation on the part of both student and teacher to temporary imbalance of parts and to ranges which limit the material used.

Learning 3: Since the voice is more limited in range and facility than in earlier years, the junior high student needs to synthesize his understandings of interpretation and phrasing so that these skills will not become dormant through lack of use. An emphasis at this time will solidify understandings which will be used in great detail and with great skill in a short time.

Learning 4: Although his production may not be as skillful as the student may wish, he should synthesize his past knowledge of intervals to develop a more complete understanding of the function of the melodic line in relation to the chordal background. Intonation is often difficult to achieve but should be stressed in order to present the best production possible.

Learning 5: Part singing should be continued and expanded. The F-clef should be explored by all students.

Learning 6: Although some polyphonic singing should be a part of earlier grades, this experience should be expanded to explore simple polyphonic singing of various periods, with additional emphasis upon the aesthetic reasons for such writing.

Singing Summary

Although new learnings are built upon old, there is noticeable exploration in singing for the junior high school student. Most of all, he is accommodating to new physical growth patterns and what these mean to voice range, facility, and timbre as well as accommodating to the literature available to him. Musical literature must represent added maturity without superceding the student's emotional and psychological level; although production in singing may be difficult, his understanding of vocal musicianship could become more acute. More interesting and complex harmony will fascinate the student so that he will be attracted by chords of all types and by the intricacies of polyphonic music.

Music Reading

Learning 1: The student will review skills in music reading learned during earlier years, will tend to organize these into a more efficient production, and will explore the F-clef and its use in three- and four-part music.

Learning 2: Most of the expressive musical symbols and musical terms will have been introduced during previous years so that a review through continued use will improve the understanding of them.

Learning 3: Commonly used rhythm patterns will have been introduced in previous grades so that a review through additional rhythmic reading will solidify these learnings. Exploration will center about the more contemporary use of polyrhythms and macro-rhythms.

Learning 4: One goal of music education aims at enabling every student to play some musical instrument, however modestly. Thus, instruments are introduced at an early grade in the elementary school to help the student directly apply musical learnings to musical production. His first learnings come through easily handled and played rhythm instruments. Later, bells and autoharp are used. The recorder can be introduced in the fourth or fifth grade, but because of finger manipulation problems, it is advisable to wait until the junior high for the guitar. Standard wind, string, and percussion instruments should be introduced during the sixth or seventh grade, and these should be accompanied in the general music class by the study of different kinds of instrumental notational needs (C-clef and scores).

Learning 5: The reading of chord symbols is begun with the autoharp. When the student reaches junior high school these learnings are reviewed and extended so that he can use them satisfactorily with guitar and piano, and in writing accompaniments.

Learning 6: Mature polyphonic music should be explored so that the introduction received in earlier grades will culminate in a realization that the complex structures of music are aesthetically oriented.

Learning 7: Mostly a review of learnings introduced at an earlier time, the emphasis rests upon the repetition of various forms in major compositions and the manner of aesthetic unity.

Learning 8: A review of forms introduced earlier, with an attempt to gain better insight into the function of the form aesthetically.

Learning 9: Since the principles of scales have been introduced at an earlier age, the junior high student reviews these learnings to assure their understanding in more advanced material.

Music Reading Summary

Music reading consists not only of an interpretation of pitch and rhythm patterns but of an intelligent approach to a score, including the single-line material to a multi-line vocal or instrumental composition. Many of the skills learned in earlier years are used again to retain their efficiency. Some skills are extended to show additional uses or to assist the student in understanding those aesthetic goals which repetition, contrast, form, polyphony, or scalar concepts can initiate. Ex-

Student-directed theory drill, Merton Williams Junior High School. Hilton, New York.
Marcia Bannister, teacher.

plorations in music reading center about the F-clef and the use of instruments: the one aids the development of the mature voice; the other assists in accompaniments and provides a greater opportunity for expression of musical concepts and learnings.

Listening

Learning 1: Although instrumental colors and characteristics are studied in early years, continued work should emphasize their expressive qualities through larger forms and more complex media. Instruments of the world, particularly those not familiar to Western civilization, should be explored and heard, and their expressive qualities discussed.

Learning 2: The junior high student is atune with contemporary popular music. With its emphasis upon folk-type music, we are assured of an excellent opportunity to broadly explore folk music. This synthesis should combine the ideas of earlier learnings of folk song into a new understanding of the material heard regularly on TV and radio.

Learning 3: Earlier introductions to the works of great composers should culminate in junior high, with new insights into these men as creators within the limits of a period in history and its culture.

Learning 4: Listening should involve more mature concepts in form and style. Contemporary forms and styles should be explored and contrasted to historic ones. This synthesis should result in a realization of the continuity of artistic efforts.

Learning 5: The new importance placed upon singing and hearing harmonically should result in an increased emphasis upon listening and on hearing a total composition: its accompaniment as well as the melodic lines. Additional listening of polyphonic sounds should increase contrast, emphasizing the homophonic structures.

Learning 6: Again, a synthesis of learning concerning rhythm should bring the student to a deeper realization of the role of rhythm in compositions. Not only will it be a pulsing or driving characteristic, but an aesthetic element as well.

Listening Summary

Most listening studies center around a synthesis of ideas presented earlier, but now the student should understand them more completely because of his increased maturity. Instruments, folk characteristics, major compositions, styles and forms, accompaniments and accompanying structures, and rhythm should all be heard in new compositions with a deeper technical and aesthetic understanding than was possible before. Exploration should involve ethnic and national instruments from little-known areas of the world, a constant exploration of forms and styles as they interrelate with historical periods and cultures, and an introduction to the way in which rhythm and accompaniment act as a basis for expression and formal development.

Creativity

Learning 1: For many junior high school students, the understanding of creative movement possibilities is more feasible than the exact implementation. Such synthesis would tend to create the appropriate image of physical movement with music rather than the movement itself.

Learning 2: Reviewing the learnings of the past, the student can create appropriate backgrounds to compositions. The guitar and the piano are new instruments for exploration.

Learning 3: The melodic instruments learned throughout the elementary school may be used to further a creative melodic expression.

Learning 4: The creative work throughout earlier years should culminate in larger compositions, with greater finesse and technical facility expressed in an understanding of variety, unity, and climax.

Learning 5: The creation of backgrounds, accompaniments, and harmony for melodic lines should be more sophisticated. Various symbol systems should be used and understood.

Creativity Summary

Most of the creativity for the general music class will review earlier learnings and will attempt to synthesize these learnings into a more complete aesthetic understanding of the creative process, whether it involves musical characteristics (rhythm, melody, form), instruments, or movement.

ADDITIONAL READINGS AND BIBLIOGRAPHY

BRIGGS, LESLIE J. *Sequencing of Instruction in Relation to Hierarchies of Competence*. Pittsburgh, Pennsylvania: American Institute for Research, 1968.

CASWELL, HOLLIS, ed. *Providing Developmental Experiences for Young Children*. New York: Teachers College Press, Columbia University, 1952. (chaps. 5, 7, & 8)

DILLON, EDWARD; HEATH, EARL; and BIGGS, CARROLL. *Comprehensive Programming for Success in Learning*. Columbus, Ohio: Charles E. Merrill Publishing Company, 1970.

HERBERT, JOHN. *A System for Analyzing Lessons*. New York: Teachers College Press, Columbia University, 1967. (chaps. 2, 3, 6, & 7)

HILLSON, MAURIE and BONGO, JOSEPH. *Continuous Progress Education*. Palo Alto, California: Science Research Associates, 1971. (chaps. 1, 2, & 4)

JACKS, M. L. *Total Education, a Plea for Synthesis*. London: Routledge and Kegan Paul, Ltd., 1950. (chaps. 1 & 5)

KUNZELMANN, HAROLD, ed. *Precision Teaching*. Seattle: Special Child Publications, Inc., 1970. (chaps. 1 & 3)

MAGER, ROBERT F. *Preparing Instructional Objectives*. Palo Alto, California: Fearon Publishers, 1962. (chaps. 2 & 3)

POPHAM, W. JAMES. *Establishing Instructional Goals*. Englewood Cliffs, New Jersey: Prentice-Hall, Inc., 1970.

RUNKLE, ALETA, and ERIKSEN, MARY LeBow. *Music for Today's Boys and Girls, Sequential Learning Through the Grades*. Boston: Allyn & Bacon, Inc., 1966. (all)

Junior high students make a sound on sound tape recording.

4

The Pentad General Music Program

Previous chapters have developed the idea that all junior high school students should have an opportunity to participate in music, and for maximum success, the teacher must be alert to its proper sequencing and level. Chapters 4, 5, and 6 describe three standard and well-known teaching procedures for general music in junior schools. This chapter concerns the Pentad approach, a method designed to be similar to that used most often in elementary schools. For this reason it satisfies well those students who may need considerable experience in music or who desire a feeling of security through the continuation of educational processes. Since many intermediate schools now include the sixth grade, the Pentad program may be a consideration during the first year of this school.

The Pentad Program

The five musical activities involved in the teaching process of the Pentad program usually include singing, rhythmic emphasis, music reading, listening, and creativity. The progress made in each of these areas in the elementary school determines a level, so that by the time the young person begins seventh grade he should be advanced enough in each of these areas that good work in music should ensue.

The young people of junior high age should be singing well, in unison and parts, with each child understanding his own voice and the artistic possibilities of that voice in some relation to the artistic demands of the composition. Appropriately, advanced music should be a part of the regular singing program. The F-clef should be explored, and discussions of the voice change should be a part of the music class in order to assist each boy and girl in understanding his physical and musical development.

Although the student has had considerable study of rhythm during the first six years of his school life, he should continue his rhythmic study to provide a precise performance of more complicated rhythms as well as those simpler rhythms found almost daily in all kinds of music, and to achieve an appreciation for polyrhythms through listening.

The young person should continue his work with music reading to improve a skill which could benefit him greatly throughout the remainder of his life. Reading should involve part work as well as those clefs used for vocal and instrumental purposes.

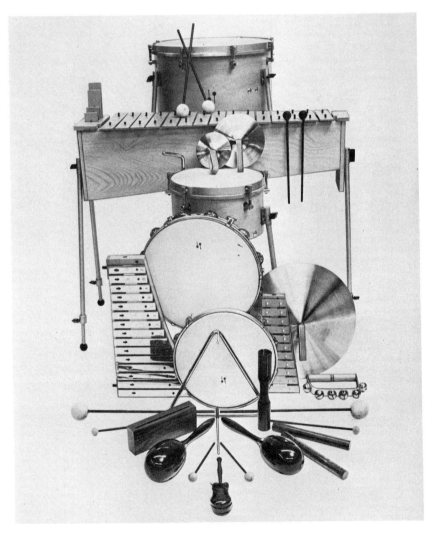

Instruments used in junior high music classrooms. Photo courtesy M. Hohner, Inc., Hicksville, New York.

The listening program should place considerable emphasis upon standard music compositions that the young person will hear throughout mature adult life. These selections should explore the various moods and aesthetic possibilities of music as well as the various forms of compositions.

Past experiences in a good music curriculum will have demonstrated to the student that creativity is an attractive facet of the program. Additional opportunity for creativity will lead to a more mature musical experience within the junior high school, including experience with a variety of instruments, compositions, lyrics and/or backgrounds.

Advantages

Several advantages exist for a continuation of teaching procedures used in elementary schools, and almost all are immediately obvious.

Sequel.   A continuous procedural program for elementary school through junior high produces logical sequels to earlier learning. By the end of the sixth grade, young people working through a good elementary music program achieve confidence and understanding that is most satisfying to themselves and the teacher. The performances and comprehensions are mature enough that musical learnings beyond the superficial can then be explored. This learning can be developed when the child moves into the seventh grade, provided the program is not disrupted. Changing the approach or permitting a discontinuance of the subject could mean a deterioration in an area that needed only some additional work to cement that learning for a lifetime of benefit. If the type of music program in the elementary school can be continued into the junior high school, the student will benefit in the higher school through the music offerings which gradually and logically become more advanced and mature.

Routine.   In the elementary school the child has established a learning routine through the procedures involving the concepts of music. A continuance of this approach assists the child in completing his learning in this field as directly as possible, while changes tend to disrupt the manner in which the child approaches the subject matter and could bring confusion in the understanding of concepts about the field.

Completeness.   A professional elementary school music program usually assures the child an approach to music that is all-inclusive as to basic concerns. Even though the young person progresses into the junior high school, he still needs a well-rounded study of music at this new level. Some junior high programs slight certain basic facets of the musical training, but this is less of a possibility with the program which continues the five activities of the elementary school.

Music series progression.   Another advantage for the continuous program involves the materials which are available. For years, the music series have published for the junior high school, music books which continued the concepts developed in the elementary school. Where teaching procedures centered around one series, the children witnessed a uniformity of approach usually not evident in other situations where no set plan was involved and no continuing music series provided appropriate materials.

Irregular backgrounds. Students in junior highs often include those with different economic or cultural backgrounds. Variances in their understanding and knowledge of music are evident in the ability of the young people. Continuing the teaching of music by the Pentad program from the elementary school permits the teacher to operate each phase of learning at a level befitting the background of proficiency of each area. Since the child is working within the framework of familiar learning areas, the teacher can plan her work to review, drill, or progress as the abilities of the students dictate.

Attention span. Even though the child has moved into the junior high, teachers notice that the attention span of the child is not particularly longer. Teaching by the Pentad program method permits the music teacher to move from phase to phase throughout the music period, keeping the interest of the child and still being assured that teaching and learning are taking place during the entire period. Since the usual junior high school period is almost double that of the average sixth grade music class, this can become a real factor in good learning and discipline.

Balance. Most importantly and related to the advantages just mentioned, this program assures the student of equality of learning in all phases of instruction. This balance may not be obtained in the same manner as it is in the lower elementary school, where the five activities should be presented each day; rather, in the junior high school, the balance may be achieved throughout the week or in a somewhat larger unit of time. An important part of the five-activity program is the symmetry achieved for the student.

Despite these advantages, however, there is much to be said against this teaching procedure. The following chapters in the text will acquaint you with some of the reasons why changes should exist in the music program as the student moves into the junior high school. Weigh these advantages against the disadvantages which will be discussed in subsequent chapters.

Sample Plans

Two sample lesson plans follow which place emphasis upon the Pentad program. These plans were originated for the junior high school music class by college students. (Learning Activities for the plans appear on page 84.)

TEACHING PLAN **A**   **Pentad Plan 1**
BALANCE AND
IRREGULAR BACKGROUNDS

I. Specific details
   A. Seventh grade—required class
   B. Mixed student group of thirty
   C. Fifty-minute period daily

II. Materials
   A. *Exploring Music,* 7, Holt, Rinehart and Winston
   B. Recordings: Ives, "Variations on America"
                  Satie, "Gymnopedie No. 1"
                  Blood, Sweat and Tears, "Gymnopedie"
   C. Rhythm instruments and bells

III. Goals
   A. Long range: (1) provide new musical experiences which build upon
                      previous ones;
                  (2) bring students to satisfactory level in three areas.
   B. Short range: increase knowledge and experiences in creativity, rhythm,
                   and form.

First Day

1. Read and discuss No. 1 and No. 2, Holt, page 55, on Theme and Variations.
   (15 minutes)
2. Divide the class into six groups of five each. Distribute various percussion instruments among the groups. (tambourine, claves, rhythm sticks, guiro, drums,
   triangle, etc.) Explain that each group is to create a composition using the
   given percussion instruments and any kind of body sound. The compositions
   are to be at least two minutes long. They are to be a theme and variations
   form. Compositions will be heard the following day; some type of notation
   might be necessary for an assist to memory. (10 minutes)
3. Sing a familiar song ("Sing Out,"* p. 62) with prepared rhythm accompaniments. (5 minutes)
   a. Practice patterns.
   b. Put patterns with song.

   * Song material follows this teaching plan.

4. Read the song "Einundswanzig"* on page 61 (Holt, page 91). (10 minutes)
   a. Read the rhythm of the song (rhythmic reading syllables).
   b. Speak the words in rhythm.
   c. Add steady beat with the feet with words in rhythm.
   d. Read pitches on "lu", or numbers; use hand to indicate pitch level.
   e. Sing with words.
5. Listen to Charles Ives' "Variations on America" (Holt, page 56). (8 minutes)
   a. Listen for melodic distinctions.
   b. Listen for rhythmic distinctions.

Second Day

1. Sing "Einundswanzig"* as a round. (5 minutes)
2. Performance: compositions created first day; students have now been composers, performers, and listeners. (15 minutes)
3. Discuss which compositions they like best and why, in relation to the questions on the bottom of page 54, Holt. Emphasize that form unifies music. Perhaps the compositions liked best will have a distinct and easily recognized form and can be titled. (10 minutes)
4. Continuation of explanation and demonstration of theme and variations (page 55, Holt, as a guide).
   a. Rhythmic variation: demonstrate with a drum; teacher demonstrates one variation of the pattern and then a student creates another.
   b. Melodic variation: using melody of "White Coral Bells," students and teacher demonstrate—
      (1) changing note values;
      (2) same note values but different pitches;
      (3) added notes to embellish;
      (4) change of meter;
      (5) change of style;
      (6) change of key or mode.

   * Song material follows this teaching plan.

5. Listen to Ives' "Variations on America," variation by variation, discussing each and using page 56, Holt, as a guide. (10 minutes)

Third Day

1. Sing "The Washing Machine,"* page 68 (Holt, page 51). (5 minutes)
2. Add a rhythmic accompaniment by students to "The Washing Machine." What sounds are appropriate? Why? (5 minutes)
3. Listen to "Gymnopedie No. 1" by Erik Satie in its original piano form. Listen to Blood, Sweat and Tears' variations on this theme. (10 minutes)
4. Discuss variants and instrumentation (Holt, page 57 as a guide). (5 minutes)
5. Create a set of variations on "Twinkle, Twinkle" or "Einundswanzig,"* using bells, rhythm instruments, and/or voices. (15 minutes)

MUSIC EXAMPLES FOR TEACHING PLAN A

Einundzwanzig

German Round

1.(Ein - und - zwan - zig, zwei- und - zwan - zig, drei und vier und funf und sechs-und -
{ Sie-ben-und - zwan - zig, acht- und - zwan - zig, neun - und - zwan - zig ___ und ___

zwan - zig.
dreis - sig.   O   lee   ay   lee   o,   o lee   ay   lee   o.

2. Einunddreissig . . .   6. Einundsiebzig . . .
3. Einundvierzig . . .   7. Einundachtzig . . .
4. Einundfünfzig . . .   8. Einundneunzig . . . und hundert
5. Einundsechzig . . .

From *Exploring Music Series* by Beth Landis, Book 7, copyright © 1971 by Holt, Rinehart and Winston, Inc. Used with permission of Holt, Rinehart and Winston, Inc.

* Song material follows this teaching plan.

Sing Out

Arr. by Hugo D. Marple

Words and Music
Steve, Paul, and Ralph Colwell

Top

Middle

Lower

Acc.

When you see the first sign of spring you want to sing out! When you

When you see the first sign of spring you want to sing out! When you

hear the fin - al school bell ring,_ you want to sing out!

hear the fin - al school bell ring,_ you want to sing out! You

F#7

It

take off for the swim-min' hole_ with your faith - ful dog and your fish - in' pole,_ It

Bm   G

seems that you can hear the whole world sing _ out!

seems that you can hear the whole world sing _ out!

D   F#7   Bm

Make a stand up land-ing from a free fall,— you want to sing out!

Make a stand up land-ing from a free fall,— you want to sing out!

When you hear the crack— of a home run bell— you want to sing out!

When you hear the crack— of a home run bell— you want to sing out!

When you see the surf-er shoot the curl,— from out in space you

it seems that you can hear the whole world sing out!

view the world, it seems that you can hear the whole world sing out!

D   F#7   Bm

For some it's Tchai - kov - sky's Con -

Loo Loo   Loo Loo

BM B7   E

cer - to; Loo Loo   Loo Loo Loo Loo Loo

Loo Loo   Loo Loo for oth - ers it's rhy - thm and blues

Loo Loo   Loo Loo   Loo Loo

A   D   G

66

67

(Good Old Electric) Washing Machine (circa 1943)

Words and Music
by John Hartford

1. Well, I sure__ do__ miss that good__ old e - lec - tric__
2. Well, I cry__ when I see that brand__ new__ au - to - mat - ic

wash - ing ma - chine, __ The one that
wash - ing ma - chine, __ 'Cause I'm sen-ti -

we ain't got__ 'round here no more, __ And I
men-tal for the old__ ma - chine still yet, __ 'Cause the

sure__ do__ miss that big round tub and them stomp - ing
old__ one__ real - ly looked like a real live wash - ing ma -

swing - ing sounds, __ And I miss them groov - y
chine, __ But the new one just looks

1.
pud - dles on the floor.

2.
more like a tel - e - vi - sion set.

TEACHING PLAN   **B**   **Pentad Plan 2**
                                                          BALANCE AND
                                                       SEQUEL LEARNING

I. Specific details
   A. Seventh grade, mixed class, integrated
   B. Compulsory class
   C. Monday, Wednesday, Friday—the eighth to tenth week of school
   D. Fifty-minute class periods

II. Materials
   A. *Exploring Music,* 7, Holt, Rinehart and Winston
      Growing with Music, 8, Prentice-Hall
   B. Recordings: Honegger, *Pacific 231*
                  Stravinsky, *Rite of Spring*
   C. Autoharp and rhythm instruments

III. Goals
   A. Long range: exposure to additional styles of music and discussion of
      their aesthetic differences.
   B. Short range: an emphasis on rhythm and style as understood through
      listening, creativity, and singing.

First Day

1. Read "All Who Sing,"* page 71 (Prentice-Hall, page 147). (10 minutes)
   a. Everyone read top line with numbers.
   b. Divide class; sing top line with scale line added.
   c. Sing with words.
2. Sing "Wade in the Water,"* page 72, in unison and parts (Holt, page 66).
   Discuss general interpretation of gospel music (Holt, pages 70–71). (10
   minutes)
3. Listen to "Dance of the Adolescents" from *Rite of Spring* by Stravinsky.
   a. Measure lines are merely organizational devices. Many times they are
   rhythmic aids (indicating points of emphasis or accents), but other times
   they are not.
   b. Play the following melodic lines from "Dance of the Adolescents" on bells
   or piano.

   * Song material follows this teaching plan.

c. Divide with measure lines, using a regular meter.
d. Divide the melodies according to musical accents.
e. Read the rhythms with rhythmic syllables.
f. Listen to the recording.
g. Discuss the rhythmic freedom and the use of rhythm to establish a mood through the frequent meter changes. (15 minutes)
4. Rhythmic study of "It'll be Comin' Round,"* page 75.
   a. Determine if it is simple or compound meter.
   b. Clap rhythms of each part.
   c. Speak the words in rhythm.
   d. Sight-read the melodic line.
   e. Add rhythm patterns; create rhythm patterns throughout.
   f. Discuss how the composer uses rhythm patterns to create a train rhythm effect and to assist the melodic line. (15 minutes)

Second Day

1. Read "Workin' on the Railway,"* page 77, emphasizing tonal independence and harmony.
   a. Half of class clap steady beat while others clap rhythm of melodic lines or parts.
   b. Sing melodic line with numbers.
   c. Sing with words.
   d. Compare the rhythmic feeling of "It'll be Comin' Round"* and "Workin' on the Railway."* Are they equally descriptive? (10 minutes)
2. Listen to Honegger's *Pacific 231*. Discuss the use of rhythm to describe. Contrast to the rhythm of "It'll be Comin' Round."* (15 minutes)
3. Study, play, and sing three different rhythmic accompaniments to "Wade in the Water"* corresponding to the three tempos and styles of interpretation (Afro-Cuban, gospel, and soul) (Holt, page 71). (15 minutes)
4. Sing "He's Going Away,"* page 79, (Prentice-Hall, page 93). Discuss the aesthetic and rhythmic differences between this folk song and "Wade in the Water."* (10 minutes) (Bells may be substituted for the oboe counter-melody if you wish.)

* Song material follows this teaching plan.

Third Day

1. Sing "Pizzicato Polka,"* page 81 (Prentice-Hall, page 134). (10 minutes)
   a. Discuss pizzicato technique on stringed instruments and how the rhythm of the music transferred this effect.
   b. Discuss use of sixteenths. Do sixteenths always produce the same effect? Is the effect established by the text?
2. Read "Yigdal,"* page 83.
   a. Read pitches with numbers.
   b. Discuss, key, appropriate dynamic levels, and style.
   c. How does this religious song differ from "Wade in the Water"?* (10 minutes)
3. Create pentatonic descants for "Wade in the Water."* (15 minutes)
4. Study "Sarakatsani Song,"* page 72 (Holt, page 141). (15 minutes)
   a. Read rhythmically; discuss the 7/8 meter.
   b. Add autoharp, finger cymbals, drums, and tambourine.
   c. Add melodic line.
   d. Discuss the rhythm in comparison to the Stravinsky recording heard earlier.

All Who Sing

Music by T. Goodban

From *Growing With Music Book 8* by Harry R. Wilson et al. © 1972 by Prentice-Hall, Inc., Englewood Cliffs, N.J. Reprinted by permission.

* Song material follows this teaching plan.

Sarakatsani Song

Greek Folk Song

Accompany "Sarakatsani Song" by playing the chords on the autoharp and these percussion patterns on classroom instruments.

Finger Cymbals

Tambourine — Repeat throughout

Drums — High / Low

Wade in the Water

Spiritual
Arr. B. A. R.

last time to Coda ⊕

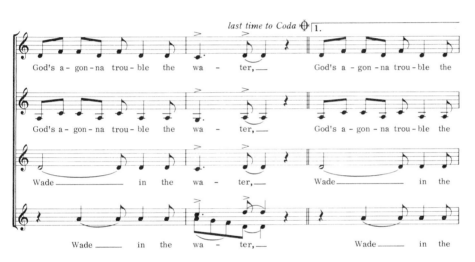

73

God's a-gon-na trou-ble the wa - ter,— God's a-gon-na trou-ble the wa - ter.

God's a-gon-na trou-ble the wa - ter,— God's a-gon-na trou-ble the wa - ter.

Wade ———— in the wa - ter,— Wade ———— in the wa - ter.

Wade ———— in the wa - ter,— Wade ———— in the wa - ter.

It'll be Comin' Round

Chu - Chu - Chu, Chu, Chu, Chu, Chu,Chu,Chu,Chu,Chu,Chu, Chu,Chu,Chu,Chu,Chu,Chu,

upper

It' - ll be com - in' a - round the moun - tain when it

lower

Loo

Piano

A

comes ———— Loo ————

Loo ———— It' - ll be com - in' a - round the moun - tain when it

simile

Verse 2: It'll be blowing the big, loud whistle when it comes

Verse 3: It'll be pulling a red caboose when it comes

Verse 4: It'll be tearing along the wide track when it comes

Workin' on the Railroad

Upper

Middle

Lower

Oh I've been work-in' on the rail - road All the live long day; Oh

Oh I've been work-in' on the rail - road All the live long day; Oh

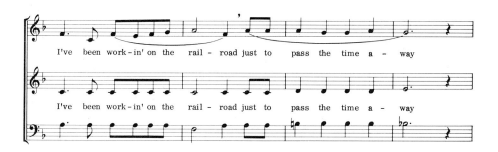

I've been work-in' on the rail - road just to pass the time a - way

I've been work-in' on the rail - road just to pass the time a - way

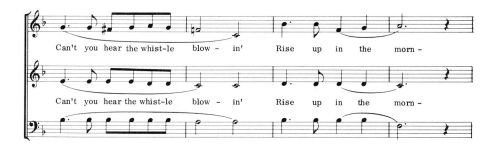

Can't you hear the whist-le blow - in' Rise up in the morn -

Can't you hear the whist-le blow - in' Rise up in the morn -

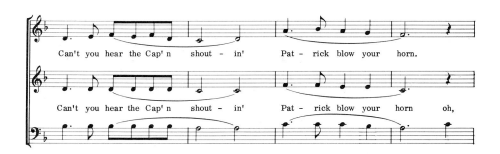

Can't you hear the Cap' n shout - in' Pat - rick blow your horn.

Can't you hear the Cap' n shout - in' Pat - rick blow your horn oh,

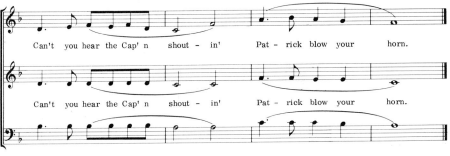

78

He's Goin' Away

American Mountain Song

1. I'm goin' a-way, For to stay a lit – tle while, But I'm
2. He's goin' a-way, For to stay a lit – tle while, But he's

com-in' back, If I go ten thou – sand miles. Oh, who will tie your
com-in' back, If he goes ten thou – sand miles. Oh, Pappy will tie my

Who will —
Pappy will —

shoes, _____ And who will glove your hands? _____ And who will kiss your ru-by
shoes, _____ And Mammy will glove my hands. _____ And you will kiss my ru-by

tie your shoes, And who will glove your hands,
tie my shoes, And Mammy will glove my hands,

Look a - way,
mp

Hm, _____

lips, When I am gone?
lips when you come back.

Look a - way,

Hm, _____

p

pp

O - ver Yan - dro.

Pizzicato Polka

Words by Marcella Bannon
Music by Johann Strauss

Pizzicato is a direction used in music written for strings. It indicates to the players that the strings are to be plucked rather than bowed. The "Pizzicato Polka" is played in this way throughout.

The word "plink" should be sung very crisply. The lowest voice part might sing this word throughout the entire performance.

From *Growing With Music Book 8* by Harry R. Wilson, Walter Ehret, Alice M. Snyder, Edward J. Hermann, and Albert A. Renna © 1966 by Prentice-Hall, Inc., Englewood Cliffs, N.J. Reprinted by permission.

Plink, plink, plink, plink, plink, plink, Comes this tune we sing to-day,

plink, plink, plink, plink, plink, Plink, plink, plink, plink, plink, plink,

plink. Plink, plink, plink, plin - ka, plin - ka, plink, plink, plin - ka, plin - ka,

plin - ka, plin - ka, plink, plink, plink, Plink, plink, plink, plin - ka, plin - ka,

1.
plink, plink, plin - ka, plin - ka, plin - ka, plin - ka, plink, plink, plink,

2.
plink, plink, plink, plink, plink, plink, plink, plink, plink, plink, plink.

82

Yigdal

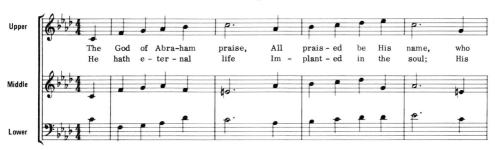

The God of Abra-ham praise, All prais-ed be His name, who
He hath e - ter - nal life Im - plant-ed in the soul; His

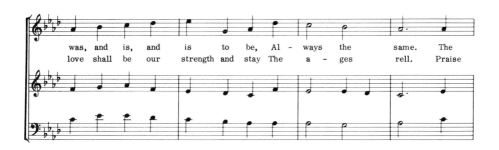

was, and is, and is to be, Al - ways the same. The
love shall be our strength and stay The a - ges rell. Praise

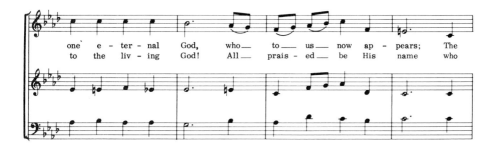

one e - ter - nal God, who to us now ap - pears; The
to the liv - ing God! All prais - ed be His name who

First, the Last be - yond all thought of time - less years.
was, and is, and is to be, For all the same.

1. Study the plans and ascertain for yourself the *level* of each activity. (See Chapter 2 as an assist.)
2. Decide where in the plan each of the musical activities is being used and what the overlap between the activities may be. Are all activities incorporated into each plan? Equally?
3. Teach one day of the material from one plan to your class. You will benefit by the preparation, and the class will better understand the phases of the plan.
4. Create a lesson plan for a seventh-grade general music class using the Pentad emphasis. Include the following six major divisions.
    a. State the specific details for the class:
       (1) required or elective;
       (2) all boys, all girls, or mixed;
       (3) daily meetings or specific days of the week;
       (4) length of class periods;
       (5) the exact grade level.
    b. List the teaching materials you will use.
       (1) List the names of the music series and the grade level of each.
       (2) List all recorded materials.
       (3) List other materials used by you or the students, including autoharps, recorders, rhythm instruments, etc.
    c. Define your goals in two ways.
       (1) Long-range goals should state those musical areas or concepts which you believe need improvement during a six-week period or semester. These are based upon recognized needs to further learning or bring students up to level.
       (2) Short-range goals should state specifically the musical details which will accomplish or practice the long-range goals—items which are specific for this lesson plan.
    d. The plan should be an outline, but state key words for each item.
       (1) create   (5) tap
       (2) sing   (6) read
       (3) play   (7) add
       (4) listen   (8) discuss
    e. Divide the plan into three or more days.
    f. Estimate the time necessary to teach each item.
       Beginning teachers often fail in the classroom by planning too long a lesson, but they usually fail because of too little lesson planning. No lesson will ever be taught twice at the same length, but you should try now to estimate the time of each item.

As a beginning teacher, you need practice in the planning of each activity. As you practice you will become more sensitive to planning each day's work so that it will have a beginning, a high point, and an end. Much like a good composition, a good lesson is planned, its form is sketched, and it is reevaluated. There are those who argue that such rigidity leads to sterile teaching, but this is no more correct than it is for the jazz artist who states clearly before an improvisation who will be responsible for it and how many choruses it will run before an ending is supplied by the group. Even though each item has been planned, the free improvisation of that item is a give-and-take between teacher and students.

5. Exchange lesson plans with your classmates. Read through the plan— marking the good points, the weak points, where you believe the planning is weak, and where the timing is in error.

6. Choose at least one member of your class to teach one day of his plan. This should provide experience for verbalizing in the classroom situation within a specific framework.

Suggested Materials

One of the aims of the early chapters in this book is to assist you in understanding the level of the student you will teach and how to move beyond his level. Part of the success of your teaching will relate in some way to your familiarity with materials for these grades. Not only as a part of developing a lesson plan but for learning for the future, become acquainted with the music series and the material found there. A list of these materials follows.

Sixth Grade Series

BERG, RICHARD C., et al. *Music for Young Americans,* 6. New York: American Book Co., 1960.

BOARDMAN, EUNICE, and LANDIS, BETH. *Exploring Music,* 6. New York: Holt, Rinehart and Winston, Inc., 1966, 1971.

CHOATE, ROBERT T., et al. "Mastering Music" from *New Dimensions in Music.* New York: American Book Co., 1970.

LEONHARD, CHARLES, et al. *Discovering Music Together,* 6. Chicago: Follett Publishing Company, 1966.

SUR, WILLIAM R., et al. *This is Music,* 6. Boston: Allyn & Bacon, Inc., 1962.

WATTERS, LORRAIN, et al. *The Magic of Music,* 6. Boston: Ginn and Co., 1968.

WILSON, HARRY ROBERT, et al. *Growing With Music,* 6. Englewood Cliffs, New Jersey: Prentice-Hall, Inc., 1963.

YOUNGBERG, HAROLD C., et al. *Making Music Your Own,* 6. Morristown, New Jersey: Silver Burdett Company, 1968.

Seventh Grade Series

CHOATE, ROBERT A., et al. "Sound, Beat and Feeling" from *New Dimensions in Music.* New York: American Book Co., 1970.

COOPER, IRVIN, et al. *Music in Our Life.* Morristown, New Jersey: Silver Burdett Company, 1959.

EISMAN, LAWRENCE, et al. *Making Music Your Own, 7.* Morristown, New Jersey: Silver Burdett Company, 1968.

ERNST, KARL, et al. *Birchard Music Series, 7.* Evanston, Illinois: Summy-Birchard Company.

LANDIS, BETH. *Exploring Music, 7.* New York: Holt, Rinehart and Winston, Inc., 1971.

LEONHARD, CHARLES, et al. *Discovering Music Together, 7.* Chicago: Follett Publishing Company, 1967.

WILSON, HARRY R., et al. *Growing With Music, 7.* Englewood Cliffs, New Jersey: Prentice-Hall, Inc., 1966.

Recordings

Exploring Music, 7. New York: Holt, Rinehart and Winston, Inc.

Making Music Your Own, 7. Morristown, New Jersey: Silver Burdett Company

Music Sounds Afar, 7. Chicago: Follett Publishing Company

Sound, Beat, and Feeling from *New Dimensions in Music.* New York: American Book Company

This is Music, 7. Boston: Allyn & Bacon, Inc.

ADDITIONAL READINGS AND BIBLIOGRAPHY

ANDREWS, FRANCES M., and COCKERILLE, CLARA E. "Elementary Music Teachers," "Why Do We Have Music in the Elementary Schools," and "Elementary School Music Content and Method" from *Your School Music Program.* Englewood Cliffs, New Jersey: Prentice-Hall, Inc., 1958.

BESSOM, MALCOLM E. "Organizing the Elementary Music Curriculum" from *Supervising the Successful School Music Program.* West Nyack, New York: Parker Publishing Company, 1969.

HERMANN, EDWARD J. *Supervising Music in the Elementary School.* Englewood Cliffs, New Jersey: Prentice-Hall, Inc., 1965. (chaps. 7 & 8)

MURSELL, JAMES L. *Music and the Classroom Teacher.* New York: Silver Burdett Co., 1951. (chaps. 4–8)

NYE, ROBERT E. *Music for Elementary School Children.* New York: Center for Applied Research in Education, Inc., 1963. (chap. 2)

NYE, ROBERT EVANS, and NYE, VERNICE TROUSDALE. *Music in the Elementary School.* Englewood Cliffs, New Jersey: Prentice-Hall, Inc. 1970.

RUNKLE, ALETA, and ERIKSEN, MARY LEBOW. *Music for Today's Boys and Girls.* Boston: Allyn & Bacon, 1966. (all)

SANDOR, FRIGYES, ed. *Musical Education in Hungary.* London: Boosey and Hawkes, 1969. (chaps. 2, 4, & 5)

SMITH, ROBERT B. *Music in the Child's Education.* New York: The Ronald Press Company, 1970. (all)

SQUIRE, RUSSEL N. *Introduction to Music Education.* New York: The Ronald Press Company, 1952. (chap. 3)

5

The Unit Plan

The unit plan has been popular in the junior high school for many years. Its characteristic qualities and strengths assure this position.

Elementary school teaching approaches subject matter in small portions so that the change of concentration comes regularly and consistently throughout the day. Considering the attention span of the student, this works to good advantage.

As the student reaches the junior high school age, the attention span lengthens. At the same time, student interests become broader while comprehension deepens, and inquisitiveness increases to question how subject matter of one class might possibly interrelate with that of another. Students are capable of study in greater detail, yet welcome an opportunity to cursorily survey breadth and interrelatedness before specialization or intense study is necessary or appropriate.

Music teachers reason similarly. During the elementary years the child is offered an attractive musical learning situation by weaving an educational pattern from a number of musical areas. Through proper sequencing, the child learns as he progresses through these various areas. Although they are not often presented in an interrelated manner, it is not necessary that they be if the emphasis centers primarily upon the learning of skills and concepts.

As a part of the general music class in the junior high school, additional maturity and inquisitiveness can assist the student in beginning to understand music as related to other fields of subject matter as well as other areas. The time is appropriate for the student to begin to understand music as a coordination of information rather than as a series of characteristics, skills, or performances that may or may not be related.

The unit plan offers this kind of opportunity to the student and the teacher, with the focus of attention not only upon music, but, in addition, on the opportunity to be involved with and study background and related materials.

Popular with junior high school students and teachers for years, the unit plan for teaching music has not been promoted recently by educational leaders as heretofore. In schools where it is well taught, the unit plan still is respected since it offers the student learning possibilities which are difficult to duplicate.

The Definition

The unit is as complete a study of one segment of music as is possible within the educational resources of the school, the teachers, and the students.

To define the scope of the unit, all information which has any relatedness to the subject chosen should be considered. This means that the teacher and the student should be encouraged to make use of all pertinent material in the school, community, and regional libraries—including recordings, films, film strips, musical materials, and references, as well as non-musical but associated items. The breadth of the subject is often determined by the extent of the resources available.

The following areas or subdivisions are usually represented in the unit plan.

Singing. Although a unit could be built involving no singing, that unit would not be as strong as if a good singing opportunity were offered. Most boys and girls enjoy singing, and if material is well chosen to fit the junior high school

Clapping rhythms, Merton Williams Junior High School. Hilton, New York. Marcia Banister, teacher.

voice, they usually participate readily. If the singing material is a part of an interesting unit, the songs could take on added meaning for the entire group and the singing will be all the more enthusiastic.

Rhythmic activities. Since rhythm is a basic element in music, the unit plan should include some rhythmic activity to be a complete learning experience. The activities used should be an outgrowth of the unit and always related directly to the singing, listening, or creative work.

Audiovisual. Most music classes in the junior high school make considerable use of the record player and the library of records owned by the school, the teacher, or the students. The unit plan provides an opportunity to involve the student in this wealth of material but at the same time not to make of it the sole focus of the teaching. The teacher's notebook from a music literature class can be a somnolent weapon in the junior high school. However, if through work on the unit, the class can be stimulated to include historical or developmental information of the recorded music, the learning will be all the more interesting and secure.

Many films or film clips, which are available through regional or rental libraries, can add much to the presentation.

Creative activities. Throughout the elementary school, young people have participated in creative tasks. Here is an opportunity to extend creative work to more advanced levels with considerable meaning. Creative activities centered around the unit topic most likely will seem more attractive to the young student.

Readings about music. The junior high school student should have acquired modest skills in reading and use of the library. In addition, his natural inquisitiveness should lead to a search for interesting and heretofore unknown facts about the unit, the latter supplying the impetus for the reading and the search. Once a little information is gleaned, the joy of discovery will often propel the student to further search.

Related activities. The unit plan gives ample opportunity for the student to become involved with activities which are only peripherally concerned with the study of music, but at the same time often carry an incentive or reward so strong that an interest in music is a by-product. Some such activities could be the compilation of a notebook, the planning and execution of a bulletin board, the drawing of appropriate maps, or the preparation of related artwork.

In addition, the unit plan offers two potential procedures which assist teachers and students in its scope and effectiveness:

Student planning. Students appreciate having some voice in those areas or concerns of music they would prefer to study. Many times this alone is an incentive for being involved, attracting the pupil who is not enthusiastic about music, or who feels insecure in his skills.

Interdisciplinary learnings. The unit plan offers the student an opportunity to begin to understand the interrelatedness of the art of music. This may take place within the music classroom; or the unit may inspire discussions, trips, lectures, or readings in other locales or involving other disciplines. When explored carefully, this facet of the program can provide worthwhile and interesting results.

Advantages

Those who have worked with the unit plan and found it an appealing method of teaching junior high school students list some or all of the following advantages.

All of the learning areas can be easily assimilated. Any good unit in junior high school music will include some instruction in all of the areas of music study, consequently enhancing the musical education of the student.

The subject matter of the unit can be appealing to students. Music teachers realize that large numbers of junior high school students profess little interest in classroom music. Of the many reasons for this lack of interest, this attitude can result from a poorly organized and poorly taught elementary program, or may be the result of an early elective program coming into conflict with certain required subjects. In working with the unit plan, the possibilities are so numerous that some cross-reference of interest can be found for almost everyone.

The students can assist in the planning. This advantage alone will carry the day in some classrooms. Students enjoy the opportunity of planning, and when they can suggest ideas and procedures, study becomes all the more interesting.

An assortment of activities can be associated with the unit. Junior high students bustle with high interest when confronted with classes including diverse procedures. When the program mirrors such variety, the interest of the student is kept at a high level.

Heterogeneity assists the poor performer. By their very nature, music classes which center upon performance skills eliminate the student with average to poor abilities or background. Students often resent the class and the teacher because of defensive feelings toward their own abilities. With the unit plan, the variety potential is so great and broadly based that every student can participate and resultantly be proud of his part within it.

The unit can include review as well as unexplored material. Because the unit cuts across grade and subject matter lines, it is often possible for the student to be involved in a review of musical rhythm, singing, theory, history, or other areas. In addition, the student sees this material in a new light since it is now within a different frame of reference; or the material is approached with an attitude that brings the student to a new realization of its value and perspective. In addition, the unit offers ample opportunity for search into new paths for new information which can be equally attractive.

Unequal emphasis can be an advantage. Although most units will contain all of the areas included in its definition, there is no effort on the part of the students or the teacher to be sure that all of these are taught every day, or that they are taught with any amount of emphasis. Where and when the unit prescribes the study of some material, it becomes appropriate and useful. If a given unit places less emphasis upon a particular facet of the music program, it will almost follow that another of the units studied later during the year will place considerable emphasis there. This unequal emphasis changes the routine in the classroom so that considerable variety ensues.

Student conductor, Merton Williams Junior High School. Hilton, New York. Marcia Bannister, teacher (at the piano).

The unit promotes a variety of classroom procedures. Since the unit often is best taught with a variety of activities incorporated in the classroom procedure simultaneously, it is possible to change the teaching procedure during the class period and from one class day to the next. Moving from singing, to a film, to library work within one day changes the pace of the classroom and keeps the interest high for the student. Field trips, which take the student out of the school building for a short time, are also a possibility. All of these learning processes are easily incorporated within the unit plan.

Disadvantages

Many teachers consider that the disadvantages outweigh the advantages.

Many units do not make use of the complete musical program for general music. Teachers often treat the unit plan as an opportunity to offer the student little in the field of music. Units can be devised with little exposure to the necessary basic emphases in music. Consequently, the music class is no longer general in scope, and the learning consists of a little outside reading followed by a film or listening lesson. The bulk of the learning is peripheral and far from the center of concern for a music program. The student is learning and doing, but much of it has little to do with music.

Limited experience prohibits good student planning. Although students can be involved with the planning of a unit, they often are not well enough grounded in music or educational possibilities to understand potentials or realizable goals. Many suggested topics are too broad and many deal with subject matter for which little or no material is available.

Non-musical activities give wrong impressions about the study of music. As he is learning about music and its relation to other fields, the student often is so active in many non-musical activities as to give the impression that music is a secondary study. Further, since the student who performs poorly is busy with non-musical facets of the unit, he comes to believe that he is doing acceptable work in an art of which he has little understanding and knowledge.

Much time is wasted. Since the unit makes it possible for the student to spend considerable time in the study of non-musical endeavors, he is wasting much time which could be used for his musical growth. Teacher-planned programs, with goals which are realistic and centered upon the music program, can offer all students more of a musical education.

Many of the activities of the unit plan are unnecessary. Special trips, notebooks, bulletin boards, library readings of related areas are often considered of little value by music teachers. Furthermore, it becomes difficult to test the child on what he has learned since much of it is non-musical.

Poor discipline could grow from the multi-activities of the students. Since the students are usually not involved in one single idea per day, the students fail to understand the personal discipline necessary to be a part of a good music program. In addition, poor classroom discipline may result.

Much planning is necessary. Since the unit, if well conceived and executed, requires much planning on the part of the teacher, music teachers often believe that it is not worth the effort involved. Using the library, finding appropriate singing material, ordering and using films, and conducting field trips are considerably more work than conducting a classroom song or activity of music.

Despite the disadvantages, and considering the advantages for the student, the unit plan is a valid approach to the teaching of music in the junior high school when well planned and executed.

Sample Unit Plans

One of the best methods of studying the unit is to read through a number of plans that have proved successful or of interest to a number of teachers. The following plans were developed in junior high music classes. How well do the units fit the characteristics discussed at the beginning of the chapter?

TEACHING PLAN	A	Unit Plan 1

THE POLKA, MAZURKA, AND WALTZ

I. Specific details
  A. Compulsory class, mixed group, seventh grade
  B. Fifty-minute period, two days per week

II. Materials
  A. *Making Music Your Own,* 6, Silver Burdett Company
     Discovering Music Together, 6, Follett Publishing Company
     Rhythms Today! Silver Burdett Company
     Magic of Music, 6, Ginn and Company
  B. Recordings: *Rhythms Today,* Record II, Silver Burdett Company
     Making Music Your Own, 6, Record I, Silver Burdett Company
  C. Additional teaching aids: maracas, tambourines, castanets, woodblocks
     The Waltz, Mosco Carner
     History of the Waltz, Edward Reeser

III. Goals
  A. Long range: to assist young people with an acquaintance of dance music from other times, and to introduce an understanding of how popular music becomes stylized and "classic."
  B. Short range: to acquaint the seventh-grade general music student with three basic European dances: the polka, mazurka, and waltz, and their background, and musical characteristics.

First Day

The Polka

1. Assist student AB in presenting a brief definition and demonstration of the polka. Use material from encyclopedia or other general source. (5 minutes)
2. Listen to parts of recorded orchestral compositions of "'Polka" from *The Bartered Bride,* Smetana, and "Polka" from *The Golden Age,* Shostakovich, with special attention to the rhythm. (5 minutes)
3. Study "The Polka" (Silver Burdett, page 4). (20 minutes)
   a. Play the composition. Assign four or eight band students to prepare this short selection before class. (Silver Burdett, page 224)
   b. Clap the polka rhythm as shown in the text, as the quartet plays a second verse.
   c. Sing and clap as the song is repeated again. Suggest that students snap their fingers for the sixteenth notes in order to give the "hopping" quality of the polka.
   d. Add the tambourine, using the rhythms given (Follett, page 63).
   e. Discuss "The Polka."
      (1) Review the term "sequence" and find examples in the song. Note that measures five-eight and nine-twelve are melodic sequences of measures one-four.
      (2) Consider key and meter.
      (3) Consider the repetition of the syncopation.
      (4) Discuss the chordal outlines in the refrain.
4. Play "Polka" (*Rhythms Today,* Silver Burdett, Record II, Side 1, Band 5). (20 minutes) Teach the basic steps (step-close-step in a gallop) and urge all to dance according to instructions on pages 110–111 of *Rhythms Today.*
5. Request four students to prepare a bulletin board emphasizing rhythm of sight lines or dance step outlines.
6. Library assignment: Read about and prepare a report on Frederic Chopin for the following class.

Second Day

The Mazurka

1. Review polka rhythm and steps. (5 minutes)
2. Relate rhythm of polka to Mondrian's *Rhythm in Straight Lines* (Ginn, page 38). Discuss how a painter creates rhythm through lines and color. (5 minutes)
3. Student BA presents a brief definition and demonstration of the mazurka. (5 minutes)

4. Piano student BB plays Chopin's "Mazurka in A minor, opus 68, number 2." Class should listen for typical mazurka rhythm. (5 minutes)
5. Discuss Chopin's life and the aesthetic characteristics of his music. (10 minutes)
6. Listen and dance to a Chopin mazurka (*Rhythms Today,* Silver Burdett Company, Record II, Side 2).
   a. Clap the mazurka rhythm as students listen.
   b. Encourage students to dance (Instructions in *Rhythms Today,* Silver Burdett, pages 146–149).
   c. Some students may wish to accompany the dances on maracas, tambourines, castanets, and woodblocks. (Refer to *Rhythms Today,* Silver Burdett, page 147.) (20 minutes)
7. Assignment: Prepare a pencil sketch emphasizing rhythm of line. Rhythm of the polka and mazurka should be recalled before work begins.

Third Day

The Mazurka and the Waltz

1. Review briefly the differences between the polka and mazurka. (5 minutes)
2. Sing and discuss "Mazurka" (Silver Burdett, page 12). (15 minutes)
   a. Consider meter and read rhythmically.
   b. Read pitches with numbers.
   c. Sing the song.
   d. Create a new verse for the song which describes the dance. Begin with the lines: "Let's go dancing, Let's go dancing."
3. Ask students to display their sketches. Discuss how some sketches fulfill the emphasis upon rhythm. (5 minutes)
4. Student CA presents a brief definition and description of the waltz. (5 minutes)
5. Discussion of the waltz. As a basis for class participation, show pictures on the opaque from *The Waltz* by Mosco Carner (pages 8, 9, 17) and from *The History of the Waltz* by Eduard Reeser (pages 19, 23, 38, 55). (10 minutes)
6. Sing "Ah, No My Dear Mama" (Silver Burdett, pages 8–9). (10 minutes)
   a. Use one girl for the mama, all girls for the daughters.
   b. Sing song in parts or refrain with entire class.
   c. Sing all four verses.
   d. Compare rhythm of this song to polka and mazurka rhythm.

Fourth Day

Waltz Continued, and Review

1. Review the definitions, rhythms, and dance steps of the polka, mazurka, and waltz. (5 minutes)

2. Student DA presents a brief biography of Johann Strauss, Jr., relating some of the musical highlights of his career. Show pictures of Strauss (*The Waltz,* Mosco Carner, page 47). (10 minutes)
3. Listen to Waltz I and Waltz II from *Die Fledermaus* by Johann Strauss, Jr. (20 minutes)
   a. Write themes on board (*This is Music,* 6, Allyn & Bacon, pages 164–165).
   b. Ask children to listen and note the themes.
   c. Discuss the aesthetic qualities of the waltz as compared to the polka and mazurka.
   d. Discuss the popularity of these dances with the people and their adoption by famous composers. Consider the songs sung in class and the recordings of Smetana, Shostakovich, Chopin, and Strauss which were heard.
4. Review through listening. (15 minutes)
   a. Ask the students to identify five compositions as either a polka, a mazurka, or a waltz.
   b. Have them write the basic rhythms of each.
   c. Use parts of—
      (1) third waltz from *Die Fledermaus* (recording for page 164 of *This is Music,* 6) Allyn & Bacon;
      (2) "Polka" from *The Bartered Bride*;
      (3) "Mazurka" from Silver Burdett, 6;
      (4) "Merry Widow Waltz" by Franz Lehar;
      (5) Chopin's "Mazurka in A minor, opus 68, number 2."

TEACHING PLAN   **B**   **Unit Plan 2**
MUSIC OF AMERICAN INDIANS

I. Specific details
   A. Compulsory, mixed, eighth-grade class of general music
   B. Second and third weeks of spring semester
   C. Two fifty-five-minute classes per week

II. Materials
   A. Songs: "The Omaha Tribal Prayer"
             "Love Song"
             "Song of the Wren"
             "Song of the Indian Coquet"
      Taken from *Indian Story and Song* by Alice C. Fletcher. Boston: Small Mahnard and Company, 1970.
   B. Recordings: *Songs of the Chippewa,* Library of Congress LC 1820–1LP

Pueblo, Toas, San Ildefonso, Zuni, Hopi, Library of Congress, AAFS
    L43

Songs from the Iroquois Longhouse, Library of Congress, AFS L6B

C. Additional teaching aids: Tape: "The Music of the American Indian"
    Audiovisual Library, City Public Schools Library

Indian Story and Song, Alice Fletcher. Boston: Small Mahnard and
    Company, 1970

Southwest Museum Papers, Number 10, Cheyenne and Arapaho Music.
    Frances Densmore

III. Goals

A. Long range: to introduce music of different aesthetics than that of West-
    ern civilization and to broaden the musical experiences in melody and
    rhythm.

B. Short range: to give the students a greater appreciation of the music of
    the American Indian; to give the students understanding of music as it
    plays a part in the everyday life of the American Indian; to give the
    students a knowledge of specific types of Indian songs and instruments
    through participation.

IV. Outline of musical study

A. Singing: sight-reading and detailed study of four songs

B. Rhythm activities: clapping rhythms, accompanying songs with rhythmic
    instruments

C. Creativity and related activities: creation of instruments, research for
    reports, and creation of bulletin board

D. Readings: readings and studying of various articles such as "Relation of
    Story and Song"

E. Interdisciplinary:

   1. American history class will study the forced migration of Indians
       from New York, Ohio, and Illinois into the open lands of the West.

   2. Art and physical education classes will study the pottery making,
       the weaving skills, and the dances of the Indian.

   3. The local library will feature exhibits of books, artworks, and
       artifacts of the Indian.

   4. Discussion in music class will emphasize the active roles of music
       and art forms in the lives of these American people.

First Day

1. Two students report on music in Indian life (reference material from school
   and city libraries). (15 minutes)

2. Listen to tape: "The Music of the American Indian" (audiovisual library, city public schools). (15 minutes)
3. Discussion of characteristics of Indian music. Reports and tape used as basis for discussion. (10 minutes)
4. Listen to two songs: "I am Going Away" (Songs of Chippewa, Library of Congress LC 1820–1 LP), "Taos War Dance" (*Folk Music of United States from the Pueblo, Taos, San Ildefonso, Zuni, and Hopi Tribes,* Library of Congress AAFS L43). Discuss briefly the musical elements of rhythm, instrumentation, intervals, and pitch. (10 minutes)
5. Assignment: Request four students to report on the background of one of the four songs to be learned in class on following days: "The Omaha Tribal Prayer," "Love Song," "Song of the Wren," "Song of the Indian Coquet."

Second Day

1. Listen to "Corn Song" and "Iroquois War Dance" (*Songs from the Iroquois Longhouse,* Library of Congress AFS L6B). Review the processes used to discuss musical elements during first day, and ask students to discuss these new songs from the standpoint of these elements. (10 minutes)
2. Distribute four songs to be studied.
   Report by student AA on "Omaha Tribal Prayer."
3. Sight-read "Omaha Tribal Prayer." Use neutral syllable. Teacher discusses pronunciation of words. Repeat song, using Indian words.
4. Presentation of report on "Love Song" by student AB. (5 minutes)
5. Sight-read song "Love Song." Clap rhythm of song; discuss rhythmic patterns; sing song, using English words.
6. Student AC and teacher present report on Indian musical instruments. Borrowed instruments and pictures are used. (10 minutes)
7. Sing "Love Song," using instruments. (5 minutes)
8. Assignment (one of the following)
   a. Make a modern version of an Indian rhythmic instrument and write a short paragraph describing its use.
   b. Write a report on one type of Indian song such as war songs, social songs, songs of the medicine man, etc. Material is available in school and/or city libraries. To be prepared for presentation in class.
   c. Make an attractive and informative display for the classroom bulletin board appropriate to the unit.
   All are due within one week.
9. Announce trip to city library (or museum) for a Friday afternoon.

Third Day

1. Review briefly the musical characteristics of Indian music. (5 minutes)
2. Sing and review "Omaha Tribal Prayer" and "Love Song." (5 minutes)
3. Read and discuss "The Relation of Story and Song in Indian Music" (*Indian Story and Song,* Fletcher). Associated with this, illustrate by playing the recording of "Zuni Rain Dance" (Library of Congress AAFS L43). (20 minutes)
4. Report from student BA on "Song of the Wren." (5 minutes)
5. Teacher explains pronunciation of language. (5 minutes)
6. Sing "Song of the Wren," using neutral syllables; then repeat, using Indian words.
7. Report by student BB on "Song of the Indian Coquet." (5 minutes)
8. Sing "Song of the Indian Coquet," using Indian words; repeat, using appropriate rhythmic instruments. (5 minutes)
9. Discussion of relationship of story of each song to the musical elements and expression of song. (5 minutes)
10. Reminder: projects are to be completed for next class period.

Fourth Day

1. Listen to "Hopi Version of Dixie" (Library of Congress AAFS L43). Have student discover the relationship with the familiar tune of "Dixie."
2. Compare and contrast the Hopi version with the original American folk melody. (10 minutes)
3. Sing and review the four Indian songs learned during the past three class periods. Students who have created rhythmic instruments may accompany the songs. (15 minutes)
4. Representative students may present reports on the types of Indian songs; those who prepared bulletin boards may describe the contents. (20 minutes)
5. Summary and general review and discussion of music in Indian culture, characteristics of Indian music, and Indian instruments. Contrast valid Indian music with that heard in movies and on TV.

TEACHING PLAN	**C**	**Unit Plan 3**

MUSIC OF THE
TWENTIETH CENTURY

I. Specific details
   A. Eighth grade, mixed class
   B. Compulsory class

C. Fifty-minute periods
D. Thirty boys and girls

II. Materials
   A. Music texts: *Growing With Music,* 8, Prentice-Hall
      Discovering Music Together, 8, Follett
      Making Music Your Own, 8, Silver Burdett
      Exploring Music, Junior Book—Holt, Rinehart and Winston
   B. Recordings: *Rite of Spring,* Stravinsky, Silver Burdett, 8, Record IV
      Piece for Tape Recorder, Ussachevsky, Silver Burdett, 8, Record IV
      Happy Birthday, Stravinsky, Holt, 1, Record 10
      Belshazzar's Feast, Walton, Holt, 8, Record I
   C. Additional teaching aids: bulletin boards display
      pictures of contemporary paintings and sculpture
      examples of contemporary poetry
      pictures from contemporary drama productions
      pictures of contemporary composers

III. Goals
   A. Long range: to work with and understand music of many periods; to build an appreciation for music of many styles.
   B. Short range: to gain an insight into twentieth-century music, its rhythm, harmony, melody, and uniqueness by means of examples, comparisons, and creativity.

First Day

1. Discussion by class after they read material on twentieth-century music (Follett, page 170; Holt, page 68–69; Silver Burdett, page 94). Main objectives of discussion: why it evolved, directions of development, musical characteristics, composers of the period. (20 minutes)
2. Listen to "Games of Rival Tribes" and "Procession of Sage" from *Rite of Spring,* Stravinsky (Silver Burdett, 8, Record IV) (Silver Burdett, 8, page 60).
3. Review points of first discussion in relation to compositions.
4. Listen to "Piece for Tape Recorder," Ussachevsky (Silver Burdett, 8, Record IV).
5. Compare to Stravinsky and previous discussions. (20 minutes)
6. Introduce song "Jabberwocky." (Follett, page 172)
   a. Use only melodic portion.
   b. Analyze rhythm as to similarities to and differences from previously learned material.

  c. Study melody by analyzing pitches which are used and their intervalic relationship.

  d. Sight-read melodic line. (10 minutes)

7. Assignment: for sixth day of unit

  a. There will be a varied collection of recordings of twentieth-century music in the listening center of the music room and school library. Students are to select one recording and use it as a basis for one of the following:

   (1) Create a 5-minute drama skit inspired by one selection of music (4 to 6 students).

   (2) Present an artwork inspired by a composition (individual students).

   (3) Compose music (individual students).

    (*a*) Tape environmental sounds, editing them to create a composition.

    (*b*) Create a composition, using only percussion instruments.

    (*c*) Create a song based upon a tone row for the class to sing.

  b. All projects should be presented to the class the sixth day of the unit.

  c. Concrete plans for each project should be submitted to the teacher by the third day of the unit for approval and suggestions, and so that a schedule may be arranged for the sixth day of class.

Second Day

Melody

1. Define and explore meaning of four characteristics of twentieth-century melody.

  a. Octave displacement (melodies not continuously in same octave). (10 minutes) Write displaced melodies for well-known tunes. Play these on piano, instruments, or bells. Can class hear and recognize melodies?

  Example

To what extent does the rhythm hold the melody into a recognizable state?

If played twice as fast, is it still as easily identified?

  Listen to "Happy Birthday," Stravinsky (Holt, I, Record 10)

  b. Inversion (turn melody upside down to create a new melody). (10 minutes) Write inverted melodies for well-known tunes. Play these on piano, instruments, or bells. Remember to consider steps and half-steps.

Example

c. Twelve-tone music (melodies and accompaniments created from all tones of the octave). (10 minutes)
Write a row and a melody from the row. Vary the rhythm.

Example

Listen to Suite, Opus 29, Schoenberg (*Theme and Variation* I) (Holt, 8, Record IV)

d. Atonality (melodies pulled out of a tonal center). (10 minutes)
Write atonal melodies from well-known tunes. Play these on piano, instruments, or bells. Try to sing some without accompaniments.

Example

2. Introduce song "What is a Much of a Which of a Wind." (Holt, page 194)
   a. Discuss poem and interpret it.
   b. Clap rhythm.
   c. Analyze melodic line.
   d. Work with sight-reading of melody.

Third Day

Rhythm

1. Define and explore twentieth-century rhythmic characteristics. (20 minutes)
   a. Irregular accents with regular meters

   b. Irregular accents with irregular meters

2. Write, speak on neutral syllables, clap, conduct, play exercises as the examples.
3. Listen to *Rite of Spring,* Stravinsky, and discuss in relation to the previous exercises. (15 minutes)
   a. "Dance of the Adolescents" (*Growing With Music,* Prentice-Hall, page 58).
   b. "Adoration of the Earth" (Prentice-Hall, pages 84 and 58).
4. Experiment with changing meter of familiar songs. (10 minutes)
5. Continue working on song "What is a Much of a Which of a Wind." (10 minutes)

Fourth Day

Harmony

1. Define and explore twentieth-century harmonic sounds (*Exploring Music,* Holt, page 77).

a. Cluster chords—experiment with clusters of sounds—
   (1) on the piano, within one octave;
   (2) on the piano, in spread position;
   (3) on instruments of like timbre (for example, all brass);
   (4) on instruments of unlike timbre;
   (5) on instruments, in spread octaves.

b. Compound thirds—experiment with ninth, eleventh, and thirteenth chords—
   (1) on piano, in same octave;
   (2) on piano, in spread position;
   (3) on instruments of like timbre;
   (4) on instruments of unlike timbre;
   (5) on instruments, in spread octaves.

c. Random chords—experiment to find the most dissonant sounds—
   (1) on piano, in same octave;
   (2) on piano, in spaced position;
   (3) on instruments of like timbre;
   (4) on instruments of unlike timbre;
   (5) on instruments, in spread octaves;
   (6) when dynamics is a factor.

d. Bi-tonality-melodies and chords of two tonal centers simultaneously
   (1) Using the autoharp
   (2) Write examples using simple well-known songs; sing these.

Example:

2. Listen to portions of *Belshazzar's Feast,* Walton (*Exploring Music,* Holt, page 78; Record I). Discuss effect of dissonant harmony. (10 minutes)
3. Review song material from previous days.

Fifth Day

Aleatoric Music

1. Define and explore aleatoric music. (25 minutes)
    a. Create composition of environmental sounds.
    b. Create compositions of singers and readers of newspaper columns.
    c. Create musical themes from telephone numbers.
2. Review singing two songs previously presented in this unit. (10 minutes)
3. Review main points of unit. (15 minutes)

Sixth Day

1. Five students present a brief review of unit in creative way.
2. Drama presentation.
3. Twelve-tone composition performance.
4. Look at and discuss several art works.
5. Percussion composition.
6. Drama presentation.
7. Composition of environmental sounds.
8. Look at and discuss two art works.
9. Review—ask students to write a paragraph on some impressions of twentieth-century music, what was new to them and what was of most interest.

LEARNING ACTIVITIES

1. Create a unit for the junior high school general music class.
    a. Work with a partner—your choice, but only two people per team.
    b. A unit is any area of study in music. Consider junior high abilities in your geographic area.
    c. All song material should be from standard junior high school or sixth-grade series.
    d. All recorded material must be listed in Schwann catalogue, be a part of the music school or music-education libraries, or owned by you.
    e. The unit must be complete. (Complete means as you would use it in junior high school, not just 4 periods from a large unit.) Your assignment is at least four junior high periods.
    f. State specific details, list teaching materials needed, and consider goals.
2. Your own background will supply many ideas for unit plans. The following may prompt you to think of others:

a. Music During the Life of George Washington
b. Tin Pan Alley's Art Songs
c. Music of India and its Use in Rock
d. Songs of the Mississippi River
e. Music of the American Psalters
f. Various Types and Uses of the March
g. Light as an Interpretation of Sound
h. Body Movement as an Interpretation of Rhythm
i. Polyrhythms as a Means of Expression

3. Educational materials centers for public schools exist in every state. Where is the one nearest you? Write for a listing of tapes, films, books, and records. Discuss with your classmates how one could best use the items indicated for junior high. Visit the center and learn how it can assist teachers.
4. Invite to your class students majoring in art education, physical education, history education, anthropology, general science education to participate in a discussion of how their areas can assist musical learnings. What other major fields should be represented?

Suggested Materials

In addition to those materials listed in Chapter 4, the unit plan will find resources in many areas.

Eighth-Grade Series

Adaptable materials also may be found in the eighth-grade books of the music series. Become acquainted with these texts and compare their offerings to those of the seventh grade since some publishers believe in a completely different approach for the two levels.

CHOATE, ROBERT A., et al. "Sound, Shape and Symbol," from *New Dimensions in Music*. New York: American Book Company, 1970.
COOPER, IRVIN, et al. *Music in Our Times*. Morristown, New Jersey: Silver Burdett Company, 1967.
EISMAN, LAWRENCE, et al. *Making Music Your Own*, 8. Morristown, New Jersey: Silver Burdett Company, 1968.
LANDIS, BETH, and HOGGARD, LARA. *Exploring Music Together*, 8. Chicago: Follett Publishing Company, 1967.
WILSON, HARRY R., et al. *Growing With Music*, 8. Englewood Cliffs, New Jersey: Prentice-Hall, Inc., 1966.

Film Strips

A number of filmstrips are available in the area of music. These usually contain pictures in color which illustrate the discussion material and recorded music on an accompanying record. The ones listed below are only samples of those available. The subgroupings indicate something of their potential for the unit plans.

Biography
    "Beethoven—a Story in Pictures." Bowmar B536
    "Haydn—a Story in Pictures." Bowmar B533
    "Mozart—a Story in Pictures." Bowmar 537
Folk Songs
    "Folk Songs of Africa." Bowmar B4001
    "Folk Songs in American History." WASP Filmstrips
    "Folk Songs of the Arab World." Bowmar B4009
    "Folk Songs of Our Pacific Neighbors." Bowmar B4006
    "Our American Heritage of Folk Music." Society for Visual Education A681SR
Patriotic
    "America"—"The U.S. Air Force"—"The Army Goes Rolling Along." Bowmar B2064
    "Anchors Aweigh"—"The Marines' Hymn." Bowmar B2062
    "Star-Spangled Banner"—"America the Beautiful." Bowmar B2052
Instrumental
    "Instruments of the Symphony Orchestra" (six filmstrips, including one each for strings, woodwinds, brass, percussion, melodious percussion, and orchestra). Learning Arts.
    "Learning to Play Musical Instruments" (three filmstrips, one each for brass, strings, and woodwinds). Learning Arts.
    "Maintaining Your Musical Instruments—Violin Family" (two filmstrips, instruments, and bows). Learning Arts.
    "Meet the Instruments." Bowmar 124.
    "Young Person's Guide to the Orchestra" (Britten). Learning Arts.

Books

Numerous reading books are published for young people. These include biographies as well as those dealing with selected topics. Many contain excellent pictures. The educational section of most city libraries will contain a good supply and some university libraries list a sample collection. Junior high school libraries should include numbers of such books. A sample list includes the following.

APPLEBY, WILLIAM, and FOWLER, FREDERICK. *The Sleeping Beauty and the Firebird.* London: Oxford University Press, 1964.

BAILEY, CAROLYN S. *Tops and Whistles.* New York: The Viking Press, 1937.

BERNSTEIN, LEONARD. *Young People's Concerts.* New York: Simon & Schuster, Inc., 1970.

BROWN, IVOR. *William Shakespeare.* Cranbury, New Jersey: A. S. Barnes & Co., Inc., 1969.

BURCH, GLADYS. *Richard Wagner.* New York: Henry Holt, 1941.

CHASE, ALICE ELIZABETH. *Looking at Art.* New York: Thomas Y. Crowell Company, 1966.

CLEATOR, P. E. *Exploring the World of Archaeology.* Chicago: Children's Press, 1966.

COUSINS, MARGARET. *Ben Franklin and Old Philadelphia.* New York: Random House, 1952.

CRAIG, JEAN. *The Story of Musical Notes.* New York: Lerner Publications Co., 1968.

CROZIER, ERIC. *The Magic Flute.* New York: Henry Z. Walck, Inc., 1965.

DAVIS, LIONEL, and EDITH. *Keyboard Instruments.* New York: Lerner Publications Co., 1968.

FABER, DORIS. *Robert Frost-America's Poet.* Englewood Cliffs, New Jersey: Prentice-Hall, Inc., 1964.

FOSTER, GENEVIEVE. *George Washington's World.* New York: Charles Scribner's Sons, 1941.

FRYER, JUDITH. *How We Hear.* Minneapolis: Lerner Publications Co., 1966.

GILMORE, LEE. *Folk Instruments.* Minneapolis: Lerner Publications Co., 1971.

GRAMET, CHARLES. *Sound and Hearing.* London: Abelard-Schuman, Ltd., 1960.

HARMON, HARRY. *Picasso for Children.* New York: Wynkyn de Worde Books, 1962.

KETTELKAMP, LARRY. *Singing Strings.* New York: William Morrow & Co., 1958.

KRISLEF, ROBERT. *Playback: The Story of Recording Devices.* Minneapolis: Lerner Publications Co., 1970.

LIEBERMAN, MARK. *Hildago-Mexican Revolutionary.* New York: Praeger Publishers, 1970.

MERRETT, JOHN. *Albert Schweitzer.* Chicago: Children's Press, Inc., 1960.

PEARE, CATHERINE OWENS. *Aaron Copland.* New York: Holt, Rinehart and Winston, Inc., 1969.

REIDY, JOHN, and RICHARDS, NORMAN. *Leonard Bernstein.* Chicago: Children's Press, 1967.

RICHARDS, KENNETH. *Louis Armstrong.* Chicago: Children's Press, 1967.

WOOD, FRANCES. *Grand Canyon, Bryce and Zion.* Chicago: Follett Publishing Company, 1963.

Bulletin Boards

Although students will create bulletin board designs based upon the unit, they may need some suggestions to assist with the decorative potential. Two books are suggested, but others may be found.

BUZZELLI, JOSEPH. *Adventures in Music Through Bulletin Boards.* New York: T. S. Denison & Co., Inc., 1966.

LEE, CARVEL, and LORITA. *The Music Bulletin Board Guide.* New York: T. S. Denison & Co., Inc., 1969.

Records

Any listing of recordings can only be representative since so many excellent releases have been made over the years. Older records may be available in city, school, or personal libraries, and may be invaluable since recording companies often discontinue a release after a few months. If the borrowing of a recording is not acceptable to the owner, consider taping the portion needed from the available source. Ideas for units of study may develop from a record list. For example, finding an old Caruso 78-rpm record in a neighbor's collection could lead to an interesting unit on early recordings.

"A Bell Ringing in the Empty Sky"—Nonesuch, H72025
"American Folk Songs"—Follett Publishing Company, L22
"China"—Nonesuch, H72051
"China"—Capitol, T10087
"The Complete Orchestra"—Music Education Record Company
"The Confederacy 1861–1865"—Columbia, DL220
"Dances of the World's Peoples"—Folkway Records, FD6503
"Essential Musical Knowledge"—Music Education Record Company
"Folk Instruments of the World"—Follett Publishing Company, L24
"Folk Songs of the Frontier"—Capitol P8332
"Folk Songs of the Old World"—Capitol, PBR8345
"Golden Rain"—Nonesuch, H72028
"House of the Lord"—Capitol, P8365
"Japan Revisited"—Capitol, T10195
"Japanese Koto Classics"—Nonesuch, H72008
"The Jasmine Isle"—Nonesuch, H72031
"Jewish Music"—Capitol, T10064
"Luiz Bonfa's Brazilian Guitar"—Capitol, T10134
"Modern Motion Picture Music of India"—Capitol, T10090
"Music from the Kabuki"—Nonesuch, H72012
"Music 100, An Introduction to Music History"—American Book Company
"People of Rhodesia"—Nonesuch, H72043
"Sarangi, The Voice of a Hundred Colors"—Nonesuch, H72030
"Sea Chanties"—Capitol, P8462
"West Meets East"—Angel, 36418

ADDITIONAL READINGS AND BIBLIOGRAPHY

COOK, MYRA B., ed. *The Come Alive Classroom.* West Nyack, New York: Parker Publishing Company, 1967.

DEAN, FRANCES F., ed. *A Selected Bibliography of Teaching Aids for Art, English Language Arts, Music, Social Studies, and Spanish.* College Station, Texas: Texas A and M University Press, 1967. (chap. 3)

KEMP, JERROLD E. *Instructional Design.* Belmont, California: Fearon Publishers, 1971. (chaps. B, 5, 7, & X)

MCMURRY, CHARLES A. *Teaching by Projects.* New York: Macmillan Publishing Co., Inc., 1920. (chaps. 2–6 & 10)

NORDHOLM, HARRIET, and BAKEWELL, RUTH V. *Keys to Teaching Junior High School Music.* Minneapolis, Minnesota: Paul A. Schmitt Music Company, 1953. (chap. 1)

PAYNTER, JOHN, and ASTON, PETER. *Sound and Silence, Classroom Projects in Creative Music.* Cambridge: At The University Press, 1970 (all)

PIERCE, PAUL, et al. *The Unit of Learning.* Chicago, Illinois: Chicago Public Schools, 1954. (all)

6

Teaching General Music Through Singing

The teaching of general music by emphasizing singing would appear to be a misnomer since it enunciates too limited a focus. Yet those who believe in this method of teaching in the junior high school consider the area of singing to be a valid center activity from which all other musical learnings stem.

Definition

A general music class, developed with an emphasis upon singing, does not replace the choir or vocal ensemble of the school. It fits the usual definition of general music in that it is a required class, it enrolls all students, and it includes a wider emphasis than singing. If properly conducted, it will not use the same vocal material as the junior high choir. The diagram on page 113 indicates how singing radiates toward several other activities, with its format including some concerns not mentioned in other teaching approaches.

Singing. Mentioned first, since in this plan singing takes the foremost position. Unlike other general music approaches, singing becomes the main concern, and the teacher and students are involved with its production most of the time.

Theory. In order to be an adequate singer, one must understand music theory. The student is given every opportunity to grow and to learn theoretical aspects through the singing program. This should include appropriate written work in the construction of chords, scales, and accompaniments, with each of these emanating from the compositions being sung. The junior high school age is interested in written theory when given a meaningful reason for its study. Theory learned in elementary school may serve as a point of departure for the general music teacher who can build on this knowledge and expand it to a more advanced level.

Music Reading. Any singing or instrumental program demands good music reading. If the student is to understand the printed page and to make it mean-

ingful in his junior high school work or in the future, he must have at least minimal skills in this area. Probably begun in elementary school, continuance of the study will aid considerably in his musical development.

Music History. To interpret a composition well and to understand its style, it is often helpful to be knowledgeable concerning the background of the composer and the place of this composition in musical history. With singing as the center of this teaching procedure, any composition may be a departure point for a study of historical information concerning that composition and its composer. Such information tends to make the student more informed and articulate.

Ear Training. A sensitiveness to the sounds of a musical score, and the aural understanding of these sounds, should be undertaken in the junior high school music program. Begun in elementary school, dictation of rhythms, intervals, and chords should continue through the intermediate years. This aids the student in listening, so that he will be a more skillful performer and a more particular listener of music. In addition, technical listening assists the student in comprehension and offers the student a base from which he can discuss in a learned and technical way those portions of the music which he has heard.

Listening. A student in a general music class should become aware of representative literature of the field, and should be guided in listening to some of the great musical compositions as they are related to his study of music history and to the singing program. Any serious music class in junior high school should accept this obligation.

Students and the composers, Merton Williams Junior High School. Hilton, New York. Marcia Bannister, teacher.

Observe that this format follows more closely those areas of the music program usually taught in colleges. This means that the student is beginning a study of those characteristics or facets of the music program which carry over directly into adult life. There is no artificial breakdown here, nor is the teacher asked to compromise his own feelings or training in any way.

Advantages

Singing as the center and main focus of a general music program could be considered problematic. However, if the young person's voice is treated with understanding, no reasons exist for pessimism. The student has been singing since early years, and if a music program of any quality has existed in the elementary school, singing has been a main concern. To continue this, then, is most logical. Considering singing, several secondary points are evident.

Singing in the general music class is a group activity. This satisfies those desires of the junior high school student to be involved with other members of his peer group, and to be active in the same type of activity.

Singing provides an opportunity for emotional expression. To observe the junior high school student alone and to observe the same student with a group of his peers will evidence different kinds of emotional expression. A hesitancy to express some types of emotion openly is merely an attempt on the part of the student to appear grown-up, while underneath, the emotion demands to be expressed effervescently. Music can assist with these dichotomies.

Vocal expression is basic to the human personality. All of us are witness to this in our desire to communicate daily; and the junior high school personality desires not only to talk but to whistle, yell, and to participate in any vocal way. Singing can be an assist to vocal expression, and the music class can take advantage of this desire.

Singing can give personal satisfaction. Often, only singing may satisfy so completely the attempt to express oneself diversely. Since the voice is so intimately personal and the pleasure so great with even the simplest of sounds or lyrics, the individual satisfaction can be great even for the hesitant singer in the junior high school.

An aesthetic experience may be achieved simply. Inasmuch as the person can be led to sing with little or no previous musical experience, and since aesthetic values are often immediately evident, some satisfying results are obtained quickly and with comparative ease not readily available in other mediums.

The class can be taught by vocal teachers. Since the emphasis is so strongly on the singing aspects of the program, any vocal teacher should be able to instruct the class. This means that no special training is required for the junior high school music teacher, placing general music on a par with most junior high classes wherein personnel trained for high school teaching are equally well qualified for grades seven, eight, and nine.

General music will prepare students for performance groups. Since the emphasis is so strongly upon singing, music reading, and ear training, the student is preparing himself for participation in the various musical organizations of the high school. Students who have a good background in general music may move into the choir or instrumental music program with comparative ease.

General music class may have a high rating with all students. Since the general music class with this focus is so similar to performance classes, it will not seem to be a secondary class for those with little talent.

The focus is upon music. Unlike some studies that become involved in peripheral material or side issues, this class continually focuses on music, on singing, and on the study of music as musicians know it.

A great carry-over exists for adult life. Everything learned in this class can be of value the remainder of the life of the student since the material is valued from the adult concept. If the student sings little as an adult, other facets of the program will assist him in being a better consumer of the art.

Disadvantages

There is too great a focus upon singing. In a true general music class, the emphasis should be upon a many-faceted program with balance. This program loses some of its general quality when it places too strong an emphasis in one direction. Although singing is important, and it has been included in all previous approaches to general music, other aspects of the program are important also and deserve more attention than they would receive in this method of teaching. The advantages listed for singing are valid, but one need not consider singing as the major focus to enjoy these advantages and yet add others to the program.

There is little need to train for performance. The emphasis in this class is to assist the student in understanding music as an art, in beginning to comprehend how his educational training assists him in this understanding, and to appreciate the relationship of music to other areas. Those who are interested in performance may join the appropriate organizations.

Well-taught courses will be well regarded. Students do not shy from any course which is well and interestingly taught. They are more apt to understand and appreciate a course which demands of them a variety of skills to assist with some insights into the subject.

Too much technical material for the time allotted. No matter what time is allotted for general music in the junior high school, if singing is a major concern, there will not be sufficient time remaining to cover but a little material in music history, theory, and ear training. To help the student understand these areas he needs adequate time regularly. It would be better to give the student a more general background, concentrating on historical and theoretical skills at a later date if interest is maintained.

The program is too nearly patterned after college curricula. Although the intent is to teach the student at his own level, this combination of theory, history, and performance is taught as if the class were a diluted college curriculum. The student of the junior high school needs courses planned specifically for him and his maturity level.

The student can learn about music from and through other disciplines. The student should begin to understand the interlinking of disciplines, and the manner in which music is a part of the entire fabric of knowledge. An introduction of this in the junior high school will assist in his understanding these points, and, at the same time, possibly point to personal interests which may not have been apparent heretofore.

Distinctive Problems of the Singing Emphasis

If the singing type of general music class is to be successful, several points need be stressed.

Each voice should be carefully considered. Early adolescence is the age of the changing voice for the boy and the girl. Although demanding some attention, the girl is not the obvious problem; the boy usually becomes the center of attention and rightly so. The treatment of the boy's voice should be a constant concern for the teacher in the junior high school. This problem will be discussed in detail in a later chapter.

Unison singing is possible only in a limited way. Because of the vocal ranges that exist in the average music class of these grades, unison singing is not possible unless the melody has a range limited to about a sixth, with some voices singing at the octave. Consequently, most materials should be in three or four parts to sustain interest, but also to avoid those range problems created by unison or two-part singing.

Boys should not always sing the lowest part. In the upper elementary school, when children learn to sing in parts, too often boys are requested or permitted to sing a lower part, ignoring the characteristics and range of the voice. This request appears logical when it is reasoned that before long they will not be singing the melody and that reading a part will be their usual lot. The boy, and some teachers, then erroneously assume that the boy should always sing the lowest part in junior high school and assign this part to him in any given piece of music. This is not at all what might be dictated by the voice range.

Music should be chosen carefully. Because of the range problem with the various voices, music should be chosen which does not exceed the range and, in most cases, the tessitura of the voices with which you are dealing. Some octavo music and many three-part songs from music series are available to the teacher, although recently music series have placed greater emphasis upon attracting the interest of the boy by considering the type of music presented rather than by being concerned about careful part writing and range considerations. Each musical number for singing should be chosen carefully, noting the following.

Text. Junior high boys and also girls are obviously particular about the lyrics they sing. If the lyrics are meaningful to them, the vocal material itself can be fast or slow, loud or soft, smooth or agitated, and they will accept the music even though it may not be their favorite song. Many lyrics which are understandable and meaningful to the adult will have little meaning for the young student. Poetry of the romantic period, easily understood and greatly appreciated by the teacher, may carry little meaning to the student. An explanation by the teacher does little to change the mind of the young person in accepting this as a valid song for him to sing. The old favorite "Stars of the Summer Night," even though a well-used male quartet number in years past, offers no interest to the young student because its choice of words is so far from that used in the latter part of the twentieth century. Love songs are appealing but they must express their sentiments in ways which sound contemporary; narrative songs, patriotic songs, spirituals, religious music, songs of the frontier, and songs expressing idealistic sentiments are always favorites of this group. One music series used the following songs on the first pages of the book to attract the young adolescent singer.

Sing Out	It's a New Day
Let the Rafter Ring	It's a Small World
We'll Find America	Get Thy Bearings
The Tree of Peace	

Difficulty of interval. Since we are working with a comparatively inexperienced voice in the general music class, the teacher must be aware of the difficulty of the intervals in the parts, particularly with those parts sung by the changing boy voice. Unusual intervals in the parts only tend to increase the insecurity of vocal production. Easy intervals include the second, third, fourth, fifth, and octave. More difficult intervals are the sixth and seventh, as well as augmented or diminished ones.

Speed of voice movement. For the same reason just given, the voices will not be able to execute the fast interval movement required in some songs. Although the voices of the soprano and the boy soprano are quite flexible, other voices are less so. The lower the voice, the less quickly it usually adapts to pitch changes. This is not to be confused with speed of articulation of words on a repeated pitch. The greater the interval of pitch change, the more difficult for the student to move quickly, and the more inaccuracy possible with the attempted pitches.

Monotony of part. No person enjoys the singing of a part which is monotonous, and least of all the young singer who, more than the experienced singer, probably gains less enjoyment from a blending, harmony part. Despite this, the overall effect will be a more telling point in the acceptance of the composition. A song with attractive words, to be sung with a proper zeal, even though the parts are less interesting, will most surely be a winner with this group.

Range. At this age, girls' voices are not mature and should be considered as one coloration and range, even though they often divide to provide harmony. Most girls will prefer to sing in the lower ranges because it requires less energy but, with a few exceptions, girls will benefit from singing the upper parts on some songs and the lower part on different material. In this way, a wider range will be utilized and flexibility will be maintained. Boys' voices may be considered as either changing or baritone. The boy whose voice is changing may sing with the lower girls on some numbers or with the changing boys on another. Boys whose voices have matured even more may be comfortable on the baritone part. Advisable ranges are given, page 119. (See Chapter 7 for additional discussion.)

Physical facilities. Since the general music class places major emphasis upon singing, it follows that the room in which it is taught should be arranged to best accommodate its purpose. Space for both classroom and rehearsal is needed.

GIRLS   CHANGING BOYS   LOWER BOYS

If only formal classroom space is provided, then the method of teaching general music through singing will be less successful than you may expect. The room should be large enough to provide space for desk chairs for the classroom activities, and risers for both sitting and standing during singing. One could eliminate the standing risers, but risers built for seating are a necessity. Properly built posture chairs without an arm desk are a requirement for the sitting-type riser.

Choir, Wooddale Junior High School. Memphis, Tennessee. Robert Mathews, conductor.

To bring as much aesthetic pleasure to the singing as possible, the teacher should be sensitive to the physical arrangement of the voices of the singers on the risers. This will depend upon the balance of the boys to the girls, the balance of the boys' changing voices to those with lower ranges, and the music which you may wish to use. No uniform rules can secure balance for any group; the teacher must experiment with the voices available. Generally, however, the lower girls have a potential for more vocal strength than other parts. This means that usually one will need more upper girls than lower. Boys whose voices have matured enough to sing baritone will have more vocal strength than the changing voice which often sings an upper male part. In fact, the changing voice may be weakest of all, and if few in number, may not balance the remaining parts. It is for this reason that many teachers prefer SAB music for the adolescent group.

The diagrams which follow will give you several options, all of which are possibilities for some classes in some schools. The emphasis in each case is to provide the boys with enough melodic and harmonic support to assist them in their singing and yet not permit their sound to be obliterated or overpowered by the girls. By placing the boys in the center of each arrangement, a better balance can be secured, and, in addition, the director will be in constant contact with those who may be having the greatest difficulty in singing because of the changing voice.

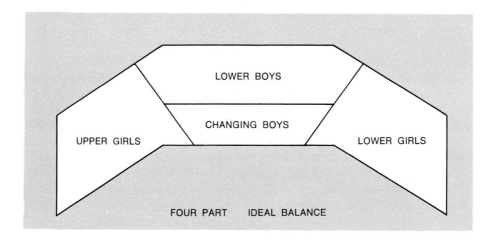

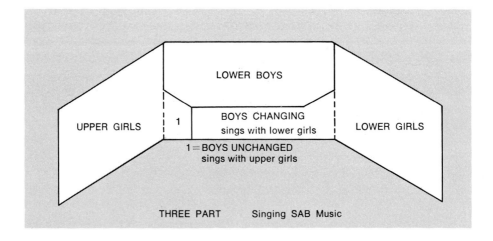

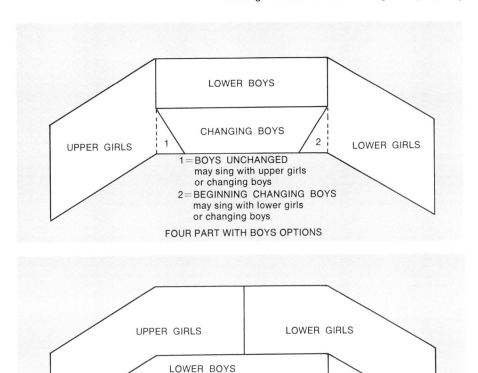

Accompaniment. Although a piano is a necessity in the music room, do not rely upon it to the point where the young singers never learn to hear music or sight sing. Each vocal ensemble must be independent enough from an accompaniment as to learn and become secure with its own blend and balance of voices. The piano constantly playing in the vocal room eliminates this possibility for most amateur adolescents. Even though the pitch may suffer, the advantages gained from the independence more than offsets this difficulty.

Choral Emphasis Planning

To be successful, the general music class which features singing cannot be another choral rehearsal, although this activity will be emphasized. Ear training, listening, theory, music reading, and music history should be planned to correlate with the singing, but each will usually not be presented daily. Rather, each should be a part of the overall work in the class, with the needs established through the song material. In other words, if the class works on five or six different vocal selections at a given time, each of these would take its turn as a concentration point for music history; each would be an invitation to listening; each would instigate some work in theory, ear training, and music reading; but this might occur over a two- or three-week period, so that each area would not be a part of every class day's activity. One, or possibly two, of the peripheral areas might be considered each day, but not all of them.

The following lesson plan will exemplify these points. The music used in this plan will be found following the plan.

<table>
<tr><td>TEACHING PLAN   A</td><td>Singing Emphasis Plan 1
CHRISTMAS SONGS</td></tr>
</table>

I. Specific details
  A. Required class of seventh-grade boys and girls
  B. Two meetings per week for fifty minutes each

II. Materials
  A. Music: "Praise Ye the Lord of Hosts,"* pages 125–26, Saint-Saens, arranged by Edward Jurey, Mills Music, 1962
    "Praise Ye the Lord of Hosts,"* page 127, Saint-Saens, *Discovering Music,* 8, Follett (page 211)
    "I Am So Glad Each Christmas Eve,"* page 128, Knudsen-Wood, Augsburg Press, 1969
    "Jesu, Joy of Man's Desiring,"* page 135, Bach-Riegger, Flammer, 1927
    "Deck the Halls,"* page 132, traditional carol
    "Fum, Fum, Fum,"* page 140
  B. Recordings: Saint-Saens, *Christmas Oratorio,* opus 12
    Bach, "Jesu, Joy of Man's Desiring,"* page 135
  C. Additional teaching aids: autoharp

III. Goals
  A. Long range: to assist young people in understanding the skills and background necessary for artistic performances in the field of music; to understand various styles of music and their interrelationships.
  B. Short range: to study various types of Christmas songs, and to understand the musical characteristics of each.

* Song material follows this teaching plan.

First Day

1. Blend: Sing slowly on "loo," phrase one and phrase five of "Praise Ye the Lord of Hosts," Saint-Saens (previously studied) (unaccompanied). Stress nasal resonance as well as throat resonance. Sing same phrases on "naw." (10 minutes)

2. Interval study: Sing intervals of a third, as found in this same composition. For review, sing the following intervals with numbers: 1–3, 2–4, 3–5, 8–6, 5–7, 3–1, 1–6, 7–5. Locate these intervals in the score. In which part? Which measure? Sing the entire phrase containing these intervals and listen for correct intonation. Sing the interval of a sixth: 1–6. Hear it as 8–6. Locate this interval in the music. Sing the entire phrase (no accompaniment for interval study). (10 minutes)

3. Sing the composition, noting enunciation, blend, and pitches (no accompaniment). (15 minutes)

4. Discuss the position of Saint-Saens in French romantic music: his style of composition, his emphasis, and his important works. (10 minutes)

5. Sight-singing: Continue work on F-clef facility with entire class. Study the melodic line of "I Am So Glad Each Christmas Eve" (top of page 5). Discuss intervals used, names of pitches; sing by number without rhythm, with rhythm, and with words. (10 minutes)

Second Day

1. Listen: Recording of "Praise Ye the Lord of Hosts" from Saint-Saens *Christmas Oratorio*. Discuss the mood, the tonal energy, the style. (5 minutes)

2. Introduce: "Jesu, Joy of Man's Desiring," Bach. Examine the form, the repetitions for the voice lines, the instrumental counter-melodies. (5 minutes)

3. Sight-sing (no accompaniment): All voices examine the soprano part, first two phrases. Discuss movement of line, and then sing with each voice singing at his own range. Examine phrases three and four, and sing on a neutral syllable. Examine phrases seven and eight; discuss, and sing on neutral syllable. (10 minutes)

   Examine baritone line, discuss, sing on neutral syllable for phrases one, two, three, and four. Examine phrases seven and eight, noting differences. Sing these on a neutral syllable. (10 minutes)

   Sing soprano and baritone lines together on neutral syllable for the above phrases, noting errors, correcting sight-reading. (10 minutes)

4. Theory: Considering the melodic line of "I Am So Glad Each Christmas Eve" for page 3, what chords could be used to accompany this little melody? Can students hear where the chords should change? Write the chords and number them (use only I, IV, and V^7). Place in an appropriate key for the autoharp and have a student accompany the group. (10 minutes)

Third Day

1. Breathing exercises with emphasis upon use of diaphragm, extending the singing phrase, and energizing the tone. (10 minutes)
2. Dictation: Have students write the following tonal patterns or phrases taken from the music which is being studied ("Praise Ye the Lord of Hosts"): (No rhythm in this dictation; use only even note values.) (List name and sound beginning pitch.)
   a. Soprano line, phrase one
   b. Bass line, phrase one
   c. Tenor line, phrase six
   d. Alto line, phrase six
   e. Alto line, last three measures (15 minutes)
3. Sing: "Deck the Hall." Since the students know this tune, read through with parts and accompaniment. Reread without accompaniment to check pitches. Combine upper and middle lines for pages 136 and 137. Add lower part. Discuss the contour of each accompanying line. Sing each line without accompaniment with entire class, then put together. (15 minutes)
4. Sing: "Praise Ye the Lord of Hosts" for polish and review of uniform vowel treatment (no accompaniment). (10 minutes)

Fourth Day

1. Blend and tune: Extract the cadence chords from "Fum, Fum, Fum." Sing on neutral syllables such as loo, noh, naw. Stress intonation of half steps and minor third in alto line. (5 minutes)
2. Sight-reading: Work on F-clef; entire class read baritone line; work on the rhythm, the note names; sing the pitches on neutral syllables, then with words. (10 minutes)
3. Sing: "I Am So Glad," final verse in unison: to review the melodic line, to learn proper diction and syllable division. Stress enunciation. Review page 130. Sight-read page 131. Discuss contour of lines. Sing alto line with entire class without accompaniment. Sing page 131. (15 minutes)
4. Music History: Discuss the types of Christmas music from the standpoint of the form: carol, hymn, chorale, anthem, and pop song. (10 minutes)
5. Sing: "Deck the Hall," concentrating upon blend while avoiding a heavy tone color. Sing entire composition with bell accompaniment for enjoyment and to have students understand how the entire composition has been put together. Discuss differences in style with other compositions which were sung during past two weeks. (10 minutes)

Praise Ye the Lord of Hosts

From the Christmas Oratorio, Op. 12
For Mixed Voices (S. A. T. B.)
With Organ or Piano Accompaniment*

Arranged by
Edward B. Jurey

by
Camille Saint-Saens

*The orchestration published under the same title may be used as an accompaniment.

126

Praise Ye the Lord

(From The Christmas Oratorio)

Camille Saint-Säens

Praise ye the Lord of Hosts, Praise and a - dore Him, Sing ye now and shout His praise,

Praise His Ho - ly Name. Sing now, ye heav - ens, on earth be ex - ul - tant,

1. Fine

Sing now and praise our dear Lord for He com - eth, Al - le - lu - ia!

2.

Al - le - lu - ia. _____

ia! Al - le - lu - ia, Al - le - lu - ia, Al - le - lu - ia, Al - le - lu -

Al - le - lu - ia, _____

D.S. al Fine

ia, Al - le - lu - ia, Al - le - lu - ia, _____ Al - le - lu - ia, Al - le - lu - ia!

Al - le - lu - ia,

From *Discovering Music Together 8.* Used by permission of the Follett Publishing Company.

I Am So Glad Each Christmas Eve

Marie Wexelsen, 1832-1911
Tr., Peter Andrew Sveeggen, 1881-1959
Alt., D. W.

Peder Knudsen, 1819-1863
Arr., Dale Wood

128   * The second verse is optional.

Star shone forth, And an - gels sang — on earth.—

The lit - tle Child — in Beth - le - hem, He was a King — in -
The lit - tle Child in Beth - le -

deed! — For he came down — from heav'n a - bove To help a world — in
hem, — Came down to help a world in

130

Deck the Halls

H.D.M.

133

Fa la la la la la la la la la la la la

Fa la la la la la la la la

Fa la la la la la la la la

Return to beginning
for 2nd and 3rd verses
Then to ending ⟶

Verse Two:
See the blazing Yule before us
Fa la la la la la la la la
Strike the harp and join the chorus
Fa la la la la la la la la.
Follow me in merry measure
Fa la la la la la la la
While I tell of Yuletide treasure
Fa la la la la la la la la.

Verse Three:
Fast away the old year passes
Fa la la la la la la la la
Hail the new, ye lads and lasses.
Fa la la la la la la la la.
Sing we joyous all together,
Fa la la la la la la la la
Heedless of the wind and weather,
Fa la la la la la la la la.

Jesu, Joy of Man's Desiring

For Three Part Mixed Chorus

From Cantata 147

Johann Sebastian Bach
Edited and arranged by
Wallingford Riegger

*The second verse is optional.

joy of man's de - sir - ing,
way where hope is guid - ing, Ho - ly
Hark, what

joy of man's de - sir - ing,
way where hope is guid - ing, Ho - ly
Hark, what

joy of man's de - sir - ing,
way where hope is guid - ing, Ho - ly
Hark, what

mp

wis - dom, Love most bright;
peace - ful mu - sic rings,

wis - dom, Love most bright;
peace - ful mu - sic rings,

wis - dom, Love most bright;
peace - ful mu - sic rings,

p

Drawn by
Where the

p

Drawn by
Where the

p

Drawn by
Where the

pp

138

Striv - ing still to Truth un - known,
Thou dost ev - er lead Thine own,

Striv - ing still to Truth un - known,
Thou dost ev - er lead Thine own,

Striv - ing still to Truth un - known,
Thou dost ev - er lead Thine own,

Soar - ing, dy - ing round Thy throne.
In the love of joys un - known.

Soar - ing, dy - ing round Thy throne.
In the love of joys un - known.

Soar - ing, dy - ing round Thy throne.
In the love of joy - un - known.

Fine

139

Fum, Fum, Fum

Spanish Carol

1. On De-cem-ber twen-ty-fifth, sing fum, fum, fum.
2. Sing with joy all men on earth, sing fum, fum, fum.
¡Vein-ti-cin-co de di-ciem-bre, fum, fum, fum!

Sing with joy this bless-ed morn, Je-sus Christ, our Lord, is born. In a
Stars a-glow in Heav'n a-bove Send the light of God's pure love. On this
Na-ci-do ha por nues-tro a-mor, El Ni-ño Dios, el Ni-ño Dios; Hoy de

man-ger cold and drear-y, He is born of Vir-gin Mar-y, fum, fum, fum.
day glad tid-ings bring-ing, Heav'n and earth to-geth-er sing-ing, fum, fum, fum.
la vir-gen Ma-rí-a En es-ta no-che tan fri-a, ¡fum, fum, fum!

Drum

Recorder

From *4 + 20 Carols*. Used by permission of The Informal Music Service, Delaware, Ohio.

TEACHING PLAN	B	Singing Emphasis Plan 2

INSPIRATIONAL SONGS

I. Specific details
    A. Required class of seventh-grade boys and girls
    B. Three meetings per week, forty-five minutes each

II. Materials
    A. Music: "A Mighty Fortress is Our God." *Sound, Beat, and Feeling,* American, page 18.
        "Simple Gifts." *Sound, Beat, and Feeling,* American, page 158.
        "Chester." *Sound, Beat, and Feeling,* American, page 269.
        "Lolly Too-dum." *Making Music Your Own,* Silver Burdett, page 126.
        "Inch Worm." *Making Music Your Own,* Silver Burdett, page 167.
    B. Recordings: Bach, Cantata 80, "Ein Feste Burg"
        Copland: Appalachian Spring or Variations on a Shaker Melody"
        Loesser: "Inch Worm" from *Hans Christian Anderson*
        Billings: *Hymns and Anthems*
    C. Additional teaching aids: Autoharp

III. Goals
    A. Long range: to assist young people with singing and the background which different songs demand; to understand that different styles of music demand different styles of singing.
    B. Short range: to become acquainted with five different inspirational songs.

First Day

1. Enunciation: Sing the words "aluminum, linoleum" rapidly, each word on a different diatonic pitch, moving upward and downward a fifth. Stress lip and tongue movement, but not jaw movement. (4 minutes)
2. Breathing and phrasing: Sing the melodic line of "Chester" in unison. Use the syllable "law" or "loo." Stress breathing at end of phrase only, and equal tone color throughout. Repeat each phrase several times or until each seems clear and definite. Use the upper octave on some phrases to increase range for the girl voices. For low voices, use the octave below exact pitch. (10 minutes)
3. Sight-reading: Read "Lolly Too-dum" with rhythmic syllables. Explain the syncopation if necessary. Clap the pulsations of the measures as you read. When this is secure, play the accompaniment as the students read the rhythmic syllables without pitches. This should give a driving pulsation to the reading

and also, indirectly, implant the harmonic background for the composition. (10 minutes)

4. Listen: Bach Cantata No. 80, final section, which is the simple harmonization of the chorale. Students should observe the chorale as the recording is played. Play at least two times. Comment upon the style of the music, its intensity, and its differences from and similarities to "Chester." (10 minutes)

5. History: Discuss Bach's style of writing in the chorale and why it became important in musical history. (6 minutes)

Second Day

1. Ear training: Dictate a number of tonal phrases taken from "Simple Gifts." Use patterns such as: 1–2–3; 3–4–5; ⑤–1; 1–2–⑦–⑤; 1–3–4–5; 5–2–3–2. (7 minutes)

2. Sight-singing: "Simple Gifts," slowly with numbers. Read the rhythm of the song; then sing the numbers in rhythm. The first reading may have been somewhat in rhythm, but some rhythms may have been lost in the concentration on pitches. Sing on a neutral syllable. Sing with words. (8 minutes)

3. History: Project the musical climate at the time of the American Revolution. Name other songs which might be known of this period. Listen to another Billings tune on record, preferably a fuguing tune. (6 minutes)

4. Singing: (a) Review the melodic line of the Billings tune being sure to observe the phrasing and the dynamics which were developed on the first day. (b) Add low voices (girls and boys). Sing the bass line while the higher voices sing the melodic line (no accompaniment). Stress the reading of the bass line while listening to the melodic line. (15 minutes)

5. Theory: Analyze the chords used in "Chester." Locate the I chords, the IV chords, the V chords. How many chords remain? Approximately what percentage of chords belong to I, IV, and V? Sing these chords through the song, omitting all others. (9 minutes)

Third Day

1. Full tone development: Use the first two measures of "Chester." Sing these chords in four parts to develop full tone for each section. Use singly, without rhythm, discussing the balance of the chord members. Finally, sing in rhythm. (8 minutes)

2. Sight-reading: Review the rhythmic reading of "Lolly Too-dum" with accompaniment. Discuss the numbers of the melodic line. Sing each phrase

without the second part. Secure each phrase before moving to the next. Finally, sing with words and with accompaniment. (12 minutes)
3. Listening: Again hear the Bach Cantata 80, final chorale.
4. History: Discuss the Bach chorale and its familiarity with the people. Consider Bach as a writer of religious music for his church and its services. (10 minutes)
5. Singing: "Simple Gifts" without accompaniment. Be sure that all intervals are correct, that words are clearly sung, and that phrasing is understood by all and correctly performed. Stress appropriate style of the singing.

Fourth Day

1. Tone Development: Using the melodic line of "Chester," sing phrases on the vowel "naw" to assist the tonal color. (5 minutes)
2. Sight-reading: Using "loo," sing the phrases of "Inch Worm" without accompaniment. Stress the chromatic intervals, their location to diatonic pitches, and correct intonation. Sing slowly in unison with accompaniment after song has been learned. (12 minutes)
3. Singing: "Simple Gifts" with accompaniment. Use autoharp. Use only two chords, and locate the chord changes by the changes in the melodic line. A number of students should be accompanists for hearing experience.
4. Singing: Review "Lolly Too-dum." Add the second part as written, but do not drill the second part alone. Do not use the solo as indicated; rather, use as a sectional solo for all boys who can sing the line at the pitches given. All voices sing those sections marked "chorus." (10 minutes)
5. Sing: "Mighty Fortress" with the recording. Have each voice sing a line appropriate to the range of the voice. (5 minutes)
   By this time "Lolly Too-dum" and "Simple Gifts" should be modestly well performed, and subsequent days will continue the work on the song material not yet learned. New material should be added regularly so that music reading, ear training, history, listening, and theory may be an ever reoccurring part of the daily work.

LEARNING ACTIVITIES

1. Write a plan for a general music class which emphasizes singing.
   a. Plan for four days of learning activities.
   b. Choose song material from the junior high series, your school library, the vocal library, the public library, or from a junior high school music library.

c. Be sure that all of the peripheral areas have been represented during the four days of the plan.

d. Try to make it as interesting for the junior high student as possible.

e. Consider a variety of musical styles and periods.

f. Be particularly careful concerning the voice ranges of the music selected.

2. Arrange a well-known favorite song for a junior high school music class. You may use SAB or SATB, but carefully work out the range of the voice parts, being sure you abide by the tessituras suggested. Choose song material which you believe will appeal to the junior high student.

3. Most school systems sponsor a junior high school vocal concert each year or a part of a program which features the junior high vocal ensembles. Attend such a program, noting the vocal qualities, the arrangement of the numbers, the arrangement of the voice parts on the risers, the type of music, and the ranges of the parts.

4. Attend a rehearsal of a junior high school vocal group. Be conscious of the seating arrangement, the vocal energy, the physical appointments of the classroom, and the vocal quality of the group.

5. A large number of junior high schools no longer use the general music class which emphasizes singing. Why would this be true? Why might some schools disagree?

6. Many teachers of junior high school music claim that they cannot find music for their classes which the young people can sing. Review one or more of the junior high school series books, and then decide if this statement is valid.

Suggested Materials

Much music for the singing class may be used from the music series. However, many teachers wish to augment these texts with octavo selections. Most states regularly compile an up-to-date listing of such music for their festivals or contests. The list from your state will be invaluable to you, and your school library probably contains copies of many of the items on past lists. A suggested list of three- and four-part music follows, but should not be considered complete. Although these have been successful in many junior high schools, additional selections could and should be added.

Three-Part

Bach-Aslanoff	Jesus, Jewel of My Faith	Theodore Presser Co.
Cain, arr.	Ole Ark's a Moverin'	Harold Flammer, Inc.
Cheyette, arr.	In Good Old Colony Times	Bourne, Inc.
Christy, arr.	Away for Rio	Hall and McCreary Co.

Davis, arr.	Goin' to Boston	C. C. Birchard and Co.
Elgar-Wilson	As Torrents in Summer	Boosey-Hawkes
Elliott	Navajo Trail	Jack Spratt Music Shop
Farrant-Davies	We Sing Our Praises Now to Thee	Harold Flammer, Inc.
Greyson, arr.	Come, Sing This Round with Me	Bourne, Inc.
Handel-Scholin	O Sing Unto the Lord	Belwin
Hart-Blight	If You Can't Sing, Whistle	Sam Fox Publishing Co.
Johnson, arr.	Green Grow the Lilacs	Hall and McCreary
Leontovich-Ehert	Ukranian Bell Carol	Pro-Art Publications
Old, arr.	St. Francis Hymn	Hall and McCreary Co.
Steele-Ades	America, Our Heritage	Shawnee Press, Inc.
Sullivan-Wiley	Come, Ye Faithful	Pro-Art Publications
Youse	Sing, Oh My Soul	Charles H. Hansen Music Co.

Four-Part

Brahms	In Silent Night	G. Schirmer, Inc.
Brahms	Six Folk Songs	Marks Music Corporation
Bright	Never Tell Thy Love	Associated Music Publishers
Donato	All Ye Who Music Love	Mills Music, Inc.
Fisher, arr.	Ye Watchers and Ye Holy Ones	Oliver Ditson, Co.
Frackenpohl	Hallelujah, Praise the Lord	Shawnee Press
Goodale, arr.	Ju Me Leve un Bel Maitin	G. Schirmer
Grant	Lazy River	Wallace Gillman Publishing
Gustafson	Keep an Eye on Me	Theodore Presser Co.
Henderson, arr.	I Went to the Market	Neil A. Kjos Co.
Kirk	O Come Loud Anthems Let Us Sing	Shawnee Press
Krones	A Song for Mary	Neil A. Kjos
Lambert	At Dawning	Boston Music Co.
Morgan	Ours Is the World	Hall and McCreary
Paxton	Breathe Soft, Ye Winds	Music Publishers Holding
Praetorius-Rikko	Joy and Good Cheer	Mercury Music Corporation
Smale, arr.	Love Somebody, Yes I Do	C. C. Birchard and Co.
Vaughan-Williams	O Taste and See	Oxford
Wick, arr.	Voices of Spring	Wick Publishing Co.
Young	Now Let Us All Praise God and Sing	Galaxy Music Publishers

ADDITIONAL READINGS AND BIBLIOGRAPHY

BENTLEY, ARNOLD. *'Monotones'—A Comparison with Normal Singers in Terms of Incidence and Vocal Abilities.* London: Novello and Co., Ltd., 1968. (chaps. 4 & 5)

FRISELL, ANTHONY. *The Tenor Voice.* Somerville, Massachusetts: Bruce Humphries Publishing, 1964. (chap. 2)

GILLILAND, DALE V. *Guidance in Voice Education.* Columbus, Ohio: Typographic Printing Co., 1970. (chap. 8)

HOGGARD, LARA G. *Improving Music Reading in the Choral Rehearsal.* New York: Fred Waring Office, 1947. (Part II)

HOWERTON, GEORGE. *Technique and Style in Choral Singing.* New York: Carl Fischer Co., Inc., 1957. (Part II)

MAYER, FREDERICK D. and SACHER, JACK. *The Changing Voice.* Minneapolis, Minnesota: Augsburg Publishing House, 1963. (all)

McKENZIE, DUNCAN. *Training the Boy's Changing Voice.* New Brunswick, New Jersey: Rutgers University Press, 1956. (chaps. 2–6)

MELLALIEU, NORMAN. *The Boys Changing Voice.* London: Oxford University Press, 1935, 1962. (all)

NEIDIG, KENNETH L. and JENNINGS, JOHN W. *Choral Director's Guide.* West Nyack, New York: Parker Publishing Company, 1967. (chaps. 5 & 9)

RICHARDSON, A. MADELEY. *The Choirtrainer's Art.* New York: G. Schirmer, Inc., 1914. (chaps. 3 & 4)

RORKE, GENEVIEVE. *Choral Teaching at the Junior High Level.* Chicago: Hall and McCreary, 1947. (chaps. 2 & 5)

Today

7

The Changing Voice

As the child who is developing physically offers potential coordination problems, as the child moving into adulthood may offer psychological problems, or as the child growing into adult society may offer social problems, so also may the young person provide a possible difficulty to the music teacher in the intermediate school because of the changing voice.

Physiological Changes

The larynx has two growth periods during a child's early years. The growth of the larynx is modestly rapid until about age six, and during this period the child may have some difficulty in producing a satisfactory singing sound. The speaking voice of preschool boys and girls is alike as to timbre and pitch, but singing voices vary greatly. After age six, the vocal bands of the larynx neither lengthen nor thicken any appreciable amount until the time of puberty, but as boys and girls use the voice during the elementary years it becomes stronger and the range increases. The voice of the fifth- or sixth-grade boy is strong over a wide range, and contains a luster and brilliance which girls do not possess; girls, although making use of similar range, often do not have the strength nor clarity heard in the voice of the boy. Such brilliance seems almost to preface the more troubled years of adolescence which lie ahead. During the years of puberty, however, there is a constant strengthening and firming of the muscles and cartilages of the larynx. This is the process which is known as the changing voice for both boys and girls.

Among the physical developments of adolescence is a growth of the larynx sufficient to make a change heard and felt by both girls and boys. For the girls, the larynx enlarges at a ratio of five to seven, or to six-tenths of an inch in length. This growth is noticeably less than for a boy. While the larynx in the male usually protrudes in the front of the neck, marking the point of the thyroid cartilage, in women the growth is less large and less seen, partly because of its size and partly because of a fatty tissue beneath the skin which softens the outline of the cartilage. The muscles and cartilages of the larynx in the female do become a bit heavier or thicker, extending the lower range but particularly adding a new magnitude in the lower register, which can also add color and depth to the upper register or head voice if used. Hearing this more mature sound in the lower part of the range leads most girls to shy from the upper notes, considering them thin and shrill. It is for this reason that the female voice benefits most satisfactorily by vocalizing from modestly low pitches to the higher ones.

With the boy the larynx develops to twice its original size, or to about one inch. Not only does the larynx double in size, but this results in the vocal cords doubling their length. This changes the pitch level to approximately an octave lower. Like the girl, the bands become heavier and stronger, and the muscles and cartilages which surround the vocal cords also increase in size and heaviness. When the larynx doubles its size, it calls into use different muscles than the boy used for singing when the voice was unchanged. The outward result is usually a voice where some lower range is evident along with most of the former range used by the boy during his intermediate years. Between these two ranges is a weak area, or non-sounding section. This is not an actual problem, nor does the du-

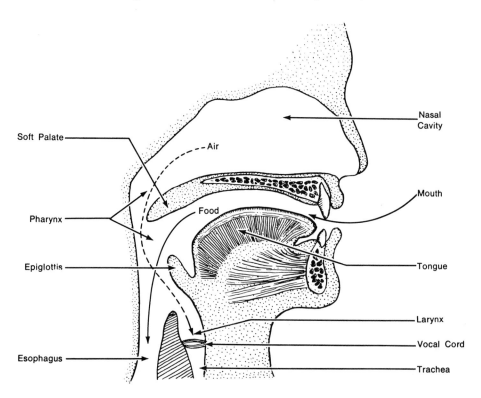

plicity of registers indicate sudden growth. It simply means that the boy has not yet learned to coordinate the necessary muscles to control his growing voice.

As you see from the accompanying diagram, the single opening at the back of the throat becomes two tubes lower in the neck. The tube toward the back of the neck carries the food to the stomach; this is known as the esophagus. The tube closer to the front of the neck carries air to the lungs. Immediately below the chin line, or at the top of this latter tube, is the larynx; the vocal cords are part of the larynx.

The larynx consists of cartilages, muscles, vocal bands (cords), membranes, ligaments, and folds of mucous membrane. Situated just at the top of the trachea, or the tube which leads to the lungs, the structure of the larynx consists of a series of cartilages united so as to ensure sufficient firmness, with considerable flexibility and pliability. The muscles act on these movable cartilages. The diagrams that follow give two views of the structure of the larynx.

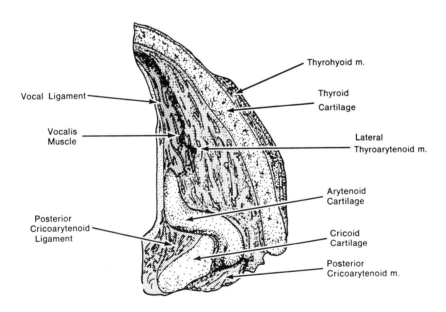

Right half of the larynx, drawn from photo in *Organic Voice Disorders,* G. Paul Moore. Copyright © 1971, p. 25. Reprinted by permission of Prentice-Hall, Inc., Englewood Cliffs, New Jersey.

Across the glottis (the opening of the tube) are two folds of tissue called the vocal cords (thyroarytenoid muscles), which are thickest and widest at their uppermost surfaces where they come together. The vocal cords are attached in front to the midpoint of the thyroid cartilage. In back, each is attached to one of a pair of small cartilages called arytenoid (hence, the name thyroarytenoid),

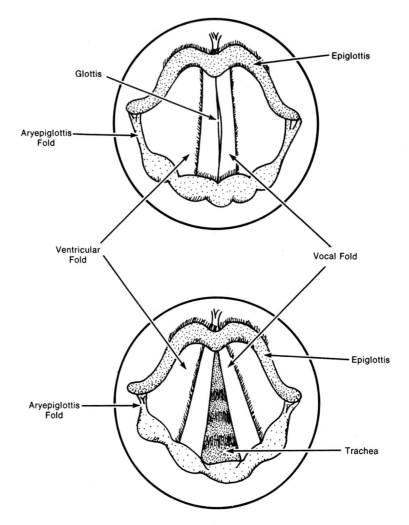

Drawn from photo in *Organic Voice Disorders,* G. Paul Moore. Copyright © 1971, p. 25. Reprinted by permission of Prentice-Hall, Inc., Englewood Cliffs, New Jersey.

which is able to move laterally, medially, forward, or in a rotary manner. The cords and cartilages together make up the voice box or the larynx. Small muscles (thyroarytenoideus) can rotate the arytenoid cartilages in such a fashion that the vocal cords are moved away from each other, forming a V, with the apex forward to the front of the neck. When this is done, the opening is wide enough so that air passes up and down without affecting the cords. A movement in the opposite direction, however, brings the vocal cords close together and parallel.

With only a narrow passage left for air, any air current moving up or down the column sets the cords into motion, thus producing a sound. When this is correctly controlled it becomes singing. The faster and more forcefully the air is expelled past the cords, the louder the sound. Furthermore, with a greater degree of tension a higher pitched sound is produced, and if the cords are relaxed some, lower pitches are heard.

As far as phonation is concerned, the larynx exists for the vibrating vocal bands. Nearly all the changes affected in the movements and tensions of the vocal cords result from the alterations in the positions of the arytenoid cartilages to which they are attached.

The muscles of the larynx are usually arranged in pairs which have opposite or antagonistic action: those which open and close the glottis and those which regulate the tension or relaxation of the vocal bands.

The thyroartenoid muscles determine the shape and tension of the vocal cords, shortening and relaxing them by pulling the arytenoid cartilages forward or backward; they also close the glottis by an inward movement of the arytenoid cartilages.

The cricothyroid muscles elevate the cricoid cartilage, thereby tensing and elongating the vocal cords.

The cricoarytenoid muscles open and close the glottis by rotating the arytenoid cartilage.

The vocalis muscle adjusts the tension of the vocal ligament along with the thyroarytenoid muscles to aid in the control of the pitch of the voice.

The arytenoideus muscles close the glottis and the laryngeal vestibule.

As we have just described, the growth of the larynx at the time of puberty causes problems for the maturing male. An irregular development of cartilage and muscle, with a consequent imbalance in the functioning mechanism, can bring sudden variations in pitch and/or loudness as well as uncertainties in their control. In addition, other growth changes also affect singing and speaking for the maturing person.

Resonating chambers add a complication with overtones which provide the voice with its quality or timbre. Since no two people have a nose, mouth, throat, and chest of precisely the same shape, no two people have a voice exactly alike in quality. Our ears detect these delicate differences in timbre, making possible the recognition of a voice.

The vocal cords alone would set up a relatively simple and faint sound. However, the nasal passages, the mouth, and the chest, acting as resonating chambers, enable us to be heard[1] and simultaneously give the voice its characteristic resonances. It is not the larynx which is crucial in the articulation of words or

1. Some primates (howler monkeys) have developed their resonating chambers to the point where their cries can be heard for a mile or more.

the singing of pure vowels; rather it is the development of the brain and nervous system controlling numerous delicate muscles which alter the vocal cords and the resonating chambers.

To summarize, the functioning of the vocal mechanism involves the size, condition, and power of the breathing apparatus, the functioning of the larynx, and the modification of the resonators. Even if a young person could adequately focus the resonators and if he had developed his breathing apparatus to support his efforts, the control of the larynx during this time of growth would offer sufficient problems. A combination of all three puzzles most adolescents. The dilemma of how to assist these young people is primary to voice use.

Approaches to the Changing Voice

Over the years several methods of approaching these problems have been used. Four of these will be discussed.

Cessation of Singing

In the recent past it was considered proper by some for the boy to refrain from singing during the change-of-voice period. This practice was probably more common in the church choirs of England than in this country. One might surmise that this practice was prevalent partly because the child voice had been maintained overly long so that a rest was physically necessary before the voice would respond well to singing the tenor or bass part.

Music teachers in this country rarely subscribed to this practice, but when a teacher realized that the music of the junior high school did not attract the male students into the class, this principle was a convenient excuse. Girls' glee clubs could be organized while the boys "went through that difficult age of voice change." In other words, although not ascribed to in practice, it became an excuse which sounded legitimate since it was based upon a prominent theory.

Although most vocal teachers today believe this method to be an improper approach for the young singer, we still find teachers who understand the male changing voice so little that their approach to the problem is frustrating to themselves and so discouraging to the boys that singing ceases.

No Singing in the Music Program

Becoming frustrated with the changing voice and its limitations, some teachers in the public schools decide to teach music with little or no singing. Some of these classes then emphasize music theory, or become an activity class. Others become a general class including music history, record listening, and the playing of simple instruments such as guitars, tonettes, and so forth. Although defended on other grounds, this type of program may indicate a lack of understanding on the part of the teacher for the adolescent voice.

The Multiphase Process

Two productive approaches exist for the adolescent voice. Both of these emphasize concern for the individual and include the young voice in a program of singing as a regular facet of the music offerings of the junior high school.

The first of these base the pedagogy upon a gradual and developed moving of the voice into adult coloration and range. Through the early years of his life and through most of the elementary school, the boy sings with a soprano-like voice. During the maturing period known as adolescence he usually moves through two intermediate vocal stages prior to adulthood: the cambiata, sometimes called alto-tenor, and baritone.

The cambiata phase of development is usually attained prior to becoming a baritone. This, as the name implies, is not alto nor tenor in range or quality. Not being an alto, the young person should not sing second soprano or alto parts in soprano, alto, tenor, bass music. Rather, specific material is required that fits the unique possibilities of this first stage of the lower male voice.

Almost all boys move from cambiata through baritone on their way to adult tenor or bass. As the voice continues to mature and becomes lower, a baritone phase is always realized. Material with correct range and tessitura is essential.

Although with the boy the evidence of voice change is more obvious, the girl also evidences an alteration based upon maturity. The voice may not lose much range, but with the gradual increase in heaviness in sound, the girl, and many times the teacher, may mistake this for a definite voice change and place the girl in the alto section even though the soprano range may still be quite secure.

In other cases the voice may become shrill, thin, and less pleasant. To mistake this quality for an ability to sing in a high range is an error. Since altos are rare in junior high, it is much preferred to consider the girls as first and second sopranos. Alternation of parts will assist in keeping the top range while exercising the lower.

To assist in classification, average ranges are helpful.

The usual tessitura of these ranges becomes important.

By observation of the range and the tessitura it should be obvious that the boy cambiata is neither an alto nor a tenor. The alto part, as found in much SATB music, contains a tessitura too high for this voice. Further, it is not proper to use this voice on tenor parts since most tenor parts are too low in tessitura, and occasionally may even run out of range. What is needed, then, is a careful observation of this voice, with a realization that the boy can sing adequately, but for his own vocal protection he must have vocal material of a range which enables him to participate without singing beyond his vocal possibilities.

Likewise, the bass parts of the usual SATB are not suitable for the immature baritone voice. If given this material, the boy will try to sing the parts, extending himself to touch the notes, but with results so unsatisfactory that proper balance will probably demand too much from the section. Thus, the singer could perform an injustice to his vocal development.

With the cambiata and the baritone, the determinate is the range, since both qualities will be somewhat husky and unclear. As the boy moves through each level into an adult voice, he should be told about this growth and given opportunity to satisfactorily participate in vocal organizations by means of these developmental stages. This is particularly true of the baritone phase. The teacher should not consider this the maturity point, since the young voice may sing baritone parts for some time but later develop into an adult tenor. This means that the correct placement of the adolescent voice by range is a protective device for the immature and mature voice. It also follows that the mature voice should be classified more upon quality than upon range, and this quality is not evident with the adolescent. The truth of this statement becomes apparent when one considers that the college voice is still within its logical development, and numerous voice teachers at the college level move voices into new classifications as the voice matures and produces its adult quality.

The Developmental Process

In contrast to the ideas above, the developmental approach to the changing voice understands that this is a process not involved with steps or stages.

The voices of boys and girls sound much alike during most of the elementary school. But this sound is deceptive since the larynx of the boy is developing with the body even though the sound has not yet altered obviously.

Small group sing, Merton Williams Junior High School. Hilton, New York. Marcia Bannister, teacher.

The developmental approach prefers that the boy not be kept in a soprano range until the change of voice becomes obvious to the listener. If such change becomes obvious to the listener or if a break should occur, the voice has been kept too long at the younger, higher range. Rather, the boy should be developing his lower tones continually during the chronological approach to the adolescent years. His ability to sing into an extended range should be explored through some lower pitch usage, so that at no time should the voice be indulged to sustain its younger status. When the boy has difficulty in singing above e^2, when a little huskiness is heard in speaking, when a new richness comes into the singing middle range, then the voice is beginning to show signs of change, and the lower ranges should receive more emphasis and be developed.

At the outset, as the lower portion of the voice develops, it is possible that only a few additional lower pitches might be added to the soprano range. However, as additional lower pitches are added, a boy may be able to sing in two ranges simultaneously: the upper range where he has been singing (now somewhat limited), and a new lower range which is developing. Both of these ranges should be used, but with increased emphasis upon the lower range, since it is this level which the voice seeks and here the boy will eventually sing.

Range classification—of little value with this plan—depends upon vocal production, experience, and training. The more important item is fatigue. Overuse of the voice limits range, while regular use of the adolescent voice, when not tired, may produce increasingly wider ranges. Using the voice carefully for small amounts of time and with little intensity will be most helpful to the growth of the voice. A wide range use will not be harmful to the voice unless it becomes fatigued through loud singing, long singing, or both.

Consequently, as the voice begins to deepen, the boy will be able to sing some alto parts and some tenor parts. As the voice continues to develop, some bass parts will be possible. Flexibility and adaptability within each song becomes more important than classification and special material. The placing of the young person into the cambiata or alto-tenor classification is unnecessary musically, and could be psychologically harmful, since the limited ranges of these parts might limit the range of the adult voice, and, probably most important, tend to imply to the singer that the quality most desired is an immature one which sounds neither male nor female. Such implications retard the quality development for the approaching mature voice. The junior high voice is not something special—it is only a part of the development from childhood into adulthood. To treat the voice at this time as a phase of specialness robs from this natural development.

Testing the Voice

No matter the approach used for the junior high school changing voice, testing should become a regular part of the educational singing process so the teacher may guide the student accurately and carefully. Some teachers check voices quickly and often; others less often, but use regular, extended testing.

Quick Classifications

Because of their experience and skill in working with the maturing voice, some teachers rely upon quick testing methods entirely; other teachers use quick test methods between extended testing. Usually a quick test will be given, with the entire class present or a number of students in the room.

The speaking voice usually will indicate that the voice is maturing. If this process is used, request the student to speak loudly and a more accurate pitch definition will result than if the student speaks softly. The pitch of the speaking voice is near the bottom of the singing range. This is particularly true of young boys who wish to sound mature.

The lowest vocalized pitch which a student can produce on a given day may be helpful. A low B-flat or C can be reached by a young baritone; if this pitch can not be vocalized, higher parts should be assigned.

A third quick test uses familiar song material. Without reference to any previous pitch, ask a young voice to sing "Jingle Bells" without accompaniment, from a pitch of his choosing. Many boys with a changing voice will begin on G-sharp or A, indicating the key of E-major or F-major. They prefer to sing in those pitches immediately below middle C, choosing these pitch centers since the song uses the three, four, and five of its scale, predominately, and the tonic note but twice. Next, ask the boy to sing "America" in any key center he chooses. Often he will pitch this song lower than "Jingle Bells" if his voice is maturing and he can begin on a lower pitch. The range limits demanded by the song will give additional information concerning the tessitura of the singer.

Extended Testing

Extended voice testing usually is conducted singly, with no other students in the room. This gives an importance to the interview, as well as a confidentiality and an opportunity for individualized informality.

For girls:

1. Begin with a single-pitch vowel or enunciation exercise on G^1.
2. Next, use a simple ascending diatonic vocalise, preferably with a range of a third. The "aw" vowel will assist in bringing the maturity of the lower pitches into the head voice.
3. Use a simple ascending diatonic exercise with a range of a fifth. Begin on G^1 and work chromatically upward.
4. When the upper limit of the range has been reached, return to G^1 and invert the exercise, working chromatically downward.
5. Although many vocal teachers prefer "aw" as the beginning vowel, the syllable "loo" will assist inexperienced singers who lack confidence and any understanding of focus.
6. After range extremities have been ascertained, arpeggios may be used to exercise the voice in different ways than step material.

For boys:

1. Begin with a single-pitch vowel or enunciation exercise on small B.
2. Use a simple descending diatonic exercise, preferably with a range of a fourth. Begin on small B and work chromatically downward. This exercise will enable you to find the lower extent of a changing voice quickly without assuming that the voice can sing low pitches.
3. If a small D is reached by exercise 2, begin again on small B, using a descending triadic exercise with small B as the fundamental, followed by the fifth be-

low and the lower third. Work chromatically downward to locate the lower limit of the range.

4. When the lower limit has been reached, return to small B and work chromatically upward, using a diatonic ascending exercise until the upper limit is realized.

5. The "o" vowel, preceded by "n' or "l," often assists the young male in achieving confidence before other vowels are practiced.

The extended test should assist the teacher in realizing not only range but the tessitura, vocal quality, intonation, vowel coloration, breath support, and posture. If desired, the teacher may extend the test to include musical examples which might indicate sight-reading ability, diction quality, vocal agility, and vocal independence against an accompaniment.

The extended test should also assist the young person in understanding his vocal development as well as providing an explanation that by failure to accept his present developmental stage or by forcing his voice into ranges not yet prepared by experience and maturity, later vocal ability and satisfaction will be curtailed.

Additional Factors Affecting the Changing Voice

Because the young person is also a most active personality, the correct choice of music will take into consideration not only voice range but will be ever mindful of uninteresting parts. The young singer appreciates singing the melody on occasion and prefers a part which moves in an interesting manner.

Related to this, the music should have interesting but not difficult intervals. Those best suited for the young male are the seconds, thirds, fourths, and fifths. Octaves are possible, but other intervals offer intonation and quality problems.

In choosing the music, consider the speed with which the young voice is expected to move from interval to interval. If flexibility demands become too great, the resultant indefiniteness of pitch will lead to intonation problems.

The type of music and the words of a song may be the deciding factor for the adolescent. Girls will usually sing songs which appeal to boys, but the reverse is rarely true. Infrequently do young people of this age prefer to sing words which portray the subtle meaning of life, although a song with strong emotions will be a favorite. The adolescent has a tender heart, but the material must not be outwardly over-sentimental or the student disassociates himself from it.

Unison singing will be most difficult for the voices of the junior high school. Only occasionally, when the composition is carefully written so that portions of it will fit the ranges of all the voices, will unison singing be possible. The mature voice may respond most easily to a unison situation, but the young adult whose voice is in the process of changing will find unison work almost impossible since he will not be able to match his own voice range with others. Attempting to sing in unison with girls of his own age or other males whose voices have matured beyond his point of development, the maturing adolescent boy may conclude that he is not a singer. It becomes necessary, therefore, to find part material which offers opportunities for the changing voice.

Summary

In the schools of this country, hundreds of boys and girls quit singing during adolescence. A lack of comprehension of adolescent voice problems by teachers of music contributes to this problem. The teacher must assist the child in understanding his vocal growth much as a physical education teacher attempts to assist the child with his physiological and biological growth. Music teachers have failed, as well, to understand the maturity level of the young people in the junior high schools, and often have excused their inabilities by explaining the need for boy choirs, or excusing the lack of boys in the program by stating the older principle of vocal rest during adolescence.

There are two current theories about active singing programs for boys in mixed vocal situations. One process believes that boys are best served when growth is directed through definite phases toward maturity. A second process, the developmental, permits the boy's voice to mature in an individual manner with certain emphases, using the mature voice as a guide.

Your work with young people in the junior high school will benefit you if you are aware of these ideas and are willing to use them with intelligence and observation until experience with the boy and girl adolescent voice directs your teaching routine in particular ways.

LEARNING ACTIVITIES

1. Invite three or four junior high boys to your classroom. At least two of these should be in the seventh grade, and at least one boy from the eighth grade. Compare these boys according to—
   a. the speaking voice;
   b. independent pitching of the first phrase of "America" or "Jingle Bells";
   c. vocalizing from the "Jingle Bells" fifth downward by step to locate the lower note of the range;
   d. vocalizing from the "Jingle Bells" third upward by step to locate the upper note of the range;

e. location of pitch where best tone color is found;

f. location of pitch or pitches where easiest loudness can be obtained;

g. the tessitura;

h. whether the voice has two ranges or a regular range and a falsetto;

i. the vocal agility of each individual;

j. each student's "feel" of singing certain pitches and his "feel" of singing now as compared to previous years.

What observations can you make after hearing and talking with these students?

2. Invite two fifth-grade girls and two seventh-grade girls to your classroom. Compare the voices in similar ways to those listed above. What observations can you make after hearing and talking with these students?

3. Invite two fifth-grade boys and two seventh-grade boys to your classroom. Compare the voices in similar ways to those items listed above. What observations can you make concerning the changing boy voice? What can you say concerning the two approaches of teaching the changing boy voice?

4. Arrange a song for the changing voice to sing as a solo. Consider text, range, tessitura, skips, and vocal movement.

5. Arrange a song for the junior high vocal class. Use SAB or SACB, but be sure you consider range, tessitura, skips, vocal movement, and text.

6. Develop a written statement, at least one typewritten page in length, on the subject, "The Many Voices of the Young Adolescent."

7. Look at your state festival or contest list of easy solos. What solos would you consider inappropriate for the changing voice, based upon your knowledge of their text, title, or range. Many music libraries can furnish sample or complete copies of such solos for your study. If not, a high school vocal teacher may be able to assist you.

ADDITIONAL READINGS AND BIBLIOGRAPHY

ASIMOV, ISAAC. *The Human Body—Its Structure and Operation.* Boston: Houghton Mifflin Company, 1963. (chap. 5)

BEALL, LEE MORRETT. "Elementary and Junior High School Voice Training." Doctoral dissertation, American University, 1958.

CARLSON, ANTON J.; JOHNSON, VICTOR; and CAVERT, H. MEAD. *The Machinery of the Body.* Chicago: The University of Chicago Press, 1961. (chap. 6)

CONRAD, ROBERT M. "Developing the Boy's Changing Voice," *Music Educators Journal* 50 (April 1964): 68.

COOPER, IRVING. "Study of Boys' Changing Voices in Great Britain," *Music Educators Journal* 51 (November 1964): 118–20.

EKSTROM, ROBERT CARL. "Comparison of the Male Voice before, during, and after Mutation." Doctoral dissertation, University of Southern California, 1959.

GUSTAFSON, JOHN MILTON. "A Study Relating to the Boy's Changing Voice: Its Incidence, Training, and Function in Choral Music." Doctoral dissertation, Florida State University at Gainesville, 1956.

HEATON, WALLACE and HARGENS, C. W., eds. *An Interdisciplinary Index of Studies in Physics, Medicine, and Music Related to the Human Voice.* Bryn Mawr, Pennsylvania: 1968.

HOLLIEN, H., and MALCIK, E. "Evaluation of Cross-Sectional Studies of Adolescent Voice Change in Males," *Speech Monographs* 34 (March 1967): 80–4.

HOLLIEN, H. et al. "Adolescent Voice Change in Southern White Males," *Speech Monographs* 32 (March 1965): 87–90.

JOSEPH, W. "Summation of the Research Pertaining to Vocal Growth," *Journal of Research in Music Education* 13 (Summer 1965): 92–100.

———. "Vocal Growth in the Human Adolescent and the Total Growth Process," *Journal of Research in Music Education* 14 (Summer 1966): 135–41.

———. "Vocal Growth Measurements in Male Adolescents," *Journal of Research in Music Education* 17 (Winter 1969): 423–6.

LANDMAN, G. H. M. *Laryngography and Cinelaryngography.* Baltimore: The Williams and Wilkins Company, 1970. (chap. 1)

MOORE, G. PAUL. *Organic Voice Disorders.* Englewood Cliffs, New Jersey: Prentice-Hall, Inc., 1971. (chaps. 2 & 3)

———. *Physiology of Hoarseness.* Gainesville, Florida: Communication Sciences Laboratory, 1962.

MURPHY, ALBERT T. *Functional Voice Disorders.* Englewood Cliffs, New Jersey: Prentice-Hall, Inc., 1964. (chaps. 2 & 6)

PUNT, NORMAN. *The Singer's and Actor's Throat.* London: Heinemann Medical, 1967. (chap. 2)

QUIRING, DANIEL P., and WARFEL, JOHN H. *The Head, Neck, and Trunk.* Philadelphia: Lea & Febiger, 1967. (chap. 12)

SHAW, J. R. "Psychological Barriers to the Voice," *Musical Journal* 26 (December 1968): 77.

SWANSON, F. JOHN. "Voice Mutation in the Adolescent Male: An Experiment in Guiding the Voice Development of Adolescent Boys in General Music Classes." Doctoral dissertation, University of Wisconsin at Madison, 1959.

TAYLOR, GAYLORD LYMAN. "The Problem of the Changing Voice and the Literature for Junior High School Musical Classes." Doctoral dissertation, Colorado State University at Greeley, 1966.

8

Theories of Growth and Development

As the human organism grows, personality patterns develop in certain but individualized directions. In the next chapter, we will come to understand that these individual traits tend to group themselves, disposing persons toward common behaviors. In this chapter, theories of personality growth are summarized to assist in understanding the adolescent struggle for maturity—the causal ingredients, as well as some determinant associations. Although attempting to be objective and as complete as possible, any theory contains certain limiting factors as to the manner of interpreting growth and development of personality.

During the last fifty years, but most particularly during the last two decades, a number of interesting theories of growth and development have emerged. To better understand the adolescent and his evolution to adulthood, and to better place your own thinking in relation to standard concepts, it would be helpful to review some of the better known theories concerning personality development. These are divided into general categories to assist in understanding and to emphasize their differences.

Psychoanalytic Theory

Through the last fifty years proponents of psychoanalytic understandings of human behavior have relied upon the writings and theories of Sigmund Freud, who is best known for his approaches to sexuality and the sexual determinants of personality.

During the adolescent age, two basic yearnings or desires are predominant: mourning and love. As the young person looks toward adult life he foresees a separation from his parents which results in a substratum feeling of sadness, emptiness, and grief. Consequently, the young person attempts to supplant the love for and idealization of parents with love for persons of his own age. As a result, friendships are overemphasized and exaggeratedly idealized.

Partly because of the result of her earlier physical maturity, the adolescent girl sheds a portion of her femininity to become an active and aggressive partner in the love game. This characteristic will be explained in more detail in Chapter 9.

The peer group takes on significant proportions because the young person relies on his peers for mental and psychological comfort; because he is able to submerge himself into the group and take on the appearances of the group at a time when his body changes cause him to be hesitant and full of wonderment as to their development; and because the group offers a release from adult pressures when these latter tend to bombard him or appear threatening. When adult pressures do threaten, the resultant rebellions of the young only underline a need for social belonging. Any group or system supplying convincing and ready answers will appear attractive to the adolescent since a certain amount of security is found within rigidity. This rigidity may be part of the adult world or, at times, the peer group. For this reason, democracy does not supply as quick an identity for large groups of young people as a more totalitarian system.

Implications for Music Teaching

During the past two decades we have seen the small pop-music group become the rallying point for numerous adolescents. Today this is less true than in past years, but it does indicate that young people consider music an excellent source of cohesion. The small group offers opportunities for personal growth and interrelationships not possible with the large ensemble or class. The junior high teacher should recognize the importance of both large and small group work, but with neither should there be a passive acceptance of aesthetic values. This means that one should not consider the rock group the only avenue of approach to musical learning; more traditional small-group work will also be accepted enthusiastically. In addition, the teacher should not be fearful of activities which are boyish in nature or which are rigid in structure. For this reason, the marching band or a strict approach to choral organizations or orchestra will be admired by the adolescent. The music class often is too loosely run so that the young student has little respect for the teacher. The teacher, although ready to listen to other points of view, should not appear to vacillate or equivocate in discussing musical likes and dislikes with young students.

Psychological Theory

Psychological theories envelop the corporeal and the outer world as related to the mind, or as they are thought to exist in the mind of the perceiver. During the growth period, these forces interact to produce in the young person a set of values or a formula by which various stimuli are categorized to become a base for reaction.

The child looks upon the outer world as a fantasy, often involving a certain amount of magic. During adolescence a more realistic understanding of life and, at the same time, a deeper meaning to life develops.

In addition, the body also matures so that motor control leading to purposeful action is added to reflex actions. To aid this striving toward maturity, we should help to develop actions of foresight and actions which involve planning. Advanced maturity may involve a creative stage.

During adolescence, a value set evolves. The more immature personalities struggle with value development by becoming involved with radical and dramatic procedures. Some personalities react less vehemently and with a greater disposition toward continuity; these gradually adopt cultural values which are held by society without greatly destroying or altering their own personality. A more mature procedure is involved in a third process wherein the adolescent achieves his goals through self-discipline and active efforts. Throughout this searching and seeking, the individual is involved with self, his feelings of loneliness, and a need to experiment with his developing self to ascertain a definite identity.

Some psychological theorists place an emphasis upon the outer world rather than the inner self since the former emphasizes interacting environmental and personal factors. Under such an emphasis, three external areas predominate. First, the immediate environment (including the parents) should be able to assist the young person by offering sufficient structure. Without this, the child will lack personality integration. Secondly, his rapidly expanding environment yields uncertain reactions. These changes in surroundings produce stresses, and, consequently, a considerable amount of disorganization even within the well-known environment.

The third external facet influencing the young adolescent is the presence of conflict points. Since the adolescent has more pressure than either the child or the adult, points of conflict will arise during this period. Although occurring within the environment, they affect the body—at least as the person perceives it. These points of conflict may not always be present in the environment, or may not be present at all times during the growth period, since the person may grow into or out of the conflict. Examples of these pressures include a conflict between social and moral values, and an awareness of differing styles of living as well as differing ideas and manners of thinking.

Implications for Music Teaching

The music teacher should recognize that he is working with the creating of values as he teaches the young adolescent. This involves not only the values of music, but social and moral values as well. The teacher who can relate socially to this age and indirectly concern himself with the moral development of the students will be well liked. Young persons should be helped to recognize that musical judgments involve value sets, and that these sets will change and possibly expand during the junior high school years. The more mature students will be attracted to and comprehend a spectrum of musical worth, while the students whose musical values are limited (in some cases superficial and, hence, radical) will be least mature.

Stage band, Le Mars Community Junior High School. Le Mars, Iowa. Dean Pelz, director.

The less mature students may appreciate the continuation plan of teaching which closely follows approaches used in the elementary school, while the more mature students will realize greater benefit from the unit approach. In some cases it might be profitable to begin the school year teaching general music with the continuation plan and adopt the unit approach as the student matures. Most junior high school students need and desire a sufficient amount of structure. Too many music teachers believe they are appealing to this age group by operating a music class with little structure, only to learn that students disparage the class to their friends.

Psychological-Sociological Theory

From what might be considered a midpoint position, Havighurst and others have defined theories which cut across two or more fields. Society expects young people to acquire certain knowledge, attitudes, and skills at certain points in their personal growth. By learning one type of task, the young person prepares for the next task or for the next level of social-psychological development. Failure to learn, or failure in learning, at one level will produce difficulty for the next, often bringing a social and personal anxiety which may retard the growth process or, at worst, produce ill effects in the form of maladjustments.

Those tasks which are more biological in nature will vary little from culture to culture, while those items based upon culture will vary greatly. For example, middle- and upper-class youth realize more anxiety since their social status defines their goals, values, and behaviors in a different manner than does the social status of lower-class youth. Particularly is this true in the areas of sex and aggression. Middle- or upper-class young people are expected to sublimate sexual and aggressive desires for long-range goals that are established specifically by the family and generally by society. Lower-class youth know they will receive no status for sublimating or postponing these desires. Many contemporary middle-class young people have adopted values of lower-class youth in many social areas on the pretext of seeking personal freedom, while many lower-class youth voluntarily become involved with values of middle-class society.

Havighurst has defined the tasks facing the young adolescent as follows: accepting one's physique and sex role, relations with peers of both sexes, emotional independence of parents, partial attainment of economic independence, making vocational choices, acquiring intellectual competence, acquiring socially responsible behavior, preparing for marriage and family life, and building a personal set of values. By reviewing these tasks, one may understand the social anxiety which can be a part of the young adolescent as he works toward maturity.

Implications for Music Teaching

Emphasis upon the learning of one type of task as preparation for the following task parallels the Level and Sequence Charts of Chapter 3. The knowledgeable teacher will understand that social-psychological growth parallels musical learnings in that each step is a prelude for the next. Failure to learn at one level produces social and personal anxiety later. This is particularly true in music.

Many students will adopt lower musical values on the pretext of personal freedom. Although obvious during the past two decades, this will continue in the future. At the same time, some lower-class students will become involved with middle-class values in music. The music teacher should guide lower-class youth

Scene from Cole Porter's "Anything Goes," Mackenzie Junior High School. Lubbock, Texas. Jeff Berta, director.

who are willing to learn, and patiently persist in aiding middle- and upper-class youth in experiencing varieties of art music which correspond to their maturity level.

The adolescent finds his relations with his peers of both sexes important, and although it may be easier to teach some classes which are all girls or all boys, the students will eventually disregard the class and the subject since it does not assist them in a major task in development. The junior high music teacher should assist these young people in extra musical areas such as the educational requirements and personal attributes necessary for musical vocations, the acquiring of intellectual competence in music which is often overlooked in music classes, and the acquiring of socially responsible behavior in regard to musical events, which should include school dances as well as formal concerts.

Sociological Theory

The basic problem of adolescence is understood to be not physical or psychological but social. Society has not accepted the adolescent and his abilities and, consequently, the social maturity of the young person does not equal his physical maturation. In fact, many young people are physically and mentally equal to older persons, and yet the adolescent is placed in a socially subserviant position. Adolescence spotlights this kind of lag for the first time. As society becomes more complex the lag could become greater, resulting in even more problems and complexities.

These lags predominate in four areas. First, they occur in the vocational area. Here status is determined by achievement, ability, seniority, or social position. Consequently, as the general standard of living in the culture is raised, the adolescent begins farther from the top on the vocational ladder. This produces obvious strains for the adolescent, for to him he appears farther from possible success and farther from the economic standards currently enjoyed by his parents in the home where he has lived.

The second area of strain in society involves sexuality and reproduction. Premarital chastity is upheld, but, in contrast, the adolescent is permitted and encouraged to associate freely with the opposite sex. Despite the sexual and physical maturity which is reached during later adolescence, he is cautioned to remain virtuous until he fully realizes an education or vocational goal.

Authority organizations produce the third area of social strain. The young person recognizes the family as a primary authority, linked to him historically and emotionally. Moving into the world, he confronts other authorities such as the school, the church, society, or government. Since these outside authorities exert limited control over the young person, family authority becomes unnecessary or unwanted. Consequently the adolescent tends to rebel against the family. Furthermore, family authority includes religious teachings, heritages, and patterns of conduct ingrained when the parents were younger. Often conflicting with the conventions of society or patterns of conduct established by law, family authority is refuted on the grounds of being outdated. To seek the independence that our society interprets as adulthood, the young person faces only one obvious and recognized escape route, and that through marriage.

Another social strain is rooted in the cultural content of society. As the frontiers of knowledge are pushed back, bringing scientific and social change, the greater the gap becomes in the cultural content between generations. Considering that social scientists and scientists usually teach in advance of their own times, and since most young people today are associated with colleges, they become involved with an institution which produces a widening of the cultural content between parent and child, adolescent and society. Advancing technology requires institutions which produce highly trained personnel and project highly specialized technical ideas. Adolescents come from school with abstract knowledge which often does not enable them to find a ready niche in society. Vocational training should be introduced into the school system along with cultural and technical information so that the young person may be able to find vocational gratification in current society as he moves through his more technical training. Production of a large number of highly trained individuals who are not readily satisfied within the current job market produces a social lag.

Implications for Music Teaching

The music teacher should be cognizant of the young person as an individual even though we often confront them in large groups. Learning a large number of names, some of their personal characteristics, and their mental attributes often is an assist. The general music class can be a social situation which accepts the young person and his abilities, for here the emphasis need not be upon production but upon development.

Being cognizant of the conflict which exists between young people and school, family, and social authority does not mean that music classes should not make demands upon students; rather, we should understand that this art form can bridge the relationship between family heritages, religious teachings, and the conventions of school and society.

The music teacher should emphasize personal growth and satisfaction in music as well as the performance and aesthetic values of music. Vocational or recreational applications of musical learnings should be enunciated, and music's relationship between the past and the present should be constantly mentioned in order to eliminate the cultural gap which appears enormous in the minds of most young people.

Biological Theory

Since the biological interpretation is the most common attempt to explain the adolescent, it consequently contains the largest number of theories. One of the simplest theories considers that the child must live through the past stages of civilization. In infancy, the sensory and motor functions are dominant. During preadolescence much of the early learning of mankind is relived. Adolescence, being a period of rebellion, parallels the human race in its transitional stage; while maturity is equivalent to modern civilization.

One of the most famous writers in the field of adolescent development is Arnold Gesell. For years his theories have assisted persons in understanding the biological growth patterns of the child and the young person. His detailed chronological descriptions of the developing human are explicit and often reassuring in that what appears to be specific behavior as seen in one youngster is often a general phenomenon. His emphasis centers upon the premise that each child develops certain personality and biological characteristics, usually during a specified age.

Although a few children may be somewhat earlier or later than the average, the characteristics, common to all, are predictable and predeterminable.

Another biological theory states that personality characteristics are controled for the most part by the body type of any individual. These body types are three: pyknic, athletic, and asthenic. The pyknic is the person with the large abdomen, usually short and squat. The athletic type is obvious. The asthenic is weak, with a slender build. The most normal personality belongs to the athletic type. Schizoid tendencies are said to appear more frequently in people with slender and tall bodies, while the manic depressive or cycloid tendencies appear more frequently in people with a stocky build. Naturally, variations exist within the three types, and personalities vary accordingly. During the time of adolescence the degree of turbulence experienced is correlated with the body type. The lean, slender young person, who has a tendency toward a schizoid personality (shy and withdrawn), will indicate more turbulence. The stocky body type, who usually is inclined toward a cycloid personality (frequent fluctuations of mood from gaeity to depression) will evidence much less disturbance during this period.

Most common of all theories of adolescent development concerns the biological change in the body during adolescence. The more pronounced bodily changes are usually discussed by the adolescents themselves in their everyday conversations. These include the sex potentials and evident personality changes accompanying body change. Linked with these, according to the biologist, are the psychological functions which are embedded in layers of the brain. The elementary emotional functions are rooted in the cerebellum, while the cognitive and intellectual functions originate in the cerebrum. There is a suggestion that a direct relationship exists between the evolution of the brain and its stratification and the development of the personality.

To be more explicit, the lowest layers of the brain are more resistant to environmental influence while the higher layers of the brain, being the newest layers, are open to environmental pressures. These lower layers are related to body functions that preserve the life, and take care of the comfort of the body and those psychological functions closely related to body organs. The second layer of the brain, the endothermic stratum, is the seat of emotions. The third layer directs the highest portion of the personality, including the ego function, cognition, and volition. This third layer organizes and directs the lower layers. With a forced or premature personality development, actions and reactions supercede the natural growth of the brain layers, resulting in negative consequences for the psychological development.

Considering brain growth, two periods of change or obvious upheaval are evident. The first comes between the ages of two and four and is often referred to by parents and psychologists as a time of negativism. During this period the integration of the two lower strata of the brain takes place. The second period of upheaval, commonly known as adolescence, takes place usually between the ages of ten and fifteen. This time the change takes the form of adventure seeking and the acting out of sexual and aggressive urges. Society sees these actions as negative, or, more commonly, as rebellion. In reality, the personality concerns itself with self-determination and independence. Biologically, the new integration between the strata of the brain involves the sexual concerns from the lower strata and love needs from the upper. These changes and personality assertions evidence that the third or upper strata is coming into focus and seeks predominence. Proponents of this theory advise that adults be tolerant of the adolescent during these periods, considering his struggle with emotional instability, disobedience, and exaggerated self-assertion, all of which point toward this transitional stage of normal development.

Implications for Music Teaching

Adolescent students enjoy looking backward to recognize the educational progress they have made and to realize their added maturity. Music can assist in this by occasionally singing or playing material from an earlier grade as a reminiscence, or by rethinking those items which have been learned. Although each individual creates his own behavior patterns, a norm does exist for adolescent development, and the norm can help bring consistency to a teaching situation. For the music teacher, personal teaching experience is helpful, but the developmental norm may act as a standard against which individual behavior may be measured.

As the student grows through the adolescent period, the third, or upper strata, of the brain seeks predominance, evidencing emotional instability, disobedience, and an exaggerated self-assertion. Music classes can assist during this period by stabilizing emotions; and through the correct choice of musical literature, the adventure-seeking drives can find some outlet which will assist the exaggerated self-assertions of this age. The unit plan of teaching can be of invaluable assistance in working with the young person as he reads, visits, listens, or activates himself in ways not possible in most classes.

Summary

By briefly highlighting these various theories of growth, one may conclude that each may sound quite plausible without being involved with another. All of these theories have been projected by scholars and men well-respected in their field. Do not try to amalgamate all of these into a single theory nor consider that you must accept them all. By presenting them to you, it is possible that your understanding of this growth period might be broadened and that the young adolescent of your classes might be better considered in a light which might not have been possible otherwise.

If one or more of these theories need further exploration or if your interest has been whetted to the point where a deeper study of them might prove interesting, the bibliography will be helpful.

LEARNING ACTIVITIES

1. Choose one of the theories of personality and define it by outlining the main points, illustrating them by factual material based upon a junior high young person you know well.
2. Organize discussion groups of five persons. Assign each person one of the personality theories so that he may defend it through illustrative examples from students he has known. Each group should choose the person who made the best presentation and that person should be presented to the class so that all may hear him.
3. Evaluate each theory and assess its worth to the junior high teacher. Which theory seems most informative to your class?
4. Invite a junior high music teacher of at least three years' experience to visit your class. Ask this teacher to discuss these theories with you from the perspective of music classes.
5. Invite a school psychologist or a guidance counselor from a junior high school to visit your class. Ask him to discuss these theories with you as a means of better preparing for teaching in the junior high school.
6. Read an Arnold Gesell description of a seventh- or eighth-grade student. How well does the description fit a younger brother or sister?

ADDITIONAL READINGS AND BIBLIOGRAPHY

ABERNATHY, ETHEL MAE. *Relationships between Mental and Physical Growth.* Washington, D. C.: Society for Research in Child Development, 1936. (chaps. 1, 4, 6 & 7)

AICHHORN, AUGUST. *Wayward Youth.* New York: The Viking Press, 1963. (chaps. 4 & 7)

BION, WILFRED R. *Transformations: Change from Learning to Growth.* New York: Basic Books, Inc., Publishers, 1965. (chap. 2)

BIRNBACH, MARTIN. *Neo-Freudian Social Philosophy.* Stanford: Stanford University Press, 1961. (chaps. 1 & 9)

BLUM, GERALD S. *Psychoanalytic Theories of Personality.* New York: McGraw-Hill Book Company, 1953.

BOSKOFF, ALVIN. *Theory in American Sociology.* New York: Thomas Y. Crowell Company, 1969. (Intro.)

BRILL, A. A., translator and editor. *The Basic Writings of Sigmund Freud.* New York: Modern Library, 1938. (part VI)

BURGESS, ERNEST WATSON. *Personality and the Social Group.* Freeport, New York: Books for Libraries Press, 1969. (chaps. 1, 2, 3, 4, 7, 10, 18 & 19)

ERIKSON, ERIK HAMBURGER. *Childhood and Society.* New York: W. W. Norton & Company, Inc., 1963. (chap. 7)

FEIGL, HERBERT, and SCRIVEN, MICHAEL, eds. *The Foundations of Science and the Concepts of Psychology and Psychoanalysis.* Minneapolis: University of Minnesota Press, 1956. (chaps. 3 & 12)

FORDHAM, MICHAEL. *New Developments in Analytical Psychology.* London: Routledge and Kegan Paul, 1957. (chaps. 5 & 7)

FREUD, ANNA. *Normality and Pathology in Childhood: Assessments and Developments.* New York: International Universities Press, 1965. (chap. 5)

GREULICH, WILLIAM WALTER. *A Handbook of Methods for the Study of Adolescent Children.* New York: Kraus Reprint Corporation, 1966. (chaps. 4, 13, 17, 18, 19, 20, 23 & 24)

JOHNSON, BUFORD J. *Mental Growth of Children in Relation to Rate of Growth in Bodily Development.* New York: E. P. Dutton & Co., Inc., 1925. (chap. 2)

JONES, RICHARD MATTHEW. *An Application of Psychoanalysis to Education.* Springfield, Illinois: C. C. Thomas, 1960. (chap. 8)

KAHN, JACK H. *Human Growth and the Development of Personality.* Oxford: Pergamon Press, 1967. (chaps. 2 & 13)

KOFFKA, KURT. *The Growth of the Mind.* New York: Harcourt Brace and Co., 1928. (I: chaps. 1 & 7)

KUNKEL, FRITZ. *What It Means to Grow Up.* New York: Charles C. Scribner's Sons, 1936. (part III)

MUNN, NORMAN LESLIE. *The Evolution and Growth of Human Behavior.* Boston: Houghton Mifflin Company, 1955. (chaps. 14–17)

RAMBERT, MADELEINE L. *Children in Conflict: 12 Years of Psychoanalytic Practice.* International Press, 1949. (II: chap. 4)

RICKMAN, JOHN, ed. *A General Selection from the Works of Sigmund Freud.* New York: Liveright, 1957. (1910, 1917)

TANNER, JAMES M. *Growth at Adolescence.* Springfield, Illinois: Charles C. Thomas, Publisher, 1962. (all)

TURNEY-HIGH, HARRY HOLBERT. *Man and System.* New York: Appleton-Century-Crofts, 1968. (chaps. 8 & 23)

VOLKART, EDMUND H., ed. *Social Behavior and Personality.* New York: Social Science Research Council, 1951. (part II)

WOLFE, W. BERAN, ed. *The Pattern of Life.* New York: Cosmopolitan Book, 1930. (chaps. 6 & 10)

WOLMAN, BENJAMIN B. *Contemporary Theories and Systems in Psychology.* New York: Harper & Row, Publishers, 1960. (chaps. 4, 6, 9 & 11)

9

The Adolescent Personality or The Young Person I Will Teach

Even before the current popularity of examining adolescent attitudes, scholars had been researching this period of physical and psychological development, realizing that within these short years great personal change occurs. Young people involved in this change evidence an in-betweenness that even they themselves do not completely understand nor appreciate.

More recently, the adolescent has been discussed in the press, over the TV, in our schools, in our churches, from the halls of government, and on the campus. Much of this added emphasis has been brought about by three situations which differ from previous years: first, the number of adolescents has increased, so that they now make up a much larger percentage of the population. Secondly, because of certain economic factors, this group now spends over a billion dollars annually, mostly upon recreation or unnecessary articles. Thirdly, the increased social acceptance of the adolescent girl as an equal member of society, along with sexual freedom granted all women, has changed a number of mores and customs.

When contemplating teaching in the middle school, be cognizant that the young adolescent of the sixth, seventh, or eighth grade differs obviously from the older adolescent who graduates from high school. This book directs attention toward the younger years in this development.

Through research a number of theories about the adolescent personality have developed. Most of these would purport to offer only a part of the complete analysis. Young teachers often believe that by understanding one facet of the adolescent personality the entire picture comes into focus. Others, realizing that the human personality is complex, disdain any study at all since each person should be met and understood on his own, without reference to studies which were not all-inclusive in obvious ways. Either approach offers problems. Examining some of the research of recent years will bring insights which could be found only in much more difficult ways.

Havighurst Analysis

This study offers numerous observations for our consideration. By defining the adolescent personality as one of five types, we have circumscribed those young people with whom we will come in contact.

Types of Personality

Submissive. A most common personality type found in the adolescent school, the submissive person with unaggressive characteristics falls in line quickly, does not initiate action, and tends to avoid conflict. Coming from a family believing in definite training, the young person usually accepts his way of life with little conflict toward his family or other authority figures. Many times awkward in social skills, this person is quite often self-critical. His academic record is rarely high and most often good to poor.

Adaptive. The most frequent personality type is the outgoing, rather confident, positive person who usually states high moral standards but may be easily swayed by the pressure of the group. Coming from a permissive family background, one observes little conflict. This person is well accepted at school, usually unaggressive, active in school affairs, and popular with the opposite sex because of well-developed social skills. Schoolwork is usually average to high and there are no signs of anxiety.

Self-directive. Of the three positive personality groupings, this category contains the fewest students, for here we find the ambitious, persistent, introspective person. Usually coming from a family background of firm convictions, some conflict of interest and action is evident between parents and child. This person, obviously active, may become a leader in school. Academically, he rates high to average, and usually drives himself to achieve more than his IQ might indicate. This person has considerable self-doubt and self-criticism, and often moves away from people and gains security through achievement.

Defiant. This is one of two negative personality types and, of the two, probably the most troublesome. Openly hostile and self-defensive, this person has a great tendency to blame society for his failures. Investigation of the family background usually indicates early and consistent family neglect toward training and responsibility; at such times when responsibility is attempted, conflict often follows. This person, unpopular at school, often quarrelsome, has a low character reputation. The intellectual capacity may range from low to high; the higher intellects tend to be leaders within their own personality group, while the lower intellects often are followers. In instances where the followers become disenchanted with the leadership provided by others, their experiment with leadership

PERSONALITY PROFILES OF ADOLESCENTS[1]

Personality Type

Area	*Self-Directive*	*Adaptive*
Social personality	Ambitious Conscientious Orderly Persistent Introspective	Outgoing Confident Positive, favorable reactions to environment
Character reputation	High Higher on F than on H & R	High Higher on H & R than on F
Moral beliefs and principles	Variable High uncertainty	High Little uncertainty Adopts current standards
Family environment	Strict family training Some conflict with family	Permissive family training No conflict with family
Social adjustment with age mates	Leader Active in school affairs Awkward in social skills	Very popular Active in school affairs Social skills well developed Popular with opposite sex
Intellectual ability	Average to high	Average to low
School achievement	High, or higher than IQ would imply	Fair to high

Personal adjustment	Self-doubt
	Self-critical
	Some anxiety, but well
	  controlled
	Concern about moral
	  problems
	Average aggressiveness
	Moves away from people
	Lack of warmth in human
	  relations
	Gains security through
	  achievement
		High on all adjustment
		  measures
		Self-assured
		No signs of anxiety
		Unaggressive
		Moves toward people

Key to abbreviations:
H = honesty
MC = moral courage
F = friendliness
L = loyalty
R = responsibility

1. Robert J. Havighurst and Hilda Taba, *Adolescent Character and Personality*, pp. 118–119. Copyright ©
1949. Reprinted by permission of John Wiley & Sons.

Personality Type

Submissive	Defiant	Unadjusted
Timid Does not initiate action Stubborn Avoids conflict	Openly hostile Self-defensive Blames society for failure	Discontented Complaining Not openly hostile
Average to high Higher on H & R than on F	Very low Higher on MC than on other traits	Low to average
High Some uncertainty	Low	Low to average
Severe family training No conflict with family	Family training inconsistent, provides no basis for constructive character formation Conflict with family Early neglect	Variable family training Conflict with family
Follower Nonentity Awkward in social skills	Unpopular Hostile to school activities Quarrelsome	Unpopular Hostile or indifferent to school activities
Low to average Seldom high	Low to high	Low to high
Fair Seldom high	Low, or lower than IQ would imply	Low, or lower than IQ would imply
Self-doubt Self-critical Submissive to authority Unaggressive	Hostile to authority Aggressive impulses Inadequately socialized Moves against people	Aggressive impulses Feelings of insecurity

is usually brief. In school this group consistently produces low grades, and, in many instances, grades lower than their capacity would indicate. To challenge or channel their potential becomes difficult and often short lived. These young people are usually hostile. Many times at school they become docile only to become obviously hostile toward the school after hours or toward society, generally, after dropping from school.

Unadjusted. This personality group needs professional psychological assistance and with such assistance, readjustment toward a positive type may be possible. Despite the usual discontent, they are not openly hostile. Coming from homes of all types, consistent conflict exists with their family because of their erratic or different desires or goals. These young people are unpopular, partly because of their unstable reaction to others, and partly because of their possible hostility or complaining. Most students are unsure with such persons and consequently assign to them a low character reputation. Rarely do these students participate in school activities. This student usually is a poor worker and his achievement is lower than his IQ would seem to imply.

The chart on pages 178–179 summarizes these five characteristics and enables comparison.

Implications for Music Teaching

This analysis interests the music teacher since the categories are easily recognizable. Most common in our elective classes and ensembles are those students belonging to the Submissive and Adaptive areas. The Self-Directive person makes up a small portion of our classes, partly because of the low percentage of this category in any school and partly because of his wide interests. Having been exposed to some music in elementary school, this student will not usually elect to continue music, not so much because of dislike for music but rather to extend his information and scope of experience.

Defiant students need music, and if the intellectual capacity is high, we should be concerned about their absence from our classes since these persons could be leaders of specific groups in adult life. This type of person will not enter the music program unless required to do so, and will be openly defiant if so assigned. We are often pleased if the Defiant students do not elect to take one of our ensembles, despite our feelings that the result could be satisfactory had the effort been made. Short-term courses or mini-courses, explained later in the book, should be a help with this group since these classes are short, focused, and place an emphasis upon individual development. Music may appeal to some of the Unadjusted students; however, their erratic approach to music's discipline could lead to disdain on the part of other students. The Pentad approach to general music, with its constant and quick changes, may be attractive to some of these students.

Ensembles usually attract students from two of these groupings. The general music program will be involved with all types, and the teacher should be prepared for each type of student when he appears in class. If possible, the music teacher may wish to make suggestions as to the grouping of students: where the defiant student might be acceptable in an English class along with all types of students, his outspoken objections or quiet nonparticipation would only breed an unproductive situation in music. Segregation of the defiant and unadjusted students into one class might yield more meaningful results.

The young musician. Photo courtesy Albion, New York, public schools.

Strang Analysis

In her book *The Adolescent Views Himself,* Ruth Strang explains four dimensions of the human personality. These dimensions are evident in all persons, but the adolescent is working toward a satisfactory amalgamation of these traits for the first time. The solution he establishes will attempt to bring his personality into focus with his environment with a certain degree of personal understanding and satisfaction.

Dimensions of Human Personality

The Individual's Perception of His Abilities. As the young person matures he continually reassesses his worth in every obvious manner. Two areas require more evaluation than others; the future vocational concern and the future social-marriage concern. Much aware of his responsibilities for the future and what this means in the way of human relationships through marriage and employment, he must grow with his abilities toward security to find a niche in the social and economic worlds. Young persons often have a tendency to belittle their own abilities, or to consider that the enormous number of young persons will blot up possibilities of employment or marriage, leaving nothing for themselves because their talents are insignificant enough to be unimpressive. Since the outer world can appear ominous, the young person needs reaffirmation in all areas, but especially in those where he looks outward toward the world and society. He needs to be led to appreciate his proper status with the world beyond home and school. The proper school environment will assist with this function. Where the home assists in this direction, it too can become an asset. Where the home conflicts with the school or any positive factor, the home will be disregarded. Although academic ability is a determining factor for some personalities, if the academic concerns of the student and his abilities come into conflict, most likely he will turn against the academic world, seeking status in areas where it can be gained, often in trivia or illegal pursuits.

The Present Self-Perception. Young people are as aware of a self-image as older persons are. They are cognizant of their lack of social poise or their outgoing nature. Many of the quick changes in personality are attempts to assert themselves in a new way by trying out a personality trait with their peers to note the reactions and feelings of others as well as within themselves. If no great discomfort was witnessed, additional explorations could be resumed. If either inward or outward uncomfortableness resulted, no additional attempts for development will probably result. The adolescent, rarely aware that his self-image is transitory or that his personality goals for himself are also transitory, constantly shifts this image in his attempt to explore his goals.

The Self-Perception As Others See It. The young adolescent greatly concerns himself with what others think. Not only is this true of himself as a person, but also in all other respects. This, in part, accounts for the tremendous peer group activity. Girls of this age use the telephone constantly to check on what others will be wearing, thinking, or if they will be participating at all. Boys, not so apt to use the phone, still have strong feelings about the same kinds of problems. Styles are most important, particularly if the style happens to be "in" or definitely "out." Teachers can be "in" as well as clothes, jewelry, or other items. Places can be "in" or "out." The place which was "in" last week can be just as far removed from their activity orbit next week. Considering what others might say

The young musician. Photo courtesy Le Mars Public Schools, Le Mars, Iowa.

if one is different absorbs a considerable amount of time, both in thinking and in discussion. Although the student spectrum will include those who are not easily swayed by group thought, the vast majority of young people are involved with peer impressions.

The Ideal Self-Impression. Young people of this age are openly idealistic. A part of this idealism involves the self-image and what the young person actually hopes to be. When this ideal becomes too romantic or too far from day-to-day reality, the young person may divulge it to no one, or only to the best friend of the moment. If the best friend betrays his trust and informs others, the friendship may cool immediately. In years past, thousands of young people held the ideal of becoming a movie star, and thousands of young people, upon gaining enough maturity, acted upon this goal. Today, the ideal is much more diverse and includes making a million before the age of twenty-five, being a rock star, having a rich husband and eight beautiful children, or moving to a quiet country place where the rest of the world does not intrude. These ideals are sometimes shared with a teacher, and when they are, should never be ridiculed. They become the raw material for realistic goals and self-direction.

Implications for Music Teaching

Often boys avoid music classes because they feel so little ego security within the demands made upon them, particularly if there is an emphasis on singing when the voice may be unstable. The student's positive assets should be emphasized so that his perception of those abilities will not become lost through his own belittling. Music, not being a formal academic subject, may offer security and refuge from scholastic emphases to a student who finds other subjects in conflict with his meager talents. In some cases, music can balance academic subjects from a student's perspective and renew his interest in standard course work.

A variety of musical activities may assist a student in his personality transitions as he tries to learn and know what it means to play an instrument, to sing, and to recreate through personal music making. Understanding on the part of the teacher should accompany these attempts.

For any elective subject, the group impression becomes important. Since the adolescent student is more often influenced by the considerations of other students, music can be an "out" subject in many schools. A required class will not face this same discrimination and will thus be placed on an equal footing with other subjects. Teachers must realize they, too, can be favorites one week and disregarded the next. The stable teacher will not permit this to affect the classroom personality or the main thrust of the program.

Since pop music is so attractive to the young adolescent, it naturally follows that these students often image an idealistic goal for themselves which is in some way attached to the pop-music field. Although highly unrealistic in the eyes of the teacher, this should be seriously discussed if the student wishes it, but never belittled. Every music teacher should be knowledgeable of the multiplicity of music vocations and the density of the market so that intelligent discussions may be held with inquiring students. The teacher should remember that the goal may be forgotten within a comparatively short time, but in the interim the goal may assist the student in beginning a genuine avocational interest in the field of music. An esteemed popular goal may cause the student to openly criticize the choice of material used in music classes since it differs from his idealization. The teacher should consider the broad perspective of the course rather than the immediate idolization by the student.

Mays' Analysis

In his book *The Young Pretenders,* J. B. Mays, a social scientist of England, has organized our young people into six categories.

Group 1. Youngsters who react aggressively against the limitation of their environment.

Group 2. Youngsters from similar socially depressed and unsuccessful stratum who do not react by open aggression against respectables.

Group 3. Made up of beats, queers, and various socially and psychologically depressed elements. Their reaction is one of withdrawal—via drugs, alcohol, or by espousal of some world-rejecting religion. They are basically inadequate types and wish to withdraw into their own world of similarly minded people, some of whom are sexual deviants; some become prostitutes and others exist on the shadowy fringe of social life.

Group 4. Angry young persons; politically leftish, strongly humanitarian, emotionally sore and sensitive. Often well educated, and in all income groups.

Group 5. New men of affluent society. Working class in origin, they do good skilled work; make high wages; suffer from few inhibitions, and are not burdened by too many scruples. Brash likable types.

Group 6. Middle class who have made a good adjustment to the realities of life and accept its goals and aspirations. Upper echelons become top business executives and managers.

The majority of young people will be found in Groups Five and Six, while Groups One to Four contain most of the deviants and failures.

There are some obvious omissions from this list, but it does contain an interesting organization of those who have or will become social failures. For teachers, this should be a constant concern.

Speaking of the failure groups, Havighurst, in his famous study *Growing Up In River City,*[2] states

> . . . the upward mobile ones, making up 19% of the age group . . . are the ones whose life chances have been enhanced by the schools and other youth serving agencies . . . The stable ones, who will lead satisfying and constructive lives . . . make up 52% of the age group. Those with whom (society) has failed, and there are a dangerous 29% of them . . . the drifters and the alienated, they have not made use of what the schools offered them, and the community has not been able to offset what in many cases was an inadequate home and in some probably an inferior biological constitution. They come from all social classes in roughly equivalent proportions, though the lower-middle class seems to furnish more than its proportional share of them. They are the elements making for instability and disunity in the society.

Implications for Music Teaching

Mays' analysis makes an interesting comparison to Havighurst. Many of the comments made in the implications for that section will be valid here. In the Mays' categories the social failures are defined in greater detail. There have been studies made which indicate that it is not that the social misfits have failed to take

2. Havighurst, Robert, *Growing Up In River City* (New York: John Wiley and Sons, Inc., 1962), p. 163.

advantage of the training offered by the schools, but that the genetic structure of the individuals in these groups is such as to preclude their benefiting from any social or educational assistance.

Tryon Analysis

This particular study asked young persons to judge themselves and their peer group by common standards and by establishing their own criteria for such personality traits as popularity, rejection, maturity, and immaturity.[3] The young people involved were asked to rate each other in terms of a number of characteristics, and the manner in which they were grouped gave the reviewer insights into the makeup of adolescent personality and what the adolescent considered of positive or little value.

The personality characteristics for this particular study are listed below with the definitions which were developed.

	Positive End of Scale	*Negative End of Scale*
Restless	Finds it hard to sit still in class; he moves around in his seat or gets up and walks around.	Can work very quietly without moving around in his seat.
Talkative	Likes to talk a lot, always has something to say.	Does not like to talk very much, is very quiet even when nearly everyone is talking.
Attention-getting	Is always trying to get others to watch what he can do or to listen to him tell about all the things he can do.	Does not care whether or not he is center of attention.
Bossy	Is always telling others what to do, bossing them.	Does not mind being told what to do, does not mind being bossed.
Unkempt	Never thinks about how clean he is or whether he looks neat and tidy.	Always thinks about keeping himself clean, neat and tidy-looking.
Fights	Enjoys a fight.	Never fights but lets other person have his own way.
Daring	Is always ready to take a chance at things that are new or unusual, is never worried or frightened.	Is always worried or scared, won't take a chance when something unexpected or unusual happens.

3. Caroline Tryon, *Evaluations of Adolescent Personality by Adolescents* (New York: Kraus Reprint Corporation, 1966).

	Positive End of Scale	**Negative End of Scale**
Leader	Always knows how to start games or suggest something interesting to do so others like to join in.	Waits for somebody else to think of something to do and always likes to follow suggestions which others make.
Active in games	Plays active games like football and basketball or likes to run and jump and so on.	Seldom plays active games like football and basketball, prefers to read or to sit and play quiet games.
Humor-Self	Can enjoy a joke and see fun in it even when the joke is on himself.	Can never appreciate a joke when it is on himself.
Friendly	Is very friendly, has a lot of friends, is nice to everybody.	Does not care to make friends, or too bashful about being friendly.
Popular	Someone whom everyone likes; others are glad to have him around.	Someone nobody seems to care much about; people do not notice when he is around.
Good-looking	Is thought to be very good-looking.	Thought not good-looking at all.
Enthusiastic	Always seems to have a good time, seems to enjoy everything he does no matter where it is—in school, on the playground, at a party, everywhere.	Never seems to have a good time, never seems to enjoy very much anything he does.
Happy	Is always cheerful, jolly, and good natured; laughs and smiles a good deal.	Always seems sad, worried, or unhappy, hardly ever laughs or smiles.
Humor-Jokes	Likes a good joke, is the first to laugh, and always sees the point.	Does not care much for jokes or has to have them explained before he sees the point.
Assured-Adults	Is always ready to talk to adults, even those he does not know well. Sometimes does the talking for young people who do not like to talk to adults.	Is shy with adults whom he does not know well; may let someone else do the talking.
Assured-Class	Does not mind reciting in class before visitors, and is calm and composed.	Always embarrassed or confused when expected to recite in class before visitors.
Grown-up	Looks and acts older than he really is.	Looks and acts rather childish.
Older friends	Likes to be with boys and girls who are older or ahead of him in school.	Likes to be with boys and girls who are younger than he and who are in a lower grade.

In working with these characteristics and the judgments by the young persons involved in the survey, several traits were found to have relation to one another. These groupings were considered as personality clusters. Some of the related groupings pointed toward immaturity; other traits toward maturity and sophistication. Even though published some years ago, this report is of interest to us because it offers information particularly focused upon those ages which concern the teacher of the young adolescent: the twelve-year-old, and the fifteen-year-old.

Twelve-year-old boys clustered the traits into these five groups:

1. Daring, Leader, Active-Games, Friendly
2. Restless, Talkative, Attention-getting
3. Bossy, Fights, Unkempt
4. Enthusiastic, Happy, Humor-Jokes
5. Popular, Good-looking, Humor-Self

The first cluster brings the most prestige to twelve-year-old boys. Admired and looked up to if positive ratings exist within this grouping, boys are ridiculed and shunned if negative ratings exist. The second cluster was one admired by most twelve-year-old boys, but if an extremely high rating was given it seemed to indicate that the boy was disorganized. Most twelve-year-olds sought a positive rating from the third cluster, which related positively with restlessness and hyperactivity. In addition, this cluster correlated well with buoyancy, good humor, and with leadership in skill games. The fourth cluster was an important one in determining prestige among twelve-year-old boys, but if scores were too high, it tended to be considered a tendency toward childishness. Boys considered this cluster related to their assurance with adults. Extreme positive ratings in the fifth cluster pointed toward certain feminine traits in the twelve-year-old. This was probably the least important of all the clusters for this age.

To review: The twelve-year-old boy has a marked tendency to prefer and to emphasize the aggressive, the boisterous, and the unkempt as well as activity of any sort. Tidiness, reserve, and submissiveness are often related to feminine behavior. High respect exists for skill in group games.

Twelve-year-old girls clustered these traits four ways:

1. Popular, Good-looking, Friendly, Tidy
2. Enthusiastic, Happy, Humor-Self
3. Daring, Leader, Humor-Jokes
4. Talkative, Restless, Attention-getting, Bossy, Fights

The first two clusters are the positive ones for the average twelve-year-old girl, while the second two are almost negative in implication. The first cluster, an important one in determining status in the group, differentiates the degree of graciousness and feminine sociability within the individual. If extremely postive in the first cluster, that girl is usually personable, amiable, demure, quiet, and lady-like; if a negative rating predominates, the girl usually is physically unattractive, untidy, and possibly bold. This grouping correlates well with cheerfulness and quiet, good humor. These qualities, demanded at this age, point the feminine personality toward womanhood.

The second cluster, also important in determining the prestige level for younger girls of the adolescent age, correlates well with ladylike behavior as well as leadership and pleasantness. The girl who rates positively will usually be pleasant, quiet, cheerful, and eager. The young lady who rates negatively will probably be depressed, sober, anxious, with some possibility toward aggressiveness.

The third cluster could be considered a negative group since it is relatively unimportant in determining status with this group. A positive score usually implies a tendency toward tomboyishness which might be acceptable in this group of girls, but not desirable. If the rating is too negative it could mean a somewhat sober and nonactive personality.

The fourth cluster also is considered a negative one by the girls. If a negative rating is evident, the girl will probably be quiet, conforming, and submissive. A positive score will mean the girl is restless and bossy, with some type of pugnacious activity for the purpose of attention-getting.

The qualities most acceptable for the twelve-year-old girl are those which indicate a tendency toward quietness, graciousness, friendliness, and unaggressiveness; with pleasant manners, quiet good humor, and a pleasing appearance.

The fifteen-year-old boy clusters the personality characteristics in the following way:

1. Popular, Good-looking, Friendly, Enthusiastic
2. Daring, Leader, Active-Games, Fights
3. Happy, Humor-Jokes
4. Restlessness, Talkative, Attention-getting

The first cluster is most important in determining the heterosexual adjustment of the fifteen-year-old male. The relation of the cluster with restlessness and hyperactivity is almost nil. A positive score in this cluster would indicate social ease and poise as well as personableness. Negative ratings would indicate lack of social ease and poise, physical unattractiveness, and probably some distasteful personal qualities.

The second cluster, also highly related to social ease and heterosexual adjustment, helps determine the prestige level within the age group. Many positive scores are related to an attractive appearance, and at this age an attractive appearance is in some way related to physical skill, strength, bravery, and/or a capacity to "take it." Negative ratings would indicate the opposite and in some way point toward physical weakness, lack of skill in games, or some fear in physical activities. If the score were definitely negative, the person might be considered a "sissy."

The third cluster is somewhat negative if too obvious. However, small percentages of this cluster could be a positive item indicating a kind of social ease, poise, and aggressiveness. If the ratings are definitely positive, the person probably would be boisterous and could be considered somewhat childish. A positive score rarely indicates a mature boy, but rather those who are too much still like twelve-year-olds. A negative rating would indicate a restrained, withdrawn, and unhappy personality.

The fourth cluster has less social significance for the fifteen-year-old than for the younger male. A positive score would point toward a disorganized type. A negative score would indicate the docile, conforming personality who lacks interest in either defying or conforming to adult demands.

With this age group, the most prestigious qualities are physical attractiveness, social ease in heterosexual situations, efficiency, and fearlessness in physical competition.

The fifteen-year-old girl clusters the characteristics in an entirely different manner than her twelve-year-old counterpart:

1. Popular, Friendly, Enthusiastic, Happy, Humor-Jokes, Daring, Leader
2. Active, Games, Humor-Self
3. Tidy, Good-looking, Older Friends
4. Restlessness, Talkative, Attention-getting, Bossy, Fights

The first grouping is the basic cluster for this age. The girl who can rate somewhat high on these characteristics will be well liked and well treated by both boys and girls. She may not have many dates, but her heterosexual development is normal. Looked up to, admired, sought after by both boys and girls in educational and social activities, her ability to get along in large or small groups and her ease within casual contacts, as well as her general social success, would be evident. This girl is the buoyant, amiable, and rather aggressive good sport. A negative rating in this cluster points to a lack of sociability and social technics with both boys and girls as well as a withdrawn, uneasy social manner.

The second cluster defines the girl who is boyish in interest and behavior. A rather high positive rating indicates that the girl is not making a good heterosexual adjustment but, instead, is sublimating such needs to skill in games and "roughhousing." A negative rating indicates one of two points: either the girl withdraws from social activity or is socially ostracized by the group; or is concentrating on another personality area and finds this cluster unnecessary.

The third cluster speaks most obviously of the girl whose interests are in her looks, her clothes, the boys, and a few older friends. This cluster has no relation to any of the other clusters; and when placed uppermost, often indicates that the girl has a limited social life and limited friendship, usually confined to older boys or men who find her glamorous and attractive because of her good looks, physical maturity, and style. Girls who receive high scores in this category may or may not be liked by other girls, may be friendly or unfriendly, talkative or quiet. Usually not rated too high socially, she has other interests. A negative rating indicates a lack of interest from boys, either because of physical unattractiveness, social charm, or immaturity.

The fourth cluster also has little relation to other clusters since it usually measures those characteristics with almost no social significance for the fifteen-year-old girl. A positive score indicates a restless, dominating, aggressive behavior. A negative score points toward the quiet, subdued, submissive, conforming person.

From twelve to fifteen, the girl personality transforms more than the boy. Her role in society changes during this time and she strives to meet these expectations. We witness a change from the quiet, ladylike, and conforming twelve-year-old to the more aggressive, more talkative, attention-getting fifteen-year-old. Her emphasis now turns toward becoming attractive to the boys, and in order to do this, the girl changes her personality to become somewhat more closely aligned to the personality of the boy. Consequently, she is more physical in her behavior, a bit louder, more friendly and outgoing, more daring, and more concerned with humor. The ability to organize activities involving both sexes, and the capacity to keep them lively and entertaining, is admired. The quality of being physically attractive to the other sex is highly considered but is not related to the other clusters.

More demands are placed upon the girls to re-orient themselves to new goals, to be flexible, and to adjust their ideals. This takes the form of emotional upheavals characterized by intermittent interest in common items of daily contact, an increase in giggling or screaming, and an egocentric interest in their own persons. Since there are very few physically-mature, socially-sophisticated boys in the ninth grade, girls who are good sports rise to prominence. Are these changes solely the result of the impact of maturity or are these changes more deeply rooted in the psyche of the female? Perhaps the role of women in society is not as clearly defined, and young girls react to this difficulty with more obvious uncertainty.

Implications for Music Teaching

Not only do these characteristics describe the changes in adolescents as they move through junior high school, they also indicate the type of class and of teacher destined to be most successful in the teaching of music. Teachers wishing to appeal to the sixth- or seventh-grade girl will conduct classes and accentuate personal characteristics so as to emphasize those characteristics (friendly, tidy, demure, quiet) considered most appealing by the seventh-grade girl. Music classes for seventh-grade boys will operate in a somewhat different manner (active, friendly, with aggressive but firm leadership). It is for this reason that many female music teachers finally conclude that they cannot reach the young adolescent boy and reorganize the music classes so as to service girls' groups only. Mixed classes are only successful if the major characteristics of the boy are considered since the girl will be moving toward those characteristics as she matures.

Music classes for upper grades of the junior high school should consider more of the "masculine" traits in approach to organization, teacher personality, and the literature used or the activities developed. The teacher should be physical in behavior, a bit loud, friendly, outgoing, daring, and with an easy humor. The teacher should in no way indicate a fear or concern for herself when with growing boys, and a jovial personality when with boys will only enhance her position with the girls as well. The class should be kept lively, but never should the teacher be immature or forget the role of a teacher and become one of the students. Such a mistake can be fatal.

Two Additional Factors

Underlying all investigations of the young adolescent are two factors which deserve mention since they take on major proportions for some individuals at certain times.

Fads. Anything may become a fad if it involves a rather novel approach to a common thing. Most common areas for fads are speech, dress, or grooming. To be effective, it must attract considerable attention by being obviously different from the usual manner of procedure, and it must be different from that usually accepted by the adult world. Fads usually spread quite rapidly through a particular section of the population, and are usually used by the adolescent to express emotions, seek status, or circumvent sexual drives. Most often fads are used by adolescents to achieve status in the eyes of their peers, since by participating in the fad they have indicated a type of resistance toward adult standards, mores, or customs. Fads are meant for the originating group. In the case of most young persons, the fad is worthless as soon as the adult world adopts it.

Peer Groups. Paul Clarke, in his book *Child-Adolescent Psychology,*[4] has stated that the adolescent may feel insecure in one or a number of areas. When this occurs he looks about for some security and will usually find this needed acceptance or security in the peer group. He uses the peer group for acceptance,

---

4. Paul A. Clarke, *Child-Adolescent Psychology* (Columbus, Ohio: Charles E. Merrill Publishing Company, 1968), p. 224.

as a maturity vehicle, and for comradeship. There are times when the peer group demands conformity, and almost always the peer group takes precedence over other group loyalties.

Three major differences exist between the adolescent and his relationship with adults as compared to his peer group.

Status. The young person is more at ease by being on a par with his peer group, consequently he is able to exercise his own judgments and attitudes. The relationship is based on mutuality, and rarely is it based upon intelligence factors or social standing. This is somewhat different from relationships within the adult world.

Emotions. The relationships with the peer group are usually not as highly charged emotionally. Not committed to his peers in the same manner as with family or teachers, he is able to move from person to person within the peer group, establishing friendships and breaking them without feeling a breach has been made in an emotional or historical relationship.

Importance. With advancing age the peer group takes on an increasingly important role with the young person. When the child is younger, the home and the adults of the home are focal. The increasing importance of the peer group typifies an unconscious realization of the need for and searching for socialization within the same age range, practicing for the adult world to come.

LEARNING ACTIVITIES

1. On the following pages you will find charts which describe particular characteristics of the young adolescent. If the school and music program is to be effective, these characteristics should guide our thinking toward particular efforts.

   a. The open columns of the chart under "Influence the School Program" and "Indicating a Musical Need For" should be completed by you.

      (1) Read the general title of the page on which you are working.
      (2) Keeping the general title in mind, read the characteristic which is found in the "Traits" column.
      (3) Complete columns two and three opposite that trait.

   This chart will assist you in your thinking of the young person and his personal attributes, but also will guide you in considering what and how the school and music program may benefit and work through such traits.

   b. After you have completed your charts, compare them with charts of your your classmates.
   c. Make a composite chart for your class. Then compare with the completed chart found in the appendix which was completed by other classes.

TWEENER CHART⁵ 1

The Tweener Wants Sufficient Knowledge and Skills Which Permit Him to Proceed on His Own

These Traits of the Tweener	Influence the School Program	Indicating a Musical Need For
An interest and an enthusiasm in gathering information and developing skills which will give meaning to him.		
A better understanding of his own ability.		

5. Texas Education Agency, *Planning for Tweeners*. Austin, Texas: Bulletin 571, 1955.

A concern about wanting to be accepted by the group.

A wide range in his skills, knowledge, physical growth, and emotional maturity.

A hesitation in participating in activities that point out his deficiencies.

An enthusiastic and persistent reader.

TWEENER CHART 2

The Tweener Desires Many Outlets for Expressing His Ideas and Feelings

These Traits of the Tweener	Influence the School Program	Indicating a Musical Need For
An intense interest in practical manipulative arts.		
A longing to participate in creative activities which give pleasure and relieve tension.		
A desire to argue with others—giving him an opportunity to clarify his own thinking and to hear the sound of his own voice.		

The copying of speech patterns similar to those of his own age group or the personality he is idolizing at the time.

The determination to try out his own ideas.

TWEENER CHART 3

The Tweener Is Concerned About His Relationships With Other People

These Traits of the Tweener	*Influence the School Program*	*Indicating a Musical Need For*
A desire to become useful and of value through affiliations with service organizations and welfare movements.		
A feeling of inadequacy toward many of the new demands of growing up.		
A difficulty in getting along with people and a tendency to blame conditions that are not the cause.		

An indifference that sometimes takes the form of cruelty toward those not in his group.

A tendency to be stubborn at home, resisting family authority.

An inclination to question the manners, morals, and ethical standards of adults.

TWEENER CHART 4

The Tweener Shows Increased Interest About Himself and His Environment

These Traits of the Tweener	Influence the School Program	Indicating a Musical Need For
A desire to learn about his special abilities, strengths, endurance, and stage of growth.		
A concern about acquiring skills, knowledge, and hobbies that will make him valuable to others.		
A shifting between feelings of superiority and feelings of inferiority.		

A desire to reconcile the realities of life with idealistic teaching.

A tendency to overreact to his successes and failures.

An urge to improve upon the realities of his environment.

TWEENER CHART 5

The Tweener Has to Adjust to Rapid and Profound Body Changes

These Traits of the Tweener	Influence the School Program	Indicating a Musical Need For
A concern about his personal appearance.		
An awareness of strange feelings that he does not understand.		
A boundless amount of energy or sudden fatiguing.		

An interest in and concern about his changing body contours.

A nervous or emotional reaction to the awkwardness that results from weight and growth changes.

An increasing amount of skill in use of large and small muscles.

An uncertain and confused feeling about sex.

TWEENER CHART 6

The Tweener Tries to Achieve Independence and at the Same Time Maintain Security

These Traits of the Tweener	Influence the School Program	Indicating a Musical Need For
A willingness to work hard to gain recognition through accomplishment.		
An insistence on having his own way and making his own plans.		
A tendency to regress to childish behavior to regain or insure security.		
A desire to be allowed to choose his own friends, clothes, hours.		

An emerging interest in vocations.

A desire for job experience.

A tendency to transfer from family to peer authority.

A desire to be grown-up—attaching undue importance to what he thinks are signs of being a mature individual: smoking, bragging, swearing.

TWEENER CHART 7

The Tweener Strives for Personal Values in His Social Setting

These Traits of the Tweener	Influence the School Program	Indicating a Musical Need For
A desire to have adults think through the problem with him.		
A willingness to accept explanations that are reached through reasoning with him.		
A desire to understand the purpose of life.		
A concern about right and wrong and a strict adherence to his code of behavior.		
A tendency to imitate the person he most admires at the moment.		

A keen sense of loyalty.

A desire to reconcile the everyday happenings he observes with idealistic teaching.

TWEENER CHART 8

The Tweener Wants to Participate as a Responsible Member of Larger Social Groups

These Traits of the Tweener	Influence the School Program	Indicating a Musical Need For
A desire to be a member of many social groups in and out of school.		
A concern about being socially accepted.		
An interest in serving school, community, and other groups.		
An urge to be a full-fledged citizen.		

A longing to be a member of one or more closely-knit groups.

A desire for direction and help in making plans and decisions, with the privilege of rejecting or accepting suggestions.

An ardent admiration for sportsmanlike behavior.

The young musician. Photo courtesy Edison Junior High School, Green Bay, Wisconsin.

2. Establish a visitation schedule with a local junior high school so that each student of your class will have an opportunity to talk with three or four junior high boys and girls. Try specifically to avoid students involved in music ensembles. Most principals will permit such discussion with students from a study hall.

    a. A sample list of questions follow. You may wish to add or delete some on the list. Be sure to obtain the approval of the principal for the questions before you begin the visitations. Avoid ad-libbing personal questions concerning family, teachers, or the school.

    b. After you have completed your interviews, answer the questionnaire concerning your visit. These questions will assist you in focusing this interview toward your own educational goals.

Questions for a Student Visit to a Junior High School

Do not tell the students your purpose unless they ask.
Do not tell the students you are college music majors unless they ask.

General

1. What activities do you like best? Least?
2. What is your favorite leisure-time activity? If sport, which one?

3. Do you know what you want to do when you graduate from school?
4. Do you think it is right to cheat a little on a test if it doesn't hurt anyone else?
5. How old are you? What grade are you in?
6. Choose a color which describes you best. Why?

Education

1. What is your favorite subject? Why?
2. What subjects do you like best?
3. Think about a teacher you admire. Why is that teacher your favorite teacher? (Personality, teaching, the subject?)
4. What do you like in a teacher?
5. What do you think you should get out of your education?
6. Do your parents make you study or do you do it on your own?
7. Do you like large or small classes better? Why? Define each.
8. What subject does your favorite teacher teach? Is it your favorite because of the teacher? Or just the subject?
9. Do parents reward you for your grades? How?
10. Are your parents concerned about the courses you take in school? About your progress? Your grades?
11. Why do you come to school?

Music

1. Do you play piano; guitar? Have you sung in church choirs?
2. How important do you believe music is as compared to other subjects?
3. Is one type of music more important than another to you?
4. Do you enjoy music?
5. Have you any desire to learn more about music?
6. Are any members of your family interested in music?
7. What is your impression of the music program in your elementary school? Why?
8. What kind of music do you like—rock, jazz, folk, country, classic?
9. Do you think music is important enough in education to be required of students?
10. Do you like the band at the football games?
11. How does music affect you? Does it make you relax? Tense? Want to move? Other effects?

Answer the Following Questions Concerning Your Interview at a Junior High School

1. Briefly describe the personality of your students. Did your short interview give you any understanding of them? Which questions helped particularly? Estimate the academic ability of your students, and their academic background.
2. What kind of teacher did these students prefer? Could you be this teacher?
3. Did your students like music? Treat it neutrally? Dislike it?
4. Why do you believe they had the attitude they did toward music? Toward home life? Former school associations? Do you believe that music teachers are to blame? Or should be praised?
5. Considering that most junior high schools require some music at this level, do you believe that you could teach the children you interviewed? Would it be easy, difficult, or moderately difficult?
6. Considering that most junior high schools require some music at this level, what do you believe you would teach them in music? What would be their interests in music? Do you believe that you could get together? At what point?

3. Study the four personality analyses. Which of the four best describes a junior high person or persons you know from your own family, from your work with Scouts, at church, or in other ways?
4. Visit a junior high from a different economic area of your city or one in a small town. Interview three or four students as stated in question 2. Again answer the questionnaire, but report to the class on the differences you found, if any.

ADDITIONAL READINGS AND BIBLIOGRAPHY

AICHHORN, AUGUST. *Wayward Youth.* New York: The Viking Press, 1963. (chaps. 7 & 9)

ALEXANDER, THERON. *Children and Adolescents.* New York: Atherton Press, 1969. (chaps. 10–12, 14)

AMES, LOUISE. *Adolescent Rorschach Responses.* New York: P. B. Hoeber, 1959. (chap. 20)

BERNARD, HAROLD WRIGHT. *Adolescent Development in American Culture.* New York: World Book Company, 1957. (all)

BERNARD, JESSIE, ed. *Teen Age Culture.* Philadelphia: American Academy of Political and Social Sciences, 1961. (all)

BLOCH, HERBERT, and NIEDERHOFFER, ARTHUR. *The Gang: A Study of Adolescent Behavior.* New York: Philosophical Library, 1958. (chaps. 1, 9, 10, 13 & 14)

BLOS, PETER. *The Adolescent Personality*. New York: Appleton-Century-Crofts, 1941. (Parts: 3, 5)

CLARKE, PAUL. *Child-Adolescent Psychology*. Columbus, Ohio: Charles E. Merrill Publishing Company, 1968. (chaps. 6–9)

COLEMAN, JAMES S.; JOHNSTONE, JOHN; and JONASSOHN, KURT. *The Adolescent Society*. New York: Free Press of Glencoe, 1961. (chaps. 1, 2, 5, 6 & 10)

ELDER, GLEN H. *Adolescent Achievement and Mobility Aspirations*. Chapel Hill: University of North Carolina Press, 1962. (chaps. 1, 2 & 4)

FRIEDENBURG, EDGAR ZODIAG. *Coming of Age in America*. New York: Random House, Inc., 1965. (chaps. 1 & 3)

GESELL, ARNOLD. *Youth: The Years from 10 to 16*. New York: Harper & Row, Publishers, 1956. (all)

GOTTLIEB, DAVID, and RAMSEY, CHARLES. *The American Adolescent*. Homewood, Illinois: Dorsey Press, 1964. (chaps. 6, 7, 8 & 10)

HATHAWAY, STARKE, and MONACHESI, ELIO D. *Adolescent Personality and Behavior*. Minneapolis: University of Minnesota Press, 1963. (chaps. 7, 8 & 9)

HAVIGHURST, ROBERT, and TABA, HILDA. *Adolescent Character and Personality*. New York: John Wiley & Sons, Inc., 1949. (chaps 12–16)

HAVIGHURST, ROBERT J. *Growing Up in River City*. New York: John Wiley & Sons, Inc., 1962. (chaps. 5–7)

———. *Youth in New Society*. London: Hart Davis, 1966.

KAGAN, JEROME, and COLE, ROBERT. *Twelve to Sixteen: Early Adolescence*. New York: W. W. Norton & Company, Inc., 1972.

KONOPKA, GISELA. *The Adolescent Girl in Conflict*. Englewood Cliffs, New Jersey: Prentice-Hall, Inc., 1966.

MAYS, JOHN BARRON. *Growing Up in the City*. Liverpool: Liverpool University Press, 1964.

———. *On the Threshold of Delinquency*. Liverpool: Liverpool University Press, 1959. (Intro., chaps. 4, 5, 6 & 8)

———. *The Young Pretenders*. London: Sphere Books, 1969.

MILSON, FREDERICK WILLIAM. *Youth in a Changing Society*. London: Routledge and Kegan Paul, 1972. (chaps. 1 & 2)

MUSGROVE, FRANK. *Youth and the Social Order*. Bloomington, Indiana: Indiana University Press, 1965. (all)

MUUSS, ROLF. *Theories of Adolescence*. New York: Random House, Inc., 1962. (chaps. 2, 3, 7 & 8)

SEBALD, HANS. *Adolescence: A Sociological Approach*. New York: Appleton-Century-Crofts, 1968. (chaps. 8, 9, 13, 14 & 17)

SMITH, ERNEST ALLYN. *American Youth Culture*. New York: Free Press of Glencoe, 1962. (chaps. 1–9)

STEVIC, RICHARD R., and ROSSBERG, ROBERT H. *Youth, Myths, and Realities*. Columbus, Ohio: Charles E. Merrill Publishing Company, 1972. (chaps. 1, 2, 3, 4 & 5)

STEWART, CHARLES W. *Adolescent Religion*. Nashville: Abingdon Press, 1967. (chaps. 6, 8, 10 & 12)

STONE, LAWRENCE J., and CHURCH, JOSEPH. *Childhood and Adolescence*. New York: Random House, Inc., 1968. (chaps. 10–13)

STRANG, RUTH. *The Adolescent Views Himself*. New York: McGraw-Hill Book Company, 1957. (chap. 2, Part II)

TRYON, CAROLINE. *Evaluations of Adolescent Personality by Adolescents*. New York: Kraus Reprint Corporation, 1966. (all)

10

Discipline

Discipline for the young adolescent has elicited more than its share of discussion. Unfortunately, the young teacher shies from these grades because of their reputation which is discussed with such regularity on all sides. And yet, every grade and every classroom has a potential for poor discipline—the first grade as well as the twelfth. With surety, problems that have been growing through the elementary school surface in the junior high school unless the teaching is good, the administration competent, and the teachers alert to those situations which lead to the problems.

Often the young teacher completes a number of education classes in college without being helped concretely with discipline. Knowing that discipline is personal so that what works for one person will not work for another, experienced teachers give only passing attention to the problem. Also, since the experienced teacher has the ability to discipline easily and has not been faced recently with any disconcerting problems, it becomes difficult to re-create the situations faced by young teachers.

Student teachers are placed in ready-made situations where the discipline is built around the critic teacher and his rapport with the students. When the discipline is weak, the student teacher can do little or nothing to improve it; when the discipline is exemplary, the student teacher has done little or nothing to develop it. Even though the critic teacher may not be present for an extended period of time, the students maintain the situation which has developed, and rarely violate it except in minor ways.

First, a few general statements, followed by specific suggestions which have been helpful to young teachers. Most of these at first reading may appear too obvious to be remembered. Yet these items contain the potential for problems which lead down an illusory path. Most situations calling for discipline appear to happen within a few minutes or even during one day, but actually are the result of irritations over a period of time. I knew a most successful junior high school teacher who often advised student teachers not to smile at students for at least six weeks. She was trying to explain in her own way that the image you build daily can be important to the larger problems.

General Considerations

Physical Conditions

Many music rooms are leftover spaces, where teachers are forced to work in poor facilities. Even though this is true, assist your own discipline by adjusting physical aspects where possible.

Chairs. Metal folding chairs do not fit the growing anatomy well and will lead to excessive noise or restlessness. In his first position, a young Wisconsin man taught where the music room was beautifully built but the chairs were a metal, folding type. These chairs offered his only consistent problem inasmuch as he was constantly requesting less noise, less bumping the chair with awkward feet, and better attention and posture. Since the school periods were one hour in length, the students began to feel uncomfortable in the chair after about thirty minutes. No matter what the lesson was, his room became noisier as the hour wore on. He was defeated in his task by the chairs in the room. A modern plastic, formed chair eliminated many problems.

Light and temperature control. Seemingly so elementary as to be self-evident, sensitivity to temperature changes, which cause students to become less comfortable, can cause some problems. If the light is not equal in all parts of the room, call this to the attention of your principal. A pleasantly bright room is necessary for good discipline.

Attractiveness. When the paint on the walls of your music room is not a pleasant color or not bright and clean, create a new atmosphere through a new coat of paint. Many a music teacher has obtained new pride on the part of the students by requesting their assistance in redecoration. Further brighten your room with a bulletin board, using drawings, pictures from music ads, magazine covers, or paper cutouts. Change the board often. Junior high students enjoy bulletin board work, especially if the teacher suggests it as a competitive team item.

Acoustics. We all know that junior high students are often noisy, and a room which magnifies sound will only increase your need for discipline. It may not be as important to have a musically acoustic room as one which aids discipline. The walls of your room may be hard, the ceiling may be hard, and the floor of concrete—impossible from the standpoint of comfort, attractiveness, and discipline. Talk to your principal about carpet, ceiling tile, wall tile, or all three. Randomly placed acoustic wall tile can be glued to existing surfaces in some attractive pattern and yet not alter the general appearance of the room nor call for a technician to apply it. Ceiling tile is difficult to install and should be placed by a professional or a maintenance crew. If the ceiling is unusually high, it can be lowered by installing tile hangers.

Many schools are using carpet throughout the building. If wall tile is impossible to install, perhaps carpet on the floor would accomplish the same result, and give a certain dignity to your room. Moving chairs about on carpet is much more quiet than on a hard surface floor. In addition, be alert to the sound of your piano around the room. If you have a tile floor, it is possible that the bright sound of the piano is magnified to an unreasonable point. A junior high school I visited a few years ago contained one of the noisiest music rooms within my experience. The wooden floor was not only sensitive to every foot movement but magnified the piano tone to a harsh and strident point. Interestingly enough, the piano sounded almost normal from the player's position, but it gave the students the idea that music class should be a place of loud and raucous noises. I advised the teacher to place the piano upon a remnant of carpet. When this was accomplished, she reported that the attention of the students improved noticeably.

Equipment. If your classroom is one used by various music classes, be alert to the irritation that music stands, unstored instruments, unfiled music, and twirler's batons can bring to students. When young hands can reach out for these pieces of equipment, sooner or later reprimands will follow. Try to assist yourself by eliminating the problem.

Room arrangement. Where chairs and desks are moveable, be sure you explore every conceivable method of room arrangement to assist with class decorum. Chairs which are too close, too far apart, or disorganized only ask students to weaken normal decorum. Your movements during teaching should help you define room arrangement, but don't hesitate to experiment. Don't place a piano between you and your students.

Self-Confidence

Even though you are a new teacher with little experience, act with sureness.

Don't become rattled. There is a game which many school students play with a new teacher. This game takes many forms, but the game is won if the teacher can be rattled. Know that the game is played with you one way if you are a young woman, and another way if you are a young man. If you can't think of anything else, smile as the comments begin. Even if the noises continue during the first day when you ask for quiet, don't become rattled. Perhaps you will need to do something, but don't get rattled.

Be prepared. Know exactly what you are going to do during the first days of your class. You should know this for each day of teaching, but it is all the more important during the early days of the semester. Don't assume that you have enough material; know that you have. Don't become alarmed if students tell you that they have never had to do this before or that the preceding teacher did not operate in such a way. Proceed; don't change your approach. It may be the wrong approach, but don't give in that easily.

Don't bluff. Junior high students often go out of their way to find questions on minutiae which might not be familiar to you. If you don't know, thank the student for the information and move on to your lesson. If necessary, explain that there are many facts which they don't know either.

Don't hesitate. Know what you are teaching each day, and how you are going to do it. Be sure the record player operates, any other equipment needed is ready, and that your lesson plan or notes are close by. Hesitations about such items produce a break in the student's attention which often destroys it for the remainder of the period. Teach until the end of the period. Students know when you are filling time. If you have no more activities for them in a given period, your pacing and planning need scrutiny. Uncertainties as to how to use last minutes of a period can lead to a long-range problem.

Probable Causes of Misbehavior

On the surface, many reasons exist for unruliness within the classroom. Many times, however, exceptional behavior is a superficial indicator of deeper concerns.

Out of caste. Within the classroom a person may feel that he does not belong with others who are there. The individual may be too old chronologically or he may be too poor to feel at ease; he may believe that he has the wrong color of skin or the wrong clothes. The teacher must be aware of these possibilities and work at making all the young people feel and believe they are welcome.

Out of talent. This affects the musical situation more than we want to admit. Believing that he knows too little about music or knows too much, the person can couple this with an age or size problem and misbehavior can result. This is common in junior high school general music. The person who knows too much for the class is impatient with other students and with the teacher, believing that he needs not be in a class which is so elementary. The person knowing less than average acts self-defensive in withdrawal or obvious overt actions.

Demands attention. Some pupils wish just to call attention to themselves. These are not always the extroverted personalities, but a need is felt so that an action follows, demanding the attention of the teacher and usually the class. An experienced teacher knows the attention is more important to that individual than the discomfort or embarrassment of being punished for it.

Fit Your Discipline to the School

The teacher who is out of place with his concept of discipline will have problems. This is true if one teacher is too tough or too lenient for a given school. The administration and the other teachers of the school create a pattern which will be difficult to change unless by common agreement. Usually the teachers in the classroom request stricter discipline than the administration is willing to impose or co-operate with. When this happens, it becomes difficult to demand more than the administration will uphold. Being out of step with discipline will produce constant problems for the teacher. Consequently, ask questions of other teachers who may guide you in your disciplinary goals.

Practical Suggestions for Classroom Control

Reduce regular activities to a routine. Almost all music classrooms have a number of small details which can be routine. Such details include the passing of music or music books. Have definite persons assigned to this task for a short or extended period of time. Decide if they will proceed upon their own or upon a signal from you. Define your seating pattern. Shall students sit anywhere in your room or in a particular position? What is the procedure for latecomers to your class? When is the class dismissed? Be sure the class understands these routines among others, and be definite and consistent. A break from definiteness or consistency always means irregularity which some young people interpret as permissiveness.

Be alert and active. Don't seat yourself at the piano and expect to have discipline. If you must play an accompaniment, make sure that you are not playing throughout the class period; rather, consider a number of activities which take you away from the keyboard. Move about the room on any pretext. If you are conducting, keep your eyes on the students most of the time, rather than on the music. In some rooms you may have to write on the board, half facing the class. Meet your class at the door, and be near the door as the class departs. Most beginning teachers are too immobile within the room. Remember, most teenagers like a bubbly person, and although this may not be your personality type, you can give this impression by your easy but fluid movements.

Plan your work. The teacher who plans well will not have the same problems which confront the optimistic teacher who has no plans. Music teachers as a group do too little planning, often relying upon their ab-lib ability, the teaching of theory, a record on the machine, or asking students for a favorite song to sing. Students know when you have no plan since most often you will resort to imitating the rehearsal approach to teaching—a procedure which doesn't adapt well to most junior high school general music classes.

Psychological and physiological aids. Enough rest, regular exercise, and some relaxation are essential to good teaching. Music requires much energy, and you must conserve yours if you are to be effective. Work hard at school and when you leave it, try to forget your concerns. Learn to associate with your teachers at school for short periods of time, but don't let the lounge or the janitor's room become an over-consuming pastime. When you are first on the job, it is easy to spend too many hours in the music room at the school. Be sure that some of your free time is spent in other than musical circles. Often musician friends understand your shoptalk and your problems, but you need other kinds of associations in addition.

Adult formality and reserve. Although you are young, don't try to be buddies with junior and senior high school pupils. Be friendly, but not their friends. Don't be aloof or formal, but know your place or they will put you in it. Don't try to dress like junior high school students. Despite this oft-stated advice, new junior high school teachers still abuse this area. Wanting to be well liked, wanting to have music become a vital part of the lives of the students, the young teacher believes that by being a friend to the student he will be a winner. Too often the teacher understands the rules as stated but believing that he will not become a victim of the situation, proceeds to fall into the trap, only to wail about this as the year progresses.

Learn the atmosphere. This may be accomplished quickly by talking to a number of teachers in your building and by visiting their rooms before or after classes to learn how they do things. Also, learn the building itself by touring the plant. Secure the texts for your classes, and if you have none, survey the music library so that you can discuss its strengths and weaknesses intelligently. Tour the school library and ascertain if it can be of any assistance to your classes. Visit the audiovisual center and ask the procedures for using equipment. Talk of your goals to the principal before too many days after your arrival have elapsed. So that they will know you are interested in their work as they should be in yours, visit the guidance counselors. Visit also the attendance officers and be sure you understand and know school policy. Make friends with the custodians; they often can be of great assistance, especially at concert and contest time. Observe the school in operation in the halls, in the study hall, and on the grounds. Size up the actions of the students singly and in groups. Finally, talk with other music teachers within the system. Above all, don't over talk. Listen a lot, and ask questions.

Know student backgrounds. Records of students are available in most school offices. Other teachers can be of some assistance, but do not accept completely the words of others. Often teachers are only repeating to you their own problems which could be based on a personality conflict, and students could be different with you and your subject matter.

Exercise self-control. Students will respect the teacher who does not lose self-control, even if they do themselves. No matter what happens in the classroom, keep control of your voice and your actions. Do not become angry. If you must take action, appear calm during the action.

Do not use sarcasm. Bitterness and unfair implications abide within sarcasm. Although the class may laugh at what you say and seem to disapprove of the actions of the disciplined student, once away from the immediate situation the students will criticize the teacher as they remember the sarcasm. It is ultimately ineffective.

Loss of face. As all of us do, students resent losing face, particularly in front of others. The teacher who pushes the student so that he feels it necessary to lie to save face or to assist other students will never be a friendly student. Students will not "squeal" on their friends for your sake.

Avoid public negativisms. When shortcomings are pointed out in public, the morale of the entire class or ensemble is surely lessened. If negative or critical remarks are necessary, these discussions are best held behind the closed door of the rehearsal room with only the class present.

Exhibit enthusiasm. Music can be uninteresting to or disliked by many students. Enthusiasm of the teacher will assist in interesting students in an area which may otherwise be filled with hesitations.

Give concise directions. Do not become quickly upset if students do not understand exactly what you wish done or how you wish it done. Students often don't understand, but this is not always the result of poor attention. If problems persist, it may help to write directions on the board, or have a student read the assignments. Explicit directions may be one thing to you, but something else to the students.

See the humor in situations. Small events during a class period may trigger the laughter of the class. It could be a misspoken word by the teacher. Don't hesitate to laugh with the group, and especially if the teacher becomes the center of the fun. On the other hand, don't try to be a joke teller. Often students won't think your jokes funny but will laugh under obligation. There will always be a few students who will misunderstand the jokester.

Work at building your self-confidence. Appear self-confident from the first day. On the other hand don't be a know-it-all. If you don't know the answer, say so. A fake answer will be recognized quickly by most students, with the teacher's possible loss of face. Be well planned for each day, including rehearsals. Do not become ill at ease if you cannot hear from the podium as well as college conductors can or cannot give pitches readily without the keyboard. You most likely will improve in these areas if you do not belabor your shortcomings. You are not expected to know everything about music. Talk with your principal regularly about your classroom problems. He should recognize your inexperience and be willing to assist. Above all, don't berate yourself before your own students. As a kind of humor at which students were expected to laugh and respond negatively, one high school orchestra director belittled himself regularly. After two or three hearings the students began to agree with him.

Avoid open personal comments. Talk to the class generally or answer an individual's question, but avoid personal comments in front of the group. Never interrupt the work of the class to talk about one student, and do not discuss the playing or singing problems of one person with another student. For a number of years one of the leading band directors of the country would turn from a particular student, and discuss the student's problem with another person or section of the band. As a result, many good musicians refused to work with this director.

Give every student the feeling he is liked. This does not mean that you always like everything which he does, but as a person he qualifies for some respect from you and some personal attention.

All of the above suggestions are intended to assist you in your classroom procedure, but none of these items implied that your classroom personality should be weak or that you should retreat from discipline when a student persists in wrong behavior. Despite the best laid plans and behaviors on the part of the teacher, there comes a time in the daily routine of the class when some kind of discipline is necessary.

When Punishment Is Necessary

If punishment is necessary the following suggestions could be helpful:

Avoid making schoolwork a punishment. First of all, don't assign additional work in music. The singing of a solo before the class, or the writing of a biography of a famous musician will not help eliminate the problem, but will help eliminate interest in music. After-school detention is helpful provided you do not ask the student to become involved with foolish activities such as writing sentences or cutting out letters for the bulletin board. One positive procedure for after-school detention is to assist the student with an assignment from another class. The concern shown as both of you work through some math or struggle with some English sentences will produce most positive results.

Make the punishment fit the crime. One junior high school teacher regularly asked students who misbehaved to polish the tubas, sometimes when the instruments didn't need it. Don't make threats which you can't carry out or will not carry out. In fact, threats are poor kinds of discipline. A teacher who is constantly verbalizing threats will almost always have poor discipline. It is best to avoid stating the punishment until you have had time to react to the situation; otherwise you may enunciate a punishment much too severe for the person and the situation. Better, establish a policy for yourself of merely asking the student to see you after class or after school, or state that you will walk with him to his next class or to the office. This gives you time to cool down, but also time to think of the correct discipline.

Don't involve the principal. Send students to the principal's or counselor's office only if you are confident that those administrators will respond in a manner appropriate to your desires. Constant are the complaints of teachers that junior high school administrative officers refuse to take proper disciplinary action with students sent to them. Many matters of different natures occupy the minds of these people so that they may fail to understand the seriousness of the situation from the classroom point of view. Much better to handle the situation yourself without involving a third party.

If at a loss, follow common sense. Some situations for which you believe you have had not previous preparation can arise within a given classroom. Only your own intuition and common sense can be your guide. Even with experience, the successful teacher may be faced with situations where he hopes his reactions were the best procedure. The inexperienced teacher should recognize the possibility of these occasions.

Corporal Punishment

In days gone by, it was common procedure for the teacher to paddle the students for a number of misbehaviors or omissions. Today, the student is rarely touched. There are those outside the classroom who are critical of this change. In some localities of the country, corporal punishment is still a possibility. A majority of college students object to a discussion of corporal punishment as if to imply that under no circumstance should a teacher consider such action. Other students believe that the absence of paddling and strapping is a loss to the general decorum of the school. A quick survey will usually find that the girls abhor bodily punishment more than the boys do, and yet they have seldom, if ever, seen it administered or have been the victim. On the other hand, the boys have been involved. The latter group usually believe that the practice should continue. In one recent class, one young man admitted freely that he would not be in college had it not been for the concern of one teacher who applied the leather strap frequently. He believed that his present orderly life resulted from her direct concern.

In some states corporal punishment is illegal. In other schools it is not considered a possibility even though legally possible. If a misbehavior is so severe as to warrant some acute correction, be sure of the local situation before becoming involved. In any event, ask the principal to be a witness to your actions.

LEARNING ACTIVITIES

1. Read the following description of a discipline problem. Then write the ending of the incident as you would handle it if the problem presented itself to you during your first year of teaching.

    When the teacher came into the room at the beginning of general music class, he indicated that class was ready to begin by waving his hands in such a way as to quiet the usual talking. As he walked toward the cabinet which housed the music books he noticed that Tom was still turned around and talking with the boy behind him. The teacher waited for a minute, assuming that Tom would finish his conversation as soon as he realized that others had ceased. When this did not happen, the teacher asked Tom to turn around in his seat and perpare to work. The teacher waited patiently and when Tom failed to respond, the request was repeated with greater emphasis. Tom ignored the teacher and continued his conversation in even louder tones. The attention of the class was now focused on this pupil-teacher situation. The teacher walked over to Tom's desk and said, "Let's get ready for class, Tom, and we'll see if I can assist you today with this problem of the F-clef." As he spoke, the teacher placed his hand in a friendly way on Tom's shoulder.

"Take your hands off me," shouted Tom.

The teacher stood transfixed by the suddenness and intensity of Tom's reaction. Tom then jumped up and pushed the teacher's arm away from him with enough force as to cause the teacher to totter backward and almost stumble against the chair in the other aisle. The teacher quickly regained balance and in a controlled but grave tone said, "Go to the office at once, and report here at the close of school."

Tom sauntered a few steps and . . .

a. How would you have reacted to this situation had you been the teacher? Perhaps you would wish to rewrite the last quotation from the teacher and the ending of the classroom scene.
b. Assuming the scene as it is written, write the ending of the classroom scene.
c. Write the conversation as you would imagine it would take place after school between yourself as the teacher and Tom.

2. Discuss the probability of your being involved with corporal punishment and under what kinds of circumstances.
3. The following problems have been listed by students as occurring most often in the junior high school; in addition, they have been categorized as simple or more complex by the students themselves. Although some may not directly affect the music class, you could be assigned study hall or cafeteria duty where such behavior could be a real possibility.
   a. Discuss each problem listed below, deciding what your best course of action might be if you were the classroom teacher or the nearest teacher to the center of the activity.
   b. Describe a situation involving one of the more serious problems. Read your preliminary description to the class, ending at a point where some action is required by the teacher. How would persons in your class respond to your problem?

Simple Problems	*More Complex Problems*
Writing on desks	Talking back to teachers
Placing gum on desks	Throwing food in cafeteria

Simple Problems	*More Complex Problems*
Running in halls	Smoking on school grounds
Excessive talking in class	Fights on school grounds
Excessive talking in study hall	Fights in halls
Horseplay in study hall	Stealing books
Unauthorized absences from class	
Smoke bomb in hall	

4. Recall a discipline problem from your junior high school days in which the teacher responded poorly, too late, in poor taste, or with the wrong punishment. Describe the incident to the class and tell why and/or where the teacher erred.

ADDITIONAL READINGS AND BIBLIOGRAPHY

ADDICOTT, IRWIN O. *Constructive Classroom Control.* San Francisco: H. Chandler, 1958. (all)

BROWN, EDWIN J. and PHELPS, THOMAS. *Managing the Classroom: The Teacher's Part in School Administration.* New York: The Ronald Press Company, 1961. (chaps. 6, 16 & 17)

BUCKLEY, NANCY K., and WALKER, HILL M. *The Modifying Classroom Behavior.* Champaign, Illinois: Research Press Co., 1970. (all)

HARING, NORRIS GROVER, and PHILLIPS, E. LAKIN. *Analysis and Modification of Classroom Behavior.* Englewood Cliffs, New Jersey: Prentice-Hall, Inc., 1972.

JAMES, KIETH FRANKLIN. *Corporal Punishment in the Public Schools.* Los Angeles: University of Southern California Press, 1963. (chaps. 3 & 9)

KOUNIN, JACOB SEBASTIAN. *Discipline and Group Management in Classrooms.* New York: Holt, Rinehart and Winston, Inc., 1970.

LaGRAND, LOUIS E. *Discipline in the Secondary Schools.* West Nyack, New York: Parker Publishing Company, 1969. (chaps. 1, 3, 5–8)

LaMANCUSA, KATHERINE C. *We Do Not Throw Rocks at the Teacher.* Scranton: International Textbook Company, 1966.

LARSON, KNUTE G. *School Discipline in an Age of Rebellion.* West Nyack, New York: Parker Publishing Company, 1972. (chaps. 5, 7, 9–11)

LARSON, KNUTE G. and KARPOS, MELVIN R. *Effective Secondary School Discipline.* Englewood Cliffs, New Jersey: Prentice-Hall, Inc., 1963. (chaps. 1, 4, 7 & 11)

MADSEN, CHARLES H., and MADSEN, CLIFFORD K. *Teaching/Discipline: Behavioral Principles Toward a Positive Approach.* Boston: Allyn & Bacon, Inc., 1970. (chaps. 1, 2, 6 & 7)

MUUSS, ROLF EDUARD H. *First Aid for Classroom Discipline Problems.* New York: Holt, Rinehart and Winston, 1964. (chap. 4)

NEA. *Discipline in the Classroom.* Washington: National Education Association, 1969. (all)

SCHAIN, ROBERT L. *Discipline: How to Establish and Maintain It.* Englewood Cliffs, New Jersey: Teachers Practical Press, 1961. (all)

SCHAIN, ROBERT L., and POLNER, MURRAY. *Using Effective Discipline for Better Class Control.* Englewood Cliffs, New Jersey: Practical Press, 1964. (chaps. 1 & 3)

SHEVIAKOV, GEORGE V., and REDL, FRITZ. *Discipline for Today's Children and Youth.* Washington: Association for Supervision and Curriculum Development, 1956. (all)

SMITH, WILLIAM I. *Guidelines to Classroom Behavior.* Brooklyn, New York: Book Laboratory, 1970.

SPIEL, OSKAR. *Discipline Without Punishment.* London: Faber and Faber, 1962. (chaps. 2, 6 & 8)

STENHOUSE, LAWRENCE, ed. *Discipline in Schools: A Symposium.* Oxford: Pergamon Press, 1967. (chaps. 2 & 5)

SYLWESTER, ROBERT. *Common Sense in Classroom Relations.* West Nyack, New York: Parker Publishing Company, 1966. (all)

WEBSTER, STATEN W. *Discipline in the Classroom; Basic Principles and Problems.* San Francisco: Chandler, 1968. (chaps. 2 & 5)

WILLIAMSON, EDMUND G., and FOLEY, J. D. *Counseling and Discipline.* New York: McGraw-Hill Book Company, 1949. (chaps. 2 & 7)

WITTENBERG, RUDOLPH M. *Discipline in the Teens.* New York: Association Press, 1963. (all)

11

Community Pressures: Metropolitanism

During the early part of the twentieth century, families were attracted to the cities of our country because of work possibilities and living conditions which included better housing along with electric lights, indoor plumbing, paved streets, fire protection, and modern transportation. The increase in the population and the demand for better education helped school officials organize the junior high school to assist the young adult with a stronger preparation for high school or with an emphasis upon job training if no more schooling were desired. The onetime advantages of the city have recently become overshadowed by disadvantages to many so that a series of conditions unique to the past two decades have accumulated to bring to the cities, as well as the schools which serve them, problems which include urbanism, inner-city deterioration, racial ghettos, suburban concentrations, accumulated retardation, school consolidations, and excessive tax structures. All of these disadvantages and others can be lumped under the one caption of metropolitanism, all demanding our attention since schools in all parts of the country suffer greatly from such problems. Auxiliary problems directly or indirectly affecting the schools include a shrinking tax base as city governments take over formerly taxable land for urban housing developments, parking lots to hold commercial interests downtown, etc.; underpaid, undermanned, and under-trained police force; growing welfare clients, slum housing, and crowded tenements; under-educated persons who find a technical society and job base moving away from their productivity possibilities; and organized crime inflicting a shadow around every corner.

Urbanism

The population of our country has been moving from a rural to an urban locale since before the turn of the century. In 1900, of the some 75 million people in the United States, 31 million lived in urban areas. By 1960 there were 178 million people in our country, of which 112 million lived in urban areas. Not only has the population increased noticeably but the percent of persons in the cities has increased from about 41 percent to 63 percent. (At this rate of increase, by the year 2000 over 25 percent of the people will live in cities of over 100,000.) This increase of 81 million people in the cities of our country has within it a basis for problems, not only for the city governments and services but also for the schools. School enrollments have increased in metropolitan areas. Of the 28 thousand school districts in 1965, 12 hundred of them enrolled 23 million pupils, or about 60 percent of the national total.

The Bureau of Census describes a metropolitan area as a city of 50 thousand or more, with its county plus those neighboring counties which are functionally bound to the city. In 1960, 65 percent of the people of the United States lived in 216 metropolitan areas which contained only about 10 percent of the land area of our country. In servicing these metropolitan areas, governments and school districts have been particularly slow in recognizing the values of metropolitan consolidation, yet inhabitants of these areas desire and seek metropolitan boundaries formed by telephones, mass media, public transportation, and other similar services. This failure to adopt a school consolidation based upon metro areas has brought problems to the schools which, even though recognized, have yet to receive a valid and plausible solution.

Suburban Concentrations

Beginning in about 1925, substantial numbers of persons with a higher standard of living began moving to the outer rim of the cities. Here, newer and larger homes could be built and larger lots could be supplied for the homes of the wage earner who had the resources for longer travel to and from his place of business. As the homes of the inner city became older, immigrants and migrants to the cities sought housing there if resources were meager, but away from the inner city if possible. Many from the rural areas, wishing to be near to the city, moved immediately outside the city limits in cheaper homes if their finances could not support urban housing. Often the growing city would overtake these make-shift areas, including them in the suburban metropolis. By 1950 it became evident that the housing of the inner city was being left to the poor, the migrant, the ethnic, and racial persons who had few marketable skills, little background in education, and low income potentials; while the white-collar worker, the educated, and the rural person of some means sought the suburb where the living style more often matched the relaxed pattern of previous days of the city or the rural community, and where, in an attempt to keep this folksiness, the size of the suburb and the restrictions of the suburb were often most limiting.

Caught in this polarization, the schools became victims of social and educational segregation. The people with educational backgrounds sought good schools for their children and were willing to increase the tax base for such schools; the tax base became a type of zoning prohibition and regulation, but at the same time enabled the suburb to build newer schools as demanded, pay higher wages to teachers and administrators, and offer greater educational services to the student. The junior high schools, or other types of intermediate schools, particularly benefited from this arrangement since it was in the rapidly growing suburb rather than in the inner city where new buildings were built for the young adolescent.

In the inner city, the students came to the school with fewer social and educational advantages, lower cognitive skills, and with a need for quality experiences in all areas of education which can only be supplied through better teaching. The inability to pay for these services through the tax base created schools which offered only minimal services, thus pushing more of the economically marginal families out of the inner city and leaving only those who had to remain. The junior high school suffered along with other educational institutions.

Inner-City Deterioration

With the property tax the basis of the school levy, the suburban areas benefited from the newer and larger homes, and still a lower evaluation per thousand could be assessed than was possible in some urban areas. In contrast, with fewer land owners living in the homes and properties of the inner city and with low income property needed by the poor, the properties of the inner city were left to deteriorate. In order to meet the cry for low-income housing and to offer the landlord a return on his money, houses which at one time had been intended for one family became multiple family dwellings. As the property evaluation dropped and as the demand and costs for city services rose, the tax dollars available to the schools became critical. Services were cut below the point where good school administration and good teaching were possible. The state governments realized the problem, but because of voting pressures from the suburbs did little to remedy the situation; the federal government, not wishing to preempt local jurisdiction, offered assistance only recently and then only under special conditions. In most instances such assistance has been too specific to be of general value.

Racial Ghettos

In years past, immigrants to the United States tended to congregate in certain sections of a city if nationalistic and/or religious ties were strong; when numbers were substantial, this created ghettos. Several differences exist between former collective living and that of recent years.

Many of the former immigrants had skilled or semiskilled backgrounds. Although they came into the city to live, they were able to support themselves almost immediately by skills which could be developed or altered to suit the American labor market. These people were assimilated quickly into the national fabric by either moving into other parts of the country or by upgrading their own living conditions within a limited geographic area.

Many of the immigrants moved from the large city concentrations into the rural areas of the country, preferring to practice their farming skills than to remain in the city.

Most of the immigration centered within the confines of a limited number of major seaboard cities and if problems existed, these were not as generally prevalent as those within the past several years.

Persons immigrating into a new country often were prepared psychologically and financially to withstand hardship for a number of years until they became established.

Most of the immigrants realized that a good schooling would assist their children in moving upward on the social and financial ladder, and supported the schools even when it meant hardship to them personally.

Ghetto living is of a different type in recent years. For the first time since the founding of our country, poor, substandard, collectivist housing is being used by natives of our own country—people who have grown up within our educational system and our social structure. They are the Puerto Rican and Mexican-American (legally migrants, although they often have severe language problems, social problems, and few marketable skills); the poor Southern white (a migrant with fewer social problems and no skin coloration differences, but with poor educational background and few marketable skills); and the Negro (most coming from the rural areas of the South with little or no educational background, with an obvious skin coloration which often leads to prejudicial treatment, and with few marketable skills). Not being able to buy or move onto the land, having benefited poorly or not at all from former contacts with education, not psychologically nor financially prepared for city living, not limited to a few seaboard cities but distributed throughout most metropolitan centers, these low income groups were attracted to the inner city because of the housing available, but it offered them little in return in the way of schooling for their children.

Broom and Glenn have statistically verified the expenditures for education for white and nonwhite populations for the states of Alabama, Arkansas, Georgia, Mississippi, North and South Carolina in *Transformation of the Negro American*.[1]

1929–1930	If whites were rated as	100%,
	non-whites equalled	25%.

1. Leonard Broom and Norval Glenn, *Transformation of the Negro American* (New York: Harper & Row, Publishers, 1967), pp. 90 and 91.

1952	If whites were rated as	100%,
	non-whites (urban) equalled	76%;
	non-whites (rural) equalled	62%.

Before desegration of public schools began, the inferiority of Negro education in Southern and border states was conspicuously evident from differences in per-pupil expenditures, length of the school term, pupil-teacher ratios, formal education of teachers, teachers' salaries, and the like. These differences are of more than historical and regional importance, since a large part of the Negro labor force throughout the country was educated in the Southern and border states during these years.

The schools, faced with this type of segregation in the inner city and with the low tax base which accompanied such segregation, were unable to effect a benefit which they needed and, in more than a few cases, sought.

Accumulated Retardation

The child of the ghetto brings to the school a meager experiential background which does not enable him to progress at the same rate as his suburban counterpart. Reading skills are poor and in some cases, such as the Mexican-American where the native language is still spoken in the home, the child is confronted with a bilingual situation. IQ's in these schools average below the national norm. All of this means that the school should provide special services in order to assist the child. Classes should be smaller but in most cases are larger than those of schools in the suburbs; psychological and guidance services should be evident; reading and skill subject specialists are needed. In order to provide an equally effective education, a higher cost per pupil base should be evident in inner-city schools rather than the usual reverse. Retardation demands special attention and when this is not forthcoming, the school services less well than it could.

School Consolidations

Not all of the economic problems, not all of the low tax base districts or the modest or poor educational opportunity schools are to be found in the inner city. Many of these are located in the rural areas of our country and a few are in thinly populated suburbs. These schools also offer services below the national standard. In 1960 the median years of education completed in metropolitan areas was eleven, while in the rural areas of our country the median was 9.5. This becomes clearer when we know that of the rural group 11 percent had fewer than five years of school while in the metropolitan areas this was 7 percent. To assist in this problem, some of the school districts have consolidated in an attempt to offer the taxpayer better schools with little increase in tax load.[2] These consolidations have been successful in many instances, but in areas where the tax base is meager, substandard education and lower salaries still predominate. Some rural schools have received a benefit over the past ten years when a few industries have moved out of the large metropolitan districts into the rural countryside, seeking "the better life" for their employees. The increase in the tax base and the concern of the professional employees brought into the community have assisted some school systems.

Excessive Tax Structures

But all is not well even in the high-income city suburbs. During the early years of the 1970s, those districts where the best schools flourished balked at added tax burdens and schools were forced to hold the line with expenditures or to cut back on services and personnel. Coming at a time when costs were at an all-time high, such taxpayer rebellions have caused considerable concern to school administrators. It would appear that these suburbs contain a certain percentage of persons who favored good schools so long as they were of relatively modest cost. Once the tax burden became excessive, these citizens quickly realigned with those who did not regard education highly and questioned whether the schools needed all of the services which have been built into them over the past number of years.

These citizen groups usually are willing to place extra emphasis upon education for the youngest children, and most high school programs seem so close to the job market that little cutting in programs is recommended. The upper grades, including the intermediate school, receive more than their share of attention from such citizen groups. Of all the courses in the school, music probably has been hardest hit.

Originating with the federal grants to education, the word "accountability" has become popular throughout the country and will continue to be so. Schools, faced with having to prove the worth of their programs and processes, were asked to account for the money given them. Citizens no longer wished to hand the schools large sums of money for the education of the young without knowing that the program produced results. Failing to achieve such accountability from the local teachers, some systems turned to the awarding of contracts to large educa-

2. School specialists, including the reports by Conant, have stated that a school system needs 2,000 pupils to warrant a curriculum suitable for contemporary needs as well as a staff to teach it. Yet in the census of 1962, after consolidations in all states over the preceding 20 years, 65 percent of the school districts had fewer than 1,800 pupils. This statistic seems less alarming when one realizes that these districts service only 10 percent of the total population.

tional corporations in order to quickly raise the performance level of certain subjects. At this point in writing, both of these areas arouse debate, yet warrant consideration and evaluation.

Some Suggested Solutions

It becomes quickly obvious through the preceding discussion that the tax
base is a major contributor toward quality of schooling. The inner city schools lack
the tax base, while suburban schools often have such a base, which enables them
to provide educational services which are considered appropriate for the times or
better than the national average. The present situation could be represented by
the accompanying diagram.

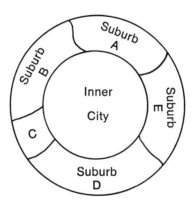

Since the suburb cannot exist without the assets and functions of the city,
one possible solution to funding would be a tax reorganization of the metropolitan
area so that the suburb would become a part of the support structure as part of
the city. No change in county, city, or suburb government need be made. This
would result in a tax base diagram as shown at the top of page 233.

As we stated earlier in the chapter, if there are families who would rather
have less quality education by paying less in taxes, this plan would enable the
person to make such a choice. At this time, the various suburbs offer this choice to
those able to consider suburban living, but the person of the inner city and the
person of modest income rarely has this choice. By combining certain suburbs
as a tax unit, and combining certain suburbs with portions of the inner city, a
graduated scale of tax base and school quality could be devised for the metropolitan area.

If the metropolitan area were not large, the tax base could be unilateral so

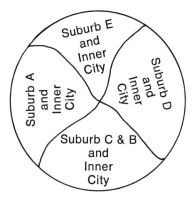

that schools could become a service such as telephone or mass media, representing the entire metropolitan area. This would mean that the suburbs would be taxed to assist the inner city or vice versa. Such a plan could be represented by the following diagram.

Metropolitan area
including inner city,
suburbs, and rural
schools in commercially
dependent areas.

Since the economic and racial disparities of the inner city and suburbs have reached a peak, the years ahead will probably find each becoming more similar to each other. For one or more reasons a few families have returned to the city, while efforts are being made to attract special groups such as retired persons and single mature adults. Cooperation between the two will be slow in developing, and the last bulwarks to fall to cooperative ventures could be government and schools.

Once established, school boundaries become calcified so that the above plans, although relatively simple in construction, would be almost impossible to adjust except by state or federal statute. The latter is more plausible since state legislatures reflect too strongly the sentiments of the upper and middle classes.

In a few instances states (New York, California, Wisconsin, for example) have enacted laws which have assisted the lower income, lower achieving schools by giving aid in inverse proportion, so that schools in wealthier suburbs receive less state aid than those in poorer rural or urban areas. Since most states have not enacted such laws during the past decade, it would indicate a reluctance on the part of most constituents to assist the schools in such a manner.

Many professionals believe that only one source, the federal government, may aid the schools in the decades to come. In 1955 a report from the Commission of Intergovernmental Relations[3] stated that the federal government had the right to support local public education under certain stated conditions when "the lower levels of government cannot or will not act." These conditions are listed below with comments in parentheses.

a. When the National Government is the only agency that can summon the resources needed for an activity. (The local governments have been opted on sources of revenue by state and federal governments. In some cities it is believed that all locally assigned sources of revenue have been used or depleted.)

b. When the activity cannot be handled within the geographic and jurisdictional limits of smaller governmental units. (The metropolis must have an educational system which supercedes the limits of city or suburban limits.)

c. When the activity requires a nation-wide uniformity of policy that cannot be achieved by interstate action. (Some believe that federal goals in education should be stated, that certain achievement scales should be used to rate the effectiveness of the educational system in order to assist in the assignment of funds where the greatest need is realized.)

d. When a state, through action or inaction, does injury to the people of other states. (Considering the tremendous mobility of the people of our country today, the ineffectiveness of education in one state acts as a penalty to another when, and if, persons from one state move to employment or for personal reasons.)

e. When the States fail to respect basic political and civil rights that apply throughout the United States. (Some believe that schools are still so dissimilar in certain states between city and rural areas and in some cases even within city limits that these schools are prejudicial toward the civil rights of those involved.)

It will be by means of and through these points that federal aid to local education most likely will be organized in the future.

The past decades have shown that the property tax has become ineffective as a school levy, particularly when it must provide most other services offered by the city. It has been suggested that all taxes be collected by the federal government, and then the states and school districts receive apportionate sums back from the one collection agency. This would tend to equalize the tax and would not offer states the opportunity of foregoing proper tax assessments in favor of lower quality education.

3. The Commission on Intergovernmental Relations, *A Report to the President for Transmittal to the Congress,* Washington, D. C.: June 1955, p. 64.

Implications for Music

Music teachers assigned to a junior high school should consider seriously the educational and sociological profile of that particular school before teaching begins. The location of the building within the metro area and its school district could affect the approach you will need for the teaching of music.

String sections in rehearsal, James Hart Junior High School. Homewood, Illinois.

In some communities there is but one junior high school; and if there is more than one, differences between them most always will exist. Such differences will be understandable in educational terms as well as socioeconomic terms. Serving several elementary schools, the junior school may enroll children from more than one social stratum. If this be true, the music teacher should analyze carefully the musical background of the students coming into the school to be positive that some part of the music program services each student. Teaching from a reference of your own background or for the young person who comes from a middle-class home and elementary school may not benefit the average student of your school. Music, better than some other courses, often can educate at several levels if the offerings and foci of the teacher are multi-purposed. Most schools will benefit from the suggestions throughout this book. Schools in the inner city may need special considerations or adaptations.

To assist you with a music program for an inner city school:

Think carefully of the teaching you witnessed as a student teacher; then, compare that school to the one where you have recently been assigned. If there are differences, do not assume that the same type of music program may service both of these schools well. Approach your work on the assumption that the differences mean some adjustment should be made in the offering and/or teaching technics.

Consider the type of training you had in the methods courses in your college. Did these speak particularly to the type of school in which you will be teaching? If not, consider other approaches.

Consider the junior high school of your own background. Can you find any similarities between the two schools? What similarities should exist in the teaching approach and subject matter?

Be resourceful, be innovative, and most of all, be involved with the approach to daily situations found in the school where you teach. Six specific suggestions follow.

Being resourceful and innovative may mean that you will have to borrow equipment, books, or music from other schools or teachers in other schools or school districts. Most music teachers are helpful and generous. Some school systems rotate equipment so as to assist many schools; other systems have a single music supply center. In addition, do not forget your state resource center.

You may well benefit the student by associating the basic skills, such as reading and math, with the teaching of music. You may find it helpful to have individual students read orally during music class as part of the music participation activities. This could entail the reading of texts of a song, with special emphasis upon word meanings; in addition, it could be biographical or explanatory material. Never consider this a waste of time if needed by the students. Many associations are possible between simple math and some explanations in music. Where it can be a logical part of music class, the teacher should welcome assisting the learning of social studies or social attitudes.

Some junior high schools should place less emphasis upon standard group performances by the students and more upon achievements in elementary basic learnings. For some schools, contests or festivals continually place the music program upon such an inferior level in comparison with suburban performing groups that the teacher never can build pride or learning into the program. Performance in these schools should be for self-expression and self-enhancement until such time when the students are ready to emphasize meticulous comparative standards which evaluate from a norm established by outstanding schools throughout the state. Inner-city schools might better cooperate with others of a similar background or similar developmental level in order to broaden musical experiences and, thus, through these experiences raise the performance level. Festivals and exchange concerts should emphasize the performance of the massed group rather than individual school performances. The former should emphasize learning and enjoying music with a large group under an inspiring conductor; the latter becomes a comparison of each school. Invariably this belittles the efforts of particular schools in the eyes of the students if their schools are not upon the rating sheets.

It would be most appropriate to consider ethnic approaches to music education. In a general music class this might lead to the inclusion of a study of several ethnic musics with appropriate singing and performance; it could mean the finding of special song material which would relate to most of the boys and girls in the school through their national or ethnic heritage; it could result in a translation of a number of songs or music materials into the native language of the students; it could make use of national or ethnic instruments, harmonic devices, recordings, songs for special holidays or religious festivals which would accentuate the cultural heritage of the students. Consider that you need not emphasize Western civilization music more than other musics; particularly would this be suggested if music could contribute to an educational atmosphere which would strengthen receptivity to learning.

The Level and Sequence charts found in Chapter 3 could be a great asset in the teaching of a junior high school in the inner city. As you will remember, these charts assist any teacher in finding the ability level of a class or a group of students, and then direct the teacher toward the next learning procedure. If students do not have abilities in specific learnings, one must begin at the beginning of the process. Address them as young people of their age, but develop the ideas sequentially, beginning at an elementary level.

Read carefully the ideas in Chapter 17. These suggestions, or adaptations of them, will assist many young people learn music where modest backgrounds exist.

If you have had good results with junior high school students during your student teaching, consider volunteering for a teaching assignment in a school of the inner city where low economic situations exist or young people come into the school with limited elementary experiences. You will learn to be a good teacher because your creativity and adaptability will be challenged; in addition, you will have assisted the students and assisted the school in being a meaningful institution to those it services.

The inequality which exists between suburban and inner-city schools has received attention in this chapter because it reflects a major concern in education in our country. It should be of interest to teachers entering the field of junior high school music. Before you initiate your professional career, seriously consider these problems as they will affect your classroom personnel, your teaching approach, and the budget you will receive for your work.

LEARNING ACTIVITIES

1. For either your home town and its county or the city where you are attending college and its county—
   a. obtain separate population figures for each decade since 1920;
   b. obtain the number and location of elementary, junior high, and secondary schools during this same period;
   c. discuss the population growth in relation to the location of schools;
   d. state how many suburban schools have been built in outlying regions since 1946; state how many of these are elementary schools; junior high schools; high schools;
   e. discuss what type of tax structure supports the schools in your survey. (See the diagrams on pages 232 and 233.)
2. Locate the oldest school building in the county where you are attending college. Who attends this school? What type of educational opportunities does it afford compared to the newest school of the same grade levels? Why are junior high schools often assigned older facilities?
3. Some states have organized their school systems on a county base rather than a school district. Debate the following proposition: Agreed that a school system organized by the county will provide a better education for all students from a tax base more fairly assessed.
4. If you could choose to have the federal government assist the local school district by providing ten dollars per student for one type of assistance only, what assistance would you choose? (Examples: teachers' salaries, or library books and materials, or remedial education, or audiovisual equipment, or others.)
5. Based on your knowledge of the inner-city school, what would you consider important background for a teacher during the four years of a college education which would better train him for such a position?
6. Visit an inner-city junior high school. How does this school differ from the one you attended? How is the music department different? Is the approach to music the same? Should it be? Why?
7. Read Chapter 9 of *Inequality* by Christopher Jencks, Basic Books, Inc., 1972. Discuss how these opinions could affect the teaching of music in the inner-city schools.

ADDITIONAL READINGS AND BIBLIOGRAPHY

BOLLENS, JOHN C., and SCHWARDT, HENRY J. *The Metropolis: Its People, Politics, and Economic Life.* New York: Harper and Row Publishers, 1965. (chaps. 1, 14 & 15)

BROOM, LEONARD, and GLENN, NORVAL. *Transformation of the Negro American.* New York: Harper and Row, 1965. (chap. 5)

CHINITZ, BENJAMIN, ed. *City and Suburb: The Economics of Metropolitan Growth.* Englewood Cliffs, New Jersey: Prentice-Hall, 1964. (Parts III, IV)

Commission on Intergovernmental Relations. *A Report to the President for Transmittal to the Congress.* Washington, D. C.: June 1955. (all)

DAHL, LEONARD J., and POWELL, JOHN. *The Urban Condition.* New York: Basic Books, Inc., Publishers, 1963.

DUNCAN, BEVERLY, and LIEBERSON, STANLEY. *Metropolis and Region in Transition.* Beverly Hills: Sage Publications, 1970. (chaps. 8 & 9)

ELIAS, C. E.; GILLIES, JAMES; and RIEMER, SVEND. *Metropolis: Values in Conflict.* Belmont, California: Wadsworth Publishing Co., 1964. (chaps. 1b, 3c, e, 6c, d, 8a, 9a, c, d)

HAVIGHURST, ROBERT J. *Education in Metropolitan Areas.* Boston: Allyn & Bacon, Inc., 1966. (all)

HAVIGHURST, ROBERT J., and NEWGARTEN, BERNICE L. *Society and Education.* Boston: Allyn & Bacon, Inc., 1962. (chaps. 2, 9 & 13)

JENCKS, CHRISTOPHER, et al. *Inequality.* New York: Basic Books, Inc., Publishers, 1972. (chaps. 2 & 3)

LONGSDALE, RICHARD C. *The School's Role in Metropolitan Area Development.* Syracuse: Syracuse University Press, 1960. (all)

MEYERSON, MARTIN, ed. *Metropolis in Ferment.* Philadelphia: American Academy of Political and Social Science, 1957. (chaps. 6, 8 & 15)

SWANSON, BERT E. *The Concern for Community in Urban America.* New York: Odyssey Press, 1970. (chaps. 2 & 3)

TIETZE, FREDERICK I., ed. *The Changing Metropolis.* Boston: Houghton-Mifflin Company, 1965. (chaps. 7, 10, 11, 29, 30 & 31)

WEAVER, ROBERT CLIFTON. *The Urban Complex: Human Values in Urban Life.* Garden City, New York: Doubleday and Company, 1964. (chaps. 1, 6 & 7)

ZIMMER, BASIL GEORGE, and HAWLEY, AMES H. *Metropolitan Area Schools.* Beverly Hills: Sage Publications, 1968. (chaps. 4, 5, 6, 7 & 8)

Periodicals

ADKINS, A. "Inequities between Suburban and Urban Schools." *Educational Leader* 26 (December 1968): 243–5.

BURNETT, J. H. "School Culture and Social Change in the City." *Educational Leader* 26 (October 1968): 12–16.

BUTTENWIESER, P. L. "Urban Teachers Need Urban Training." *Perspectives on Education* 3 (September 1970): 5–13.

DAVIS, D. L., and SHAVER, J. A. "New Ideas in Urban Education: Five Proposals for Big City Schools." *Nations Schools* 83 (March 1969): 67–82.

DERR, R. L. "Adoptive Strategies or Urban Schools." *Intellect* 101 (November 1972): 88–90.

DOUGLAS, L. "Community Education: An Imperative for Urban Areas." *Phi Delta Kappan* 54 (November 1972): 189.

ECHSTEIN, M. A. "Schooling in the Metropolis: A Comparative View." *Teachers College Record* 73 (May 1972): 507–17.

ERLACH, J. W. "Curricular Development for Urban Education." *Urban Review* 5 (May 1972): 23–9.

ESTES, N. "Answers for the Inner City." *California Teachers Association Journal* 64 (May 1968): 12–13.

GRAMBS, J. D. "Training Administrators and Teachers for Urban Schools: Some Outrageous Proposals." *Urban Review* 5 (June 1972): 27–31.

HALLIBURTON, W. J. "Inner City Education; Studying the Studies." *Perspectives in Education* 6 (Spring 1973): 14–19.

HARRINGTON, F. W. "Making Education Relevant to the Inner City." *American Vocational Journal* 47 (May 1972): 30–1.

HERMAN, B. E. "Training Teachers for Inner City Schools." *Education* 92 (September 1971): 52–53.

LEVY, B. K. "Is Oral Language of Inner City Children Adequate for Beginning Reading Instruction?" *Research in Teaching English* 7 (September 1970): 51–60.

LEWIS, M. "Weave Music into the Fabric of City Life." *Music Educators Journal* 56 (April 1970): 64–6.

LUCCO, A. A. "Cognitive Development after Age Five: A Future Factor in the Failure of Early Intervention with the Urban Child." *American Journal of Orthopsychology* 42 (October 1972): 847–56.

———. "Music in Urban Education." *Music Educators Journal* 56 (January 1970): 32–111.

OGILVIE, L. L. "Creativity: Its Nurture in the Negro Urban Junior High School." *National Association of Women Deans and Counselors Journal* 31 (Summer 1968): 186–7.

OWENS, R. G., and STEINHOFF, C. R. "Strategies for Improving Inner City Schools." *Phi Delta Kappan* 50 (January 1969): 259–63.

PAPPANILCOU, A. J. "Educating Teachers for the City." *Education* 4 (Summer 1951): 33–51.

ROBERTS, W. "Battle for Urban Schools." *Education Digest* 34 (January 1969): 4–7.

SMITH, C. H. "Teaching In the Inner City: Six Prerequisites to Success." *Teachers College Record* 73 (May 1972): 547–58.

———. "Urban Culture: Awareness May Save Our Skins." *Music Educators Journal* 56 (January 1970): 36–51.

URY, C. M. "Current Issues in Urban Education." *Catholic School Journal* 69 (March 1969): 44–6.

12

The Educationally Disadvantaged and Retarded

During the 1960s an increased awareness was evidenced toward two often related problems, the disadvantaged and the retarded. Such cognizance came partly as a result of intense educational pressures, partly through the unrest of sections of metropolitan areas; and because a large segment of the population was involved, it came also through the rhetoric of the politician.

Much has been written, stated, and heard upon these subjects. No young person growing up during the past two decades could have avoided them easily. They were a disputatious point for politicians and the subject of some TV productions. As is usual with problems of major proportions, real solutions which assist education have been slow in emendation. This chapter will deal with only little of the background of the problem of the educationally disadvantaged and retarded, but at the same time try to effect a position which could be of some value to the prospective teacher of music.

The Socially Disadvantaged and Retarded

Definitions often become difficult to formulate when the problem is multifaceted. The word "retarded" throughout this chapter refers to substandard norms in established school subjects and activities, while "disadvantaged" implies opportunities below a national norm in formal education or informal learning situations. At one time, disadvantaged persons were not quick to recognize their position nor accept it; some persons still refuse such a category. More recently, both terms have received wider acceptance, particularly if special considerations or financial assistances followed such a definition. Both of the terms, then, when in some focus with social conditions, imply that because of past or present situations, students or adults have not reached a particular norm established by society generally or the school in particular. Numerous reasons could be offered or apologies could be made in behalf of such persons; numerous faults may be found with any system of definition, whether it be based upon the norm of income, the norm of IQ, or the less statistical, subjective information of society's judgment. Holding all such statistics in abeyance, the fact remains that a large segment of the population could be considered disadvantaged (estimates claim 15 percent to 25 percent, depending upon definitions), rarely reaching potentials in scholastic or non-scholastic attainments.

Robert Havighurst, eminent educator of the University of Chicago, has defined the educationally disadvantaged as they relate to certain social characteristics.

1. They are at the bottom of the American society in terms of income.
2. They have a rural background.
3. They suffer from social and economic discrimination at the hands of the majority of society.
4. They are widely distributed in the United States. While they are most visible in the big cities, they are present in all except the very high income communities. There are many of them in rural areas.

Two elements stand out in the above: meager income offers a serious deterrent to attainment; and rural background has been a limiting factor toward realizing educational goals. In the past, some adults, realizing the limitations of a rural background, sought urban living for the family. If this move was accompanied with a low urban income, it would seem that no advantages were realized.

Havighurst defines further the educationally disadvantaged in terms of racial and ethnic backgrounds and place of abode.[1]

1. *Urban whites.* Children of Caucasian parents, some of them being old American families who have been living in urban places for generations, while others are recent immigrants from Europe, and still others are recent migrants from rural areas to the cities.
2. *Urban Negroes.* Most of them are children of rural migrants to big cities.
3. *Rural Negroes.* Most of them are living in the southern states.
4. *Rural whites.* They live about equally in the southern states and in the rural northern states.
5. *Rural Spanish-Americans.* Some are of long established families in the southwestern states while others are children of recent immigrants from Mexico. These are Caucasians but are distinguished from the other "whites" by their Spanish origin.
6. *Urban Puerto Ricans.* They are mostly Caucasians, but are distinguished by their Puerto Rican origin and by their concentration in a few urban centers.
7. *American Indians.* Many Indians are well established and well adjusted on their tribal lands, but many of those who live away from the tribal lands are disadvantaged with respect to the labor market and the educational and social expectations of their new environment, especially if it is a big city.

1. Joe L. Frost and Glenn Hawkes, eds., *The Disadvantaged Child,* pp. 20, 21. Copyright © 1966. Used by permission of the publisher, Houghton Mifflin Company.

The unique background and the diversity of potential which such persons may possess seems stifled and unable to find an outlet within the demands of today's society, within the processes of the school, and within the economic functions of the market place. Although each group listed above may have specific assets, these become lost unless they are given social worth and personal value balanced with social adaptability. These problems have been outlined by the Baltimore Area Health and Welfare Council.[2]

1. Many do not understand, or are not in contact with, modern urban living.
2. Many are participants in subcultures, the values and customs of which are different from urban middle-class values and experiences.
3. Many, particularly children and youth, suffer from the disorganizing impact of mobility, transiency, and minority group status.
4. Many have educational and cultural handicaps arising from backgrounds of deprivation.
5. Many are members of families with many problems: divorce, desertion, unemployment, chronic sickness, mental illness, retardation, delinquency.
6. Many lack motivation or capacity to cope with their problems or to improve their situations.
7. Most lack opportunities or motivation to become responsible citizens for the maintenance or improvement of their neighborhood or community.

Implicit in the above problems are two or three items which speak of situations which are probably different from those of the socially disadvantaged as they have come to our large cities over the past 100 years. Our country, and specifically the large city, still contains an allure; yet once a person arrives, the largeness of the metropolis and the impersonalness of this largeness appears to demand an overly large immediate adjustment. In times past, subcultures could thrive within the city while the young gradually acclimated themselves to the situation through education; today the size of the subculture and the disregard by people of a common background for one another have negated the value of subcultures, leaving the newly arrived with little or no social foundation. The lack of community within an ethnic or racial group disintegrates the racial or ethnic values. The relationship between the rural or ethnic background today is in greater contrast to a similar background some years ago. Finally, the deterioration of the family unit has left some children at the mercy of thieves, muggers, sexual perverts, and other corrupt segments of society.

But all is not negative; there are certain positive characteristics within these disadvantaged and retarded groups, and certain processes for assistance have been begun. Time to develop these assistances and assess them is needed, although the

---

2. Health and Welfare Council of the Baltimore Area, "A Letter to Ourselves," 1962, p. 3.

demands of such groups are immediate. Many of these people possess physical and mental resources which, although somewhat different from the average, bespeak quality. Some of these are cultural in nature, some are skills which have been learned in order to survive in a society, which, although often cruel, has promoted individual development. Others are physical in nature, where the brute strength of the body or gross skills such as running or fighting are highly developed. Any one of these, if developed, can enable the person to move into society with a higher degree of social acceptance. A good example of physical skill development is witnessed in the number of Negro athletes who now play professional sports. Their coordination and their bodily rhythm make them a valuable asset to many teams at salaries and social standing well above the national average for many occupations. Although this vocational range is not without limits, the schools must attempt to assist these disadvantaged persons by developing them for areas which could make use of their skills, cultural background, or resourceful qualities. This vocational assistance until now has been out of the bailiwick of the educational function.

Some schools, either completely on their own or with special fund assistance through governmental agencies, have sought to develop programs within one of three areas.

Compensatory education has attempted to make up deficits in knowledge, but mainly in experience. This requires special considerations and often special teachers to work with these young people. Most of the compensatory educational programs have centered upon the early levels of education and few have focused upon the adolescent school.

Other school systems have attempted to emphasize developmental processes, but this becomes more difficult since most schools are organized to assist the child who moves somewhat regularly through the various grades. Non-graded schools could more easily focus upon developmental approaches, but even here it becomes difficult if a variety of backgrounds exist within one school. Music has an advantage here if teachers will explore and use it in this way.

A third method is even more difficult and, in some ways, even more necessary: life adjustment education focuses less upon usual subject matter and more upon values, social situations, the expression of personal ideas, and an interplay between these and the individual. The school has become little involved with these ideas formally; few teachers understand them and use them. Although of potential service to all students, they fail to suffice for the person who has high vocational goals and must prove subject attainment and achievement to reach these goals. Consequently, if the schools are to service the disadvantaged in this manner, they would be compelled to function on a double track, with specially trained personnel required for the concentration in life adjustment. Music could be a vital part of such a program, but most music teachers have not been afforded an opportunity to work in such a team.

Effect Upon Music

Because of social or educational conditions, the disadvantaged and retarded persons have not been associated significantly with the music program. In the junior high schools where music is an *elective,* the music teacher has comparatively few students from the disadvantaged and retarded, especially if the school contains a mixture of social strata. In such schools, general music is aimed at the middle class, and it is these same students who are interested in vocal or instrumental music and have the money to participate if payment for instruments is necessary. Schools servicing only the disadvantaged may enroll a minimal number, but not in the same percentages as those servicing students with greater advantages.

In schools *requiring* music, the disadvantaged and retarded students have been involved only minimally, and as many other young people do, have taken the requirements and moved on to other subjects as soon as possible. Only recently have the music teachers considered course content which might appeal to the disadvantaged and retarded. Here, however, the program is rarely focused on their background; some interest may be generated when the music teacher has included in the course popular music which overlaps with the interests of most young people. However, the question persists as to how much we are servicing the group educationally and how much we are appeasing a low priority, partial interest.

Considering the implications of the material from the points detailed by Havighurst on page 242, it would seem compelling to develop specialized courses in music which would—

1. assist the young person in understanding his own culture in relation to that of others;
2. aid in the beginning of some understanding of intellectual music and why its appeal is so universal;
3. begin an understanding of the contribution ethnic and racial groups can make to the general field of music;
4. assist in understanding the general vocational field of music, what it means to hold a job and what is required in particular occupations;
5. assess how education in several fields contributes to vocational requirements in music and how music adds to the vocational requirements of other fields;
6. examine the role of worthwhile recreation and how music becomes a part of it.

Although music has made some inroads in these directions, we need specially trained personnel in junior high music if we are to become more effective with the young adolescent who is socially disadvantaged or retarded.

The Culturally Disadvantaged and Retarded

A clarification should be made concerning the culturally disadvantaged. Although all of the socially disadvantaged might conceivably be a part of the culturally disadvantaged group, yet the culturally disadvantaged group contains a much larger portion of the population, many of whom are not economically, racially, nor ethnically different nor judged below educational averages. The schools of our country have been negligent in providing a good musical education for most young people. Music education in most schools has consisted of some instrumental lessons, and although good within themselves, these often are not significant culturally. Many elementary schools have employed poorly trained teachers in order to give a semblance of a musical education, so that students leave the elementary school with little or no cultural foundation in music. Most students, consequently, come into the adolescent school with such a meager background in cultural concerns that the teacher of the arts does not understand what is to be done to achieve any degree of education in this area. A common agreement as to what is a standard, and a major effort toward this goal, are needed by music educators. Where understandings have been clear and goals have been explicit, programs have implemented steps in this direction. The music profession has been lax in supplying all but the most nebulous goals, the like of which would not be acceptable by other disciplines. Consequently, millions of young people in our schools are culturally disadvantaged and retarded. In this regard, the schools have served them poorly if at all.

Most persons concerned with education can readily understand a statement which claims that the socially disadvantaged may be educationally retarded as compared with other children of a similar chronological age.

In addition, these same persons would readily understand that children whose mental ability is deficient may have difficulty in progressing to the same level of competence in most school subjects.

It seems difficult for most persons to comprehend an allegation which maintains that a child is retarded in music and not in other areas. The reverse may be true—a student could be retarded in one or more of the basic educational skills and not be retarded in music.

Since these statements seem insignificant or incredulous, with little need of concern to most educators, music should have separate but equally well-defined standards of reporting deficient learnings to parents and school administrators. Music programs would make rapid progress in assisting the culturally disadvantaged if these ideas were generally accepted.

Widely used standardized tests assist educators in understanding levels of general intellectual accomplishments in relation to age; these are usually known as intelligence quotients (IQ) tests.[3] Music could benefit from a musical quotient

3. Because standardized IQ tests measure only one kind of intelligent responses, they have often been denounced as of little value for the disadvantaged and retarded. Yet they do measure something, usually the type of information taught by schools. As we know, this information is used as an entrance guide by colleges and many professions and as an indicator of achievement in basic learning as well as of aptitude for future learning. To eliminate them, eliminates the information they can supply. To use them

(MQ) which would assist educators in understanding an approximate level of attainment and comprehension in relation to age. To establish such standards is a necessity.

With a general acceptance of such a term and test, educators could evaluate any student, compare him to others of his age, and relate the individual deviations to established norms. When music tests advise precisely—at least as well as certain standardized tests for reading or other common subjects—we then could build a standard musical curve for the population and speak of an MQ in terms of normal or disadvantaged musical growth. No matter what the deterrent or stimulus—be it social, cultural, intellectual, or musical—we could evaluate a person's MQ with the same allowance toward accuracy deviations as other subject areas.

Assuming the above, is it not plausible to consider that some young people would fall in the one or two standard deviations above the national norm? In most IQ tests the mean is registered at 100. Following this system we could speak of students having an MQ of 110, 120, 140, etc.

As with the IQ, we would then be able to locate points below the mean. These might conceivably fall into the same categories as those used for standard academic areas indicating the disadvantaged, retarded, or slow learners.

If the child were in the slow-learner group, we could then assess his particular music learning disability and work with one or several specific remedial patterns. At the present time we do not know how young people learn music, and given particular problems, we are at a loss as to how these might best be remedied. We must assume, however, that once we became sophisticated enough to analyze the specific problem, it would not be too long before steps could be made toward proper learning processes.

To summarize, the young person who is culturally deprived or disadvantaged has not had the opportunity to live up to his potential in music because of a skimpy musical education. He could probably perform at a higher level or comprehend aesthetically with deeper significance than he presently indicates. The socially disadvantaged may fit the descriptions of the early part of the chapter. Although not always true, usually these people will be culturally deprived also. Some assistance which is not everyday classroom procedure should be given these children. For the slower learners in verbal or mathematical comprehensions who might have a better than average talent in music, we should recognize that their musical responses might be developed beyond a level indicated by standard school subjects. If such development is not possible, they at least need the opportunity to participate in an art which can give them an emotional experience beyond their limited verbal experience.

---

as the sole indicator of intelligence fails to consider abilities or potentials in nonverbal, nonmathematical fields, or many areas of general information. The music profession has fallen into this trap repetitively concerning musical comprehension, achievement, and abilities.

If special assistance can be given the child who needs help in the reading of the printed page or in the simple calculation, then we in music should also consider special assistance for the child with cultural disadvantages in music.

Implications for Music

In considering the music program for the disadvantaged and the retarded, general considerations will be more helpful since specific plans or ideas would most often serve but one particular situation.

The disadvantaged student is usually a physical learner, a young person who prefers to be active rather than read, think, or talk about. Singing is not considered doing something, since it does not seem to use the body. The music room can be an active room by using motion with musical material, or using film strips or films along with recordings or with singing. The old "Follow the Bouncing Ball" films could be an example. Many of the Carobo-Cone aids, such as plastic notes or floor staves, might assist the young learner. Instruments, including the electronic piano, could be helpful. Role-playing can be important, for the young person appreciates becoming the teacher so that he may conduct, imitate, and teach. The student as teacher has only been begun in some areas and very little in music.

The disadvantaged child usually learns more slowly. To push conformity of learning speed or to judge him as other students is inappropriate. Since he usually concentrates upon one thing at a time, a lesson plan which coordinates several musical ideas may not be successful. The teaching should fit the mental style of the student. Learning items which are usual for younger children could be the rule, and the Level and Sequence charts of Chapter 3 should be helpful.

Make the school as masculine as possible. The disadvantaged student prefers aggression to nonaggression, unkemptness to neatness, independence to dependence, and individualism to conformity, since he considers these traits as masculine. The music room need not always be neat, can help children become independent through individualized types of learning projects, and can permit students to act as individuals. Most music classes operated by women defeat the masculine approach which this young person prefers. The unit plan, described in Chapter 5, could assist these young persons, while the band would more often appeal than other types of ensembles.

Many disadvantaged young people do not discriminate well what they hear. Their background in home or community has led them to disregard much of the sound which comes to them. Consequently, they fail to distinguish accurately verbal as well as musical sounds, often becoming inattentive during talking or music listening. The lecture type of classroom, as well as the extended listening found in many music classrooms, will produce poor results. Because of this trait, these children must be taught to respond musically to instrumental teaching. Specifically they do not—

1. recognize identical sounds;
2. discriminate between sounds;
3. enunciate what they have heard;
4. sing sounds well;
5. follow directions;
6. quickly overcome enunciation problems;
7. distinguish between timbres.

The teacher must expect the child to learn. The teacher who comes to this school only as helper, whose sympathy directs him to the inner city or the rural school because of his willingness to be of service, will usually be of minimal assistance. The teacher must understand that this school, like all others, is for the purpose of learning. The teacher has an obligation to consider it an educational institution and should instruct and require progress of the students. There can be no self-serving attitude or condescension.

The school should be flexible:

1. Period lengths should vary throughout the day.
2. The groupings of young people should vary.
3. Most classes should be small, although a few should be larger.
4. The school day and week should include field trips to broaden the background of the student.
5. Special rooms should exist to assist the child with homework, to provide educational TV, games, quiet, or to provide an opportunity for bodily activity.
6. A special summer school should involve the students for more hours per day and more days per week than the usual summer offering.

Music can add to the flexibility of the school for the disadvantaged student. It can work with short or long periods; it can vary the size of groups dependent upon the type of music taught; it can be involved with field trips to many places throughout the community where music is used. Music's learning spaces are of different types; and music can be a part of a summer school which could assist the young person with art, industrial art, social studies, music, math, science, and physical education.

Through surveys it has been found that teachers in the junior high school appeal less to the young person than those in the elementary school. Too often the teacher in the upper schools takes on too professional and unconcerned a posture which does not aid the young student. The disadvantaged students prefer teachers with three major characteristics: warmth, organization, stimulation. As one author has stated: "A mature, well integrated person who respects his difficult, unmotivated, and apparently unteachable pupils" will succeed. "Ordered flexibility"[4] should be the motto.

1. What social condition would you assume to have the greatest negative effect upon a music program? Why? The greatest positive effect? Why?
2. In times past in our country, the poor were often the makers of music. For example, the poor of the Southeastern mountain country or the poor black after the Civil War. Does this not seem to be true today? Why?
3. How would you ascertain the musical quotient of a person? What would you consider a valid check on a junior high school student to determine a MQ?
4. *a.* Many students of our country are disadvantaged in the area of fine arts and/or music but not in other learning areas. To what would you accredit this?
   b. Define a musically disadvantaged or retarded person by stating his deficiencies in musical terms. Which deficiencies would you consider most general?
   c. What would be your evaluation of a remedy for this problem?
   d. Is it possible to rectify a deficiency with a junior high school student which has begun in the lower elementary school?
5. Examine the January 1970 *Music Educators Journal*. Read one of the articles on the disadvantaged and make a written report which includes a comparison with a junior high school in your background.

ADDITIONAL READINGS AND BIBLIOGRAPHY

AYRES, LEONARD PORTER. *Laggards in Our Schools*. New York: Charities Publications Committee, 1909. (chaps. 2, 8, 9, 10, & 14)

BLOOM, BENJAMIN S.; DAVIS, ALLISON; and HESS, ROBERT. *Compensatory Education for Cultural Deprivation*. New York: Holt, Rinehart and Winston, Inc., 1965. (Part II)

BOTTOM, RAYMOND. *The Education of Disadvantaged Children*. West Nyack, New York: Parker Publishing Company, 1970. (chaps. 4, 5, 9 & 12)

BURKE, ARVID JAMES; KELLY, JAMES A.; and GARMS, WALTER I. *Educational Programs for the Culturally Deprived*. Albany: State University of New York, 1970. (C1, C2)

CAIN, ARTHUR H. *Young People and Crime*. New York: The John Day Company, Inc., 1968. (all)

4. William F. White, *Tactics for Teaching the Disadvantaged* (New York: McGraw-Hill, 1971), p. 53.

COLE, LARRY. *Street Kids.* New York: Grossman Publishers, Inc., 1970.

COLEMAN, JAMES SAMUEL; JOHNSTONE, JOHN W. C.; and JONASSOHN, KURT. *The Adolescent Society; The Social Life of the Teenager and Its Impact on Education.* New York: Free Press of Glencoe, 1961. (all)

CONANT, JAMES B. *Slums and Suburbs.* New York: McGraw-Hill, Inc., 1961.

CONTE, JOSEPH M., and GRIMES, GEORGE H. *Media and the Culturally Different Learner.* Washington: National Education Association, 1969. (all)

CROW, LESTER DONALD; MURRAY, WALTER; and SMYTHE, HUGH H. *Educating the Culturally Disadvantaged Child.* New York: McKay Publishers, 1960. (chaps 1, 4 & 5)

DEUTSCH, MARTIN; KATZ, IRWIN; and JENSEN, ARTHUR. *Social Class, Race and Psychological Development.* New York: Holt, Rinehart and Winston, Inc., 1968. (chaps. 1, 2 & 4)

Educational Policies Commission. *Education and the Disadvantaged American.* Washington: Educational Policies Commission, 1962. (chaps. 1 & 2)

GENTRY, ATRON, and JONES, BYRD. *Urban Education: The Hope Factor.* Philadelphia: W. B. Saunders Company, 1972. (chaps. 1, 2 & 3)

GORDON, EDMUND W., and WILKERSON, DOXEY A. *Compensatory Education for the Disadvantaged.* New York: College Entrance Examination Board, 1966. (chaps. 1, 2 & 3)

GOTTLIEB, DAVID, and RAMSEY, CHARLES. *Understanding Children of Poverty.* Chicago: Science Research Associates, 1957. (all)

GREENE, MARY FRANCES, and RYAN, ORLETTA. *The School Children Growing Up in the Slums.* New York: Pantheon Books, Inc., 1965.

HIRSCH, HERBERT. *Poverty and Politicization.* New York: Free Press, 1971. (chap. 6)

HUNT, JOSEPH McVICKER. *The Challenge of Incompetence and Poverty.* Urbana: University of Illinois Press, 1969.

JENCKS, CHRISTOPHER, et al. *Inequality: A Reassessment of the Effect of Family and Schooling in America.* New York: Basic Books, 1973. (chap. 5)

LORETAN, JOSEPH O., and UMANS, SHELLEY. *Teaching the Disadvantaged.* New York: Teachers College Press, 1966. (Part I)

MOSTELLER, FREDERICK, and MOYNIHAN, DANIEL P. *On Equality of Educational Opportunity.* New York: Vintage Books, 1973.

ORNSTEIN, ALLAN C., and VAIRO, PHILIP D. *How to Teach Disadvantaged Youth.* New York: McKay Publications, 1969. (any)

PASSOW, A. HARRY, ed. *Education in Depressed Areas.* New York: Teachers College Press, 1963. (Part IIb, IVa, b)

PRINGLE, MIA LILLY KELLMER. *Deprivation and Education.* London: Longmans, 1965.

RIESSMAN, FRANK. *The Culturally Deprived Child.* New York: Harper and Row, Publishers, 1962. (chaps. 2, 4, 8 & 9)

ROBERTS, JOAN I., ed. *School Children in the Urban Slum.* New York: Free Press, 1967. (Parts IIb, IVa)

STONE, JAMES CHAMPION. *Teachers for the Disadvantaged.* San Francisco: Jossey-Bass Publishers, 1969. (chap. 6)

TATE, EL FLEDA JACKSON. *Teaching the Disadvantaged.* Palo Alto, California: Peek Publications, 1971. (Part 2)

WEBSTER, STATEN W., ed. *The Disadvantaged Learner.* San Francisco: Chandler, 1966. (any)

WHITE, WILLIAM F. *Tactics for Teaching the Disadvantaged.* New York: McGraw-Hill Book Company, 1971. (chaps. 2, 8 & 10)

Periodicals

Askew, Mayard. "Music Aids Deprived Children." *Music Educators Journal* 29 (November 1971): 22.

Bromwish, R. M. "Young Children's Language and Effective Learning." *Elementary English* 49 (October 1972): 826–31.

Clary, D. H. "Music and Dance for the Disadvantaged." *Instructor* 79 (February 1970): 56–7.

Cohan, S. A., and Cooper, T. "Seven Fallacies: Reading Retardation and the Urban Disadvantaged Reader." *The Reading Teacher* 26 (October 1972): 38–45.

Gallegos, A. M. "Gifted Poor." *Educational Leadership* 30 (May 1973): 749–53.

Havighurst, R. J. "Curriculum for the Disadvantaged." *Phi Delta Kappan* 51 (March 1970): 371–3.

Kaplan, L. "Ain't No Such Thing as Cultural Disadvantage." *Instructor* 81 (June 1972): 16–18.

Larson, R. G. "School Curriculum and the Urban Disadvantaged: A Historical Review and Some Thoughts About Tomorrow." *Journal of Negro Education* 38 (Fall 1969): 351–60.

Michel, D. E. "Youth Concerts: Compensatory Education for the Disadvantaged?" *Music Educators Journal* 58 (October 1971): 29–31.

Michel, D. E., and Farrell, D. M. "Music and Self-Esteem: Disadvantaged Problem Boys in an All Black Elementary School." *Journal of Research in Music Education* 21 (Spring 1973): 80–4.

Reed, J. "Sequential Program Meets Special Needs of Students." *Business Education Forum* 27 (May 1973): 38–40.

Reid, C. R. "Relative Effectiveness of Contrasted Music Teaching Styles for the Culturally Deprived." *Journal of Research in Music Education* 20 (Winter 1972): 484–90.

Renzulli, J. S. "Talent Potential in Minority Group Students." *Exceptional Children* 39 (March 1973): 437–44.

Reyes, R., and Klingstedt, J. L. "Middle School Educational and Cultural Conflicts Experienced by Chicano Students." *Man, Society, and Technology* 31 (September 1971): 20–1.

Richmond, B. O., and Norton, W. A. "Creative Production and Developmental Age in Disadvantaged Children." *Elementary School Journal* 73 (February 1973): 279–84.

Schultheis, R. "Emerging Concepts in the Education of Disadvantaged Youth." *National Business Education Quarterly* 38 (May 1970): 33–40.

———. "Successful Teaching: Demand of Yourself All That It Takes." *Music Educators Journal* 56 (January 1970): 66–79.

Today
and
Tomorrow

13

Reorganization of the School for Early Adolescents

During the last few years in our country there has been considerable interest and debate over the role and organization of the school for the early adolescent. Evaluation results from a hypothesis that the junior high school is not now organized to meet the needs of today's young people, possibly because the goals of the young people have changed, or perhaps the junior high school never did meet the needs of this age group well.

Discussions on the political, social, economic, or educational scene indicate that forces are abroad today which have not existed in previous decades. Businesses agree that changes must be made quickly or competition will force extinction. Social institutions have already altered their pattern or succumbed to little or no use. Unchanged schools could be one of the last bulwarks of another generation. Those who seek change in education believe that the reorganization of the structure of compulsory education is necessary.

This generation of young people, more than any other, have altered their pattern of recreation, socialization, and expression, emphasizing all the more that the schools have not evolved to give them educational experiences which they understand to be relevant for the present or a foundation for the future. Many statistics for the year 2000 indicate that more than half of the employment will involve positions not known at this time. With statistics such as these facing the youth of today, it is little wonder they believe that changes in the secondary, and perhaps even the elementary schools, should take place.

The Junior High School: Pro and Con

To look at the raison d'etre of the junior high school at the time of inception is to attempt an understanding of this familiar educational unit.

Some course work of the secondary level should be introduced at an earlier age. The colleges of that time were seeking to elevate the admission standards of the incoming student, and, consequently, wished that the high school be devoted more extensively to pre-college training. Since pre-college work needed more emphasis, it was suggested that the secondary school include grades seven through twelve so that six years of pre-college work could be included. This was in direct contrast to the then existing procedure in which grades seven and eight were used almost exclusively as a review of elementary work in preparation for employment.

Students dropping from school before completing high school should have certain basic skills. It was believed that the junior high school would offer a most logical cutoff point, and provide a student with minimal skills by this time.

Saleable skills should be included in a basic education for those students not interested in college preparatory courses. Increase in the industrialization of the country during the first part of the twentieth century led to a demand on the part of agriculture, labor, and industry, to include some skill courses in a new school then being organized.

Urbanization brought a tremendous influx of students into the school system. This increase in population placed a heavy burden on existing physical facilities. The reorganization of the school system offered an opportunity to build new high schools, and to use the older buildings for a new school, the junior high.

Classes would be organized in the manner of the high school so that a student could more easily move into the high school program. The basic unit of instruction, known as the Carnegie Unit, was the prevalent method of organizing instructional material for the high school and became the unit for the junior high school.

There are those who believe that the junior high school has never had a proper opportunity to develop during the last fifty to sixty years, thus concluding that the school and its potentials should not be abandoned. Rather, now is the time to be firm in re-declaring goals for this school, making every effort not to permit the high school to dominate the educational function so completely. The junior high school could become successful and is able to meet the challenge of this generation.

Those who believe that this is impossible and not at all what the present school generation needs, argue that:

What we need for the young adolescent is not at all an imitation of the high school. A new concept of organization is needed so that a different approach to education will be realized. For example, it is argued we need to eliminate the earth science in grade seven, the following biological science from grade eight, and physical science from grade nine since these courses are obviously a watering down of courses from the high school. Instigate instead a science program built just for the young adolescent. Again, world history in grade seven, American history in grade eight, and civics in grade nine is too immitative of later grades to be helpful.

What we need for the young adolescent is not the Carnegie Unit. Inasmuch as some high schools are questioning this approach to organization, many educators are convinced that the young adolescent should have a school which is not graded and not organized in the usual one-course-to-the-year type of structure.

What we need for the young adolescent is not course work which is geared specifically for the pre-college student. This relates closely to point one immediately above. Students in the junior high school today are too often confronted with the pressure that they pre-consider high school courses while they are in seventh grade, with the reminder that their entrance into some colleges could be determined by their choices. Broad based learnings seem more appropriate.

What we need for the young adolescent is not a consideration of the educational program being terminated at the end of grade seven or eight.

What we need for the young adolescent is not a group of saleable skills, but an introduction to skills which could lead in many vocational directions. For example, the student should be introduced to typing during seventh grade. This will be an assist in the educational process as well as a possible skill for the secretary of the future. Or, foreign language skills should be introduced which could assist the pre-college student as well as the young person entering the business world immediately after high school.

Some other practical matters have pushed the decision for consideration of reorganization of the junior high school.

Grade nine is most logically located with the senior high. Even though the ninth grade is placed in the junior high school, educationally it continues to be considered a part of the high school. Such consideration offers problems in junior high scheduling, organization, and educational content.

The educational content of ninth grade is determined by the senior high, and if it is located within the junior high school, the ramifications for the other grades are continuous and unavoidable. In some instances, ninth grade subject matter is introductory to courses in the senior high. Classes such as algebra, biology, and foreign language are examples.

Many high schools consider ninth grade personnel a vital part of athletic or musical teams. In some systems the students are housed in the junior high school for most of the day, but move into the senior high school at the end or the beginning of the day for participation in special activities. With a reorganization, more efficiency in the use of student time and energy would be possible.

Buildings and the use of space have most often been the determining factors in the organizational system for a given community. Only after a system has been in operation for a number of years might the junior high schools move from an older building into a facility designed especially for these grades. Boards of education in various communities locate tax dollars much easier for the building of a senior high school, no matter what its organizational plan, than any other school. Elementary school buildings stand second in line, while the school for the adolescent comes last in appropriations. In many communities, the new building for the junior high school has never come. Reorganization may assist some communities with a building program which will be more easily financed through bond issues.

Most parents and psychologists agree that the child is maturing earlier than previously. (The actual facts in the case seem to be debatable.) If this be true, the ninth grader may be physically and psychologically more at home with students of the high school. At the same time, one or more of the upper grades from the elementary school might be considered a part of the school for the early adolescent.

Although some studies made by educators and psychologists indicate that today's youth are maturing earlier than before, some critics of these statements point out that these statistics are misleading. Measurement of physical and emotional maturity of parents and previous generations are not uniformly available so that the estimates used by the researchers are not comparable. In some cases, physical maturity and mental maturity have been confused.

Bases for a New Organization

With this as a background, let us examine a number of suggestions which have come to the fore over the past decade. The most common term used for designating change in this area is to claim the establishment of a "middle school." The problem facing the serious student of reorganization is to understand what is meant by this term, since it is used loosely by many educators and communities to cover almost anything which in any way differs from the present junior high plan. We should be more definitive with our considerations.

Four concerns dominate the thinking of persons requesting a reorganization of the school for young adolescents. The configuration of these concerns defines the uniqueness of each plan:

1. A school which considers the physical development of the student.
2. A school which considers the learning environment of the student.
3. A school which considers the intellectual development of the student.
4. A school which considers the content and methodology used in the learning process.

Suggested School Organizational Plans

The Original Elementary School (Eight-Four)

This arrangement would not be at all satisfactory to the contemporary critic of school organization since it has difficulty meeting the four criteria well. This plan does little to consider the unique physical development of these students in that they are housed with early elementary grades. Since this plan is the old elementary school idea, if it exists today, students are probably housed in old buildings and these physical facilities probably do not give the student specialized spaces for specialized activities. Schools could be built for the eight-four plan which would give special attention to the environment of the student, and where special teachers would assist with the understanding of each age grouping. The eight-four plan was abandoned since the original purpose for grades seven and eight was to review the material of the first six grades, using similar content and methodology as the earlier years.

By restructuring, this plan might service the young person today, but this organizational plan was deserted because it met so poorly those objectives of great concern to the educator, parent, and student.

The Junior High School (Six-Three-Three)

To most of us this is the usual school for the young adolescent. Those who have respect for the plan believe that with minor changes it still will service young people better than any other. The problem with the present junior high school organization may not be in the concept itself, but in the manner in which it has been executed. With more attention to the specific needs of its clientele and less attention to the demands and goals of the high school, the junior high school would take on added value and prestige.

Proponents of the junior high plan believe that this school does consider the physical development of the student by offering him an opportunity to mature with his own peer group during an uncertain and uncoordinated period. Through segregation it offers the student an opportunity to develop physically and mentally in classes where demands are focused on him. To many, the ninth grade student is still more closely akin to seventh and eighth graders than to students of the upper high school.

The point is well taken that present junior highs have too often emulated the senior high school in academic programs so that the intellectual development of the student has not been as specifically oriented as it could be. This, then, is the correct time to make these adjustments.

To blame poor educational content and methodology upon the six-three-three organizational plan seems unfair since the junior high school offers many of the same possibilities, and perhaps even better possibilities than some other systems. To eliminate the junior high school rather than solve its educational problems will not cause the problems to disappear. The junior high school should be retained and corrections made which will bring the content, methodology, and intellectual climate into perspective for the contemporary scene.

Arguments to offset these points have been made in an earlier portion of the chapter.

In summary—although the junior high school is now interested in the social, emotional, and intellectual development of the pupils, the original main concern of this school focused upon problems of physical development of the student and the effects and implications this has for education.

The Middle School (Five-Three-Four)

Studies and surveys of elementary and early adolescent youth indicate that young people are maturing at an earlier age than previously believed. If we are to consider the earlier maturing age of the young student, and to provide him with a school organization which fits his needs, we could adopt the middle school plan containing the three grades of six, seven, and eight. This would provide an environment in which the student will learn more readily and with more ease since he will be associating with students of similar maturity. Proponents of this plan believe that the sixth-grade child is ready to accept greater responsibilities earlier and move into a socially more advanced situation.

The middle school usually is proposed as an ungraded school, where the student learns with an emphasis upon subject matter rather than grade level. Similar to all of the new organizational suggestions, these schools are built for, and are ready to adopt, contemporary media processes as a part of the daily learning pro-

Two junior high students performing "Country Road" for an all-school talent show. Parrish Junior High School, Salem, Oregon.

cedures. By placing more emphasis upon exploration and self-help studying than is possible in the elementary school, the child is brought into contact with these learning procedures at an earlier age.

In addition, since the elementary school is usually a neighborhood school and the middle school is usually a regional school, this means that the child could be given the opportunity of working in a multi-class or multi-racial school at least one year earlier than would have been provided by the junior high school.

This plan places the ninth grade in the high school, satisfying one of the major concerns of all those interested in organizational change.

In opposition to these arguments, psychologists are not at all sure that their studies on the early maturing of students is based completely on reliable information and statistics since earlier data on previous generations could not be as refined or accurate as recently. Secondly, there are those who believe that such an organization as the five-three-four plan only pushes the child too early into educational and social situations where the demands are too great. Finally, eliminating one year from the elementary school robs the average child of finesse and security with the basic skills.

The Intermediate School (Four-Four-Four)

By considering grades five, six, seven, and eight as one unit, the public school system would adopt the same organizational approach as churches and collegiate departments of education. For years, churches have featured a primary and an intermediate division in their educational training; schools of education have trained teachers with primary and intermediate emphases.

One suggested organizational design for this school involves the child with "planned gradualism." In such a plan, his fifth-grade year centers around a "home" or self-contained classroom. During the sixth grade, a transition takes place in which the grade is considered a "neighborhood." Although assigned to one room most of the school day, the student moves to other rooms of his grade, taking advantage of different kinds of learning situations in both large and small groups, depending upon the educational needs of the student as recognized by a team of associated teachers. Here, the student gradually becomes acquainted with several teachers and a number of students, even though most of the work is carried on in one room with one teacher and a familiar group of children. Years seven and eight are operated much as a departmentalized school wherein the students move from teacher to teacher for each subject, with teachers and students making use of educational spaces best suited to the day's activities.

Another suggested plan of operation for the intermediate school permits the student to have a home teacher, but upon his demand, to move out through the school for special information and/or laboratory centers. This type of organization is used throughout the upper four grades whenever the child needs this type of instruction or is ready for it. Presumably then, as the child matures educationally and socially, the need will be greater. One fifth-grade child might use school-wide assistances little; another fifth grader, advanced educationally or more mature, could use other teachers and other learning facilities as much and as often as a seventh or eighth grader.

A third operational idea, developed in some schools with a four-four-four system, uses a teacher advisor plan which centers the student around one teacher for many different kinds of educational or co-curricular questions or problems. At the same time, he is advised to seek the assistance of other teachers for some classes and some experiences. This plan also controls the student's movements, based upon educational needs and maturity.

As if to sympathize with these ideas, for a number of years some of our schools of education have emphasized depth rather than breadth by training intermediate teachers with only two or three areas of emphasis so that they can better teach in today's departmentalized schools. For example, while in college, the teacher is not expected to prepare to teach all of the courses of the upper elementary curriculum, but rather to be prepared in considerable depth in two or three coordinated areas. Thus, a teacher could elect science as one area of specialty and would be able to teach any or all of the sciences. What makes this different from the usual program in science is that this training features the interrelationship of all the sciences and a teacher is prepared to show this interrelationship to the students by structuring courses which are not organized into the usual elementary biology, chemistry, or physics courses.

Critics of the intermediate school believe that the effort to introduce "planned gradualism" into the school is misplaced. They contend that if the child were not being pushed to accept these kinds of social responsibilities along with his educational procedures that much of the school time need not be focused upon teacher planning for and supervising of maturity growth.

On the other hand, but still from a critical position, some parents maintain that an emotionally secure first-grade child should be able to move throughout the school, taking advantage of the various teachers and learning situations. Waiting until sixth or seventh grade for this kind of educational experience is limiting and unnecessary. Their main point is that the process of "planned gradualism" is artificial. Although educational experiences may divide themselves into primary and intermediate levels developmentally, the school should be less structured from first grade on.

The "advisor" plan is not seen as a complete educational procedure, but merely as an effort to appear to be supervising the child when in reality he is left quite unstructured. Such emphasis upon individual educational responsibility is premature and could lead to poor basic skill development.

The Double School (Six-Six)

This school serves the smaller communities probably better than the large cities. Placing the elementary students in one school, traditional or experimental procedures may be used as desired while the upper six grades of the school become the upper school or high school. Students normally in the junior high school are taught by upper-grade teachers, make use of high school gym facilities, music facilities, the library, and science laboratories. In this way, students of the seventh and eighth grades are given the highest quality education the community can provide without the cost of duplicating facilities within a special building.

At first, this plan may seem to be only at the convenience of the tax base. However, proponents of the plan cite the educational advantages for the seventh and eighth grader: first-rate teachers rather than those who have been placed, sometimes unwillingly, into a junior high school; the best facilities which the town can provide; the possibility for participation in advanced or special classes which would not be open to him in the three- or four-year adolescent school.

Considering the student's maturity, advocates of this plan point to outside-the-school unsupervised activities where the student is drawn to persons of his own maturity level from a group of acquaintances which often include boys and girls older and younger than his three or four year span. If, outside the school, the student seeks friends from a composite group and is capable of participating in multiage activities, then school situations should not offer the problem that educational authorities have predicted. This school offers the possibility of a flexible educational situation based upon the readiness of the student with social activities in a more adult-like age block.

Critics of the plan focus their attention solely upon the upper six grades, believing that the child may participate in the school physically, but not be a true part of the school until the last three years. This school contains the possibility for a caste system based upon restrictions of some social activities for the younger student. In addition, it is argued that most students are not prepared educationally to take advantage of the advanced learning which this system offers, and, consequently, these features are not an asset. A special school for the young adolescent supersedes the suggested educational and social advantages.

The Diphase (Six-Two-Four)

This plan developed as a result of criticism pointed toward some of the previous plans. It contains certain advantages in that it places the ninth grade in the high school, yet keeps the young student in the elementary school until his basic skills are sound, and until his maturity specifies a readiness for a departmentalized and socially advanced school situation.

In recent years where this plan has been operational, a great emphasis has been placed upon special kinds of learning for the adolescent, with particular emphasis upon interdisciplinary concepts usually involving audiovisual centers which feature contemporary media instruction such as teaching machines. It places high emphasis upon individual instruction through teacher conferences, student-planned goals, and individual learning rates. The student plans his schedule and his learning sequences for some of the school day. The assumption here is that the student has had adequate-to-excellent training in basic skills through the six grades of the elementary school, while the high school years of the future will be used for some requirements plus in-depth study of particular areas. During these two years of the diphase school the student may develop his particular interests and, at the same time, learn interdisciplinary concepts which may not be taught at any other time.

This plan evokes criticism around two main points.

First, it comprises really nothing new that other schools for this age could not include. Containing only two grades, it limits the enrollment so as to de-emphasize school activities which often bring pride to the student and some renown to the school. In the case of the latter, parents are usually referring to athletics or music.

The athletic program does not have the student constituency upon which to draw for competitive sports. Proponents of the plan maintain that their purpose in abandoning the junior high school was to eliminate those activities and educational procedures which emulate the high school. Consequently, a highly developed interscholastic sports program is much more important to the student. In the area of music, the student has an opportunity to participate in large organizations in high school, therefore, the emphasis at this level can well be placed upon the smaller ensemble such as the string quartet or the clarinet choir.

Secondly, critics point to the unstructured day as being next to meaningless for the student. Given free rein in establishing a schedule—even though teachers are available for advice—the usual student will not probe those areas which he knows least, but will waste much valuable time working upon well-known or peripheral material. In the meantime, many of the skills developed through the elementary school deteriorate so that the student enters the high school less well prepared than expected.

Organization Doesn't Matter

One final idea should be mentioned. Some educational thinkers believe that the organization of the school matters little. The important aspect of any education is the teacher and the manner in which the teacher aids the student. Consequently, the teacher should be well trained for the young adolescent school. Secondary school training is no longer adequate.

Summary

In some ways one might assume that the organizational structure doesn't matter. Approaching the problem in another way, it could be posited that some plans could work in some communities while others work better elsewhere. Currently, we are involved in a period of change, the main emphasis of which is a substitution for the current adolescent school because that school has not worked well enough in most communities.

Each school system must make some evaluations choosing a plan which fits its needs. We as teachers must understand the various organizational plans and be prepared to fit our music programs to them. To assure this, we must not have rigid ideas of how to teach young people; rather, take advantage of the system where we teach, not permitting the system to defeat our potential.

LEARNING ACTIVITIES

1. Organize a debate. Proposed: the junior high school is adequate to meet the need of the contemporary young adolescent.
2. Divide the class into six groups, with each group assigned one of the organizational plans for discussion. Argue the pros and cons of each organizational plan from the vantage point of the music teacher. List the advantages and disadvantages; then, have each group report to the entire class.
3. Invite a member of the education school or department of your campus to speak to your class concerning these organizational plans. Do the plans really make a difference in the educational processes of the young student or are these artificial concerns?
4. The 8–4 plan seems to be of little use in contemporary thinking. How could this plan be adjusted to meet well the four concerns of the educational process? What similarities exist in this plan as compared to the open concepts schools?
5. Discuss how the junior high school (6–3–3) could better service the four concerns of the educational process.
6. The following pages contain a checklist of items which are meant to assist you with an evaluation of the music program for the adolescent school.
    a. Honestly evaluate the junior high school which you attended. Compare this evaluation with that of others of your class.

b. Considering the organization plans discussed in this chapter, assess them in relation to this evaluation chart as best you can imagine they would evolve under actual working conditions.

c. After completing this class, use this chart to evaluate the school where you are a student teacher.

EVALUATION CHECKLIST

Since it is the business of the school to see that opportunities are given each pupil to participate in many phases of musical experience, any good music program should be adapted to the early adolescent's stages of physical, mental, and emotional growth, and should be translated into those details which may provide for such concerns.

	None	Some	Much
1. The program offers opportunities for all pupils to participate in some musical activity.	☐	☐	☐
2. First-year pupils entering the adolescent school take part in general music courses.	☐	☐	☐
3. Various opportunities are given in both vocal and instrumental music to meets the needs of talented pupils.	☐	☐	☐
4. General music courses meet in the regular school day.	☐	☐	☐
5. Special groupings or clubs for talented pupils meet regularly.	☐	☐	☐
6. Elective music courses are offered for qualified students.	☐	☐	☐
7. Elective courses in music are scheduled during the regular school day.	☐	☐	☐
8. Group instruction in the study of various musical instruments is offered for those desiring it.	☐	☐	☐
9. Voices are checked for development during adolescent changes.	☐	☐	☐
10. The general music classes—			
a. take care of individual differences among pupils;	☐	☐	☐

EVALUATION CHECKLIST *(Continued)*

	None	Some	Much
b. develop singing as only one of the fundamental activities of the class;	☐	☐	☐
c. develop increased independence in dealing with musical elements, knowledge, and skills;	☐	☐	☐
d. provide for stages of voice development;	☐	☐	☐
e. provide many opportunities for exploring music;	☐	☐	☐
f. provide experiences with a variety of musical instruments;	☐	☐	☐
g. provide a program of music through listening to records of many types and forms of compositions;	☐	☐	☐
h. encourage creative expression through pupil activities and performances;	☐	☐	☐
i. accelerate development of discrimination in musical taste;	☐	☐	☐
j. help the pupil to orient himself toward music as a personal experience.	☐	☐	☐

11. Elective courses provide the following:

	None	Some	Much
a. boys choruses, all grades included	☐	☐	☐
b. girls choruses, all grades included	☐	☐	☐
c. mixed choruses, all grades included	☐	☐	☐
d. ensembles, vocal and instrumental	☐	☐	☐
e. bands of varying sizes	☐	☐	☐
f. orchestra	☐	☐	☐
g. instrumental classes, including piano	☐	☐	☐

12. The physical equipment of the music room includes:

	None	Some	Much
a. pianos in good condition	☐	☐	☐
b. instruments for pupil use	☐	☐	☐
c. recording equipment	☐	☐	☐

EVALUATION CHECKLIST (Continued)

	None	*Some*	*Much*
d. a phonograph	☐	☐	☐
e. a radio, FM and AM	☐	☐	☐
f. music stands	☐	☐	☐
g. correct-posture chairs	☐	☐	☐
h. staff-lined chalkboard	☐	☐	☐
i. a bulletin board	☐	☐	☐
j. cabinets for instruments and supplies	☐	☐	☐
13. Members of the vocal music department have had vocal training and know the technics involved in training the adolescent's voice.	☐	☐	☐
14. Members of the instrumental music department have had training in instrumental music and have acquired the skills necessary to perform in band and orchestra and to know a number of instruments.	☐	☐	☐
15. All music teachers have had training in vocal music.	☐	☐	☐
16. All music teachers have had training in instrumental music.	☐	☐	☐
17. Music teachers have a broad and practical type of musicianship.	☐	☐	☐
18. The music program contributes to school and community welfare.	☐	☐	☐
19. Instructional activities—			
a. provide for individual differences in physical, mental, and emotional development;	☐	☐	☐
b. provide general and specific objectives for music education;	☐	☐	☐
c. provide freedom of expression through voice, body, and instrument;	☐	☐	☐
d. provide opportunities for discrimination and selectivity through listening and performing;	☐	☐	☐

EVALUATION CHECKLIST *(Continued)*

	None	Some	Much
e. provide increasing independence in dealing with musical elements, knowledge, and skills;	☐	☐	☐
f. provide for pupil-teacher sharing in making plans;	☐	☐	☐
g. develop qualities of leadership;	☐	☐	☐
h. provide for developing a sense of responsibility to the group and the individual;	☐	☐	☐
i. provide for opportunities which make the pupil aware of the relationships between music and other subject areas;	☐	☐	☐
j. provide for increased emphasis upon cooperative achievement and less upon competition;	☐	☐	☐
k. provide for assembly singing and participation in many assembly programs;	☐	☐	☐
l. provide experiences which will correlate with other departments in the presentation of school and community programs;	☐	☐	☐
m. provide for pupils to do creative work through composition and performance.	☐	☐	☐
20. A music library is provided for the instrumental and vocal departments.	☐	☐	☐
21. Recordings of a wide range of musical selections are available for student use.	☐	☐	☐
22. Pictures, charts, games, and other teaching aids are available to aid music learning.	☐	☐	☐
23. A pitch pipe is available.	☐	☐	☐
24. Musical periodicals and pamphlets are provided and placed in the main library for distribution.	☐	☐	☐
25. Staff-lined notebook paper is supplied.	☐	☐	☐
26. Biographies of musicians and stories of operas are available in the library.	☐	☐	☐

EVALUATION CHECKLIST (Continued)

	None	Some	Much
27. Tests are used to explore musical aptitudes.	☐	☐	☐
28. Evaluation activities are used to help pupils comprehend their progress.	☐	☐	☐
29. Provisions are made to assist pupils and teachers through competent supervision.	☐	☐	☐
30. Evaluation procedures are used to detect strengths and weaknesses in the music program.	☐	☐	☐

Commendable Features of the Program

1. _____

2. _____

3. _____

Areas Needing Improvement

1. _____

2. _____

ADDITIONAL READINGS AND BIBLIOGRAPHY

ALEXANDER, WILLIAM M., and others. *The Emergent Middle School.* New York: Holt, Rinehart and Winston, Inc., 1968. (all)

BANDER, PETER, ed. *Looking Forward to the Seventies: A Blue Print for Education in the Next Decade.* Gerrards Cross: Smythe Publishers, 1968. (chaps. 5 & 24)

BERMAN, LOUISE M. *New Priorities in the Curriculum.* Columbus, Ohio: Charles E. Merrill Publishing Company, 1968. (chap. 11)

BONDI, JOSEPH. *Developing Middle Schools.* New York: MSS Information Corporation, 1972. (all)

CLARK, DONALD HENRY, ed. *The Psychology of Education; Current Issues and Research.* New York: Free Press, 1967. (chap. 10)

COLE, HENRY P. *Process Education: The New Direction for Elementary and Secondary Schools.* Englewood Cliffs, New Jersey: Educational Technology Publications, 1972.

Committee for Economic Development. *Innovation in Education: New Directions for the American School.* New York: Committee for Economic Development, 1968. (chaps. 1 & 2)

DEVITA, JOSEPH C. *The Effective Middle School.* West Nyack, New York: Parker Publishing Company, 1970. (all)

EDWARDS, REESE. *The Middle School Experiment.* London: Routledge and Paul, 1972. (chaps. 2 & 4)

EICHHORN, DONALD. *The Middle School.* New York: Center for Applied Research in Education, 1966.

EURICH, ALVIN CHRISTIAN. *Reforming American Education; The Innovation Approach to Improving Our Schools and Colleges.* New York: Harper and Row, Publishers, 1969. (chaps. 1, 4, 5, 9 & 13)

FALLON, BERLIE. *Fifty States Innovate to Improve Their Schools.* Washington: Phi Delta Kappa, 1967. (any Part I; Part II: nos. 593 to 602)

GRAMBS, JEAN D. *The Junior High School We Need.* Washington: Association for Supervision and Curriculum Development, 1961. (all)

HAVELOCK, RONALD G. *The Change Agent's Guide to Innovation in Education.* Englewood Cliffs, New Jersey: Educational Technology Publications, 1973. (Part I)

HIRSCH, WERNER Z., and others. *Inventing Education for the Future.* San Francisco: Chandler Publishing Company, 1967. (chaps. 1, 2, 5, 16, 17, 18 & 19)

HOWARD, ALVIN W., and STOUMBIS, GEORGE C. *The Junior High and Middle School: Issues and Practices.* Scranton, Pa.: Intext Educational Publications, 1970. (chaps. 8–10, 17, 18)

JOYCE, BRUCE R. *Alternative Models of Elementary Education.* Waltham, Mass.: Blaisdell Publications, 1969. (chaps. 8 & 9)

LAWLER, MARCELLA, ed. *Strategies for Planned Curricular Innovations.* New York: Teachers College Press, 1970. (chaps. 2, 3 & 8)

STOUMBIS, GEORGE C., and HOWARD, ALVIN W., eds. *Schools for the Middle Years.* Scranton, Pa.: International Textbook Co., 1969. (Part IV)

United States Educational Resources Information Center. *Pacesetters in Innovation.* Washington: Government Publication Office.

Periodicals

ALEXANDER, WILLIAM M. "What Educational Plan for the In-Between Ages?" *NEA Journal* 55 (March 1966): 30–32.

———. "The New School in the Middle." *Phi Delta Kappan* 50 (February 1969): 355–57.

———. and STRICKLAND, JOANN H. "Seeking Continuity in Early and Middle School Education." *Phi Delta Kappan* 50 (March 1969): 397–400.

ATKINS, NEIL P. "Rethinking Education in the Middle." *Theory Into Practice* 7 (June 1968): 118–119.

BRIMM, R. P. "Middle School or Junior High? Background and Rationale." *National Association of Secondary School Principals Bulletin* 53 (March 1969): 1–7.

BRUNETTI, FRANK. "The School in the Middle—A Search for New Directions." *School Planning Laboratory Circular,* June 1969.

BURT, CARL W. "High Schools Just for Freshmen Reduces Discipline Problems." *Nations Schools* 76 (July 1965) : 27–28.

CURTIS, THOMAS E. "The Middle School in Theory and Practice." *National Association of Secondary School Principals Bulletin* 52 (May 1968) : 135–40.

DOUGLASS, HARL R. "What Type of Organization of Schools?" *Journal of Secondary Education* 42 (April 1967) : 169–174.

HOWARD, ALVIN W. "Which Years in Junior High?" *Clearing House* 33 (March 1959) : 405–408.

————. "Recommended Grades or Years in Junior High or Middle Schools." *Bulletin National Association of Secondary School Principals* 51 (February 1967) : 68–70.

KATCHER, NAOMI Z. "The Junior High School: Whose Failure?" *New York State Education* 55 (October 1967) : 40–43.

PUMERANTZ, PHILIP. "Relevance of Change: Imperatives in the Junior High and Middle School Dialogue." *Clearing House* 43 (December 1968) : 209–212.

REGAN, EUGENE E. "The Junior High School is Dead." *Clearing House* 42 (November 1967) : 150–151.

SHIRTS, MORRIS A. "Ninth Grade Curriculum Misfits?" *Bulletin National Association of Secondary School Principals* 41 (November 1957) : 135–137.

SCHUMAN, R. BAIRD. "Reorganization in Public Education." *Peabody Journal of Education* 40 (May 1963) : 339–344.

STRICKLAND, VIRGIL E. "Where Does the Ninth Grade Belong?" *Bulletin National Association of Secondary School Principals* 51 (February 1967) : 74–76.

VARS, GORDON F. "Change and the Junior High." *Educational Leadership* 23 (December 1965) : 190–193.

WILLIAMS, EMMETT L. "What About the Junior High and Middle School?" *National Association of Secondary School Principals Bulletin* 52 (May 1968) : 126–34.

14

Changes in Teaching Procedures

From the standpoint of the public or concerned observers of the education field, educational institutions notably resist change. Teachers consistently consider such reticence the fault of the institution, which is represented in their eyes by the administration. On the other hand, those who observe the schools, such as concerned parents or professionals in the schools of education, often consider the teacher as slow to change as the institution.

Modifications in organization are often instituted by the administration in response to pressures from crediting agencies or citizens groups; or it is determined by tax bases, or an honest attempt to service the young people with a better school. Changes in teaching procedure are often instigated by principals, but more often by the teachers themselves in response to a felt need for better instruction or a more efficient organization.

Some changes, philosophically based, are attempts to improve conditions for the individual in the belief that the child can better learn or better be led to learn under certain prerequisites. The antithesis, a system analysis approach, attempts to make the organization more efficient. Unfortunately, too often these factions war with each other over appropriateness, proper function, or correct philosophy. Both are important, and each has a role to play. The following changes in teaching procedure qualify in one of these two categories. Rarely are they restrictive or complete enough to satisfy both camps.

Expanded-Period Day

One of the more simple approaches to the solving of numerous educational problems is the expansion of the school day. For years, the fifty- to sixty-minute period was the standard, with the six-period day accepted as ideal. Despite pressures which have eliminated the six-period day in many schools in our country, thousands still accept its limitations.

Six periods limit the number of course options, activities, and educational experiences. Administrators often defend the system on the grounds that they are able to offer the basics during the six-period day and that the average child can rarely benefit from more. In fact, most young students are able to handle well only four solids, with the remaining two periods as study halls. Adding additional study halls only increases the problems most schools find with these leisure periods.

Those who do not favor the six-period day suggest that most students would be willing to and should have the opportunity to engage in other kinds of educational opportunities than solid courses; they suggest that study halls do offer problems; and, consequently, the student should be given options for social, community, or personal-centered educational activities.

In some school systems where the six-period day is not satisfactory, the school has expanded to seven or eight periods. Such periods are only a bit shorter than the usual fifty to sixty minutes, and the day is only some longer in total time. No common lunch hour exists. Usually in one of the periods there are regularly scheduled school activities, including clubs, student council, homeroom, or numerous other student-centered concerns.

Band rehearsal, Wooddale Junior High School. Memphis, Tennessee. Tom Swayzee, conductor.

The Module

The extended-period day prompted a look at the module unit as the basis for learning divisions. Coupled with electronic scheduling, this type of school planning and arrangement has altered the teaching situation in numerous schools around the country.

The module is any regular unit. In the case of the school, this unit is time. Most schools which have adopted the module idea accepted the twenty-minute unit, although some few schools employ up to a thirty-minute module or downward to a fifteen-minute module. The module school builds schedules around and considers the unit as one period. In some schools, the appropriation of each module changes every month; in some schools every week. Those who purport to understand the system best maintain that a module school minimizes its value to the learning situation unless schedules are revised daily. Most schools which revise schedules daily use a computer to make time assignments and to check conflicts. However, articles in educational literature describe the use of daily schedule changes in small schools without the aid of computer.

Even where schedules change regularly, students and teachers both have a voice in the making of schedules. A student requests one or more modules for each course in which he needs assistance or wishes to work. The teacher requests individuals or small groups of students, based upon the needs of the students understood by the teacher; or large groups of students, as demanded by the subject matter outlined by the teacher for the course.

For example, if a student in mathematics is slower than his classmates, the teacher may request one or more modules for individual or small-group work with this student. If the student had also realized the need, his request and that of the teacher would coincide. If only the teacher had recognized the need, the teacher's request for time to assist the student would supersede the request of the student to be scheduled into free periods or activity modules during the day. In some cases no conflict would have been realized so that students could have both mathematics and activities.

The work of a class might follow individual patterns, small-group patterns, and some large-group patterns. Where large-group patterns exist, usually a large-group lecture given by one teacher to as many as two hundred students would satisfy a particular class for a week or more. Between times, small-group instruction may take place; individual instruction may take place; or in the case of students who are moving smoothly and easily through the course, no formal instruction may be scheduled. In other words, the needs of the students are cared for, partly by the recognition of the student, and partly by the recognition of the teacher.

Since the module school day has as many as twenty-one units of time, it is possible for the student to use one, two, or more modules in any one of a number of ways. Some of this time may be spent in individual study, some may be spent in educational activities, some may be spent in library work, and some in large lectures or presentations. Teachers may have time for more planning, for more individual work with those who are not moving at a rapid rate through the material, or for work with small groups in ways which best would assist some students.

The advantages of the system seem obvious. Some of the disadvantages were seen shortly after the system had been placed in operation. (1) In some schools where the module plan has been adopted it has been found that students do not know how best to use their time. When students were required to remain at school only during an educational activity or class, many problems developed, some of them in the business section of the cities involved. The educational atmosphere improved when no student was permitted to leave the school grounds until the end of the school day. (2) Teachers did not know how best to organize their teaching when they were not expected to teach every person each day. Much wasted time resulted, and during the early years of the plan, many teachers could not meet their own goals. Many teachers opted for more time with students than the students could use well; and at other times they did not request enough modules to complete the work. Adjustments in this area were made, but some teachers reacted slowly. (3) Teachers as well as students seemed greedy; the students, in areas where they had built some skills, avoiding those areas where necessary backgrounds were needed but where learning had always been difficult; the teachers, in thinking that their subject regularly needed the large blocks of time they always had used.

Where teachers and administrators have persisted, the module school has resulted in a challenge and educational experience to all students.

Team Teaching

For some it is impossible to consider the module without team teaching. In other schools, team teaching has been used for a number of years without the module unit.

Team teaching, whose meaning is almost obvious from its title, uses more than one teacher for a particular subject or subject matter area. This idea purports to locate the best qualified teacher for each particular portion of the subject taught. Originally the attempt was to strengthen the quality of instruction by requesting that more than one teacher be involved with a subject or a subject matter area. In this day of advanced knowledge and intense specialization, it behooves the junior high school, or even the elementary school, to offer the young person the best available information concerning a subject.

Two examples will suffice. In the area of English it is feasible that one teacher could best teach grammar while another could best handle literature. A team approach to this class would offer the student the best parts of two teachers and a much better class. In the area of general science in the junior high school, some units could best be taught by a person who majored in physics, other sections of the class by a teacher who trained as a chemist. Again, the student will benefit by the interplay of staff rather than by one teacher working through the subject matter throughout the year.

Problems which one foresees with this idea include the careful scheduling of a teacher's time so that no lost time is built into the schedule. Never intended to result in lighter teacher loads or in less teaching time, its aim from the beginning was to assist the student in securing a better quality education. A disadvantage to some students, however, has been the change of teaching style and the insecurity felt with a change of teacher. The student who responds well to one personality may not to a new teacher who enters the class for a specified amount of time. Grading and the manner of handling class details offer some little concern for administrators and particular students.

Those who accept this idea state that the advantages definitely outweigh the disadvantages.

Core

According to the United States Office of Education, the term *core* should be used when two or more subject areas are combined or fused in some way. For some educators, the fusion of subject matter can best be handled at two points on the learning scale: one point near the beginning, when the student can benefit from such amalgamation to see the broad spectrums of knowledge; a second, much later, after some specialization has been witnessed, the student again can benefit from courses which show the interrelatedness of subject matter.

Junior high schools have used the core idea for a number of years. Recently, the core has awakened new interest because of its possibilities in several specific areas and its success in assisting the young student in seeing relations which have not been considered important until recently. For example, in the field of science, for years the single courses were promoted by the specialists in the field. Recently, and particularly with advances in medicine, psychology, brain surgery, and space exploration, the scientists themselves have been advocating a more unified approach to the sciences in an attempt to acquaint the citizen with a better access to contemporary living and to acquaint the student with a foundation for later study in his field.

The most common core has always been literature and social studies. These two areas seem to have a natural unity since literature is almost completely an interpretive art, relying heavily upon society for its subject matter.

Junior high schools which teach core courses believe that they better prepare the student for specialization courses which are to follow in high school.

For many schools, the core involves team teaching. The core, with its duplicity of ideas, becomes a natural for the team-teacher concept. Thus, in some schools literature and social studies are taught by one person, yet in other schools two teachers are involved with one class. If correctly used, this is not a presentation by one teacher for one week or unit of time, to be followed by a second teacher for a second unit of time. Rather there is a commingling of teachers and subject matter continually. In order to maintain loads and time-teacher schedules, usually such core courses, taught by more than one teacher, involves large sections of students. To some this is a disadvantage. In other schools this seems a minor problem, considering the benefits gained.

Non-Graded Schools

Although the non-graded schools are more common at the elementary level, some junior high schools use the idea to indicate that students are not bound to a rigid yearly curriculum.

In most junior high schools, a specific social science and a specific science are scheduled for the seventh and the eighth grade student. In the non-graded school, these courses are not considered a part of the graded system; rather, the student is offered courses dependent upon his ability, his past record of accomplishment, and his maturity. In such a school no grade lines are evident, but a two- or three-year sequence is offered which can be of assistance to the learning patterns of the student. No lockstep courses are evident. Although some courses are required, the exact time to meet these requirements is not specified.

Dual Progress

In an attempt to better service the young junior high school student, to better prepare him for senior high school, to act as a true transition school, some junior highs offer a mix between the elementary school and the senior high school in their course operation and organization.

The dual-progress school offers two types of school organization simultaneously. Courses in English, writing, reading, and social studies are offered during one-half of the day, and the student is involved with his grade in a formal classroom situation, with a single teacher and small classes. During the remainder of the day, sciences, mathematics, physical education, and the arts are offered on an elective basis, with a non-graded approach. Thus the student who is ready for advanced mathematics in the form of algebra in seventh grade is given the opportunity for this during the afternoon when he may be associating with other seventh graders, but more often, eighth and ninth graders. He spent the morning, however, with his classmates of the seventh grade in reading, writing, literature, and social studies.

Some schools believe that this combination school has much to offer, especially to the average and below-average student.

Accountability

Taken from the business world, the term *accountability* has become a new concern for the educator during the past ten years. It originated in those federal projects which, having been funded by the Office of Education, attempted to evaluate the amount of educational progress per pupil for the money spent.

Recently, citizens' groups have taken up the term, applying it to local situations in an attempt to ascertain the amount of education the system is producing for the amount of money spent.

Although there are those who maintain that a teacher's worth cannot be measured, that a student's learning cannot be given a price tag nor evaluated by objective means, some administrators, but, particularly, many more parents, are demanding that some kind of measure be given for the amount of dollars spent.

Often associated with situations wherein a wide divergence of background is evident, this idea has affected many schools educationally. Parents of the most successful students usually assess the progress of their children as being satisfactory. In the same school, and often within the same classroom, other children may be learning next to nothing. Most parents believe that every child should be taught to move from his current level, and that progress should be seen in all children; that every child should make some progress, and perhaps the child who needs the most should receive the most attention, in time, in effort, and thus in dollars spent.

In some ways, accountability only looks practically at some of the other ideas which we discussed earlier in this chapter. Many teachers and administrators have been concerned with this problem and have attempted to deal with it in different ways. Their failure or success has been the result of a large number of factors. Accountability focuses the attention of the teacher and the taxpayer upon the child and asks that some measure of improvement be evident. To prove progress, some administrators have turned to a number of different procedures. During the next decade, this problem will be continually with us, whether it be called by this name or not. It will affect the teacher and the teaching situation by always bringing to the fore the need to show progress with the students of the schools, all the students of all the schools, from some level upward.

Concepts and Behavioral Objectives

Education has been involved with goals for an extended number of years, at first quite simple and then more complex. Past goals, generally, have been either

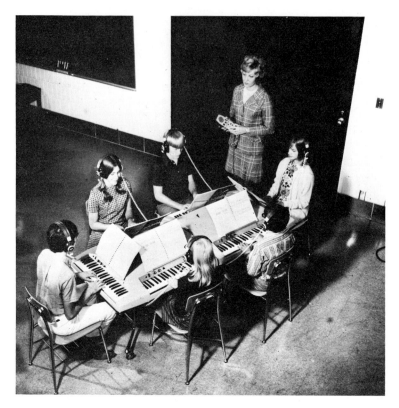

Learning musical concepts through class piano. Photo courtesy Musitronics, Inc., Owatonna, Minnesota.

vague, abstract, or narrow so that they tended to limit the focus of education to no more than the development of skills.

With the increase in the diversity of backgrounds of young people, with the increase in the diversity of reasons for seeking instruction within the formalized institution of the school, and with the increase in the complexity of the society which needs to be serviced by the school, goals seemed no longer to suffice. If man was to live well in a society in which there was a rapid advance of knowledge, more than an understanding of a series of skills would be necessary. Consequently, goals have given way to concepts.

Concepts are not another name for goals. Although including goals, they go beyond to also include the organization of material in some manner so that it simplifies the environment or enables the person to build upon it during further use. Concepts amalgamate like kinds to promote ease and speed of use or derive premises based upon generalization.

An examination of approach to the importance and learning of concepts provides an overview of educational concerns and directions, but it also provides a brief insight into two main approaches to education: ontogenetic and behavioristic.

Ontogenetic Concepts

The main proponent of this direction for education, J. Piaget, has become famous, particularly during the past decade, through commentaries on his observations of the learning of young people. Minimizing maturation, experience, and social transmissions, he believes that a person learns through a process of "equilibration," which means the reducing of disequalibrium between the individual and the environment. A person desires a state of balance, which differs with each personality, and will learn in order to achieve this. As the person develops, concepts come into focus through three periods or phases of growth, and as the person learns, his conceptualization in one phase prepares him for the next. These phases are the sensory motor, during the first eighteen months of life; the concrete operational, from about eighteen months to eleven or twelve years, wherein the thought processes develop only in relation to concrete objects handled or imaged; and the formal, age twelve and beyond, during which hypotheses are forming and consequences are deduced.

The order of the phases is the same for all persons, but are not developed necessarily at the same time or in the same manner. When a stage is acquired, the person becomes competent to conceptualize from a number of seemingly unrelated operations. Each stage contains the attainment of one phase and the starting point of the next. A diagram, such as the following, might assist in visualizing such a description.

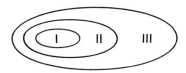

Behavioral Objectives

Behavioristic goals and procedures have been evident for a number of years. The famous stimuli-response approach to learning and educational direction is not new. Test grades, grading, reward and punishment, personal gratification through social aggrandizement, and a number of other items are common to most students. Through all of this, the main emphasis was placed upon skill learning; upon the acquiring of information, facts, and/or responses for the reward promised through stimulation, motivation, and reinforcement.

Recently, the behavioristic approach to education has developed behavioral objectives which move beyond the limitation of goals. This developed partly because of the emphasis on concepts through ontogenetic studies and partly as a result of the behaviorist's realization that his control over the response of students could go well beyond the factual and into the realm normally considered as conceptual. Consequently, educational circles have been considering behavioral objectives in a new light.

But problems have developed. We have yet to investigate well enough three conditions which affect the instructional process: sequencing, ways of interacting with subject matter, and practice. Teachers have responded to the behaviorists' new concept approach in a superficial manner, as if they once again were emphasizing goals, so that much of the rephrased behavioral objectives have been treated as goals only. This occurs because teachers have not fully understood the impact of the three conditions of the instructional process previously listed. Nor have they realized how difficult it is for the experimental analysis of behavior as outlined by scientists to be built into strategies and technics of instruction that can be used by teachers. Application of these strategies and technics usually come from teachers who are intelligent, sensitive to the needs of the students, persevering, creative, and alert to learning theory and its procedures.

Psycholinguistics

Standing as a bridge between the two theories discussed above, psycholinguistics offers an approach to the development of concepts which could be applicable to either, or create an independent hypothesis.

Experiments have pointed in the direction of language and its use as being the impetus for the development of concepts. Without secure language skills only elementary concepts are formed and those not securely. In studies with children, it has been found that where language is more advanced, concepts were accelerated and arrived at more quickly. At the primary age, it has been found that children respond mentally and overtly to the stimulation received from their own verbal responses, while behavior established without verbal associations is relatively unstable. From numerous studies and experiments, it would appear that the verbal factor is a most important one in the establishing of concepts.

The attention to concepts, but particularly to behavioral objectives, has changed teaching procedure considerably. As noted earlier, perhaps much of this is superficial since too little is known of the manner of teaching for conceptual organization. However, children and young people do form concepts consistently; the aim of education, then, should be to bring such formulation of concepts more regularly and more consistently toward a larger number of subject matter areas for a larger number of persons. The professional organizations in education understand the need and have provoked an attentive audience for this concern. It is hoped the future will supply additional definitive answers.

LEARNING ACTIVITIES

1. Organize a debate within the class. Resolved: the teaching machine would produce better musicians than other approaches to learning do.
2. Many music teachers believe they have no concern with accountability since their productions speak for them. Prepare a short talk for members of a Parent Group who have no children in a performing group, outlining for them precisely what the music program of the junior high school is teaching their children and how their children are making progress.
3. Divide your class into five groups, each group to be responsible for a presentation to the class of one of the following. Each group should state clearly the assets of the educational plan and its possibilities for music teaching in the junior high school. Be sure to consider the complete music program.

   Extended-period day   Team teaching (horizontal and vertical)
   Module time periods   The core
   Dual-progress schools

4. One junior high school organized its day according to the following diagram, using 14 periods per day. Each student could move from extended to regular periods as desired, giving the student mini-periods for study, eating, relaxing, or library work. Subjects such as English, math, history, etc., were taught during the regular periods of 45 minutes; courses such as home economics, physical education, music, or typing were taught for the extended 60 minutes. Discuss how this plan would affect the school generally, and music specifically.

8:30 a.m. to 9:15 a.m.	9:15 a.m. to 10:00 a.m.	10:00 a.m. to 10:45 a.m.	10:45 a.m. to 11:30 a.m.	11:30 a.m. to 12:15 p.m.	12:15 p.m. to 1:00 p.m.	1:00 p.m. to 1:45 p.m.	1:45 p.m. to 2:30 p.m.	regular periods
8:30 a.m. to 9:30 a.m.		9:30 a.m. to 10:30 a.m.	10:30 a.m. to 11:30 a.m.	11:30 a.m. to 12:30 p.m.	12:30 p.m. to 1:30 p.m.	1:30 p.m. to 2:30 p.m.		extended periods

This is an example of an extended-period day. Can you describe other plans which would also fit this subheading.

ADDITIONAL READINGS AND BIBLIOGRAPHY

ALMY, MILLIE CORRINNE; CHITTENDEN, EDWARD; and MILLER, PAULA. *Young Children's Thinking: Studies of Some Aspect's of Piaget's Theory.* New York: Teachers College Press, 1966.

BAIR, MEDILL, and WOODWARD, RICHARD G. *Team Teaching in Action.* Boston: Houghton Mifflin Company, 1964. (chaps. 5 & 6)

BEARD, RUTH MARY. *An Outline of Piaget's Developmental Psychology for Students and Teachers.* New York: Basic Books, 1969. (all)

BEGGS, DAVID W. *Team Teaching.* Bloomington: Indiana University Press, 1964. (chaps. 4 & 10)

BISHOP, LLOYD L. *Individualized Educational Systems, the Elementary and Secondary Schools.* New York: Harper and Row, Publishers, 1971. (chaps. 2, 3 & 6)

BOYLE, D. G. *A Student's Guide to Piaget.* Oxford: Pergamon Press, Inc., 1969. (all)

BREARLEY, MOLLY, and HITCHFIELD, ELIZABETH. *A Guide to Reading Piaget.* New York: Schocken Books, 1966. (chaps. 1 & 4)

CHAMBERLIN, LESLIE J. *Team Teaching: Organization and Administration.* Columbus, Ohio: Charles E. Merrill Publishing Company, 1969. (chaps. 10 & 11)

DAVIS, HAROLD S. *How to Organize an Effective Team Teaching Program.* Englewood Cliffs, New Jersey: Prentice-Hall, Inc., 1966. (chaps. 1, 3 & 5)

DIEVES, Z. P. *Concept Formation and Personality.* Leicester: Leicester University Press, 1959. (Intro. 1)

DRUMHELLER, SIDNEY J. *Handbook of Curriculum Design for Individualized Instruction.* Englewood Cliffs, New Jersey: Educational Technology Publications, 1971. (chap. 2)

————. *Teacher's Handbook for a Functional Behavior Based Curriculum.* Englewood Cliffs, New Jersey: Educational Technology Publications, 1972. (chaps. 3, 5 & 8)

DUNHAM, J. L.; GUILFORD, J. P.; and HOEPFNER, RALPH. *Abilities Pertaining to Classes and the Learning of Concepts.* Los Angeles: University of Southern California, 1966. (all)

DUNN, RITA, and DUNN, KENNETH. *Practical Approaches to Individualizing Instruction: Contracts and Other Effective Teaching Strategies.* West Nyack, New York: Parker Publishing Company, Inc., 1972.

FAUNCE, ROBARD CLEO, and BOSSING, NELSON L. *Developing the Core Curriculum.* Englewood Cliffs, New Jersey: Prentice-Hall, Inc., 1958. (chaps. 6, 10 & 12)

FRANSETH, JANE, and KOURY, ROSE. *Survey of Research on Grouping.* Washington: Government Printing Office, 1966. (all)

FREDERICK COUNTY MARYLAND BOARD OF EDUCATION. *Core Bulletin.* Frederick, Maryland: 1959. (chaps. 2, 3, 9 & 14)

FURTH, HANS G. *Piaget for Teachers.* Englewood Cliffs, New Jersey: Prentice-Hall, Inc., 1970. (chaps. 2, 3, 6, 8, 10 & 12)

GINSBURG, HERBERT, and OPPER, SYLVIA. *Piaget's Theory of Intellectual Development.* Englewood Cliffs, New Jersey: Prentice-Hall, Inc., 1969. (chap. 5)

GLASSER, JOYCE FERN. *The Elementary School Learning Center for Independent Study.* West Nyack, New York: Parker Publishing Company, 1971. (chaps. 3, 6, 7 & 9)

HANSLOVSKY, GLENDA; MOYER, SUE; and WAGNER, HELEN. *Why Team Teaching?* Columbus, Ohio: Charles E. Merrill Publishing Company, 1969. (chap. 7)

HASLERUD, GEORGE M. *Transfer, Meaning, and Creativity.* Minneapolis: University of Minnesota Press, 1972. (chaps. 7 & 10)

HUNT, EARL B. *Concept Learning: An Information Processing Problem.* New York: John Wiley & Sons, Inc., 1962. (chaps. 1, 3 & 5)

INHELDER, B., and PIAGET, JEAN. *The Growth and Logical Thinking from Childhood to Adolescence.* London: Routledge and Kegan Paul, 1958.

JOHNSON, ROBERT HENRY, and HUNT, JOHN J. *Recipe for Team Teaching.* Minneapolis: Burgess Publishing Company, 1968. (chaps. 1, 6, 8, 9 & 11)

KOHL, ROBERT R. *The Open Classroom.* New York: Random House, Inc., 1969. (all)

LEWIS, JAMES A. *Contemporary Approach to Non-Graded Education.* West Nyack, New York: Parker Publishing Company, 1969.

MARTORELLA, PETER H.; JENSEN, ROSALIE S.; MCKEAN, JOHN; and VOELKER, ALAN. *Concept Learning; Design for Instruction.* Scranton: Intext Educational Publishers, 1972. (chaps. 2, 5 & 9)

MCCARTHY, ROBERT J. *How to Organize and Operate an Ungraded Middle School.* Englewood Cliffs, New Jersey: Prentice-Hall, Inc., 1967.

———. *The Ungraded Middle School.* West Nyack, New York: Parker Publishing Company, 1972.

MOLTZ, HOWARD, ed. *The Ontogeny of Vertebrate Behavior.* New York: Academic Press, Inc., 1971. (chaps. 1, 4 & 11)

NOAR, GERTRUDE. *Individualized Instruction: Every Child a Winner.* New York: John Wiley & Sons, Inc., 1972.

Ohio State University School. *A Description of Curriculum Experiences in Grades Seven through Twelve.* Columbus: Ohio State University, 1952. (chaps. 1, 8, 9, 12–14)

PETREQUIN, GAYNOR. *Individualized Learning Through Modular-Flexible Programming.* New York: McGraw-Hill Book Company, 1968. (chaps. 1–6)

PHILLIPS, RICHARD CLAYBOURNE. *An Historical Study of the Concept Curriculum.* Doctoral dissertation: Northwestern University, 1962.

PIAGET, JEAN. *The Origin of Intelligence in the Child.* New York: International Universities Press, 1952. (chaps. 4 & 6)

POLOS, NICHOLAS C. *The Dynamics of Team Teaching.* Dubuque, Iowa: Wm. C. Brown Company, Publishers, 1965. (all)

———. *Team Teaching and Flexible Scheduling for Tomorrow.* New York: MSS Educational Publishing Co., 1969.

ROLLINS, SIDNEY PHILIP. *Developing Nongraded Schools.* Itasca, Illinois: F. E. Peacock Publishers, Inc., 1968. (chaps. 1, 2, 3 & 5)

ROYCE, JOSIAH. *The World and the Individual.* New York: Macmillan Publishing Co., Inc., 1900. (chap. 7)

SAXE, RICHARD W. *Opening the Schools: Alternative Ways of Learning.* Berkeley: McCutchan Publishing Corporation, 1972. (chaps. 15, 17–19)

SHAPLIN, JUDSON T., and OLDS, HENRY F., eds. *Team Teaching.* New York: Harper & Row, Publishers, 1964. (chaps. 5 & 9)

SIGEL, IRVING E., and HOOPER, FRANK H. *Logical Thinking in Children.* New York: Holt, Rinehart and Winston, Inc., 1968. (Parts 2, 3)

SMITH, LEE L. *Teaching in a Non-graded School.* West Nyack, New York: Parker Publishing Company, 1970.

THASS-THIENEMANN, THEODORE. *Symbolic Behavior.* New York: Washington Square Press, 1968. (Parts I, II)

TOOPS, MYRTLE DEWEY. *Working in the Core Program in Burres Lab School.* Muncie, Indiana: Ball State Teachers College, 1955. (all)

VARS, GORDON F. *Common Learnings: Core and Interdisciplinary Team Approaches.* Scranton, Pennsylvania: International Textbook Company, 1969. (all)

WALLACE, JOHN GILBERT. *Concept Growth and the Education of the Child.* New York: University Press, 1965. (chaps. 1 & 3)

Periodicals

CAHILL, H. E., and HOVLAND, C. I. "The Role of Memory in the Acquisition of Concepts." *Journal of Experimental Psychology* 59 (1960): 137–144.

CALLANTINE, M. F., and WARREN, J. M. "Learning Sets in Human Concept Formation." *Psychological Reports* 1 (1955): 363–367.

DETAMBEL, M. J., and STOLUROW, L. M. "Stimulus Sequence and Concept Learning." *Journal of Experimental Psychology* 51 (1956): 23–40.

ELKING, D. "Quantity Conceptions in Junior and Senior High School Students." *Child Development* 32 (1961): 551–560.

GREEN, E. J. "Concept Formation: A Problem in Human Operant Conditioning." *Journal of Experimental Psychology* 49 (1955): 175–180.

HANFMANN, E., and KASENIN, J. "A Method for the Study of Concept Formation." *Journal of Psychology* 3 (1937): 521–540.

HEIDBREDER, E. "The Attainment of Concepts: III, The Process." *Journal of Psychology* 24 (1947): 93–138.

LOVELL, K., and SLATER, A. "The Growth of the Concept of Time: A Comparative Study." *Journal of Child Psychology and Psychiatry* 1 (1960): 179–190.

MARTIN, W. E. "Learning Theory and Identification: The Development of Values in Children." *Journal of Genetic Psychology* 84 (1954): 211–217.

NELSON, P. A. "The Acquisition of Concepts of Light and Sound in the Intermediate Grades." *Science Education* 42 (1958): 357–361.

———. "Concepts of Light and Sound in the Intermediate Grades." *Science Education* 44 (1960): 142–145.

ROYER, F. L. "The Formation of Concepts with Non-Verbal Auditory Stimuli." *American Journal of Psychology* 72 (1959): 17–31.

SKEMP, R. R. "Schematic Learning and Rote Learning." *Mathematics Teaching* 21 (1962): 9–12.

STAPLES, I. EZRA. "The Open Space Plan in Education." *Educational Leadership* (February 1971).

15

Music and the Reorganization of the School

In Chapter 13 several organizational plans for the intermediate school were examined. Some advantages and disadvantages of each were mentioned. In this chapter we will examine these ideas from the perspective of music and the music teacher, thus adding a dimension rarely discussed in classes or educational circles.

The Original Elementary School (Eight-Four)

Although in a definite minority, an eight-four structure may be found in some localities. If a holdover from the early 1900s, its existence may be the result of financial problems or status quo boards of education; if newly reconstituted, some educators may believe this arrangement is advantageous for their community, other plans notwithstanding.

Advantages

In this school, the music program could realize some advantages not open to other arrangements. If the system were small, it would most certainly offer a unification of teaching staff and students, providing certain facilities and class arrangements which might not be possible otherwise. One music room could centralize musical activity for all students from grades one through eight. Likewise, one teacher could provide the musical instruction for this school and if that person were equally well trained in vocal and instrumental procedures, the music offerings would not suffer.

A more modern term for this kind of situation is the school with a self-contained music program. Where the teaching is good, this kind of situation is most satisfactory. Even if the self-contained music program were not possible, this arrangement could offer certain housing advantages for a small staff. The vocal teacher conceivably could teach all elementary and intermediate levels, providing a completely unified program. The young people would enter high school with a sequenced program which would be a welcome advantage.

The continuity offered by the extended length of the elementary school system would also produce a similar continuity for the instrumental program. Students could begin instrumental instruction in grade five, or as late as grade seven or eight, without losing the possibility of entering beginning classes at any time within the continuity of the school structure. Since the eight grades normally work together on many events, a beginning instruction class that included fifth through eighth graders would not seem unusual. Ability grouping rather than grade distinctions could be more completely built into the program. If a sixth-grade trumpet student were the best in the school, his being chosen to represent the school, to play in an assembly, or sit in the first chair would seem most logical to all the students.

Disadvantages

Even though all eight grades are housed in one building, some kind of division often pulls the upper grades from the lower. Because older students wish a prestige built upon age and activity, the music program could suffer because of social situations. In addition, buildings which house all eight grades are most often old and ill suited for music. Small rooms, poor acoustics, and lack of storage space are common.

The Junior High School (Six-Three-Three)

This arrangement of grades is the most common throughout our country and so only a few advantages and disadvantages will be mentioned. Your experience probably will provide additional ones.

Advantages

Since the school operates as a social and educational entity, programs can be unique. In music this means that special kinds of offerings can be arranged, such as a male ensemble or an uncommon approach to the general music class. At this school, students begin a more serious kind of musical study, usually taught by a specialty teacher. After a required introductory course, music electives are open to all having interest and talent.

Ensembles become an integral part of the junior high school serving the student educationally, but providing a medium for school spirit, prestige, and social outlets as well. Also their popularity is due in part to the learning independence these give the junior high student.

If the student has begun an instrument in the elementary school, classes and ensembles are usually provided for students of his grade. If the student wishes to begin an instrument at this later date, he may join with others who are also beginners. In some school systems, no attempt is made to introduce instruments in the elementary school, but all beginning classes are held in the junior high school. In such situations it is reasoned that students are able to make more definitive choices of instruments, able to progress more rapidly through the early learning problems, and able to participate in this activity as a part of the junior high school program where other new items are also evident in the educational offerings.

Brass choir, Edison Junior High School. Green Bay, Wisconsin. Roger Bintz, conductor.

Disadvantages

The general music class usually has been a requirement for all students and, consequently, a catch-all of various backgrounds and abilities. Students from a number of elementary schools usually make up the music classes in a junior high school, occasionally including some from city schools and some from outlying areas. This educational discrepancy leads to such a heterogeneous grouping of musical interest and talent that some music teachers feel unable to cope with the situation and, thus, little or no music is taught. If not well taught, students conclude this class to be a repeat of six years of elementary school. They express their dissatisfaction in word and action, and where possible, do not elect it.

Vocal ensembles create specific problems for the junior high school because of the maturing male voice; in addition, the girl voice, through change, often becomes less effective. These factors lead to personal problems introducing an insecurity toward singing. The change of school, the change of teacher, and the introduction of the new only offer an opportunity for the student to drop his musical activity.

In the instrumental program, a change of teacher from the elementary to the junior high school may cause students to feel lost with new methods and procedures, or to feel insecure with larger facilities and a redistribution of familiar associates. Furthermore, the intermediate usually matures in taste as well as physique and comprehends that the junior high ensembles lack the quality which he can respect. This may lead to restlessness, dissatisfaction, or disinterest. At best, the ensemble might have a respectable quality but be small in size and instrumentation, leading to a feeling of inferiority on the part of some participants. This is difficult to overcome by any music teacher. In ability groupings, such as instrumental ensembles tend to be, the difference in performance and musical maturity between the seventh grader and the ninth grader can be tremendous. The seventh grader with modest ability and the ninth grader with outstanding ability are probably farther apart musically than at any time on the educational scale. Performing music which can be profitable to both presents a problem.

The Middle School (Five-Three-Four)

One of the major characteristics of this plan is the inclusion of the ninth grade in the high school. This offers certain advantages to any system where the size of the musical ensemble is a factor. However, other advantages might be more important than this one.

Advantages

The proponents of this plan believe that the individual matures earlier now than previously. If this be true, the sixth grader more logically belongs with the seventh and eighth grader, while the ninth grader belongs with his high school friends. A general music program probably could be defined which would be more homogeneous for grades six, seven, and eight than for grades seven, eight, and nine of the junior high school. Musically, this plan could be defended only if the music program were energetic in the first five grades of the elementary school.

From the standpoint of the vocal teacher, the changeable years of grades seven and eight might better be handled along with the sixth grade which could give a measure of stability to any performance by supplying ample high voices. In addition, recently some teachers have found a substantial number of changing voices in the sixth grade, and conclude that this level should be placed in the middle school so that vocal problems could be more carefully handled while not presenting an opportunity for a feeling of maladjustment by younger elementary students.

Instrumentally, the program could be a success since in our country sixth grade is the most common one for the introduction of instruments. If this introduction could take place as the student enters the middle school, a most beneficial climate could ensue wherein the child would have the same teacher and the same learning situations for the following three years, providing sufficient musical maturity and sufficient experience for later high school participation.

Disadvantages

Since the child is moved into the middle school at the end of his fifth grade, some teachers believe that he loses one vital year where fundamental musical concepts are secured. It is rarely possible to teach within five years as complete a program as needed.

If the child voice can be best cared for in the elementary school, then by placing the student into the vocal ensembles of the middle school one year earlier, the voice could be pushed downward too soon, offering more problems in the vocal area rather than eliminating those we now have. Music teachers are ensemble-prestige conscious, and the middle school will only place the same pressure now witnessed in the junior high school upon this middle school with its less mature voices. The results could be problematic for the senior high ensembles.

In the instrumental field, the combining of grades six, seven, and eight could produce ensembles which are even farther away from the maturity of the high school, offering increased problems for the teacher.

The Intermediate School (Four-Four-Four)

As explained in the preceding chapter, this school has taken several emphases (planned gradualism, school-wide assistance, and a teacher-advisor plan) in order to assist the child in his learning climate, all of which stress the need of the student for gradually increasing educational horizons, and leading him to some independence of activity and thought.

Advantages

If the assumption exists that music is not only a mass performance skill but that the child may learn musical ideas without always involving himself with a group of his peers, then this plan will lead to exploration in music much as in other fields. With the music room as an area of resource, with the teacher as the assisting resource person, and with the library and its collection of records and films on musical subjects, the child can progress most satisfactorily along a learning path which will be invigorating and helpful. Whether one follows planned gradualism, the home-teacher idea, or the teacher-advisor plan, the student becomes a part of the music program somewhat as a result of interest, somewhat as a result of ability, somewhat as a result of group incentive with his peers; but most importantly, he is able to develop some concerns which are particularly his. This most likely would develop the musicianship of the student at least as much as procedures which are more teacher guided.

This student would have more time for practice on the instrument of his choice or more time in which to experiment in a choice of instruments. More private practice or lesson time on the instrument might prove an advantage. In addition, the instrumentalist would also have staff and library resources at his fingertips, which would enable him to go beyond just the involvement with the instrument alone. The instrumental program would most logically be instituted when the child entered his fifth grade, giving him four years of intermediate school study, and thus enable him to progress further by the time he reached the high school ensemble. This would be a particular advantage in the eyes of teachers of string instruments.

Disadvantages

Educators concerned with the general music learning of the child quickly would point out that this plan most certainly would bring a curtailment of basic music at the end of grade four. School administrators could argue that a logical break point for the general music program should be a the end of the elementary school, thus offering only four years of basic music for the child; then beginning with grade five, offer him only specialty opportunities which so often service best a smaller percentage of the student population.

Since this school places a greater emphasis upon the child and his own desires and initiative, this means that a large number of students would not have the same quantity contact with music as in another type of school organization. In addition, it is more difficult for students to learn music as an independent subject, and this would prove discouraging to most. The child would suffer vocally since his contact with music could be less regular and less well planned as compared to systems comprising longer elementary school music programs. The fifth grader is not ready to assume the self-determinance of his older classmates, but needs a longer basic training before his sole musical experiences are independently structured or consist of an ensemble devoted to part singing and performance.

If the emphasis in the instrumental program is placed upon the individual, then those who have interest and ability will do well while those having either less interest or less ability or both might not survive musically in this atmosphere. Our high school organizations contain a number of students who learned early music tasks quite slowly. Still others benefited obviously from the beginning class and the encouragement and drive which this kind of participation and competition offered. If this school provides any less of these, then instrumental programs will attract fewer students.

The Double School (Six-Six)

Advantages

Since this plan aids the smaller school system, it would follow that the music program would benefit as well. The small high school could benefit by having six grades in one building, with the musically trained students participating in vocal and instrumental ensembles. This could mean that elementary basic music would be offered only in the first six grades, while the upper school would concentrate on speciality courses and ensembles. The student who begins an instrument in the seventh grade will have an incentive for development leading immediately into the high school's major ensembles. Two types of ensembles would be beneficial in the upper grade unit. The first would be a training group which would take into consideration the problems of the young student. The second would use the more mature voices or players. Both would be conducted by the same person, permitting an easy flow from one to the other. A lack of duplication in equipment and facilities would assist the small system.

Disadvantages

Several objections may be stated briefly. Economic savings are considered above all else; the young adolescent is better served by a separate facility; the delay of initiating an instrumental program until the beginning of the seventh grade may not be advisable; the lack of the usual general music class or specialized classes for the young student would be a retrogression; the inclusion of the young seventh grader with the senior high student will offer a number of problems for teacher and students.

The Diphase School (Six-Two-Four)

Advantages

The general advantages listed in Chapter 13 are appropriate also for the music program.

This plan keeps the child in the elementary school until basic skills are as secure as possible. On the other hand, it places the student of the ninth grade in the high school where his participation in the music program can be advantageous to him and to the school. Rarely do schools offer or require general music for ninth graders. Consequently, the student might better be located in the high school where he can participate in more advanced programs.

This school offers instrumental instruction for only two grade levels. If the student has participated in beginning instrumental classes in the elementary school, he then will be prepared to participate in the seventh and eighth grade classes and ensembles. These grades are similar enough in ability required that a good ensemble would result. In addition, this school places major emphasis upon small ensemble participation, enabling the student to understand musical independence, blend, and musical responsibility, all of which train him well for more advanced participation.

A good general music program could be planned which would involve these two grades, and one could require such a course for both years with benefit for both. A vocal ensemble for those who wish it would be a possibility. Since these two years envelop most of the changing-voice problems, the ensemble director could define his work most specifically. A voice class could be a valuable educational asset for these young people.

Disadvantages

Being homogeneous, this school attracts special kinds of programs and experiments. Since the nature of the school determines the strength of the music offerings, unsoundly based concepts could lead to weak music possibilities; thus, constant change in design may frustrate specialty programs more quickly than basic programs. One such experimental program centered upon individual instruction possibilities through student scheduling, precluding large ensembles. No vocal program and only a weak instrumental program was the result.

If the school is not involved with student scheduling, it could be that with only two grades, the school could not support a proper instrumentation distribution; or a vocal ensemble composed so completely of changing voices might offer the student little in aesthetic development or diversity of literature.

Summary

After consideration, one or two plans might offer possibilities superior to the others. Throughout the coming years, as these plans become realized in more of our communities, the music teacher should be prepared to offer his advice, taking a position which will direct the attention of the community toward the general educational advantages and disadvantages, and at the same time, being alert to them from the standpoint of the music program. Parents and students are sensitive to the demands of the music program if these demands are reasonably stated with an understanding of the complete educational picture.

LEARNING ACTIVITIES

1. Choose the school plan which you believe best accommodates the teaching of junior high school general music. Discuss your reasons with your classmates.
2. Choose the school plan you believe best accommodates the teaching of instrumental music for the young adolescent. Do others share your point of view?
3. Your first music position will probably be in a smaller community. Does any one plan suit itself more logically to the smaller community than to the larger city system?
4. Debate with your classmates on the following topic: Resolved: the junior high school should be replaced by a newer organizational plan.
5. Many of these plans exist in communities of our country. Which plans are now in operation in your area? Would a visit to a junior high school assist in your understanding one or more of the plans and the advantages and disadvantages for the music program?

ADDITIONAL READINGS AND BIBLIOGRAPHY

BACKEN, J. J. "Flexible Scheduling: Facts, Fantasies, and Fads." *English Journal* 60 (March 1971): 363–368.

BAKER, R. M. S. "Innovation and the Beginning Teacher." *Pennsylvania School Journal* 119 (November 1970): 157.

CONNALLY, J. A., and HOAGLUND, M. L. "Adapting Instruction to School Objectives and Student Needs." *Educational Technology* 12 (April 1972): 31–4.

FRANKLIN, MARIAN POPE. *School Organization: Theory and Practice.* Chicago: Rand McNally & Company, 1967. (chaps. 2, 4, 10 & 11)

HILFIKER, L. R. "Factors Relating to the Innovation of School Systems." *Journal of Educational Research* 64 (September 1970): 23–7.

HILLSON, MAURIE, ed. *Change and Innovation in Elementary School Organization.* New York: Holt, Rinehart and Winston, Inc., 1967. (Part IIe, IIId, IVd, Va, b, c, VIb, d, e)

McGLASSON, M. A., and PACE, V. D. "Functions of Junior High Schools and Middle Schools." *Viewpoints* 47 (November 1971): 2–14.

―――. "Preparation of Teachers for Junior High and Middle Schools." *Viewpoints* 47 (November 1971): 108–26.

McISAAC, D. M. Jr. "Flexible Modular Scheduling by Computer." *Business Education Forum* 25 (May 1971): 17–19.

ODETOKE, T. O., et al. "Organizational Structure and Student Alienation." *Educational Administration Quarterly* 8 (Winter 1972): 15–26.

STANBROOK, J. R. "Preparing Teachers for the Intermediate Schools." *Clearing House* 46 (January 1972): 284–7.

―――. "Student Reactions to Three Innovative Facilities." *Audio-Visual Instructor* 15 (October 1970): 47.

UDINSKY, F., and GEORGIADES, W., eds. "Four Major National Innovative Programs." *Journal of Secondary Education* 46 (April 1971): 148–88.

WILEY, W. D. "Flexible Scheduling; Some Considerations." *Business Education Forum* 25 (May 1971): 15–17.

16

Music Reacts to Changes of Teaching Procedures

Music teachers usually react unfavorably when confronted with teacher committees or administrators requesting a searching inquiry into teaching methods. The public, the usual watchdog of the school systems, knowing little of the field of music teaching, usually will cry for change in academic areas, but trail off to silence when confronted by music directors. Even the professional educators in schools of education, who often push for change through state agencies or national organizations, know little of music and only hesitantly estimate how contemporary teaching procedures could or would affect the music program. Consequently, the music teacher claims irrelevance when changes are suggested, and offers the success of one or more performing groups as an antidote; and for the most part, these arguments are accepted as valid. Most suggested changes are not adaptable to music teaching without some adjustment. Rather than work to adjust, the musician more often holds out for no change or minimal change, believing this procedure to best promote existing programs or personal understandings.

In situations where change has been considered a school-wide concern and pushed upon the music teacher, some music directors resist so vehemently they would prefer to stunt or kill the program than change, crying, to camouflage their stubbornness, that their demise was instituted by an unknowing administration who thought music was a subject "just like all others."

The professional college music educator has been of little assistance in this educational quagmire. He has not been asked for advice by public school authorities when he could have been an excellent resource. On his own campus, often he is relegated to a position of heretic because he dares to differ with ensemble directors, studio teachers, and classroom teachers of theory or literature whose procedures are only imitations of teachers they have seen, whose procedures, in turn, were copies of their teachers, etc.—a chain of teaching ideas which have come from the European studio-conservatory system of the later nineteenth century.

Consequently, school music holds the fort against change, partly through the ignorance of the public, and partly through fellow teachers of the school system who work with the music teachers, and administrators who try to assist the ongoing school programs. Since the music teacher has had little professional work in the field of psychology, sociology, child development—and, specifically, learning theory—opinions are based almost entirely upon the experiences of rehearsal-learning situations and the studio-learning procedures. Even in music classes of colleges, little contemporary teaching exists. College students who might wish for more contemporary teaching are quickly advised that this is not possible in music.

The best which could be hoped for has been some attention to a more efficient organization, often instigated by commercial interests. Efficiency, here, evolves around such technical matters as a better way of filing music, choir robes, band uniforms, storing instruments, or teaching improvements in the use of mouthpieces, reeds, and fingering. To their credit, commercial companies have understood a few pedagogical developments and their educational representatives have promoted them.

An examination of changes developed in the schools of our country will give a more detailed look at the dilemma of music. It would be unfair if we did not agree that music does have certain differences from academic subjects and if we did not recognize these differences justly and honestly; at the same time, we should admit when music has been resistant to change rather than honestly attempting to evaluate itself and adjust.

Recently, music education has found itself in the midst of forces so strong that changes are beginning. Similar to the evolution of some years ago called "new math," music teachers face "new music." One difference exists: no one direction or series of changes predominate in music. Rather, a variety of ideas involving such items as electronic music and equipment, popular music with its various styles, and some emphasis upon special groups such as the handicapped, preschoolers, or non-Western cultures have all clamored for attention. Teachers without a concern for perspective or knowledge of the complete picture may alter the program and believe they have satisfied the situation. Teachers not sensing the basis for change within a particular school system may still be out-of-step and again deplore the lack of understanding for the music program on the part of administrator and taxpayers.

Expanded-Period Day

Music stands to lose considerably in a school organized by the six-period day. First, students interested in both sports and music find this arrangement not versatile enough and too limiting. In junior high or middle schools, students have not yet determined a major activity, and administrators should emphasize the advisability of breadth rather than depth.

Secondly, students interested in music often are highly intelligent and desire a full schedule of academics, including more highly specialized courses or honors classes which might be offered. When these are in conflict with the music program, it is the six-period day which gives the fewest solutions for the music teacher and the interested student.

Thirdly, many students interested in music, and talented in the field, deserve the opportunity to participate in general music and one or more ensembles; a talented instrumentalist might wish to play in both band and orchestra. These requests are not often possible with a limited number of periods. Too many students whose schedule will not permit music could become effective participating members if more periods were possible in the school day. A well-rounded music program may be developed if the more talented students and a larger percentage of students are serviced. A six-period day will be of little or no assistance.

The Module

Most music teachers are not fond of the module system. This is not based upon a study of possibilities, but rather upon a word-of-mouth opinion which has circulated through the profession from those who would prefer not to become involved with this change. Directors of ensembles do not understand how it could possibly bring anything but deterioration to their group.

From the standpoint of the general music teacher in the adolescent school, the module could be a workable situation. Just as any other teacher, he would be faced with large-group lectures, small-group discussions or explanations, and individual assistance times. Exactly how this would work for the music teacher can only be surmised, since the module is most effective when it applies directly to a specific class or group of students. The demand for small group or individual instruction units would be impossible to foretell without knowing the students and their learning problems.

The general music class servicing the average or general student should have no more difficulty in teaching by the module than a class in English or mathematics does. The adjustment would be difficult for the teacher only in that he would have to rethink his course structure and how it applied to the specific students he was teaching in any given class.

Ensembles could also find the module an interesting and rather exciting possibility, although most ensemble directors are so committed to the daily hourly rehearsal that it becomes difficult for them to consider the advantages or feasibility of such a system. Imagine, if you will, a large instrumental ensemble in the adolescent school. Because of the module system in the school, the ensemble would meet as a large group only once each week. This meeting might be staggered as to

Band in concert, Wooddale Junior High School. Memphis, Tennessee. Tom Swazee, conductor.

the day of the meeting so that one week it could assemble on Tuesday but the following week on Thursday. During the interim, the teacher would be busy with small group meetings or classes as well as individual assistance classes. For example, a small group, which in this situation might consist of all of the brasses, might meet twice between the large rehearsals. In addition, the trumpets might meet alone three times for two modules each, while the trombones, who needed additional assistance, might be called for four times, at two modules each. The tubas, needing less assistance, would be requested but once, for three modules. Further, certain performers might be in need of special assistance; consequently, they would be scheduled to meet with the teacher one or more times depending upon the progress of each individual. It would be difficult to imagine this group reassembling without some obvious progress having been made.

We in music have not explored well enough two items which bear upon this situation. First, we do not really know the effect of strong sectional rehearsals upon only an occasional total rehearsal. At the present time, most ensemble directors have good-to-poor small-group rehearsal possibilities, but regular large ensemble rehearsals. If the reverse were true, the result might be equally satisfying, or even improve upon the present. Second, we do not really know the effect of practice upon the large ensemble. Musicians do emphasize practice, and practice is necessary. The exact nature of the practice has yet to be ascertained if we are to reach maximum efficiency.

Team Teaching

In the adolescent school, team teaching would be a natural for the general music class. In some schools, assembled groups are too large for one teacher to be continually effective; in others, smaller classes mean constant repetition of teaching throughout the day. The teaching of music with a team of two or three teachers would be ideal in many respects. The subject matter and the students could be well handled while each teacher taught his specialty. Large groups of students could be scheduled, but during special projects, smaller groups could work effectively with the supervision of a staff member.

A teaching team is a combination of qualified specialists. The ideal setup would place each specialist in a proper teaching assignment. Some opportunities of service include a master teacher and assisting teacher; some teams may include paraprofessionals, interns, and clerical aids.

Team teaching may yield an increase of quality in content, organizational benefits, and stimulation of team ideas and evaluation. The first criterion in organizing a learning team is to establish the content for which each team member is to be responsible. The second is the identification of instructional procedures.

The Vertical Team

Consisting of two or three teachers from the same department, this group works together to instruct a common set of students. This approach usually fits within the conventional class schedule and, consequently, is more quickly organized and more often used.

In some schools at the present time, the music department has taken advantage of the vertical team teaching idea, using several members of the staff to assist with large ensembles. Usually only one person is the regular director, but other teachers assist with details of instruction or administration. In addition, teachers in a team may move from school to school to work with the beginner or the near beginner—the woodwind teacher providing good instruction for his beginners, while the brass and percussion teachers assist students in those areas. The same team teaches in the junior high school to provide sectional or group instruction as needed. In the large rehearsal, one person conducts while two teachers move through the organization to assist the young player with details.

Few if any schools have used the team for choral ensembles, although the situation, as with instrumental groups, could be equally profitable.

The Horizontal Team

The horizontal or interdisciplinary team consists of teachers from different disciplines who are given a common block of time to use as the team sees fit for the instruction of a common set of students in classes of flexible size.

In the horizontal situation, music teachers often have difficulty working on a team. For many, heavy schedule demands make it impossible to be a true team member. The ensemble director, for instance, faced with numerous deadlines of a concert nature, can little afford to miss group or individual instruction which is needed for the progress of his ensemble in order to participate with a team teaching a broad subject matter course. In addition, for most music teachers there exists little concern for the broad areas; training has been narrow in scope, and the teacher does not have a background which will permit participation comfortably.

School-Within-a-School Team

Consisting of teachers from all disciplines, this group becomes responsible for the instruction of the same body of students over an extended period of time, such as one to three years. In larger schools this approach compensates for the mass of students involved, enabling the individual to find security and self-identity through a smaller group.

The Core

The preceding paragraphs explained some of the problems faced by team teaching. While the team clusters teachers, the core clusters subject matter; and in some cases these are combined. But, as with the team, music has difficulty in adopting a vertical core approach, and even more difficulty with the horizontal core.

In the vertical core, the various areas of music would be combined into one course to be taught by one or more teachers. Theory, applied music, literature, musical science, and ensemble would be considered as one course. In reality, these areas are included in the general music class which has occupied the attention of teachers of music in the junior high school for years. But, as we have noticed in our previous discussions, all subareas of music are seldom given a balance. Teachers are not developed well enough to teach effectively across the entire scope of music. To illustrate, it has been only during the past twenty years that the area of music theory has been considered a core and taught in a unified manner. Even today, music teachers will argue that it is impossible to teach sight-singing if one must have the students writing and considering the rules of harmony.

In the horizontal core, where music combines with one or more disciplines or arts, the music teacher has reluctantly embraced this possibility. In our junior and senior high schools, the most commonly known humanities course often includes art, music, and literature, although other combinations have been used. Beyond a comparatively few schools, humanities courses have not been particularly successful. To create a workable situation, the teachers themselves must be convinced that this type of offering can and will be a success and a valuable asset to the student and the curriculum. Anything less than total commitment will be the beginning toward elimination of effectiveness and possible dissolution of the horizontal core.

In addition, the music teacher who works with the horizontal core must have a background of some breadth as well as an interest in other humanities areas. Too often the musician wishes to enter the course only for those times when music may be taught and no true amalgamation with other courses is evidenced in his mind or in the minds of the students.

Many humanities courses have relied too heavily upon the historical approach so that the student sees little value in the offering or little relevance to himself. All teachers of art, music, and literature have been taught the historical approach almost exclusively in college classes, so they believe that unless a student is taught in this manner he will not understand the art form. Also, the historical or style period is explored too deeply and relied upon too greatly. One humanities course in an Eastern junior high school began with a three-week sequence on pop music, but moved immediately to Greek and Roman times and then progressed chronologically back to the present. The teachers had one good thought, but ended their originality there. If the humanities classes are to be effective, they must work from a base where all the areas involved can have almost equal effect and equal contribution to the topic chosen.

Non-Graded Schools

Music is often non-graded. In some junior high school ensembles, grade lines mean very little. However, other schools operate an eighth-grade chorus or band and a ninth-grade group, following a timeworn schedule. Unfortunately, the music program probably suffers. Traditionally, teachers of music preferred the general music class for seventh graders, and special classes for eighth- and ninth-grade groups. Some schools open a chorus only to ninth graders. All of these limitations would not exist in the non-graded school.

Instead, junior high chorus membership would depend upon scheduling or talent, with the latter preferable. Instrumental groups in some adolescent schools operate successfully upon such a plan. General music should not be limited to the seventh grade. In the non-graded school such a system would be feasible, and the class would not be taught as an extension of the elementary program, but would use more mature understandings of the art of music in as many different ways as possible since it would not be limited to only the seventh-grade student.

Other musical offerings could be given, including special classes in the science of music, the recreation of music, and class piano, to name only a few. The non-graded school offers considerable benefit for the music program, and most music teachers should welcome this approach to their classes.

Dual Progress

By reading the description of dual progress in a preceding chapter, one may readily understand certain advantages for the music program. Similar to the non-graded school, it permits students to choose musical activities without being held to grade lines, and places music with a respectable academic group of elections. In addition, it eliminates some of the required course conflicts which are inevitable under the standard system. As a group, musicians have not been aware of this type of offering for the adolescent school and have not heard of the advantages it could offer to the music area.

Accountability

Only a few restricted school systems have introduced the word accountability into the educational process. In principle, music should have little difficulty in accepting accountability. However, in practice it will be difficult to come to grips with this idea, for music teachers as a group are not fond of definite scales or testing gradations to prove growth and maturation. Traditionally, music teachers accept subjective judgments of playing or singing, yet other evaluations are not attempted since it is generally agreed that true knowledge and understanding of music comes from the feelings, which are not easily evaluated. This is true at the present time since the music profession has done little to come to grips with this question, and educational testing specialists are rarely well enough trained in music.

In years past in the schools, music contests existed in which students were expected to memorize facts about music such as composer's names, names of compositions, or their movements. These were rightfully abandoned as bearing too little upon the true value of the understanding of music or its effect upon the individual. However, with modern testing devices and unlimited response possibilities through computer storage and processing, new horizons in the testing of sensitivities will be forthcoming which will enable the musician to make evaluations not believed possible before.

Accountability attempts answers for the administrator, the parent, and the taxpayer. If all of these groups consider music only as a performance medium, then the music teacher will have little difficulty in accounting for his work through the usual concerts or contest ratings. However, if growth toward music's meanings and feelings are to be the guide, then other roles and avenues must be explored. If we are to state on the one hand that there should be music in some form for every child, then on the other, we should be ready to defend and supply evaluations of our teaching and the results we achieve. Such acceptance would go beyond the performance group and into the general music class of the adolescent school as well as into other types of offerings such as the humanities classes or the specialty classes in music theory or history. These classes offer a particular challenge as to accountability, and it is possible that music teachers will be forced into reconsidering the methods used and materials taught. It also could force the music teacher to consider the testing and evaluating process to a degree not realized at this time.

Notably, music budgets exceed those of other subjects in the school. This results from costly equipment and for some schools, from the low student-teacher ratio. At first, music teachers might hestitate to publicize the exact cost of the instruction. They have little to fear provided they satisfy parents concerning the learning-cost ratio. Consequently, it behooves the music profession to work diligently to justify through appropriate means those learnings which do take place in many music classrooms.

Music is poorly taught in many schools. As a profession, music has not been contemporary in adjusting to the recent curriculum developments known generally as "modern math" and "modern language." Music too often is an undirected series of experiences based upon the concert, the contest schedule, or specific directions of the teacher. Accountability will undoubtedly force the music teacher to plan a sequenced learning schedule which will benefit the students involved. When this occurs, music will no longer hide behind the skirt of contest ratings but be more willing to work with accountability demands.

Concepts and Behavioral Objectives

The music teacher rarely involves himself with the development of the human personality to the extent necessary if he is to understand growth processes as related to learning. The following two approaches are not equally understood.

Ontogenetic Concepts

Of the two subdivisions of learning theory, that one dealing with the needs of the maturing child is least often considered. The music teacher, although aware that the child grows, has not examined these growths in terms of developmental stages and his own teaching processes. Most music teachers believe that formal music instruction, particularly on an instrument, should be begun as early as possible. Even among the profession it is accepted that early learning can best begin with the piano.

Music could benefit from an adaptational study of the learning stages and the conceptual development as proposed by Piaget. Although many elementary music teachers do consider gradation of material, they are not in a position to adjust this learning to the development of the children. Current classroom music procedures are often on such a mass basis that many children are passed by before even the most elementary music ideas are grasped. The preparation of the child for musical learnings has been little considered—including those preparations which could well precede instrumental work. Instrumental teachers, particularly piano and string teachers, are convinced that the earlier the instruction begins, the better, not realizing that certain concepts could well precede production upon an instrument.

Further, the music teacher has only begun to understand the role of music, with its organizational and reactional qualities through rhythm and sound, in the psychological growth of the personality. Such understandings come only from arduous work with an observation of young children or the slow learner.

The reverse of such concern asks if certain kinds of sounds can be psychologically detrimental to such developments. It is entirely possible that children react in a neutral or negative manner to musical instruction because they are not in the proper conceptual stage as the demands of the material. A greater knowledge of the student, his growth, his learning, and the effects of music will be a larger part of the training for the music teacher in the future.

Behavioral Objectives

Rather than considering the child as a changing personality reacting individually to his needs or disequalibrium, behavioral objectives imply that the teacher and the school environment coordinate to bring the personality to a specific point of reaction or development. The environment, then, is either overtly or indirectly controlled so that certain learnings will take place.

During the past decade, the music education profession has become concerned, tenacious, and overly directed in the development of behavioral objectives for various facets of the music program. Almost every state and national convention has its sessions for the development of these objectives in terms of musical development. In schools around our country, administrators have demanded that such objectives be developed for each course and learning activity within the school. Reluctantly in most cases, teachers are attempting to define these processes as they befit overall structures and substructures of learning categories. Even after the objectives have been defined, teachers may be at a loss as to the sequence which should be used to attain them. In some cases a former goal has been rewritten to include more contemporary language but with little other change or understanding. True behavioral objectives are difficult to write since they require definition, presentation and observation, and redefinition. Some teachers decry the usefulness of such objectives, claiming irrelevance for music classes. Since the arts are so personal and so intimate a learning, it is impossible to create objectives which fit them. Such claims, espoused to be based upon aesthetic concerns, have little validity in fact. When teachers cannot write behavioral objectives which accurately lead the student to desired results, it only points to their lack of knowledge of the learning process, to their brief attempts to analyze it, and to their misunderstandings of the manner in which behavioral objectives are conceived. Behavioral objectives are difficult to search out, requiring working, reworking, and refinement until the exact demand placed upon the young personality in musical learnings will be defined, extrapolated, and brought to focus.

Psycholinguistics

Two ideas need to be explored by the musician. First, does language development influence the receptivity of musical learnings? Second, with music being a language, could it be approached as a language for learning purposes?

Many studies indicate the development of language as a determiner and an indicator of learnings in other areas. Language development would seem to be based partly upon intelligence, upon the extent to which the young child has been engaged in conversation, upon the receptivity of language attempts by the young child, upon psychological growth, upon movement development, and upon protein and food supplies for body and brain energy. Could these also affect music learnings? The music listener? There is also reason to believe that in some ways music may assist with language development. This latter idea has received some speculation but little experimentation.

Considering that for years musicians have explained music as a language, it seems surprising that this connection has not been developed more strongly. If we consider music as a language, then why not consider it much like verbal learnings in regard to teaching and response. To do so would recognize two aspects of language and the respective problems of each: the patterns of language, and patterns and their context in various situations. Musicians have discussed musical patterns in some learnings, but have not explored seriously the learnings in music as related to patterns for the young child or the novice; nor have they considered what learnings could be developed with these patterns in numerous contexts.

Patterns as related to language infer the combination of sounds which, when given meaning, become words. In musical expression, sounds become motive fragments acting as the basis of other structures. It is in the recognition of word patterns that the child realizes a vocabularly which he uses by selection and understands from others. In music this same situation could probably be realized. As with language, what is used and what is heard and understood become two facets of the vocabulary. Patterns in musical form, small or large, are also possible patterns which the young person should know from use and from hearing.

With language, the context places new or different meanings upon these patterns. Music also contains similar possibilities wherein tonal and rhythmic patterns can be reorganized by context to produce different meanings. The task of the teacher becomes one of assisting the person in adopting patterns into the musical vocabulary and then adapting those patterns to new contexts so as to realize meaning in a particular composition.

In order to be successful with the ideas above, the person must be successful in both a musical and a non-musical way. These operations, which differ in unlike occasions of communication, require a general intelligence and a special ability to work within the musical language. This latter could be called a special linguistic ability or musical ability, and is the result of both innate potentialities and learning conditions.

If we recognize music as a language then we should also understand that its development would be essential to cognitive understandings in the field. Therefore, in order to develop music's language skill it becomes important for the person to exchange musical ideas with other members of his peer group. At every level of development, the child must not be cut off from expression—no matter if the pattern development is slower in one person than another. The understanding of these patterns in various contexts will expand through such exchange and if the hearing is followed by oral expression. Written expression is only feasible if the oral has been developed.

Conclusions

Although moving now with considerably more determination in some quarters, music has been and is slow to consider the need for changes in teaching procedures. Some changes in organization have been sought by music teachers only to be negated by administration; other organizational changes have been executed only after considerable pressure upon the music teacher to move into line with other academic areas. Those changes based more obviously upon philosophical determinations usually are little understood or of little interest to the average music teacher. As we approach the future, the music teacher will find these of a greater necessity if he is to play his proper role as teacher in the school system, and if he is to understand such changes as are sought by parents, administration, and the student.

1. The following vertical team-teaching plan was developed for the young adolescent.
   a. Study plan A, the outline, and the detailed three-day plan.
   b. Write your own vertical team-teaching outline.
2. The following excerpt, a modification of a plan from the Alpine School District of American Fork, Utah, uses the horizontal core.
   a. Read through outline B and imagine how this material or similar material would be made appropriate to a junior high school in your area.
   b. Devise a horizontal core program for a middle school.
   c. Using this outline as a guide, write a one-week detailed lesson plan for one of the units.
3. Some teachers are convinced that the module school best teaches the concept approach.
   a. Read through outline C on the following pages.
   b. Using the concepts listed, write your own three-day sequence for a different part of the outline. Use a plan in which all students are required to participate simultaneously, but once per week.
   c. Write a plan for a performing organization under the module plan. Use a two-week sequence of time; plan for one full rehearsal each week; use sectional and individual rehearsals; state precisely the literature and exercises you would use, along with the literature to enhance its learning potentials.
4. Sensitive to the problems of the Mexican-American student in our schools, plan D emphasizes the teaching of general music in a non-graded middle school.
   a. Read the outline and study the three goals discussed in detail.
   b. Write a similar outline, using a different minority group.
5. Conceptual teaching need not involve school reorganization as Plan E indicates.
   a. Using sections of Plan E as a guide, create your own concept outline for a similar rhythmic idea or a completely different rhythmic idea.
   b. Following section D as a guide, write the concept pages which precede the teaching of the whole-tone scale.
   c. Write a series of pages which you could use to develop another melodic concept for your class.

TEACHING PLAN   **A**   **Vertical Team**
HOW MAN USES MUSIC IN HIS
LIFE AND WORK

The following plan for a vertical team includes a large-group lecture and instruction, a small-group assignment, and individual study projects. The large-group presentations should indicate course goals and suggest a means of direction toward their attainment. An example of a large-class lecture is included.

a. Lectures should be crisp and easy to remember, and should have continuity. Each must be a precise lesson within itself while being correlated within a broader unit which will be dealt with in follow-up activities. The teacher should build the following mechanisms of learning into the lecture where possible: classification, association, assimilation, and memorization. Areas for further study, thought, and exploration should be presented during the lecture. Illustrations should accompany lecture presentations, and artistic illustrations could be used to dramatize the main points. An outline of the lecture should be given each team member.

b. The small group should be student centered and aim for active learners rather than passive listeners. The purposes are to clarify points from the lecture, share interpretations, broaden and enrich ideas and concepts of the topic, encourage active participation and discussion, and develop critical reading and thinking. The following activities should be observed within the small group: verbalization of understandings, questioning and challenging of ideas, applying basic information to new problems, moving beyond the lecture with reports, listening, and evaluations. Student notebooks should be checked periodically.

c. Independent study enlarges the student's self-development through personal accomplishment and productive work which leads to self-satisfaction. The teacher has a responsibility to motivate the student, to offer suggestions for improvement, and to serve as a resource person for pertinent readings. Individual study provides a program of instruction while bridging the transition from elementary school to the more sophisticated senior high school.

The following diagram depicts the plan of scheduling used in this project.

MONDAY	TUESDAY	WEDNESDAY - THURSDAY			FRIDAY
Planning and staff consultation Teachers: A, B, C	Large-group lecture Teachers: A, B, C present Each teacher presents those lectures most appropriate to his training and background. The following outlines uses teacher C	A small group	B small group	C small group	Independent study Teachers: A, B, C Assist students with ideas and projects most closely aligned to teacher's background and training

Outline: How Man Uses Music in His Life and Work

I. Man uses music for working

II. Man uses music for recreation

III. Man uses music for dancing

IV. Man uses music to express inner emotions
    A. Love of nature
        1. Folk songs
        2. Choral music
        3. Intellectual music which portrays nature
            a. Music which leads to Impressionism: Debussy, Ravel, Griffes
            b. Program music
            c. Symphonic poem

The following lesson plan will concentrate upon section IV-A of the outline. The main topics preceding it were listed to indicate previous work; additional ways for music to express inner emotions will be developed to complete the semester or year. The main goal is to assist the student in becoming aware that music is a vital part of his existence in today's living, and that all types of music can offer a means of expression and depict life around him.

Lesson Plan for One Week

> Goals for this week: The students should (1) learn how to relate music to their everyday lives as they see the possibilities of music's expressing nature; (2) learn more of the form and technic of music in an applicable situation; and (3) learn additional repertoire and examples of different styles.

Materials
A. *Discovering Music Together,* 8, Follett
   Making Music Your Own, 8, Silver Burdett
B. Recordings: Debussy, *La Mer,* (Third Movement) Follett Record 8
   Ravel, "Mother Goose," Bowmar No. 57
C. Film: *What is the Symphonic Poem?* Coronet Productions
D. Visuals: Slide projector
           Slides of "Cliff at Etretat" and "View of the Thames"

Tuesday—Large-Group Lecture and Instruction

A. As students enter, they find material on each desk; their attention is directed to the screen at front of room, on which is projected correct procedures.
   1. Using a ruler, make guidelines at center top for title: Man Uses Music to Express His Inner Emotions.
   2. Using a ruler, make guidelines at center bottom for name and class section.
   3. Second and third overhead give directions for folding and gluing large sheet making a folder. (Immediate class participation is important.)
B. Show slides of nature ("The Cliff at Etretat" and "View of the Thames"), accompanied by the playing of Debussy's "Dialogue of Wind and Sea" (Follett, 8). (5 minutes)
C. Questions: What is the general idea of these music and art examples? What first impressions were received? (3 minutes)
D. Introduction to: Man uses music to express love of nature.
   1. Goals and how we will achieve them in the following weeks.
   2. Explanation of folder.
   3. Text references: Follett, pages 80–85; Silver Burdett, pages 84–87. (10 minutes)
E. Repeat slides and Debussy: Look at themes (Follett, page 84); discuss mood, timbre, melody, and orchestration (Follett, page 85). (10 minutes)
F. Introduce symphonic poem: definition, origin, use in intellectual music. (5 minutes)
G. Film: *What Is the Symphonic Poem?* Coronet Productions. (11 minutes)
H. Introduction to "The Moldau": brief discussion of themes and format of composition (Silver Burdett, pages 86–87). (5 minutes)
I. Listen to portions of "The Moldau" which use themes discussed. (5 minutes)
J. Summary of lecture, followed by a preliminary statement concerning the Wednesday and Thursday study of tone color. (5 minutes)
K. Distribute handouts on tone color and the symphonic poem which have been revised by Teacher A for the junior high level. (2 minutes)

Wednesday and Thursday—Small-Group Sessions with Teachers A, B, and C

A. Clarify any points from Tuesday's lecture.
B. Singing about nature
   1. Folk songs and contemporary popular songs
      a. Discussion of how the texts comply with the topic of study
      b. Discussion of how the music fits the texts
   2. The simple choral selection

      a. "For the Beauty of the Earth" (Follett, page 80) (5 minutes)
      b. "Bendemeer's Stream" (Follett, page 81) (5 minutes)
        (1) Stress dynamics, phrasing, and identify all musical elements.
        (2) Analyze harmony, consider chromatic chords, discuss instrumental accompaniment.
      c. "New Hungarian Folk Song" Bartok, (Silver Burdett, page 205). (5 minutes)
        (1) Discuss variants of meter.
        (2) Read rhythmically.
        (3) Consider accompaniment.
  C. Define tone color. (15 minutes)
    1. Introduce vocabulary and implications of overtone and harmonic series.
    2. Class participation (Silver Burdett, page 288).
      a. Select five students to stand behind class; choose two at random and without revealing their identity, have them read phrases from the board to illustrate tone color and changes in the overtone series. "What voices did you hear?" "How did you recognize the voices?" "Did holding the nose or cupping the hands in front of the mouth make a difference?"
      b. Listen to portions of Ravel: *Mother Goose,* "The Conversation of Beauty and the Beast." Version 1, piano; version 2, orchestra. (Follett, Record II)
      c. Discuss differences of two recordings. Discuss tone color of instruments.

Friday—Individual Conferences and Projects

    This time will be devoted to personal contact with the students and to assist them with projects.

    The teacher's time should be flexible but not completely unstructured. Each student should be contacted with some regularity by at least one of the team. Where projects are concerned, a student should be assigned to the teacher who can best assist him. Three examples follow:

Teacher A: Lloyd has a growing talent for writing songs; he plays the piano and guitar but has difficulty in notating what he wants to express. The teacher suggests he create a song from three suggested poems on nature (use the one poem of his choosing), being sure the melody and harmonic structures fit the mood and meter of the poem.

Teacher B: Curtis has a keen ear as he listens to music and was interested during the listening presentation of the large-group lecture and small-group sessions. He needs to be motivated to seek further examples of recordings in this area, studying in depth their characteristics in tone painting, and either making a report or writing a paper.

Teacher C: Beverly is rather slow in music but loves art and creates well with art mediums. After counseling with Beverly's art teacher, it was planned to suggest that Beverly correlate her drawings with the musical topic. In addition, she may be interested in locating additional art works which could correlate with music examples to present to the class in a large group lecture.

TEACHING PLAN   B   **Horizontal Core**
                                                FINE ARTS IN THE SCHOOL,
                                                HOME, AND COMMUNITY

The following plan for a horizontal core includes three examinations of the arts for the junior high school student.

a. The fine arts in the school.   For many seventh grade students the junior high class schedule is a new and unusual experience, and most students seek to explore its newness and understand its possibilities. Beginning with a study of "Arts in the school," each student may familiarize himself with the place the arts have in the curriculum. Through a gradual expansion of this horizon, the student will have the opportunity to find how the arts constantly enrich his life. It is expected that most class members may profess primary interests in areas other than the arts; however one or more of the arts may prove to be of importance to these persons every day of their lives.

b. The fine arts in the home.   The arts can be a great source of pleasure in the home. Family members can participate in arts of all types and at various levels. Such activities do much to create a feeling of unity in the home. One of art's greatest values is in making worthy use of leisure time. Because there are numerous ways to enjoy these activities, many families are able to participate together and establish worthwhile interests which last a lifetime.

c. The fine arts in the community.   Utah, for instance, has an extended history in the use of the arts through the pioneers who crossed the plains and settled the early towns. Many young communities had activities which introduced and furthered artistic endeavors. Today, Utah has several outstanding performing groups of professional quality, including the Utah Symphony, the Mormon Tabernacle Choir, and the Valley Music Hall. Many guest artists travel to Utah cities, giving concerts, plays, and lectures which are of value and interest to local audiences. Junior high students should become aware of the artistic history and the present cultural advantages in Utah.

Outline: the Fine Arts in the School, Home, and Community

Part I

OBJECTIVES

1. The student should become acquainted with his opportunities as a student in the junior high school.
2. The arts are related to many subjects within the curriculum.
3. The arts have a place in the future of the student.

I. Student fine arts background survey

II. School classes in the arts
   A. General music
   B. Art survey
   C. Literature survey
   D. The arts curriculum in junior and senior high school
      a. Pottery, basketry, drawing, and painting
      b. Instrumental and vocal groups
      c. One act plays: comedy, historic, and tragedy
      d. Folk, ballet, and ballroom dancing
      e. Creative writing and poetry

III. The arts are related to other school subjects
   A. Science
   B. History
   C. Current events
   D. Mathematics

IV. The arts and the school library

V. Careers and hobbies in the arts
   A. Teachers
   B. Performers in drama, ballet and dance, music, art
   C. Repairmen and restorers
   D. Technicians of sound, museums, design, lighting, and sets
   E. Researchers
   F. Historians
   G. Composers, painters, authors, playwrights, dance creators
   H. Conductors and directors

I. Librarians
J. Amateur performers, artists, writers, and dancers
K. Collectors of art, books, records
L. Audiences and observers.

Part II

OBJECTIVES

1. The arts can be used as a family activity.
2. The arts may be a great source of pleasure.
3. The arts are a worthy use of leisure time.

I. Home arts survey

II. The arts for observation and pleasure

III. Participating in the arts at home

IV. The arts as an avocation
  A. Work which becomes pleasure
  B. Art which assists work

V. Changes in perspective through age

Part III

OBJECTIVES

1. There should be an increase in the students' knowledge of their own state's artistic heritage.
2. The student should become acquainted with Utah's outstanding artists.
3. Utah has made several contributions to the artistic world.

I. Background to Utah's arts
  A. Pioneers and their arts
    1. Journey westward
    2. Mormon battalion
    3. Early settlers and their artifacts, songs, dances, plays, and literature
  B. Growth of the arts in Utah
    1. Painting, literature, theater, dance
    2. Mormon Tabernacle Choir and Organ

C. Utah state song

II. Utah's outstanding art groups and display
   A. Tabernacle choir and organ
   B. Utah Symphony and bands
      1. Instruments of the band and orchestra
   C. Opera, musicals, and ballet groups
      1. Utah Valley Opera Association
      2. Valley Music Hall
      3. University groups
   D. Contemporary drama
      1. University groups
      2. Summer stock
   E. Museums
      1. Three museums in Salt Lake City
   F. Architecture and famous buildings
   G. Famous statuary

III. Utah's contribution to the arts
   A. Osmond Brothers, King Sisters, Red Nichols, Clinger Sisters, The Letter-men, The Three D's
   B. Grant Johannesen, Reed Nibley, Alexander Schriener
   C. Robert Cundick, Maurice Abravanel, Richard Condie, Crawford Gates

IV. Guest artists and their concerts in Utah
   A. Current season
   B. Famous artists of the past

TEACHING PLAN   **C**   **Concept-Centered Plan 1**
TONE COLOR (MODULE)

This concept-centered curriculum services a module school based on the five-three-four, or middle school, plan but could be used for any intermediate system. The student's conceptualization of the basic elements of music—rhythm, melody, harmony, form, and tone color—will be the basis for this program. Each concept studied will involve singing, creating, playing instruments, movement, and music reading as applicable. An example from contemporary popular music and other selections will be used for each concept. The idea is to relate former periods of music to the music of today.

Because of the module schedule, planning could be the biggest problem.

Music will be required of all students in grades six through eight, with at least one twenty-minute module of music twice weekly and two or three modules on particular days. If the student needs more time on one lesson because he does not understand or because he wishes to learn more, additional time may be scheduled when he can repeat the material or move ahead to new examples under guidance of the teacher.

The following plan defines two twenty-minute classes and one class of two modules. No individual assignments are given.

Outline: Concept-Centered General Music Class

I. Concepts concerning rhythm (9 weeks)

II. Concepts concerning melody (9 weeks)

III. Concepts concerning harmony (9 weeks)

IV. Concepts concerning form (4½ weeks)

V. Concepts concerning tone color (4½ weeks)
   A. Characteristic qualities of sounds are determined by the types of voices or instruments which produce them.
   B. When instruments are played in different ways, they produce different sounds.
   C. When individual instruments are combined, new effects of tone color are created.
   D. When formal structures call for repetition of themes, variety may be achieved by use of contrasting tone colors.

Lesson Plan for Three Sessions from Concepts Concerning Tone Color

First session—one module—twenty minutes.
Goal: the student will be able to identify certain characteristics of musical sounds as elements of tone color.

I. Concept A—Characteristic qualities of sounds are determined by the types of voices or instruments which produce them.
   A. First experiences
      1. Hear a pattern of nontonal sounds and compare with the same pattern produced by a single pitch.

    a. Play

    b. Play

    c. Compare tonal and nontonal sounds.
2. Hear a pattern of nontonal sounds and compare with the same pattern played on a variety of pitches.
    a. Repeat 1 a. above
    b. Play

    c. Compare tone color and pitch. Describe differences.
3. Hear a short pattern of tonal sounds and compare with the same pattern when the quality of the sound has been changed.
    a. Play first phrase of "Spinning Wheel" on a trumpet (*Exploring Music,* Holt, page 35).
    b. Play the same with a mute.
    c. Compare. Difference is quality of sound.
4. Hear a melody played by two highly contrasting tone colors of two instruments.
    a. Play melody of the last movement of Beethoven's *Ninth Symphony* on a flute (*This is Music,* 6, page 38).
    b. Repeat on the oboe.
    c. Discuss the difference created by tone color.
5. Experiment with percussion instruments and discover characteristic sounds.
    a. Tambourine—hit and shake
    b. Bells—use different mallets and different ranges
    c. Snare drum—snares off and on
B. These experiences should culminate in the ability to identify the following characteristics of musical sounds as elements of tone color.
   1. Tonal or nontonal
   2. Pitch
   3. Quality of sound (timbre)

Second session—two modules—forty minutes

Goal: the students will experiment with their speaking and singing voices to discover the variety and range of sounds individuals can produce; they will become aware of different types of voices as to range and timbre.

C. Vocal experiences
1. Discover, identify, and describe the difference between speaking and singing sounds.
   a. Speak: "Oh, say can you see . . ."
   b. Sing: "Oh, say can you see . . ."
2. Compare the sounds of a pattern or phrase when sung by an individual elementary child with the sound of the same pattern or phrase sung by an intermediate individual or a group.
   a. Have one student sing one phrase of "Joy to the World."
   b. Have half the class sing "Joy to the World."
   c. Compare the two.
3. Discover and describe differences in quality between boys' and girls' voices.
   a. Listen to "Everything's Alright" from *Jesus Christ Superstar.*
   b. Listen to Cherubino in *The Marriage of Figaro,* Mozart (woman).
   c. Listen to Ottavio in *Don Giovanni,* Mozart (man).
4. Recognize the differences in tone color when the loudness of a musical sound is altered.
   a. Sing: soft—loud (note narrow range of loudness on part of adolescent as compared to teacher).
   b. Play oboe: soft—loud. (Is the difference great or modest?)
   c. Play piano: soft—loud. (Is this a wide or modest range?)
   d. Play drum: soft—loud. (Why is this greatest?)
5. Recognize, identify, and verbalize the differences in tone color which are evident when the same melody is sung an octave higher or lower by a male or female voice.
   a. Teacher sings "America" in two octaves.
   b. Have students try this to feel and hear differences.
6. Recognize differences in quality among a variety of vocal ranges from recordings or live performances.
   a. Coloratura: "Queen of the Night," arias. *Magic Flute,* Mozart
   b. Dramatic soprano: "Return Victorious," *Aida,* Verdi
   c. Lyric soprano: Pamina's aria, "Ah, I Feel It," *Magic Flute,* Mozart
   d. Mezzo soprano: "Witches' Ride," *Hansel and Gretel,* Humperdinck

> *e.* Contralto: "Cresent Noon," The Carpenters, *Close to You*
> *f.* Tenor: "Celesta Aida," *Aida,* Verdi
> *g.* Baritone: "Largo al factotum," *Barber of Seville,* Rossini (*Making Music Your Own,* 6)
> *h.* Bass: Caiaphas, "This Jesus Must Die," *Jesus Christ Superstar*

7. Recognize and identify particular qualities of sound as appropriate or inappropriate to particular expressive purposes.

   Example: Discuss a tuba playing or a bass voice singing a musical composition about little birds flying in the air. What would be more appropriate for this kind of sound?

8. Listen to recorded performances of sacred and secular music performed by choruses. Example: *Robert Shaw Chorale Sings* (RCA LM 1784)

Third session—one module—twenty minutes

Goal: the student will recognize that percussion instruments have definite pitch, indefinite pitch, or no pitch, by using them in the following activities.

D. Instrumental experiences.
   1. Discover that percussive sounds have definite, indefinite, or no pitch.
      a. Use melody bells.
      b. Use cymbals.
      c. Use claves.
   2. Identify the following and group the sounds. (Introduce at random.)

Definite Pitch	Indefinite Pitch	No Pitch	
autoharp	cymbal	conga drum	claves
melody bells	finger cymbals	bongo drum	coconut shells
resonator bells	gong	bass drum	maracas
tympani	jingle	snare drum	pompons
	temple blocks	tambourine	sand blocks
	triangle	woodblock	tom-tom
		guiro	tone block

   3. Sing songs which invite instrumental accompaniments.
      a. "Spinning Wheel." Create patterns with sand block, drum, tambourine (*Exploring Music,* Holt, page 35)
      b. "Marine's Hymn." Use rhythm sticks, drums, cymbals. (*This Is Music,* 6, page 227)

4. Experiment with a variety of percussion instruments evaluating their appropriateness to the song.
   a. Use tonal or definite pitch instruments.
   b. Use indefinite pitch instruments.
5. Identify and select from among a variety of sounds those most appropriate to a given environmental sound. Examples:

> bell chiming (finger cymbals)
> clock ticking (rhythm sticks)
> feet marching (snare drum and guiro)
> horse trotting (coconut shells)
> waves lapping (pompons)
> wheels turning (sand block)
> wind blowing (pompons)
> sleigh bells (jingles)

Students may wish to create others, using definite and indefinite pitched instruments.

TEACHING PLAN   **D**   **Educationally Deprived (Non-Graded Schools)**
MUSIC OF TWO CULTURES

This plan is prepared for a non-graded intermediate school, with special consideration for the educationally deprived student.
   a. The non-graded school will have students in phases instead of the traditional grade levels. A student may at any time advance to another phase according to his individual progress in a particular subject. Overall achievement will not be the deciding factor.

Phase I: students who lack basic skills
Phase II: students who are developmental
Phase III: students who are statistically average
Phase IV: high ability students, more often those who could be college bound
Phase V: a quest phase, students who wish individual or independent study

A student may be in Phase I in one subject and in Phase V of another. This type of encouragement is especially applicable to the bilingual, educationally deprived student.

b. The educationally disadvantaged student is often considered "culturally deprived." This is a misleading term, since many of the people so labeled are part of an ancient culture which includes highly developed music, art, politics, and religion.

An educationally neglected people in the United States are the Chicanos, or Mexican-Americans. Many educational problems in the school systems stem from the inability of teachers to understand the Spanish language and the culture it describes. Since a majority of teachers are not able to communicate with these students whom they are supposed to teach, problems develop.

In a non-graded school, the educationally disadvantaged student may not experience the failure which he has come to expect in the traditional school system. The non-graded system will relieve the pressures of competing with other students and will enable him to concentrate on his own abilities or inabilities. In experiencing no failure, the educationally disadvantaged student will not develop a negative self-concept. Any music program includes students of many capabilities. A non-graded music program can be more relevant for the student by speaking directly to his level.

The following outline is specifically geared to the Chicano student in a non-graded school system. Students of Phase I and II should be in one class, while students of Phases III, IV, and V should be in another.

Outline: The Music of Two Cultures

I.   Introduction to music
     A. Early music of the Western hemisphere
     B. Gregorian chant—how it relates to early Indian civilizations

II. A comparison of the music of historical cultures
     A. The music of the Aztec culture
         1. History and background
         2. Structures of music
         3. Types of instruments
         4. Religious ceremonies
     B. The music of the American Indian
         1. History and background
         2. Structures of music
         3. Religious ceremonies
         4. How music reflected a way of life
     C. Music of the Renaissance
         1. History and background
         2. Structures of music
         3. Types of instruments
         4. Religious ceremonies
     D. Music of the baroque era
         1. History and background
         2. Structures of music
         3. Religious music
         4. How music reflected a way of life

III. Music and nationalism
   A. The music of Mexico
   B. Nationalism in Europe
   C. A comparison of European and Mexican music

IV. Music since 1900
   A. Mexican music
   B. European music
   C. Music in the United States
   D. Music of the contemporary Chicano—a combination
      1. Folk music
      2. Emotional music
      3. Intellectual music

A series of classes focused upon IV D will enable the student to comprehend how Chicano music is a combination of many cultures. The sequence will include an introduction to folk, emotional, and intellectual music of the Chicano. This portion culminating the entire plan will relate to the semester's work requiring the student to synthesize, organize, and remember; for example: the contribution of the American Indian, and of the baroque period.

I.   First goal: to explain differences and similarities of contemporary folk music
   A. A comparison of styles
      1. Chicano to European, Mexican to United States, United States to Chicano
      2. Structure and instrumentation
      3. Vocabulary introduced, discussed, and compared
         a. Corrido, Mariachi, Segunda, Tersera, Gitaron
         b. Modernization of corrido explained
      4. Recordings of Texas Chicano artists: Little Joe y La Familia, Sunny Ozuna and the Sunliners, La Revolucion Mexicana, Agustin Ramirez
         Chicano artists who sing in English
   B. Summary and review

II. Second goal: to explain differences and similarities of contemporary pop music
   A. A comparison of styles
      1. Chicano to United States blues, rock, and ballad

2. Structure, instrumentation, and style
3. Style and rhythm vocabulary introduced and defined
4. Recordings: Rene and Rene, Santana, Vicki Carr, Jose Feliciano

B. Summary and comparison of folk and pop music

III. Third goal: to explain differences and similarities of intellectual music
    A. Comparison of styles
        1. Mexican to United States and European electronic, aleatoric, and atonal
        2. Structure, instrumentation, form, and style compared
        3. Special notation, theoretical organization, and procedures introduced and explained
        4. Reading: portions of *Twenty Centuries of Mexican Art* by Carlos Chavez

TEACHING PLAN	**E**	**Concept-Centered Plan 2**

RHYTHMIC DEVELOPMENT

Emphasis upon concepts has been begun in our schools, and students have reacted favorably when teachers understood this type of teaching.

The following material, taken from the *Guide for Teachers* for the junior high schools of Milwaukee, Wisconsin, proposes concept development through units of work. The concepts are outlined, but the precise daily processes are not, the latter being developed by the individual teachers. The experiences and the music examples used to help the student understand the following concepts are included:

Part A: Concept of steady beat and underlying beat
Part B: Concept of triple and duple meters
Part C: Concept of a combination of duple and triple

Part D: Concept of whole-tone scale

Part D was chosen to offer a contrast with A, B, and C, while the first three show a development in the rhythmic learning of the student. This last concept, the whole-tone scale, taken from a later section of the guide, considers a melodic concept contrasting to the rhythmic ideas of the preceding concepts.

ELEMENTS OF MUSIC: RHYTHM

Concept	Experiences	Musical Examples	Symbolism
PART A			
Steady Beat	Sing song with definite beat feeling.	*Havah Nahgeelah, Making Music Your Own,* 7, Silver Burdett *Upward Trail, Birchard Music Series,* 7, Birchard	Subnumber in Time Sign ? 4
Underlying beat or Basic beat	Tap a steady beat accompaniment with drum or woodblock.		
	Show beat notes on chalkboard.		
	Devise bodily rhythm accompaniment in duple meter (hand jive). ex. Tap knees twice Clap hands twice Snap fingers twice left Snap fingers twice right		
	Add percussion instruments: Drum, tambourine, claves, maracas.		
	Use hand jive to accompany listening selection.	Prokofiev: *Summer Day Suite,* "March," *Adventures in Music,* Record 1, Victor	
	After first hearing, try hand jive backwards during **B** section to show ABA form of selection		

PART B

Meter can be triple

Discover that triple meter "fits" songs.

Listen to recording in triple meter.

Accompany listening selection.

ex. castanets

♩ ♩ ♩ ♩ (3/4)

tambourine

♩ ♩. ♩ (3/4)

tap shake

De Falla: *Spanish Dance* first section, *Adventures in Music*, Record 6, Victor   (3/4)

Meter can be duple

Sing song in duple meter with rhythm accompaniment.

ex. tambourine (c)

finger cymbals (c)

Jikel 'Emaweni, *Making Music Your Own*, 7, Silver Burdett   (2/4 4/4   c)

Elements of Music: Rhythm—Continued

Concept	Experiences	Musical Examples	Symbolism
PART C			
Meter can be combinations of duple and triple	Play a selection in 5 meter.	Brubeck: *Take Five*	$\frac{5}{4}$
	Discover the division of the 5 beats, 3–2 or 2–3.		
	Accompany first section of recording with percussion instruments:		
	cymbal woodblock		
	Play other selections in 5 meter.		
	Discern groupings of duple and triple.	Holst: *The Planets*, "Mars. Bringer of War," *Making Music Your Own*, 3, Silver Burdett	
Compound meters	Listen to a composition in 4 meter.	Tschaikovsky, *Symphony no. 6*, 2nd mvt. (2–3)	$\frac{4}{4}$
Duple-duple	Play drum on first beat.	Herbert: *Natoma*, "Dagger Dance," *Adventures in Music*, Record 3, Victor	Quarter notes
	Play woodblock on first and third beats.		
	Show beats and accent on chalkboard as:		

Concept	Experiences	Musical Examples	Symbolism
PART D Whole-tone scale	Form whole-tone scale from the chromatic scale. C D E F# G# A# C		whole tone
	Sing a familiar song in the major scale.	*Lovely Evening*	
	Play the same song on the bells in the whole-tone scale. Class sing with bells		
	Form tone clusters using alternate tones C E G# and D F# A#		tone clusters
	Accompany class singing of song on whole-tone mode with alternating tone clusters. ex.		
	G# A# G# A# E F# E F# C D C D		
	Tremolo for impressionistic effect.		tremolo
	Discuss the fact that a dissonance occurs without stridency because of the lack of tonal center feeling.		
	Listen to an example of whole-tone mode.	Debussy: *La Mer*, "Play of the Waves," *Adventures in Music*, Record 6, Victor Debussy: *Voiles*	

ADDITIONAL READINGS AND BIBLIOGRAPHY

BAIR, MEDILL, and WOODWARD, RICHARD E. *Team Teaching in Action*. Boston: Houghton Mifflin Company, 1964. (chaps. 6 & 8)

BEGGS, DAVID W. *Team Teaching*. Bloomington: Indiana University Press, 1964. (chaps. 4 & 11)

BRAMELD, THEODORE. *Minority Problems in the Public Schools*. New York: Harper and Brothers, 1946.

BROWDER, LESLEY H. *Emerging Patterns of Administration Accountability*. Berkeley, California: McCutchan Publishing Corporation, 1971. (Part Ia, c, IVd, g, h)

CHAMBERLIN, LESLIE J. *Team Teaching*. Columbus: Charles E. Merrill Publishing Company, 1969. (chaps. 2 & 6)

CUMMINGS, PAUL, ed. *Fine Arts Market Place*. New York: R. R. Bowker Co., 1973.

DENSMORE, FRANCES. *The American Indians and Their Music*. New York: Womans Press, 1936. (all)

DUNHAM, J. L. *Abilities Pertaining to Classes and the Learning of Concepts*. Los Angeles: University of Southern California, 1966. (all)

FLETCHER, ALICE. *Indian Story and Song from North America*. Boston: Maynard, 1900. Repr. of 1900 ed. AMS Press, Inc., New York, 1970. (all)

FRENCH, WILLIAM COLE. *The Principal and Staff in the Crowded School*. New York: Bureau of Publications, Teachers College, Columbia University, 1965. (chaps. 3b, 4, 5)

GOTSHALK, DILMAN W. *Art and the Social Order*. New York: Dover, 1962. (chaps. 1 & 3)

HANSLOVSKY, GANDA; MOYER, SUE; and WAGNER, HELEN. *Why Team Teaching?* Columbus: Charles E. Merrill Publishing Company, 1969. (chaps. 2 & 3)

HUNT, EARL B. *Concept Learning*. New York: John Wiley & Sons, Inc., 1962. (chaps 1, 3, & 5)

LEON-PORTILLA, MIGUAL. *Pre-Columbian Literature of Mexico*. Norman: University of Oklahoma Press, 1969. (chap. 2)

MARTORELLA, PETER H. *Concept Learning*. Scranton: Intext Educational Publishers, 1972. (chaps. 3 & 10)

MILLER, JAMES E., and HERRING, PAUL D., eds. *The Arts and the Public*. Chicago: University of Chicago Press, 1967. (chaps. 4 & 11)

MYERS, BERNARD S. *Art and Civilization*. New York: McGraw-Hill Book Company, 1957. (chaps. 9, 22, 24–27)

POLDS, NICHOLAS C. *Team Teaching and Flexible Scheduling for Tomorrow*. New York: MSS Educational Publishing Co., 1969. (chaps. 1, 6 & 7)

RAVICZ, MARILYN. *Early Colonial Religious Drama in Mexico*. Washington: Catholic University of America Press, 1970. (chaps. 1 & 2)

SCHULTZE, LEONHARD. *Old Aztec Songs*. Stuttgart: W. Kohlhammer, 1957.

STEVENSON, ROBERT M. *Music in Mexico*. New York: Thomas Y. Crowell Company, 1952. (all)

TOFFLER, ALVIN. *The Culture Consumers*. New York: St. Martin's Press, 1964. (chaps. 6 & 14)

UNDERHILL, RUTH. *Singing for Power*. Berkeley: University of California Press, 1968. (chap. 1)

WALLACE, JOHN GILBERT. *Concept Growth and the Education of the Child.* New York: New York University Press, 1965. (chaps. 1, 2 & 3)

WEINSTOCK, HERBERT. *Mexican Music.* New York: W. E. Rudge's Sons, 1940. (all)

Periodicals

————. "Accountability Umbrella." *Music Educators Journal* 59 (September 1972): 42–73.

ANDREWS, FRANCES, and DEIHL, NED C. "Development of a Technique for Identifying Elementary School Children's Musical Concepts." *Journal of Research in Music Education* 18 (February 1970): 214–222.

BEICHEFF, K. A. "Costing Out the Music Program." *Music Educators Journal* 59 (September 1972): 71–3.

BENN, OLETA H. "How Music Concepts Are Developed and How They Are Applied." *Music Educators Journal* 56 (February 1970): 54–60.

CREWS, KATHERINE. "How Musical Concepts Become Understandings." *Instructor* 80 (December 1970): 37–38.

DEL ROSSO, C. F. "Can We Justify Instrumental Music in Today's Crises Curriculum?" *School Musician* 43 (December 1971): 46–8.

EVENSON, F. "How Music Concepts Are Developed and How They Are Applied." *Music Educators Journal* 56 (February 1970): 54–60.

FLOM, J. H. "Investigating Growth in Musical Facts and Concepts, Musical Discrimination, and Vocal Performance Proficiency as a Result of Senior High School Musical Experiences." *Journal of Research in Music Education* 19 (Winter 1971): 433–42.

HAACK, P. A. "Study Involving the Visual Arts in the Development of Musical Concepts." *Journal of Research in Music Education* 18 (Winter 1970): 392–8.

IHRKE, WALTER R. "Modular Stations for Automated Music Training." *Educational Technology* 11 (August 1971): 27–29.

————. "I is In; Individualization in Music Education." *Music Educators Journal* 59 (November 1972): 18–54.

KAISER, L., and MEREDITH, H. "Wide Open Music; a Team Teaching Experiment." *Music Educators Journal* 59 (March 1973): 66–67.

KAPFER, M. B. "Behavioral Objectives in Music Education." *Educational Technology* 17 (August 1971): 30–33.

LARSON, R. L., and BOODY, C. G. "Some Implications for Music Education in the Work of Jean Piaget." *Journal of Research in Music Education* 19 (September 1971): 35–50.

MICHALSKI, S. F. "Development and Evaluation of a Visual-Aural Program in Conceptual Understanding of the Basic Elements of Music." *Journal of Research in Music Education* 19 (September 1971): 92–97.

MONSOUR, SALLY. "How Music Concepts are Developed and How They Are Applied." *Music Educators Journal* 56 (February 1970): 54–60.

NOBLE, R. F. "Effects of a Concept Teaching Curriculum of Performance Achievement in Elementary School Beginning Bands." *Journal of Research in Music Education* 19 (September 1971): 209–215.

O'BRIEN, J. P. "Music in Early Childhood." *Music Educators Journal* 58 (September 1971): 34–5.

O'KEEFE, V. "What Are Behavioral Objectives All About?" *Music Educators Journal* 59 (September 1972): 50–55.

SCHMALSTIEG, E. B. "Individualize in Junior-Senior High." *Music Educators Journal* 30 (March 1972): 70–71.

SCHMITT, C. "Thought Life of the Young Child: Jean Piaget and the Teaching of Music." *Music Educators Journal* 58 (December 1971): 22–6.

SHECKLER, L. R. "Putting the Efficiency Engineer on the Right Track." *Music Educators Journal* 57 (February 1971): 55–6.

TRIMILLOS, R. D. "Expanding Music Experience to Fit Today's World: A Conceptual Approach to Ethnic Musics." *Music Educators Journal* 59 (October 1972): 90–4.

WOODRUFF, AZUL D. "How Music Concepts Are Developed." *Music Educators Journal* 56 (February 1970): 51–4.

ZIMMERMAN, MARILYN. "Percept and Concept: Implications of Piaget." *Music Educators Journal* 56 (February 1970): 49–50.

ZIMMERMAN, MARILYN, and SECHREST, L. "Brief Focused Instruction and Musical Concepts." *Journal of Research in Music Education* 18 (September 1970): 25–36.

17

Music Does Some Innovating

Pressured somewhat by administrators, somewhat by associations with young people and by the times in which we live; pressured by thinking music educators, and somewhat by the ever-haunting realization that junior high music has not kept the interest which was generated by the elementary school, but, more often, has eliminated students from the program—music teachers have turned to innovations.

Unlike those of a broader nature discussed in the preceding chapters, these innovations deal almost entirely with the presentation of music itself, and they seldom affect the overall school program. Some of these innovations fit into schedule or organizational changes which have been developed by the school system. However, rarely are they connected directly to them. Some of the changes have been adopted in what otherwise might be a conventional school and have been successful.

Some basic educational, psychological, and learning concepts underlie these changes:

1. An adolescent has keen interest in his peer group.
2. Freedom of movement and individual learning speed lead to more meaningful development than restrictive physical environments and regimented class routines.
3. Discovery is a more meaningful learning approach than being told.
4. The adolescent has a learning span directly related to a growing, active body.
5. Recreational instruments often lead to serious study.
6. Music as a means of communication or as a language conveys feelings and emotions rather than ideas.
7. The young person holds membership in the twentieth century and recognizes this more than his teachers suspect.

Pop and Rock Music

As late as 1966, the author proposed to the Conference Planning Committee of the North Central Regional MENC that teachers be appraised of the background of pop and rock music so they could intelligently discuss this field with the young people of our schools. Those years witnessed millions of adolescents organizing rock groups, creating song material, and teaching themselves the guitar. This great musical movement was outside of the school and the influence of the music educator. It became impossible for the educator longer to ignore these realities.

Students learn contemporary pop rhythms through playing as well as listening.

At the present time two approaches to rock music exist in the schools. The first approach teaches folk and rock as a legitimate musical style; teaches its instruments, its recorded music, its folk ways, and forms. The second uses rock or popular folk music as a stepping-off point for more traditional music. Rock music uses many of the compositional technics found in older compositions, and teachers are bridging this musical gap by explaining the musical ideas first in terms of rock music, followed immediately by showing a relation to a composition by a composer of a different style. The hope is that the student will not only understand the musical concept but will comprehend it in terms of more than one style or period.

The Problems

As seen from the eyes of the administrator and the music teacher, several problems exist. Even schools using one of the approaches mentioned above quickly admit to one or more of the following.

The pop-rock field changes so quickly it requires a devoted teacher in this area to keep abreast of the developments and be able to use them in classes.

Is it the function of the school to offer the young student, and label as education, only those experiences which he hears and finds continually around him? Should the school only provide the student with the popular and common? Does the school have a responsibility for the historical perspective of music, the promotion of quality?

If pop-rock were to be the basis of junior high school music, would the emphasis be mostly upon listening, or should creativity and ensemble participation also be considered?

If pop-rock be the basis for the study of music for seventh graders, will the music program attract large numbers but perhaps lose the talented student in music whose skills, and often his tastes, go beyond the popular?

If pop-rock were used as introductory material for other music, won't this seem too obvious a sop to the young person who becomes attracted into music class only to be led down a different path once he has enrolled?

Can the average teacher quickly adjudge the entire pop-rock field and select those items which contain aesthetic experiences to develop the young person past his immediate level? Will the class limit the artistic development of young people?

The answers to these questions are not to be found in a general consensus, but rather, in the minds of the teachers in the adolescent school and the administrators who assist in establishing general educational directions. As younger men and women move into the teaching profession, many are attuned to the pop-rock field as they knew it when they were part of the high school or college scene. Their own familiarity leads them to capitalize upon what they know; but with a field which changes so rapidly, they, too, quickly find themselves out of step.

One serious problem faces the music educator in this regard. Does the teacher have a responsibility to lead the young person to understand and appreciate the artistic in art forms, or is he only a person who introduces the student to ideas, leaving the young person to make any choice he may wish? This affects the pop-rock field as well as more traditional arts. To restate the issue: Does the teacher have the responsibility to assist the young student in evaluating a preference in pop-rock (as well as in other styles of music), based upon an artistic expressiveness within the composition; or should the teacher offer all types of music, leaving the choice to the student?

Previously, when the teacher and student discussed only well-proven art pieces, this question was almost nonexistent. This question arises with the introduction and performance of popular forms in the classroom.

The Assets

1. The music teacher may begin with that music which the student knows and move into other musical areas immediately.
2. The interest of the young person is captured by that music which speaks to the adolescent of his time and experience.
3. Because the student knows the music well, musical concepts can be explained easily and with understanding.
4. Since the school is using the art form of the present, the student will take his learning from school with him and could explore it each time he hears pop-rock.
5. The use of pop-rock does not require a special school organization in order to achieve maximum success.

Electronic Music

The electrical production of sound has developed rapidly over the past ten years. Prior to that time this field had produced the electronic organ and technical equipment used almost entirely in physics laboratories. The development of the electronic music synthesizer has altered compositional technics, as well as the source and the effect of music. At first restricted to the scientist and the avant garde musician, cheaper models have enabled purchases by secondary and middle schools for use in classrooms with young people.

What once had been the large general music class taught along conventional lines now may be fragmented into several small groups working with synthesizers. The tape recorder also has become a device of composition, particularly since the introduction of stereo. The junior high student whose music class features electronic music is as well informed about oscillators, saw-tooth wave, mixers, white noise, and filters, as he is about the latest scores of the local sports teams.

In some schools, entire junior high music programs center about electronic music and its composition. The creative act of composition attracts some students, while the active manipulation of switches and dials appeals to others. The technic to be learned is not that of a musical instrument, but rather of an electronic machine. These skills are of a less technical-artistic nature than those required for a musical instrument and consequently more rapidly assimilated by a larger number of students.

Other schools consider electronic composition a part of the music program, but open only to those who elect it. Students may elect this class each year of

Electronic music synthesizer. Photo courtesy ARP Instruments, Inc., Newton, Massachusetts.

the junior high school. For others, electronic music becomes one part of a general music class.

The Problems

1. Although the cost of synthesizers has been reduced recently, the price still exceeds the budget of some schools. Teachers interested in their purchase will argue that they cost no more than one piano or other large instruments. Yet, this could be prohibitive for some systems. In contrast, some junior high schools own two or three smaller models and one large model, thus offering a complete program of electronic music.
2. Even though students are interested in this type of music class, should the musical experience be limited to this approach and this experience? Should the student view music only from the standpoint of the composer for an electronic synthesizer, and learn only of electronic music?
3. Some schools have limited the musical experience for the junior high student to one class of eight-to-twelve weeks duration during one year of the junior

high school. Such an arrangement enabled the students to enroll in electronic music class and still not overtax the class or the facility. Is this kind of limitation a true service to the school? Does such a replacement of the general music class satisfy a fine arts requirement?

The Assets

1. The young person becomes interested in the musical process. During the young adolescent years, continued involvement is critical and a program which replaces the lethargy in other learnings should be promoted.
2. Musical learning advances most quickly during the compositional process. The young person learns about music more quickly during the electronic class than in any other manner open to him at this age. Electronic composition learnings are basic though rapid.
3. Learning is secure. Students voluntarily spend many free hours in the electronic lab and learn musical concepts as well as machine technics.
4. The young person will be involved with contemporary music the remainder of his life. Learning about it firsthand will continue the interest.
5. When schools offer this type of learning along with other musical learnings and expressions, a broad knowledge of the field results.

Aesthetics

American education has never placed a high priority upon the arts. Observing the quality of life during the latter part of the twentieth century, some educators have voiced the opinion that the educational system of our country needs to concern itself more completely with the arts. Every child needs an aesthetic education woven into the general education curriculum to give him an opportunity to understand the linkage of the arts with other subject matter areas—in fact, with all of life. Although this was not a new idea to some, a reemphasis and refocus was needed since so much education in the arts in the schools has been either peripheral or has emphasized the technical and its production.

During the years of 1964 to 1966, the Arts and Humanities Program in the Office of Education instigated a series of conferences, seminars, and symposia to stimulate a discussion of the arts, and identify directions and issues in research. Not only were artists involved but teachers and researchers in the social and behavioral sciences were also involved. Throughout this series of conferences and work sessions there evolved a concern for developing a sequential aesthetic education program within the context of general education. Such a sequential program should have two main goals: to produce students who can perceive, analyze, judge, and value the things they see, hear, and touch in their environment; and to heighten those vital sensitivities which enable individuals to make informed judgments about things which matter to them. No concern was given to the training of architects, painters, writers, or musicians, though such aesthetic goals might lead some students in a professional direction.

It should be emphasized that aesthetic education is not a replacement for classes and study in the arts disciplines; rather, it is an attempt to consider the focus of such work and to augment that work in such a way so students will understand the artistic as a real part of life, and not consider the arts separate from other learnings, and restricted in scope.

CEMREL

Out of this concern developed the *C*entral *M*idwestern *R*egional *E*ducational *L*aboratory, now CEMREL, Inc. CEMREL has considered four focuses for the public schools and has concerned itself with the development of materials for exploring these four areas.

Aesthetics in the physical world. Investigates the aesthetic qualities of time, space, motion, sound, and light. Because some or all of these elements are basic to every art form, they provide a starting point for aesthetic education. A basic goal attempts to lead students to an awareness that anything recognized by the senses may be involved with one or more of the aesthetic qualities.

Aesthetics and arts elements. Contrasts and relates the aesthetic elements present in the environment with works of art. The emphasis is on recognition of the elements within each arts discipline and of the relationship of each to the structure of a work of art. This is the beginning of the development of the critical and descriptive skill necessary for making aesthetic judgments.

Aesthetics and the creative process. Presents methods which artists use to organize the elements through the creative process, transforming them into works of art. The student puts elements together, thus creating his own work of art, and in the process, practices making aesthetic judgments.

Aesthetics and the artist. Emphasizes the artist as a person and shows the student who he is, how he works, and what he produces.

Aesthetics and the culture. Attempts to consider behavior patterns and attainments and how these are supported in value by the aesthetic. Through his understanding of the basic aesthetic qualities, the young person is assisted in understanding aesthetic values in various cultures.

Although music educators have been slow to become a part of this thrust, a few comprehend the consequences of developing aesthetic concepts which are not present in much of the music education in our country. Gradually music teachers are assessing the lack of aesthetic understanding and feeling on the part of students in our public schools. While many pupils possess knowledge and great technical skill, their aesthetic understandings and feelings are often minimal. For other young people who declare little interest in music, such disinterest might be traced to a lack of aesthetic experiences with music at some time during their earlier educational associations.

To alter this situation, an attempt is being made to emphasize the aesthetic qualities of music along with analytical and technical learnings. For some this brings an increased emphasis upon understanding form; for some it could stress musical composition and creativity; while others concentrate upon the feelings and underlying meanings of music through listening and performance. Although many teachers approach the teaching and study of aesthetic concepts rather simplistically, continued discussion with teachers, convention sessions, and graduate courses will assist their educational concern in the future.

Contemporary Music Project

The single most influential innovation of the past twenty years has been the multifaceted Contemporary Music Project, with nationwide interest running from the elementary school through college. Although phased out of existence during the early seventies, it included and interested hundreds of teachers and students during its existence, and it continues to influence the musical thinking of the current decade because of the breadth and extent of its concerns.

Its beginnings date to 1957 when the Ford Foundation began an examination of the place of the arts in contemporary society and particularly in the educational system. Two years later, as a part of this concern, young composers were placed in a selected number of school systems to effect an artistic influence upon the students and the community and, simultaneously, to emphasize in diverse ways the creative process and contemporary music. These artists found that most music teachers knew little of contemporary music, its organizational structures and technics, and that the students were not being exposed to learnings which would enable them to become concerned consumers during their adult life.

In connection with the Ford Foundation, the Music Educators National Conference sponsored the Contemporary Music Project for Creativity in Music Education which influenced an ever-growing number of teachers in elementary schools, secondary schools, and colleges through special conferences, workshops, and pilot projects. The purpose of the program was to (1) increase the emphasis on creativity at all levels of music learning, (2) provide a climate for the acceptance of contemporary music in the public schools, (3) reduce compartmentalization in music and music education, and (4) discover creative talent among the students in the schools. After exposure to these goals at a workshop, music teachers attacked the problems of building an understanding of and a need for the analysis and performance of contemporary music through new teaching methods which increased creativity and placed an emphasis upon the elements of sound and comprehensive understandings.

A conference at Northwestern University in 1965 reevaluated the music education provided for teachers. From this conference came three main suggestions which defined a comprehensiveness:

1. Teach items which are basic and essential to the understanding of all musics.
2. Build technic which will help novices develop as listeners, producers, and teachers.
3. Involve music of the past, present, and future.

As the emphasis upon comprehensive musicianship which evolved, three main categories defined the thrust of the concern.

1. Common elements approach
   a. Understanding of relationships of style and culture based upon basic principles.
   b. Emphasis upon the physical characteristics of sound and their organizational elements.
   c. Concern for the concepts developed in elementary school: rhythm, melody, harmony, form, and expressiveness.
2. Musical functions include a gamut of activities.
3. Educational strategies
   a. Integration: the student should recognize relationships between all of music's categories—theory and literature, styles or periods, ethnic or nationalistic.
   b. Breadth and depth: teachers should choose those areas where depth is desired, but breadth should always be included.
   c. Involvement: students should be active learners.
   d. Independence: student-centered learning should include emphasis upon personal and group evaluation.

Those persons coming into the project with little background of its main concerns too often captured only one facet of the program and, failing to see its comprehensiveness, believed it carried only a singular emphasis. Although the effects have been widespread and obvious, the impact of the project is still to be realized since much traditional teaching still exists throughout our school systems. Without a CMP headquarters, some of its continued effect may be lost to diluted efforts or to newer emphases which regularly capture the efforts of music teachers.

MMCP

Originally known as the Manhattanville Music Curriculum Project, this program also centers upon creativity and composition. Again the emphasis is the student, his manipulation of the sound source, and his inquiry into sound and its organization. Based upon the conceptual approach within a phenomenological field, the young person, by means of the creative process and his own curiosity, is led through a series of sixteen cycles in a Bruner-type spiral.

The MMCP music room is not the conventional one with chairs and desks, but an open area which includes carrels, practice rooms, a listening center, recital space, skill stations, and work tables.

Five musical factors dominate each cycle: timbre, dynamics, form, rhythm, and pitch. Strategies are developed which assist the student in arriving at a musical concept by means of the problem presented, an investigation and experimentation of the problem, and the analytical and creative thought demanded to solve the problem.

In this curriculum, the teacher attempts an unintrusive posture while he acts as a guide, the creator of problems, a resource person, and a stimulator of musical thinking.

The student becomes involved with composing, performing, evaluating, conducting, and listening. No two students need be on the same cycle, nor need they be involved with the same strategy if on the same cycle.

The Problems

1. Can a school adopt such a program which relies so heavily upon individual creativity without restructuring the entire curriculum? Would this plan only be feasible in a module school? Can it handle large numbers of students?
2. Considering the student with little experience, could there be enough strategies devised to keep the student interested and occupied and yet keep him from feeling as if he were obviously behind others in his group?
3. Is it possible for the average music teacher to devise enough strategies for the class? On the other hand, would it not be possible that some students would outrun the cycles and demand more advanced materials?
4. Although the students are capable of performing the problems assigned, will they, in turn, understand the concepts which they exemplify so that they are translatable to standard compositions as well as to those of their own devising?

The Assets

1. The child is encouraged to work continually with five basic musical factors.
2. The focus centers upon his own learning and doing.
3. Musical activities can be devised which adapt to student skills and understanding.

4. The student learns to understand music from the viewpoint of composer, conductor, and listener.

Sample cycles and strategies will be found at the end of the chapter.

Mini-Period or Mini-Course

By the time the student has reached the junior high school or early adolescent age, certain patterns of interest and skill are beginning to develop. The general music class, although planned to recognize these differences, expects each child to participate in each area taught. On the other hand, the mini-period approach to adolescent music permits the student to elect three or four areas during the school year which might contain special interest for him. The number of music electives possible is determined partly by the manner in which the music department of the junior high school divides the school year and partly by the length of such courses as decided by the music staff or the school administration.

The student is asked to choose a specified number of classes from a list of offerings. The student participates in his first choice during the first time unit of the school year, in his second choice during the second time unit of the year, and so forth. Class size is limited to the type of class and the facilities. Over subscribed courses require students to delay that class until a later year or to make a different choice. Students may offer suggestions to the music faculty as to the nature of courses they would prefer in a later year.

Some schools have developed art, home economics, shop, and other courses along a similar format. Then, for example, the student may elect one class of music, followed by a class in art and perhaps a course in manual arts. The student may be expected to complete two or three courses in music and two or three in art during a three-year period. Other schools offer different arrangements with mini-courses.

The following list of courses exemplify those offered by adolescent schools:

four-part singing	contemporary pop music (listening and analysis)
barbershop quartets	rock
pop vocal group	jazz
class piano	country and Western
electronic music (see Plan B)	folk
composition (tonal approach)	creative musical productions
recorder	musical commercials and speaking chorus
guitar	Christmas show
bell ringing	opera or operetta
developing a record library	music of other cultures
music in the community	guided listening (standard repertoire)
	Match Box

It should be noted that the preceding list includes listening, creative activities, and performance activities which have an emphasis upon serving the person who has had little background in music or does not wish to participate in the standard musical ensembles. Some students elect to participate in ensembles as well as one or more of the classes listed above.

The Problems

1. Does the student really learn much about music, or is the entire program focused too heavily upon the light, the pop, and the entertainment aspects?
2. Does this program not require a large staff with many specified talents, thus eliminating the smaller junior high from such a program?
3. In so short a time, does the student learn much about the values of music, or does this not become a superficial treatment of junior high school music, resulting in little understanding of a lasting nature?

The Assets

1. Each student, although required to participate in music, may choose areas in which he has some interest and concern.
2. Not all students are expected to participate in the identical activity or learning structure.
3. The program can be geared in a most contemporary manner, while at the same time retaining some traditional approaches.
4. Teachers may choose courses which match their interest and teaching skills.
5. The plan has certain advantages of scheduling for some students so that music need not be taken for one complete year.
6. The student may be scheduled to elect some music for each of his years in the adolescent school rather than complete one year of a required course in sixth or seventh grade and not be involved with music again until high school, if then.
7. A teacher may instruct four mini-courses during one year and be involved for only one period per day.

Summary

Music teachers are concerned with the teaching of music. When pressured for change by external situations, preference focuses upon the structure of music teaching. On the other hand, music teachers often are reticent to become involved with educational concepts and formulations which involve the entire school. Some of the considered changes proposed through the educational structure are not seen by music teachers as involving the music program realistically, advantageously, or directly.

Despite the changes outlined in this chapter, most teachers have not accepted these except in small ways or in part, so that the overall teaching structure of music and its place in the curriculum has changed but little. In addition, music teachers are too greatly influenced by the historical approach to music, the historical literature, and the stylistic period. Although these ideas are important for an in-depth study of the art, they are of little interest to the adolescent whose concern and concentration focuses almost entirely upon his day-to-day existence.

LEARNING ACTIVITIES

1. Teaching Plan A includes two commercial publications which service the young adolescent in the area of pop and rock music.
   a. Choose a pop tune which you believe contains teaching potential; develop a student form for your tune, using the questionnaire by Mr. Bennett of Memphis as a model.
   b. Write a section of material which you believe might be used as part of *Pipeline*. How would these materials differ?
   c. Plan a lesson using one of the chapter headings in the Fox text. How were you able to use pop music and standard repertoire together?
2. To develop Musique Concrete is time consuming but completely enjoyable. Read the material given in Teaching Plan B; then proceed through the following steps.
   a. Prepare a tape of approximately three minutes in length which uses only speed changes.
   b. Splicing of tape from previous recordings is an interesting method of obtaining a new composition. Record a number of items, and then splice the tape in a way which interests you. Can you explain to your class the reason for your composition, or was it merely chance at work?
   c. If your school has a synthesizer, arrange for a demonstration on the instrument so that you will be able to understand completely its possibilities. If possible, create a short composition for the instrument.
   d. If your school does not own a synthesizer, ask your teacher to arrange for you to visit where one is located so that you may become acquainted with its possibilities.
   e. After your visit, write a lesson plan for the synthesizer, using the one in Teaching Plan B as a model. What steps would you use as first learning experiences for a junior high student?

3. Teaching Plan C presents an outline based upon one of CEMREL's focuses for aesthetic education.

   a. Plan an outline using one of the other focuses.

   b. Prepare a discussion for your class on the topic: Aesthetic education is a most important education for the young adolescent.

   c. Do young people have a feeling for the aesthetic? Is this feeling pronounced or subdued in most young people? Is it similar to the aesthetic feeling of college-aged persons? Why do you believe this to be true?

4. The Contemporary Music Project is a wide-based program.

   a. Create an outline for teaching junior high students which would be completely different from that given in Teaching Plan D, and yet one which would exemplify the goals of the Contemporary Music Project. Solve as many of the educational strategies or concerns as possible.

   b. The Contemporary Music Project has a concern for the training of teachers for the public schools. How would you organize the college curriculum if you were to consider the educational goals of CMP? How would classes be organized? Would any classes be eliminated? Combined? Expanded?

5. Read through the material on pages from the MMCP Synthesis in Teaching Plan E. Be sure that you understand the process and the procedures developed there.

   a. Write your own ideas for cycles two and three, based upon timbre and form; the skills you would develop, and the sample strategies you would use to secure this development.

   b. Read through the material on pages 383, 384, 385, and 386. Write the cycle outline, the skills and the strategies you believe necessary to immediately precede cycle six for expression.

   c. Following the same procedure as in step two, write the cycle outline, the skills, and the strategies you believe should be cycle seven for expression.

   d. Choose another of the areas within cycle one or six. Complete the outline, the skills, and the strategies which you believe appropriate.

6. The mini-course has become increasingly popular throughout the schools of our country.

   a. What are the reasons for this as you understand the possibilities? Why would students prefer mini-courses to standard year-long music classes? Why would students not prefer mini-courses?

   b. Read through the outlines of the mini-courses suggested in Teaching Plan F. Write a lesson plan for one of the items which does not have a teaching plan in the text.

   c. Read through the information in Teaching Plan F, noting those areas which are new to a junior high school music program. Write a teaching plan for two of these areas. How does your plan differ from that suggested in the text? Why?

d. If you have never sung in a Barbershop quartet (male or female), organize one from the students in your class, learn from the experience what it means to sing this type of music. Could you arrange a tune in this style?

e. Sing through the arrangements for the pop vocal groups and then write an arrangement of at least twenty-four measures, using one of the styles suggested. Sing the arrangement for your class with some of your class members.

f. Visit your class piano laboratory and experiment with the instrument to ascertain a teaching process for one aspect of the general music class which could not be called piano technic. Consider the intercom system built into the pianos.

g. If you have never played a recorder, borrow or buy one and play it, using simple tunes. Be sure to play the tenor and the bass instruments. Their breath requirements are so different that it is impossible to imagine what is required unless you play one.

h. Before teaching in the junior high school, every teacher should be familiar with the guitar. Using the symbols and strums in Teaching Plan F, play and sing a song which uses at least two chords.

i. If your school owns a film strip-cassette guitar method, listen and watch the learning progression, ascertaining how it would fit the slow learner of the junior high school.

j. Visit a church where handbells are used. Request the director to speak to you of their choir, the bells, and request to see some of the arrangements. Play some of the arrangements with your music class. Can you imagine why these would be so popular with junior high school students who have little or no background in music?

k. Using members of your class, devise a speaking and singing commercial to be performed in class. The commercial must be at least thirty seconds, but no more than one minute.

l. Construct a MATCH BOX which you believe would be of interest to a junior high school. To test your educational judgment, take it to a junior high school, asking the teacher to complete the assignments with the young people.

TEACHING PLAN	**A**	**Pop and Rock Music**
		LISTENING AND
		STUDY GUIDES

As stated in the chapter text, two approaches to pop and rock music exist in the schools. One promotes the performance of the music by organizing school groups as a performance medium, using periods of the school day for practice, with teachers acting as coaches. Invariably this leads to performances by the groups at concerts or assemblies, PTAs, or other school or community associated meetings.

The more common approach uses pop and rock music as a basis for reaching the general student, attempting to help him understand the music which he considers the benchmark of his age group, with an aim to appreciate music generally through the learning of some theory, some form, and comparison of elements of style.

These approaches, although rare at one time, have grown to include large numbers of schools, students, and teachers. Some schools teach classes which make use of this material as the sole content (see mini-course Teaching Plan F); other schools introduce pop and rock music into the general musical offerings. Because of such wide acceptance, no outline of procedure nor sample lesson plans will be given; rather, three published approaches to the teaching of pop and rock will be described, and some samples of the material will be provided.

A. Sidney Fox and Thomas MacCluskey (Follett Publishing) have developed a teaching procedure entitled *The World of Popular Music: Rock*. This program consists of a student workbook, a teacher edition which includes aids, questions, directions, and suggestions, a four-record album of illustrative music, and a poster. The teacher's edition contains the entire student text with answers and additional suggestions overprinted in color, suggestions for using the program, a guide to setting up a music lab for nonperformers, as well as a history of popular music in the United States.

The chapter headings will explain the developmental approach used by the authors toward the subject.

> The Roots of Rock
> The Nature of Music
> Rhythm
> Intervals
> Melody
> Harmony
> Form
> Rock and the Masters

Although the last two chapters are short, containing too little discussion, the earlier chapters include ample material. Using rock as a departure point toward a broader base, any teacher could make constant references to other musics with little difficulty. This book, simple and straightforward, could service well those students who have little or no background, but whose attraction for the current pop sounds instigates an interest in music.

B. Michael D. Bennett of Memphis, Tennessee, has developed a listening guide for the intermediate student. Concerned with all types of pop music, this monthly publication assists the young person in progressing beyond the superficial aspects of his listening habits. The material focuses upon two recordings (four sides) which are part of the monthly packet along with student work sheets and a teacher's supplement. The student work sheet approaches the recordings at three progressive levels, each developed with more detail. Students who have less experience will be able to learn from the easier, first two portions of the listening guide; those with more maturity and/or more musical experience or background will benefit from working through the easier as well as the more advanced material. In all three sections, the students are requested to answer questions concerning the music, reacting to its various characteristics.

The *Pop Hit Listening Guide* for February 1974 follows this discussion.

C. *Pipeline,* edited and published by Silver Burdett, features music of all types, including standard repertoire. The student edition, a six-page publication, features two-tone printing, pictures, a main article, a description of a new pop-rock group, a short biographical statement of a contemporary pop composer, questions involving the top-forty, and an editorial comment which provides unity and camaraderie for the readers. Although all types of music are discussed, the takeoff point is pop and rock, with the top-forty as the focus. Such a focus may be more pertinent for those students from the larger cities than from the smaller communities. The *Teacher's Supplement,* a four-page, black-and-white publication, gives the essential information from the student paper, but in addition keeps the teacher coordinated from issue to issue as well as uniting the ideas of any one issue. Each month *Pipeline* issues a recording which includes pop items, movie sound tracks, standard repertoire, and ethnic musics where applicable.

A sample of the material is given on page 358.

Suggested Readings and Bibliography

BELZ, CARLA. *The Story of Rock*. New York: Harper Colophon Books, 1969.
COHN, NIK. *Rock from the Beginning*. New York: Pocket Books, 1971.
DAVIES, HUNTER. *The Beatles*. New York: Dell Publishing Co., Inc., 1968.
GARLAND, PHIL. *The Sound of Soul*. Chicago: Henry Regnery Company, 1969.
HEMPHILL, PAUL. *The Nashville Scene*. New York: Simon & Schuster, 1970.
LYDON, MICHAEL. *Folk Rock*. New York: The Dial Press, 1971.

Filmstrip

ROSSI, NICK. *From Jazz to Rock*. Keyboard Publications.

POP HIT LISTENING GUIDE No. 74–2   FEBRUARY, 1974

Name _____

I SHALL SING *(Art Garfunkel)*

Read Questions 1–4, then listen to the entire song. You should be able to answer all the questions by the time the song is over.

1. The beginning and the end of the song are naturally at opposite ends of the tune. What happens in an opposite manner at the beginning and the end?

   Beginning: _____

   End: _____

2. The featured instruments used in the song's accompaniment belong to what two groups or families of instruments.
   ☐ brass   ☐ woodwind   ☐ percussion   ☐ string

3. What instruments used did not belong to the above groups?
   ☐ trumpet   ☐ guitar   ☐ electric piano   ☐ banjo   ☐ bass guitar

4. Which element or elements of music helped make the song interesting for you?
   ☐ rhythm   ☐ harmony   ☐ melody   ☐ tone color
   WHY? _____

Answer Check:

5. Most of the lyric phrases in the verses end with pairs of words having opposite meanings. As you listen again to just the first two verses, write each pair of opposite words. Don't be fooled, some pairs are not opposites! Listen.

   Verse 1: _____

   Verse 2: _____

Answer Check:

6. Your teacher will now play just the introduction, several times. List all the different sounds you hear. Be as specific as you can, because if you name every

sound correctly (verified by your teacher) I will send you a free 45 record. Honest! Ready?

_____

_____

Well, even if you didn't win a record you had fun trying. (To be honest, most college students miss two or three, too.)

Now we'll discover how Garfunkel's singing has been made more varied through multiple recording techniques. As you listen to the song write the letter or letters of each vocal combination you hear in the blocks next to each section. Read the choices carefully now so you won't have to hunt around while you listen.

Chart 1—VOCAL COMBINATIONS CHART

Section		CHOICES
Introduction		A. Verse melody in unison
Verse 1		B. Verse melody in harmony
Chorus		C. Chorus "la-la" in unison
Interlude 1		D. Chorus "la-la" in harmony
Verse 2		E. Verse countermelody*
Chorus		F. Chorus countermelody
Interlude 2		G. No singing at all
Verse 1 (repeated)		H. Short "happy sound" vocal sounds
Chorus		
Chorus		

* A *countermelody* is a melody that goes along with the main melody, but is not the most important one.

Answer Check:

7. The combined patterns of rhythm played by the various percussion instruments give *I Shall Sing* an interesting "Mambo-Rock" feeling. Now we will learn how to play the rhythms played by the basic percussion instruments to get an even better feel for the music. The rhythms repeat every four beats, so we'll call them *ostinato* rhythms, repeating rhythms. Chart 2 shows the _____ rhythms of the conga drum, bass guitar, and clappers heard in the verse sections. The chart shows two *measures* of rhythm for each instrument. In this piece, each _____ contains four beats. As soon as you can put the parts together you will play along with the combo.

Chart 2—VERSE OSTINATO RHYTHMS

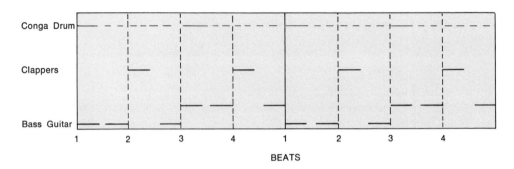

8. Not bad. Let's look at Chart 3 now. This chart shows a _____ measure rhythm pattern for the clappers and cowbell. In the chorus sections these rhythms are used along with the same conga drum and bass guitar rhythms used in the verses. Since the patterns repeat over and over they can be called _____ rhythms. Learn your assigned parts now. When you can put these together with the conga drum and bass guitar parts you will be ready to play along with the chorus sections. (Watch out for measure 4 clappers!)

Chart 3—CHORUS OSTINATO RHYTHMS

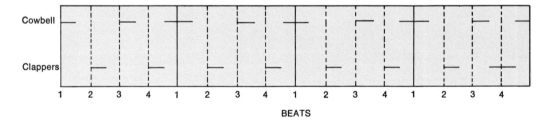

OK, time to play your parts with the entire song. The rhythm parts in the introduction and interludes are similar to the parts you have learned, but just for variety do not play there, let the band "take it." In the final chorus, clappers and cowbell players play your parts twice as fast—your teacher will show you. Play tastefully, don't crash around. Ready?

IMPORTANT TERMS TO REVIEW: countermelody, ostinato, measure

SUPPLEMENT

Last month we heard Paul Simon's *American Tune* which was based on a 250 year old church chorale by J. S. Bach called *O Sacred Head*. Believe it or not,

Bach is back! On the flip side of *I Shall Sing,* Art Garfunkel uses another Bach chorale as the middle part of *Feuilles-Oh/Do Space Men Pass Dead Souls On Their Way To The Moon?* (Pronounce the first word "fuay," to rhyme with away. It is a French word for leaves.) The name of this chorale is *Thee With Tender Care.* Bach used it in his *Christmas Oratorio,* written in 1734. The chorale melody and text are written below.

Follow the Bach melody as you listen to the Garfunkel version and answer the questions about the topics listed. You will hear the Garfunkel chorale several times.

1. The melody: Place an "x" above each note that Garfunkel leaves out.
2. The harmony: Using multiple recording again, Garfunkel starts off in unison, then he adds a second part, then a third part. Place a 2 and a 3 above the melody where the two-part and three-part harmony begins.
3. The dynamics: The Bach chorale calls for different levels of loudness to help convey the meaning of the text. How is Garfunkel's use of dynamics different from Bach's? _____

Your teacher will help you sing the Bach chorale. Can you help your teacher sing the Garfunkel chorale?

Thee with Tender Care

POP HIT LISTENING GUIDE No. 74–2   TEACHER'S GUIDE

I SHALL SING *(Art Garfunkel)* Columbia Records 4–44983

Objectives: By completing this listening guide students will be able to:

A. identify the primary accompanying instruments used in the song
B. determine the vocal combinations used in each section of the song— unison, harmony, melody with countermelody

C. define the term ostinato rhythm
D. perform the rhythm patterns utilized by four of the rhythm instruments in the verses and chorus sections of the song
E. determine how Garfunkel alters the pitches and dynamics of *Thee With Tender Care* in his adaptation of the chorale
F. indicate on the melody score where Garfunkel begins two-part and three-part singing
G. determine how Garfunkel alters Bach's phrase scheme (optional)

Simon and Garfunkel in back to back listening guides? Really, it was just a coincidence—both guys are doing well on their own these days. The fact that both records use a Bach chorale is even stranger. (Could the pop field be running out of material?)

Questions 1–4, Presentation Suggestions

I am assuming that your students have been exposed to the "families" of instruments and the general concepts of rhythm, harmony, melody, and tone color. If I am wrong you will need to prepare Questions 2 and 4.

Ask students to read the four questions, then play the record.

Answers:
1. Beginning: begins softly and gets louder (also adds instruments) End: gets softer from a loud level, fades out
2. woodwind, percussion. The solo alto sax does sound like a trumpet at times because of the hard manner in which it is played.
3. guitar, bass guitar
4. The answers may vary with individuals but the most usual answers will be rhythm and/or tone color.

Question 5, Presentation Suggestions

This is not an essential musical problem but it is fun to solve, since critical listening is required—a skill worth developing by any means you can.

Start the record at the end of the introduction and stop it after verse two.

Answer 5. Verse 1: right-wrong; night-day.

Verse 2: young-old; high-low; fast-slow. NOTE: I do not think that heart and soul are opposites but some might think so if the heart represents the human and the soul represents the spiritual foci of man—a good problem for advanced classes.

Question 6, Presentation Suggestions

My offer should stimulate some attention. The question really is quite difficult. Play the introduction no more than four times, keeping shared answers to the
minimum possible. Allow a few seconds between playings. Remind students that
the exact names of the sounds are required. Exact order of entry is not required.

Since some instruments are recorded on only one channel, reverse playback
channels after two playings to give the class an equal hearing. If your amplifier
does not have a reverse switch you can do it manually by reversing the two phono
plugs coming from the record player.

Answers. conga drum, bass guitar (or electric guitar), guitar (two really; both
are acoustic, not electric guitars; the answer "guitar" is OK), baritone sax, tenor
sax, alto sax (two are present but "alto sax" is OK), timbale (not bongo or tom-
tom) clappers, cowbell.

Chart 1, Presentation Suggestions

If your class has been doing listening guides since September do not tell them
when each section begins—expect them to use the discriminations learned earlier.
If you started the listening guides in January you may need to cue. Tell students
that there may be more than one answer in some sections. In order to accomplish
this task in one listening make sure students know the meaning of unison, harmony,
and countermelody.

Answers: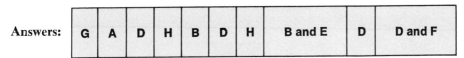

Question 7—Chart 2, Presentation Suggestions

Teach the groups by rote from the record, one group at a time. Then ask the
groups to "read" the rhythms from Chart 2. Reading from the "full score" should
help keep them together. When you put two, then three parts together practice at
no more than half tempo at first. Instrument parts should be played on desk tops
(conga players using both hands) until the patterns are learned. If you do not have
"real" instruments the following work well.

Conga drum: large cardboard box, top folded shut or large soft plastic waste
basket.

Bass guitar: medium and small cardboard boxes, top folded shut with holes
about ⅛ the top area torn out (resonates better) to simulate the B and F♯. (B is
the first pitch represented on the chart.) Boxes should be held between the legs and
struck on the ends with the side of the thumbs or with sticks. Also, two students
could play B and F♯ in the bass range of your piano. Plead with the class not to beat

wildly. If you have a large class you probably should have some students sing, then change roles after some have played instruments.

When the class can play the three parts at tempo, play the beginning of the record, cueing the group when to begin at the first verse. Cue them out for the chorus and interlude, then back in for the second verse. Stop here and do it again or add the chorus rhythms if the performance was good.

Answers. ostinato, measure.

Chart 3, Presentation Suggestions

The same learning procedure described above can be used here. When the cowbell players and clappers learn the chorus parts put these two parts with the conga drum and bass guitar parts before playing with the band. Practice the parts in song order, making sure the groups start and stop correctly, 8 bars verse, 8 bars chorus.

You can make a nice cowbell from a one pound coffee can, hit it with a stick. OK, you're on your own.

NOTE: You have probably wondered what is making the soft rapid rhythm at the beginning of the second interlude. So have I. Expert opinion has not produced a consensus, but here are the views: 1. a guy panting close to the mike
2. a gourd being rubbed with a slightly abrasive substance

Personally, I think it's a St. Bernard rejected from *The Walton's* because it slobbered too much. Anyway, you should have some fun with this one. (Am I losing my grip?)

Supplement, Presentation Suggestions

This page is intended for older classes having minimum skills in music reading. Before passing out page 4 why not play *Feuilles-Oh* and ask students to listen carefully to the middle part to determine if they have ever heard a composition that sounded a little like this. They may not think of *American Tune,* but they might think of a hymn. Either one would be a good lead in for you.

When you pass out the sheet and allow a few minutes reading time have the class hum along with Garfunkel to find out which pitches he leaves out or changes. A total of four playings should enable most groups to answer the three questions.

Answers: 1. "x" should be placed above one of the first two "C's" in bar 1 and above one of the "F's" in bar two. The high harmony line sounds like it is the melody during the final four beats, but the melody is still there below the louder line.

2. The 2 should be placed above the third beat in bar 2. The 3 should be placed above the third beat in bar 5.

3. Garfunkel's dynamics are a rather constant F, slightly increasing toward the end.

Naturally, it would be a good idea to have your class sing the chorale and listen to it performed in *The Christmas Oratorio.* It has been transposed from G to C, the key Garfunkel uses. He sings it as written on the student's page 4, not an octave lower.

Supplementary Activities

A good extra task for sharp groups would be to determine how Garfunkel alters Bach's phrases. Bach's phrase structure, in beats, is: 10, 8, 8; 10, 8, 8: two periods of three phrases each. Garfunkel's phrase structure, in beats, is 8, 8, 8; 10, 8, 6. He achieves this by cutting two beats out of the first and last phrases. Interesting changes in the flow of the music result from this change.

Another interesting task would be to have your class write new words to either Bach's or Garfunkel's melody. Pick a theme of current interest and urge the class to either use Garfunkel's rhythm plan or invent another one.

Thee with Tender Care

J. S. Bach

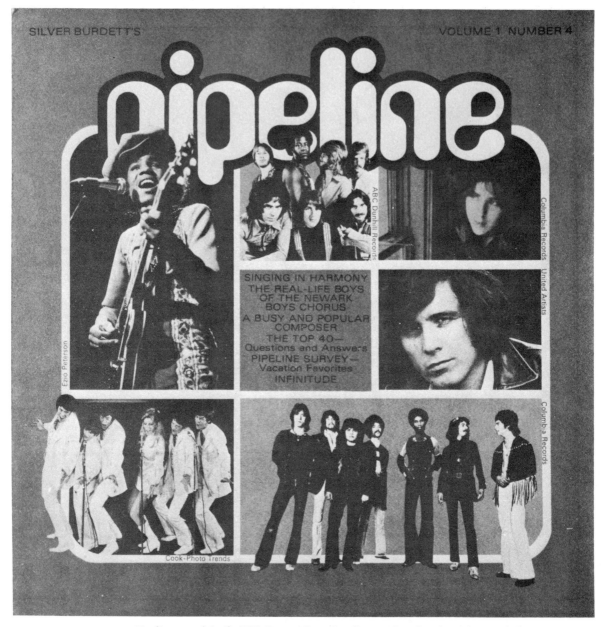

Pipeline copyright © 1972 General Learning Corporation. Reprinted by permission.

Photographs used with permission: Jackson Five, Ezio Peterson; Three Dog Night, Caribou Management Corporation; Laura Nyro, CBS Records; Don McLean, Herbert S Gart Management Inc.; Santana, CBS Records; Nancy Sinatra and the Osmond Brothers, Photo Trends; the Newark Boys Chorus, Gurtman and Murtha Associates, Inc.

SINGING IN HARMONY

If you were asked which instrument is the most expressive of all instruments, what would you answer? The trumpet? the violin? the piano? That's a difficult question to answer!

Consider the human voice as an instrument and think about the question again. Now it's easy to give an answer.

The human voice can produce a wide range of tones with different qualities. At the same time it can convey ideas with words.

The voice must be THE most ancient musical instrument. Through the ages, mothers have sung to their children. People have used their voices to express happiness; people have used their voices to show sadness. The most personal feelings can be expressed through song.

At some point in history, man discovered the totally new sound created when a second vocal part was added to the first, and slowly part singing as we know it today developed.

It can be really exciting for the performer when he sings in harmony. If you've had the experience of singing even a simple round, you know what a good feeling it is to hear harmony and to experience it closely by producing it yourself.

Some of your favorite groups sing in harmony. HOW they use and blend their voices contributes to their particular sound—a sound you can easily identify. For example, you turn on your radio and you hear a warm, clear voice with no vibrato. The group of four in the background are supporting the lead singer in block harmony. Then the group, one by one, starts singing short solos, commenting on what the lead singer is saying, in a kind of gospel style. You listen for a couple of seconds and whether you know the song or not, YOU KNOW it's the Jackson 5. Why? The quality of the voices. The style of singing. The arrangement of harmony between the voices. If it had been the Partridge Family instead of the Jackson 5, the background voices might have just been a choral fill-in of the harmonies.

Some groups write out the harmony parts, and the singers learn their parts from music. In other groups, the singers improvise, creating the harmony parts as they go along. Some people seem to have a special talent for this. There may be students in your class who can do this easily, or

can even harmonize in imitation of their favorite groups.

Can one person sing in harmony? It's possible on a record! By recording on many tracks, one artist, such as Stevie Wonder, can sing in harmony with himself. First, the artist records the melody on one track. Then, while he listens through earphones, he records another track, harmony this time. He does this as many times as necessary to achieve the total sound he wants. And when all the tracks are played simultaneously, guess what—a whole choral sound with all the voices having the same quality. On his album "American Pie," Don MacLean sings a beautiful round, "By the Waters of Babylon," by himself. The result is a unique sound.

One piece you will hear on PIPELINE Recording 4 may remind you of music for a science fiction movie. This piece was used as background music for *2001: A Space Odyssey*. This part of the movie is about the voyage of the lunar explorer team searching for the mysterious monolith. The music was composed for a chorus, without accompaniment, singing in sixteen different parts. The Latin title, "Lux Aeterna," means eternal light. When you listen to this, try to discover how the composer created this eerie mood.

In PIPELINE Recording 4, there are examples of singing in groups.

1. "I Met Him on a Sunday" (Nyro & Labelle)
2. "Para los rumberos" (Santana)
3. "The World Goes Rolling On" (Kingsley)
4. "Save the People" (Godspell)
5. "Lux Aeterna" (Ligeti)
6. "Sanctus" (Poulenc)
7. "Sanctus" (Mozart)
8. Ghana Game Song

As you listen to the recordings, try to determine which of the examples listed above are most accurately described by each of the following statements. Keep in mind that the statements may describe more than one piece. A word of warning—you may be fooled by the sound of the voices in one of the examples. Your teacher will give you the answers.

A. Women's voices are featured.

_____

B. Men's voices are featured.

_____

C. Boys' voices are featured.

_____

D. Solo voice is contrasted with chorus.

_____

E. There is a part in which one syllable is sung to *many* notes.

_____

F. Voices are unaccompanied.

_____

G. Mixed chorus is featured.

_____

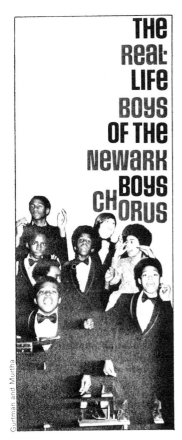

THE Real- LIFE BOYS OF THE Newark BOYS CHORUS

Gurtman and Murtha

Looking at the boys playing baseball in the local park wouldn't give you a clue. Watching them shoot baskets in their school's backyard wouldn't be anything out of the ordinary, except that they are good basketball players and almost always beat the competi-tion. They look and act like ordinary boys—but when they sing! That's something else.

The Newark Boys Chorus has its own school and teaching staff. The boys are accepted into this school only by audi-tion. All of them come from the Newark, New Jersey, area and attend the Chorus School on full scholarship. No one pays.

There are almost fifty boys in the school, and thirty of them are in the concert group now. Ranging in age from eight to fourteen years, they all spend a long day in school, a day that starts and ends with a re-hearsal. They study academic subjects at the school, and when they tour, their teachers travel with them.

They sing gospel, spirituals, and rock. They sing Mozart, Schubert, and Brahms. In fact, their rehearsals and programs include an extremely wide va-riety of musical styles.

Listen to the Newark Boys Chorus sing "The World Goes Rolling On," PIPELINE Re-cording 4. A smaller group from the Chorus sang "I'm Gonna Sing" on PIPELINE Recording 3. A lot of hard work during rehearsal time goes into this kind of achievement. The direc-tor of the Newark Boys Chorus, James McCarthy, never settles for second best.

The boys have appeared on TV; they have sung in concert with Harry Belafonte, Roberta Flack, with the New York Phil-harmonic, the Philadelphia Or-chestra, and the New Jersey Symphony. Recently, as guests of the Bahamian government, they gave a concert in Nassau.

They have toured extensively in the United States and are now planning a European tour. Where do they sing? In concert halls, in schools, in hospitals, in New York's City Hall, on Wall Street, and in Chicago at the International Amphitheatre. They are liable to show up any-where. And wherever they do, they wow their audiences with their fantastic musicianship and discipline.

If you would like to sing "The World Goes Rolling On," the fol-lowing chords may be used on Autoharp or guitar.
(Introduction)
Verses 1 & 2: C / C / E7 / E7 /
    a min. / a min. / g min. / C7 /
F / G7 / C / a min. / F / G7 / C /
Interlude ://
Verses 3 & 4: F / F / A7 / A7 /
    d min. / d min. / C♭ / F7 /
B♭ / a min. g min. / F / d min /
    B♭ / a min. g min. / F /
Interlude ://
Coda: B♭ / a min. g min. / F /
    d min. / B♭ / a min. g min. /
    F / F //

A Busy and Popular Composer

The multi-talented composer of "The World Goes Rolling On" is Gershon Kingsley, who is currently enjoying international fame with his hit, "Popcorn." A master of many musical trades, Mr. Kingsley has conducted and arranged music for Broadway shows, composed and arranged for ballet companies, and written music for films and TV commercials. In addition, he has composed a number of major religious works.

Mr. Kingsley has created many works for the electronic synthesizer. These include the record album *The In Sound from Way Out*, with Jacques Perrey (Vanguard VSD-79222), and an album of Gershwin music recorded with Leonid Hambro, pianist, and the Moog Synthesizer (AVCO 33021). He is the founder of a very unique group—the First Moog Quartet, which tours the United States. (Imagine, *four* Moogs together!)

His musical education includes study at Jerusalem Conservatory, Los Angeles Conservatory of Music, Columbia University, and The Juilliard School.

And now, in addition to his busy schedule, he is hard at work on a new musical play.

THE TOP 40/Questions and Answers

Q: What does "Top 40" mean?
A: These are the hit singles and long-playing records that are chosen, very scientifically, by *Billboard*, *Cash Box*, *Record World*, and other similar magazines on a weekly basis.
Q: How do these magazines choose the Top 40 every week?
A: Over 50 radio stations and over 75 record stores in the large cities are surveyed by phone each week and asked what the top records are—based on air play for stations, and over-the-counter sales for records. Then these figures are compiled and published weekly.

Q: What are these magazines for, and who reads them?
A: These are music trade magazines. For the most part, they are subscribed to and read by people in the music industry who want to keep up with the latest trends and facts.
Q: What album has the all-time record for being longest on the charts?
Guess. It was one of these:
1. Carole King: Tapestry
2. Beatles: Abbey Road
3. Johnny Mathis' Greatest Hits
(Clue: It ran for almost 400 weeks!)

Answer: Number 3

PIPELINE SURVEY
Vacation Favorites

No, my guess for your vacation favorite wasn't right. However, two of the three songs I guessed for your favorite *were* in *your* Top 10.

When your replies began arriving, the first check showed that "Coconut," "Puppy Love," "Lookin' Through the Windows," and "Alone Again (Naturally)" were named the most times. Now, as PIPELINE Number 4 goes to press, the Top 10 voted as vacation favorites are these:
1. Black and White 2. Lean on Me 3. Alone Again (Naturally) 4. Brandy 5. Lookin' Through the Windows 6. Puppy Love 7. School's Out 8. Coconut 9. Ben 10. Saturday in the Park

We'd like to share this with you: The first replies came from the state of Florida. So far, students from 22 states have answered. Individual replies have come from 482 students, and many classes have each voted as a group. Rock is the favorite of most students, followed by soul, country, gospel. Your ages range from nine to seventeen.

As more replies come in, we'll let you know in a future issue of PIPELINE if the order of the Top 10 changes. PIPELINE thanks you all for your replies.
—J.K.H.

A Comment by the Composer • You may enjoy working out something similar to "Lux Aeterna," just for fun. "Infinitude" may sound like nothing you've ever heard before, but don't let it fool you. It's real music, meant to capture the sounds I hear in my mind when I think of outer space. The notation used here is called "graphic" notation, and many composers are using it. The composer draws a "picture" of the sound he wants, and the performers make the sounds the "pictures" suggest. Sometimes they have to work on it! But that's all part of the fun of making music.

"Infinitude" is organized into sections. How many do you think there are? Can you find any relationship between the sections? There are words, too, believe it or not. Can you tell what they are?

INFINITUDE

David Eddleman

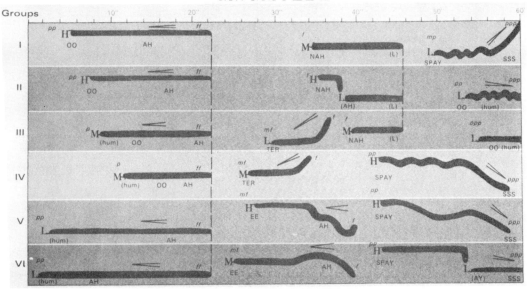

Divide class equally into six groups. Groups I and II are higher voices, groups III and IV are medium voices, and groups V and VI are lower voices. Each segment is about 10 seconds long. Timing is approximate.

For all groups: H̶ any high note in *your* voice range

M̶ any medium note in *your* voice range

L̶ any low note in *your* voice range

Capital letters indicate sound you are to sing.

Standard symbols are used for dynamic marks.

After you are assigned to a part, read through it to get an idea of when and how you are to sing.

A conductor will signal at 10-second intervals. Notice that at 22" (indicated by broken lines), there will be silence for about 2".

The second time you sang the piece together, did it sound the same as the first time? Will it ever sound the same twice? Why?

Silver Burdett/Pipeline/Published by General Learning Corporation/250 James Street, Morristown, New Jersey 07960/© 1972 General Learning Corporation/All Rights Reserved/Printed in the United States of America/Published simultaneously in Canada/This publication, or parts thereof, may not be reproduced in any form by photographic, electrostatic, mechanical, or any other method, for any use, including information storage and retrieval, without written permission from the publisher.

Editor—JANE BEETHOVEN
Managing Editor—JAY K. HOFFMAN
Chief Consultant—CARMAN MOORE

SILVER BURDETT'S

TEACHING GUIDE

Silver Burdett/Pipeline/Published by General Learning Corporation/250 James Street, Morristown, New Jersey 07960/© 1972 General Learning Corporation/ All Rights Reserved/Printed in the United States of America /Published simultaneously in Canada/This publication, or parts thereof, may not be reproduced in any form by photographic, electrostatic, mechanical, or any other method, for any use, including information storage and retrieval, without written permission from the publisher

Editor—JANE BEETHOVEN
Managing Editor—JAY HOFFMAN
Chief Consultant—CARMAN MOORE

In this issue of PIPELINE, the emphasis is on group singing. As in PIPELINE Numbers 1, 2, and 3, there are activities in which your students can participate. The main thrust, however, is discovering something about choral style by listening to the musical examples presented on PIPELINE Recording 4. Each piece will be considered separately first. Then it can be compared with any other piece, using the chart on page 2. It may be most effective to begin by comparing a piece with another that is markedly different, then with one that is very similar.

Do not distribute the students' copies of PIPELINE until they are needed.

SINGING IN HARMONY

Ask: All the pieces you will hear have something in common. What is it?

○ Play portions of PIPELINE Recording 4, Side 1 Bands 1, 2, and the middle of 3. Acceptable answers would include singing together, singing in groups, singing in harmony.

☐ Have class read "Singing in Harmony," students' PIPELINE, page 2. **Before students write their answers to the quiz:**

○ Play the complete selections on PIPELINE Recording 4. Possible answers to the quiz:

A—1, 5, and 8°	E—5 and 6
B—2	F—5 and 6
C—3	G—4, 6, and 7
D—1 and 4	(°This is difficult)

♭ ASSIGNMENT: Have students bring to class recordings of their favorite groups. These probably will include the Jackson 5, the Partridge Family, the Osmonds, Chicago, Three Dog Night, and Bread. Have duplicates eliminated before the recordings are submitted to you. Play portions from a number of the selections without announcing titles or names of groups. See if students can tell, from listening for the style, which group is singing. The differences and the similarities in style can be discussed.

ADDITIONAL RESOURCES

Making Music Your Own, Book 7: Lesson 6 (Harmony)

Making Music Your Own, Book 8: Lesson 1 (The Voice) Lessons 10–12 (Choral Styles)

1

	STYLE	VOICES	HARMONY	TEXTURE	RHYTHM	ACCOMPANIMENT	WORDS
Side 1 Bands 1, 2, 3							
1. I Met Him on a Sunday	mostly call and response	women's voices	repetitive; simple	thin	metrical; use of syncopation	at first, light rhythm accompaniment only; added small group—piano and percussion prominent	original; have folk quality
2. Para los rumberos	Latin rock	men's voices	repetitive; in thirds; moves in parallel motion	thick, heavy	Latin beat	prominent; percussion and horns	Spanish ("for those who do the rhumba")
3. The World Goes Rolling On	folk rock	boys' voices	consonant; a few chromatic harmonies; verse 1 unison	builds to thick	simple; uses syncopation; folk rock beat	piano, percussion, electric organ, strings	original
Side 2, Bands 1, 2, 3, 4, 5							
4. Save the People	rock musical	male solo; mixed chorus	open	builds to thick	metrical; use of augmentation when chorus comes in	piano prominent; guitar; percussion	religious (original)
5. Lux Aeterna	contemporary vocal style	women's voices	dissonant; tone clusters used	thin	sustained; no beat felt	none	religious
6. Sanctus (Poulenc)	neoclassical	SAATTBB	open sounds; mildly dissonant	light; ethereal	alternates $\frac{4}{4}$ and $\frac{3}{4}$ repeated pattern	none	religious (from Mass)
7. Sanctus (Mozart)	polyphonic	SATB	consonant; diatonic	contrapuntal parts clearly defined	very metrical	orchestral	religious (from Mass)
8. Ghana Game Song (an "adenkum")	Ghana circle game song; call and response	women's voices	close; consonant; frequently in thirds	builds to thick	metrical but steady; several cross rhythms used	hollowed gourds and other percussive instruments	Twi language; made up

2

"I Met Him on a Sunday" (Laura Nyro and Labelle: *Gonna Take a Miracle*, Columbia KC30987)
○ Play PIPELINE Recording 4, Side 1 Band 1. Lead class to discover that this piece is basically *call and response*.
1. With class, recall briefly some of the sung call and response activities from PIPELINE Number 2 (Teaching Guide, page 3), or let class improvise new ones. Have students work in small groups. In each activity, the response should be in harmony. Students may use neutral syllables.
2. Have each group perform its improvisation.
3. Have class listen again to first part of the recording, paying special attention to the rhythmic accompaniment. Let them create a similar accompaniment for their call and harmonized response. Keep the rhythm steady.

"Para los rumberos" (Santana, Columbia KC30595)
○ Play PIPELINE Recording 4, Side 1 Band 2. For discussion:
1. Notice close parallel harmony — in thirds.
2. Notice the many repetitions of same pattern.
3. Instrumental part seems as important as the vocal part.

ACTIVITIES
1. Divide class into two groups and sing a scale in thirds, then in sixths. They will discover that this makes a pleasing consonant sound. After they have done this successfully, start the scale again, but after about three notes, have them move up or down on signal from you.
2. Have first group make up a short diatonic melody. When they feel secure singing it, start the second group a third higher. Then start the second group a sixth higher, or lower.

ADDITIONAL RESOURCES
Review songs with harmony mostly in thirds and sixths, such as:
Making Music Your Own, Book 6: "Beside the Sea," "Joy to the World," "Kum Ba Yah," "Silent Night," and "Song of Friendship"

"The World Goes Rolling On" (Gershon Kingsley, Kingsley Sound Recordings, (KS6018)
○ Play PIPELINE Recording 4, Side 1 Band 3. Ask: Where does the vocal harmony begin in this piece? Listen to the accompaniment. What instruments are used with the first verse? with the succeeding verses?

Students may wish to sing along with the recording. Some students may be able to improvise harmony or copy the harmony from hearing the record. For some, it may be easier to pick up harmony notes from a chord accompaniment. Easy chords for Autoharp or guitar are given in students' PIPELINE, page 4.

In most of the examples on PIPELINE Recording 4, the harmony occurs below the melody. Lead students to discover that at the end of verses two, three, and four, the harmony occurs above the melody. Let students experiment with both kinds of harmony.
☐ Have class read "The Real-Life Boys of the Newark Boys Chorus," students' PIPELINE, page 4, and "A Busy and Popular Composer," page 5.

"Save the People" (*Godspell*, Bell 1102)
○ Play PIPELINE Recording 4, Side 2 Band 1. Listen for call and response, lengthened note values (augmentation) in choral section, ragtime-style piano accompaniment, contrast of full harmony with open.

"Lux Aeterna" (Ligeti, from *2001: A Space Odyssey*, Columbia MS7176)
○ Play PIPELINE Recording 4, Side 2 Band 2. The complete selection is scored for SATB, four parts each. In this excerpt (the beginning), only women's voices are heard. In the movie, the piece was used as background music for the voyage of the lunar explorer team searching for the mysterious monolith.

Lead students to discover how the composer created the mysterious mood of this piece. They should hear the following.
1. The use of dissonance. (They may say it sounds like someone singing wrong notes!)
2. The dynamic level stays about the same.
3. The piece moves very slowly. Because there are so many voice parts, it is hard to tell when and how it moves. (The score directs the chorus to sing without accents and to make all entries *very* gently. Bar lines have no rhythmic significance and meter is not emphasized.)
4. There are few skips in any given voice part.
5. There is no accompaniment.

3

ACTIVITIES

This will be a challenge:

1. Divide class into three groups. Give first group the pitch of F. Ask them to sing and sustain the tone, breathing as necessary. Bring the second group in on F#, then the third group in on G. The dissonance created is really a tone cluster and is largely the type of dissonance used in "Lux Aeterna." (See PIPELINE Teaching Guide 3, page 3, under BACKGROUND INFORMATION concerning Henry Cowell.)

2. If the class has been able to do this activity, start them again, but let them move up or down a half step at a time, on signal from you. Ask them to describe the sound created. Some may even have a physical reaction to this dissonance.

"Sanctus" (Poulenc: *Mass in G*, Lyrichord LL 127) ◯ Play PIPELINE Recording 4, Side 2 Band 3. Discuss the open sound of this harmony and the mild dissonance. The music moves along, and the dissonance is not emphasized as it is in the sustained tones of "Lux Aeterna." The piece is scored for unaccompanied SAATTBB voices. Your class should be able to clap the opening rhythm, which is heard over and over.

"Sanctus" (Mozart: *Requiem* K. 626, Columbia ML5160) ◯ Play PIPELINE Recording 4, Side 2 Band 4. Contrast this "Osanna" section of the "Sanctus" with a piece of homophonic music, such as a Bach chorale. (For example, *Making Music Your Own, Book 8:* Lesson 11, Choral Styles II.)

Ask the class if any of them have had a singing experience in which harmony was created by two or more voices, but *when heard separately* each voice part had its own individuality. Some students may have sung such songs in chorus. Others should at least be able to identify a round as this kind of piece. Or perhaps they have sung with their friends two different songs that sounded well together because the songs had the same basic harmonies.

For an example of polyphonic texture on an instrument, play PIPELINE Recording 3, Side 2 Band 2, 3, or 4 (Bach: *Two-Part Invention* in D minor).

Ghana Game Song (An "adenkum" performed by the Ghana Dance Ensemble)

◯ Play PIPELINE Recording 4, Side 2 Band 5. Have class listen especially to the close parallel harmony, typical of much African music. Lead them to discover that often the harmony is in thirds, and that it is call-and-response style. The main percussive sound is made with hollowed gourds.

Activities from "I Met Him on a Sunday," page 3, may be extended. Let students create words to use this time, and harmonize the response in thirds.

This game song was taped for PIPELINE, courtesy of the Institute of African Studies, University of Ghana, Legon-Ghana; special thanks to Institute Director, Professor Kwabena Nketia and Bertie Opoku, Director of Dance and Music.

"Adenkum" is not a title but refers to a circle game played by the Ghanian women. Sung in call-and-response style, the words are in praise of the first Ashanti king and his achievements. The game continues with more tributes in song.

Performing "Infinitude" (students' PIPELINE, page 6).

Examine instructions to students carefully. Note that H, M, and L indicate register for *each voice*.

The composition is in three sections: A—long tones hummed or sung on vowels; B—"eternal" sung on slowly contoured lines with concluding long tones relating to A; C—"space" sung on both long tones and contoured lines from A and B, plus a new vocal idea in the slow, wide vibrato. Humming and the wordless vowels from A end the piece.

In some instances, students will be unable to sustain a tone for the requested length of time, but "staggered" breathing should overcome this.

You, or your student conductor, armed with a stopwatch, or a watch with a reliable sweep second hand, may want to give some audible signal at each 10-second interval. This is permissible for rehearsal only, but the signal should not be a definite pitch. A clap will do, or a ruler tapped on the desk.

Most important is the attitude with which the piece is approached. In other words, HAVE FUN!

ADDITIONAL RESOURCES

Making Music Your Own, Choral Series (Mixed Voices): "Kyrie from Mass I," page 32

Making Music Your Own, Book 8: pages 64–65 (graphic notation of score for electronic performance)

4

Electronic Music
INTRODUCTORY CLASS

An introductory course in electronic music may profitably deal almost exclusively with Musique Concrete, a process which records acoustical sounds and then manipulates the resulting magnetic tape. This process, featuring involved sounds, produces good-sounding electronic music with little expense and modest effort. After such a beginning the student, if interested further, can pursue electronically produced sound—the study and manipulation of highly controlled, simple sounds.

The objectives of such a course are to involve the student in developing a concept of electronic music, to offer an opportunity to demonstrate his creativity and interest, and to gain a knowledge of some devices and technics used in electronic music—all of which can assist in further study or in listening to contemporary music.

The basic process is to record any and all types of sounds and then manipulate them on the tape recorder. Essential equipment includes a microphone, a tape recorder, tape to tape recording jacks, and tools for tape splicing. The following information may be helpful.

Speed Change.   Almost every tape recorder offers at least two forward speeds; some recorders offer four speed possibilities. Sounds recorded at one speed may be played back at a different speed, altering the frequencies of the sound. A few recorders offer continuously variable speed controls which enable changes between the usual 15, 7.5, 3.75, or 1.875 ips.

Retrograde.   Full-track recorders will play the tape backward if the tape is turned over, radically changing the sound since everything is heard from back to front. Such a process becomes more difficult or even impossible on most half- and quarter-track recorders.

Collage.   One sound may be placed over a previously recorded sound either by disconnecting the erase head or bypassing it. (See the following figure) Normally, all previously recorded material is erased by the erase head immediately before a current recording. However, if the erase head is inoperable, then the new sound will record over the old. In some cases this double sound has been used by a person singing a duet with himself (Danny Kaye), or playing a piano accompaniment for his own viola solo (Hindemith). In Musique Concrete, the double or triple sounds are usually in contrast to each other and become two independent, simultaneous sounds rather than the completion of the same composition during two recording sessions.

Reverberation.   If the output of a tape recorder is fed back to its own input, an echo or reverberation effect can be achieved by placing the same material recorded in one place on the tape about two inches later on the same tape. If again picked up and recorded about two inches later, a triple reverb is created.

Tape recorders for audio use have three heads over which the tape passes. These are positioned as shown below.

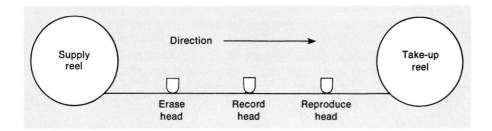

The purpose of the erase head is to eliminate previously recorded material from the tape before it is used again. The record head places material onto the tape if the machine is recording. The reproduce head will play a tape for listening. If recording, the reproduce head will immediately play the tape and permit one to hear what has been placed on it.

Any of the four technics listed above may be completed by a machine at any one time. However, if you wish to use two or more of these items on any one tape, an additional machine could be helpful.

The following electronic music outline could be used for students as an introduction to a tape recorder and other simple equipment.

Outline: Introduction to Electronic Music

I.   Introduction to course
     A. Simple demonstration of recording and use of tape recorder
     B. Introduction to tape recorder with diagrams and charts

II. Beginning technic
     A. Introduction to speed change with student experimentation
     B. Introduction to retrograde sound with student experimentation
     C. Experimentation of speed change with retrograde
     D. Introduction to reverberation with student experimentation
     E. Experimentation of speed change, retrograde, and reverberation

III. Introduction to other types of equipment
     A. Speakers, amplifiers, microphones, and phase shifter
     B. Visit to electronics equipment store

IV. Further steps of technic
     A. Introduction to tape splicing

B. Introduction to collage

V. Steps to creativity
    A. Groups begin work on tape creations using all previous technics
    B. Emphasis upon form, mood, and expressiveness

The detailed lesson plan below uses Part I and portions of Section II from the preceding outline, illustrating the development of electronic technics coordinated with listening and general musical learning.

I. Day One
    A. Welcome students to class with introduction, purpose, and a few simple demonstrations.
    B. Play tunes from Beetles' *Magical Mystery Tour:* "I Am the Walrus," "Blue Jay Way," and "Flying."
    C. Explain electronic devices employed in the songs.
        1. "I Am the Walrus" ends with radio tuning cacaphony overridden with pieces of voice fragments and other sounds.
        2. "Blue Jay Way" and "Flying" use technic of retrograde sound (backward vocal and instrumental passages).
        3. Play "I Am the Walrus," calling attention to points previously discussed.
        4. Replay other selections, reviewing the items.

II. Day Two
    A. Review basic introduction to electronic music, using class participation.
    B. Using tape recorder, teacher demonstrates simple technics.
        1. Speed changes
        2. Retrograde sound
    C. Demonstrate these technics while volunteer student sings "Jingle Bells."
    D. Concentrate upon retrograde and speed changes while listening to "Third Stone from the Sun" from *The Jimmi Hendrix Experience.*
    E. Discuss: retrograde rhythms, half-speed voices.
    F. Play record again.
    G. Discuss how rock music makes use of electronic devices.

III. Day Three
    A. Review of technics found in "Third Stone from the Sun."
        1. Speed changes
        2. Retrograde
    B. Creative experience using spoken word and instrument
        1. Teacher will have recorded preceding discussion.

2. Play tape at half-speed.
3. Simultaneously record an instrumental improvisation.
4. Demonstrates
    a. Contemporary music's use of two different but simultaneous sounds
    b. A common characteristic of the recordings heard during Day Two
C. Give a brief introduction to Edgard Varese and play portions of his music—
    1. *Desserts;*
    2. *Offrandes;*
    3. *Ionisation;*
    4. *Poeme Electronique.*
D. Play portions of recording "Ummagumma" by Pink Floyd.
E. Discuss the electronic effects superimposed on the live music sections.
F. Relate recording to music of Varese.
    (Call attention: at one point in the record a voice calls out, "Do Ya dig it, Edgar Varese?")

IV. Day Four
    A. Review of how rock music employs electronic technics and devices.
    B. Explain how electronic music is a form within itself.
    C. Play *Electronic Study #1,* Davidowsky.
    D. Discuss the recording from the standpoint of form, technics, and expressiveness.
    E. Discuss how electronics may reproduce conventional sounding music
        1. Play portions of "Switched-On Bach."
    F. Review all items discussed in order to prepare for creativity.
        1. General definition of electronic music
        2. Retrograde and speed changes
        3. Electronic music integrated with rock
        4. Electronic music integrated with conventional music (Varese)
        5. Electronic music performing conventional sounds
        6. Electronic music as a creative medium.

Suggested References and Bibliography

CROWHURST, NORMAN. *Electronic Musical Instruments.* Blue Ridge Summit, Pa.: TAB Books, 1971.
DORF, RICHARD H. *Electronic Musical Instruments.* New York: Radiofile, 1968.
DOUGLAS, ALAN. *Electronic Music Production.* London: Pitman Publications, 1973.
EATON, MANFORD L. *Electronic Music: A Handbook of Sound Synthesis and Control.* Kansas City: Orcus Operational Research Company, 1971.

RUSSCOL, HERBERT. *The Liberation of Sound.* Englewood Cliffs, N. J.: Prentice-Hall, Inc., 1972.

SEAR, WALTER. *New World of Electronic Music.* New York: Alfred Publishing Co., 1972.

STRANGE, ALLEN. *Electronic Music: Systems, Technics and Controls.* Dubuque, Iowa: Wm. C. Brown Company Publishers, 1972.

Film Strips

————. "Electronic Music." Pleasantville, New York, Educational Audio Visual, Inc., 1973.

ROSSI, NICK. "Electronic Music: Pathways to Music." Keyboard Publications.

ROSSI, NICK, and MODUGUO, ANNE D. "Creating Music with Tape Recorder." Key-Board Publications.

TEACHING PLAN	C	Aesthetics Education

The following outline indicates the first two aesthetic focuses by title only. The third, aesthetics and the creative process, is developed into three subdivisions as samples of the types of creativity suggested for young intermediates. This is not a daily course of study for a given amount of time as much as a statement of approach to activities which could be developed along with or in a number of different classes or school situations. This outline does imply, however, that items I and II have been explored and developed with the young person to insure an aesthetic approach and comprehension from these experiences.

I.   Aesthetics in the physical world

II. Aesthetics and arts elements

III. Aesthetics and the creative process
    A. Relating sound and movement
        1. Moving the body in place with sound
            a. Rhythm instruments and movement
            b. Vocal sounds and movement (no texts)
            c. Recorded sounds and movement (non-pitch)
            d. Recorded sounds and movement (standard recordings)
        2. Hand shadows and sound
            a. Early recordings (the twenties) and movement
            b. Speed changes and movement (Music recorded at 45 played at 78; music recorded at 78 played at 45, etc.)
        3. Stick men and music

        a. Draw stick men on old movie film (See page 473 for suggestions)

        b. Use with movie projector

        c. Music to fit action taken from player-piano rolls

  B. Arranging sound with magnetic tapes

     1. Prerecorded tapes

        a. Student edits from eight tapes

        b. Cut and splice tapes to demonstrate form, tempo, harmony, and expression

     2. Prerecorded tapes and recordings

        a. Combining to produce satisfactory result

        b. Collage

  C. Controlled environment in enclosed room or cubicle (light, sound, motion)

     1. Enable person to control light in small space

        a. From dark to very light

        b. Overhead lighting only

     2. Enable person to control sound

        a. Student may choose from a series of sound tracks

        b. Music and natural sounds

     3. Enable person to control motion

        a. Student may choose from a series of light projectors

        b. Light reflected around room by mirrored ball

        c. Speed of ball controlled by student

Suggested Readings and References

MEYER, LEONARD B. *Emotion and Meaning in Music.* Chicago: University of Chicago Press, 1956.

MEYER, LEONARD B. *Music, Art and Ideas.* Chicago: University of Chicago Press, 1967.

REIMER, BENNETT, ed. *Toward An Aesthetic Education.* Washington: Music Educators National Conference, 1971.

SCHWADRON, ABRAHAM A. *Aesthetics: Dimensions for Music Education.* Washington: Music Educators National Conference, 1967.

Periodicals

ALBERSHEIM, GERHARD. "Ludus Atonalis and the Future of Music Education." *Journal of Aesthetic Education* 4 (January 1970).

BROUDY, HARRY S. "Aesthetic Education in a Technological Society." *Journal of Aesthetic Education* 1 (Spring 1966a).

BROUDY, HARRY S. "The Preparation of Teachers of Aesthetic Education." *Art Education* 20 (March 1967).

COLWELL, RICHARD. "An Approach to Aesthetic Education." *Bulletin of the Council for Research in Music Education* 17 (Summer 1969).

FOWLER, CHARLES B. "Music Education: Joining the Mainstream." *Music Educators Journal* 54 (November 1967).

LASLO, ERVIN. "Fostering Musical Talent." *Journal of Aesthetic Education* 3 (January 1969).

REIMER, BENNETT. "The Development of Aesthetic Sensitivity." *Music Educators Journal* 51 (January 1965).

REIMER, BENNETT. "Developing Aesthetic Sensitivity in the Junior High School General Music Class." *Journal of Aesthetic Education* 2 (April 1968).

SCHWADRON, ABRAHAM A. "Aesthetic Values and Music Education" in *Perspectives in Music Education: Source Book III*. Washington, Music Educators National Conference, 1966.

SCHWADRON, ABRAHAM A. "Structural Meaning and Music Education." *Journal of Aesthetics Education* 3 (October 1969a).

TEACHING PLAN	D	Contemporary Music Project

The following teaching outline stems from the common elements approach to music learning and understanding. Emphasizing integration and breadth as well as depth, it helps students understand the organization and interaction of elements which produce music. Specifically, the following outline deals with the components of melody or the range of frequencies.

Using students of the class to teach other students concerning these components, the class is divided into teams, with each team concentrating upon one type of melodic organization or frequency organization which acts as the basis for melody. The individual assignment for each group is to study the background of the component; experiment with the sounds; create melodies with the sounds— noting the possibilities and the limitations; listen to recordings of the component; and finally, prepare a demonstration for the class, using this component as a basis. As the students work and listen to other group demonstrations, they will have integrated theory and literature, will have studied one idea in depth while hearing related ideas from others, giving breadth to the information, will have become involved, and will have evidenced some independence of study. All of these processes stem from the requirements of the CMP program.

I. The division of the class into groups for each component
    A. Tonal organizations of less than five pitches
    B. The pentatonic organization
    C. The hexatonic organization
    D. The diatonic organization
    E. The twelve-tone organization (no row)
    F. Tonal organization using quarter tones
    G. Tonal organization using the sweep

II. Background of each tonal organization, including some ethnic musics where applicable

III. Creation of melodies, using each tonal arrangement
   A. Aesthetic effect
   B. Limitations
   C. Instruments best suited for each arrangement

IV. Recordings of compositions using these arrangements, or short compositions using these arrangements which may be sung or played in class. (See elementary and junior high series for examples of ethnic or limited resource music.)

V. Demonstration for class with explanation

TEACHING PLAN   E   *MMCP Synthesis*

The following material taken from *MMCP Synthesis —1970* explains in detail the manner of operation for this innovative procedure.

Included in Cycle 1, which begins the learning process, are explanations of the cycle, a summary of skills, and two sample strategies for the cycle.

Cycle 6 and Cycle 7 also include explanations of the cycles, summaries of skills, and sample strategies for the cycles.

NOTE: Cycles are not grade levels, and should not be considered as such. However, it does presuppose that a child has completed cycles one through five before beginning cycle six.

By reading a sample of a beginning and a later cycle, one can image the development for the student. If intermediate students have not been involved with *MMCP* prior to junior high school, they would benefit from a program which begins with CYCLE 1 since most of the student-centered activities of this innovation are not normally used in elementary schools. In addition and most important, the learnings will present a progression of ideas which most students have not organized.

Suggested Materials

Manhattanville Music Curriculum Program, Ronald B. Thomas, Director. USOE #6-1999. *MMCP Synthesis—1970,* Manhattanville College, Purchase, New York, 10577.

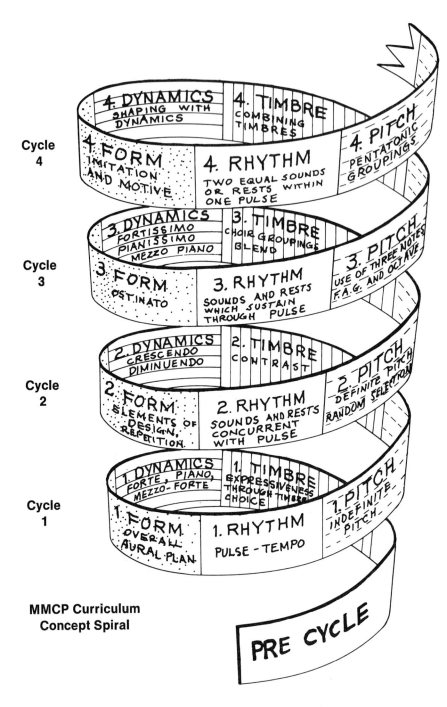

Cycle 4

Cycle 3

Cycle 2

Cycle 1

**MMCP Curriculum
Concept Spiral**

Used by permission of Ronald B. Thomas, Director, Manhattanville Music Curriculum Program.

376

Cycle 1—Parameters of Cycle

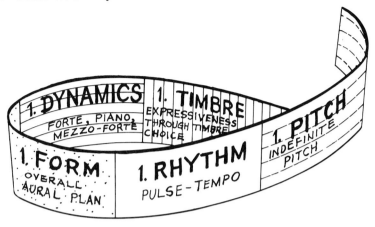

Timbre

The quality or color of sound, the timbre, is a major factor in the expressiveness of music. The timbre may be shrill, intense, dulcet, silvery, nasal, smooth, bright, or dull. Choosing the timbre which best expresses what the composer has in mind is one of many decisions which he must make when creating music.

Pitch

The comparative highness or lowness of sounds is also determined by the composer. Initially, his choices will deal with sounds of indefinite pitch such as those produced by a triangle, a cymbal, a drum, etc. In such cases, highness or lowness often depends on preceding and/or following sounds. (A cymbal sounds low after a triangle but high after a large drum.)

Dynamics

The degree of loudness or softness, the volume of the dynamics of the sound, also must be determined by the composer. Music may be loud, *forte* (f), soft, *piano* (p), or medium-loud, *mezzo-forte* (mf). The volume of the music or any one part of the music will affect the total expressive result.

Form

The plan, the shape, the order, the form of a piece of music is another determination made by the composer. Form refers to the aural design, the way the sounds are put together. The composer's plan or form is based on his expressive intent.

Rhythm

Tempo is that characteristic of music which makes it appear to go fast or slow. The pulse is the underlying beat (sometimes not heard but only sensed) that may help to create a feeling of motion in music. These items are the choice of the composer.

Cycle 1—Skills

Aural

Identify the general and comparative pitch characteristics of sounds of indefinite pitch (differences between drum sounds, cluster sounds, sounds made by objects, etc.).

Identify various timbres used in the classroom and the instruments used to produce them.

Identify volume differences in student compositions and in illustrative recordings.

Identify pulse and changes in tempo.

Recognize simple sound sequences.

Dexterous

IN PERFORMING

Produce sounds (vocal or instrumental) at the instant they are demanded and control the ending of the sound.

Produce the desired tone quality (vocal and instrumental).

Produce sounds of three volume levels (f, p, mf) when allowed by the nature of the instrument.

Maintain the tempo when necessary.

IN CONDUCTING

Indicate precisely when to begin and when to end.
Indicate pulse, where appropriate (not meter).
Indicate desired volume.
Indicate general character of music (solemn, spirited, etc.)

Translative

Devise graphic symbols, charts, or designs of musical ideas which allow for retention and reproduction. Such visual translations should represent the overall plan, include distinguishing signs for different instruments or timbres, and relative durational factors. Volume should be indicated by the standard symbols: f, p, mf. Words designating the character of the music, such as quietly, forcefully, smoothly, or happily, should also be used.

Vocabulary

Timbre	Form	Indefinite pitch	Volume
Dynamics	Tempo	Aural	Improvise
Forte	Pulse	Devised notation	Composer
Piano	Pitch	Cluster	Conductor
Mezzo-forte			Performer

Cycle 1—Sample Strategy

The quality or color of sound, the timbre, is a major factor in the expressiveness of music.

Each student selects an item or object in the room with which he can produce a sound. Preferably, the item or object will be something other than a musical instrument.

After sufficient time has been allowed for students to experiment with sounds or selected objects, each student may perform his sound at the location of the item in the room.

Focus on "listening" to the distinctive qualities of sounds performed. Encourage students to explore other sound possibilities with the item of their choice.

Discuss any points of interest raised by the students. Extend the discussion by including the following questions:

How many different kinds of sounds were discovered?

Could the sounds be put into categories of description, i.e., shrill, dull, bright, intense, etc.?

After categories of sound have been established, experiment with combinations of sounds.

Is there any difference between sounds performed singly and sounds performed in combination?

In listening to the recorded examples focus on the use of timbre.

How many different kinds of sounds were used?

Could we put any of the sounds in this composition into the categories we established earlier, i.e., bright, dull, shrill, etc.?

Were there any new categories of sounds? Could we duplicate these?

Assignment

Each student should bring one small object from home on which he can produce three distinctly different sounds. The object may be a brush, a bottle, a trinket or anything made of wood, metal, plastic, etc.

Suggested Listening Examples

Steel Drums—Wond Steel Band; Folk 8367
Prelude and Fugue for Percussion—Wuorinen, Charles; GC 4004
Ballet Mécanique—Antheil, George; Urania (5) 134

Cycle 1—Sample Strategy

The plan, the shape, the order of a piece of music is determined by the composer.

Each student may perform his three sounds at his own desk. Focus on "listening" to distinctive qualities of sounds performed.

Encourage students to focus attention on other exploratory possibilities by investigating the sound producing materials with greater depth.

Can you produce a sound on your object that is bright, dull, shrill, intense, etc. How is this done?

Discuss any points of interest relative to the activity. Extend the discussion by focusing on the following questions:

Why is silence in the room necessary for performance to be effective?

How did sounds vary or seem similar?

Which objects produced the brightest, dullest, most shrill, most intense sounds?

What makes a sound dull, bright, intense, and so forth?

Divide the class into groups of 5 or 6 students. A conductor-composer should be selected by each group. He will determine the order of sounds and the overall plan of the improvisation. Conducting signals should be devised and practiced in each group so that directions will be clear.

Allow approximately 10 minutes for planning and rehearsal. At the end of the designated time each group will perform.

Tape all improvisations for playback and evaluation. Discussion should focus around the following questions:

Did the improvisation have a good plan? Did the music hold together?

What was the most satisfying factor in this piece?

How would you change the improvisation?

What are some of the conductor's concerns?

In listening to the recorded examples focus attention to the overall shape or plan of the music. In listening to a single example two or three times students may map out a shape or a plan which represents the composition. These plans can be compared and used for repeated listenings.

Suggested Listening Examples

Construction in Metal—Cage, John; KO8P-1498
Poéme Electronique—Varèse, Edgar; Col. ML5478; MS6146

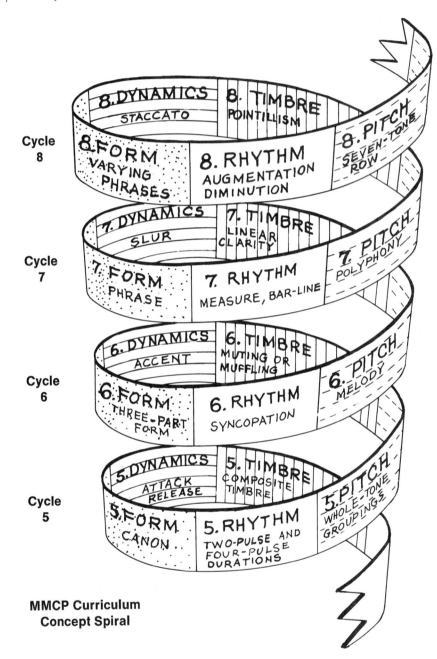

Cycle 8

Cycle 7

Cycle 6

Cycle 5

**MMCP Curriculum
Concept Spiral**

Cycle 6—Parameters of Cycle

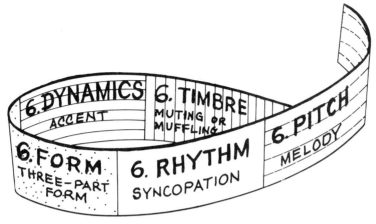

Timbre

The normal resonance of a sound-producing agent may be decreased through the use of dampers (mutes attached to the bridge of stringed instruments or inserted into the bells of brass instruments). Percussive sounds may be changed by altering the striking agent. (Bells struck with a metal mallet sound harsh; when struck with a soft mallet they sound mellow.) Blend may be improved by muting too prominent sounds.

Pitch

Melody is a coherent series of pitched sounds which serve a predominant role in many compositions. The pitches used may be drawn from a narrow or a wide pitch area. They may or may not incorporate words. Melodies may sound alone or may be combined with other musical factors. They may include repetition, imitation, or motive, and they may be the basis for an entire composition or only a part of it.

Dynamics

Pulse carries with it the concept of accent. Sounds which begin on a pulse are reinforced by the stress of the pulse and are therefore somewhat louder. However, any sound, whether it begins on a pulse or not, may be designated for accent by the composer. By adding accents to certain sounds, the character of the music can be changed.

Form

In a composition, when a musical statement, idea, or section is followed by a different musical statement and then by a return to the original idea, the form is said to be ternary or *three-part*. The return, which may be a modification rather than repetition of the original section, is the significant factor. Each section of this ABA form may be short or long and need not be the same length as any other section.

Rhythm

Sounds which begin before a pulse and continue through it or through following pulses are said to be syncopated. The most common syncopation figure is short-long-short (a short sound on a pulse, a longer sound which begins before the next pulse and continues through, then another short sound just before the third pulse). The figure may be varied by adding more than one longer sound after the initial short one or by eliminating either the final short sound or the initial short sound. The effect of syncopation is that of working against the pulse. The longer sounds, when used in this way, give the impression of setting up their own new pulse but are only really effective if the real pulse continues to be felt.

Cycle 6—Skills

Aural

Identify muted sounds of instruments used in class.

Recognize notes which receive an accent.

Identify three-part form: The original statement or idea, the different statement, and the return to the original.

Identify rhythmical figures which are syncopated.

Dexterous

IN PERFORMING

Produce accents when they are indicated in the music or by the conductor.

Play and sing syncopation figures with attention to real pulse.

IN CONDUCTING

Indicate real pulse in syncopation.

Gain control of conducting techniques sufficiently to indicate accents in situations where the performers require specific directions from the conductor.

Translative

Notate and read syncopation using quarter- and eighth-notes.
Indicate sounds of particular stress with accents.

Vocabulary

Mute	Syncopation	Open sounds
Accent	Tie	Largo
Three-part	Melody	Presto
Ternary		

Cycle 6—Sample Strategy

By adding accents to certain sounds, the character of the music can be changed.

Each group of four or five students will plan an improvisation that describes the imagined feeling of floating through space. Teacher or students may determine the selection of instruments to be used. The objective is to create a piece of music which has no audible points of stress or dynamic accent.

Following an appropriate amount of time for planning and rehearsal, each group should perform for the class. If transparencies are available, use the overhead projector to view scores during performances.

Tape all improvisations for playback and evaluation. Discussion should focus on the musical factors that contributed to the character of the piece in terms of pitch, duration, dynamics, and timbre. The discussion could be extended with the following questions: Are sudden jerks of sounds or motions appropriate in maintaining the character of this piece? What were some of the difficulties in performing this piece?

Using the *same* musical material, each group will change the basic character of the piece. As opposed to the feeling of floating in space imagine yourself as a bowling ball dropping to the floor, rolling down the alley and hitting some of the pins—all of the pins—none of the pins.

Introduce the accent symbol as a notational device for stressed sounds.

When students have completed their compositional plans and have had time to rehearse, all compositions should be performed for the class.

Tape all performances for playback and evaluation. Once again, focus discussion on the musical factors that contributed to the character of the piece in terms of pitch, duration, dynamics, and timbre. Extend the discussion with the following questions: What outstanding musical factor contributed to the change of character in this piece? What were some of the difficulties in using the same music for a piece of a different nature?

Focus attention on the various uses of accents in the listening examples.

Suggested Listening Examples

> Pictures at an Exhibition, Ballet of Unhatched Chicks—Moussorgsky, Modest; Columbia ML 4700
> Seven Studies on Themes of Paul Klee, Twittering Machine—Schuller, Gunther, Victor LM/LSC2879

Cycle 7—Parameters of Cycle

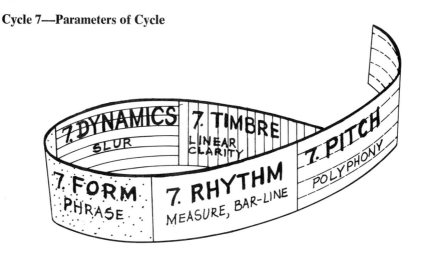

Timbre

The composer may wish to give prominence to certain musical lines or melodic situations in a composition. If his timbral resources are similar in sound, he can best accomplish such desired clarity by separating the line to be stressed from the pitch area of the other sounds. If he has several different timbres available, choosing the most penetrating one for the line to be highlighted will accomplish his purpose. If he has more than one melodic line occurring at the same time, contrasting timbres will give him greater clarity for each line.

Pitch

Two or more different melodies may occur at the same time. They may begin and end together or be of differing lengths, some beginning after others have started and continuing after they have ended. Each melodic line should be strong enough to function as a melody if heard alone. In combining melodies, the composer will find that lines which overlap have less clarity, that lines which meet on the same pitch change timbre with each meeting, and that if they continue together on the same pitches, they lose their individual identity.

Dynamics

Groups of different pitches which, after an initial attack, move from pitch to pitch without a break, without separate attacks for succeeding pitches, are said to be slurred. Sounds which are connected by slurs seem more closely bound together than grouped sounds which are separated. Slurs are used when more than one pitch is to be sung to a single syllable, or smoothness of sound is desired. They may connect both small or large groups of pitches.

Form

Musical phrases are often compared with the clauses and phrases of sentence structure. They represent ideas or thoughts expressed musically through unified longer groups of pitches or rhythmic factors. Phrases are longer than motives. Many, in fact, incorporate one or more motives in their structure. A melody will often contain a group of phrases. Phrases may be of varying length.

Rhythm

Groups of pulses may be separated from each other by bar-lines. The resulting unit which appears between bar-lines is called a *measure*. The separation is made and the bar-line positioned so that the first pulse in each measure will receive the predominant natural accent, one which is stronger than other natural accents in the measure.

Cycle 7—Skills

Aural

Identify musical phrases.
Identify sounds which are slurred from those articulated differently.

Aurally recognize the logical positioning of bar-lines in pieces of consistent meter.

Recognize the basic aural characteristics of simple polyphony.

Dexterous

IN PERFORMING

Follow the composer's indications of phrasing and slurring accurately.

In singing and instrumental performance maintain accuracy in pitch, dynamics and rhythm of line when performing simple polyphony.

IN CONDUCTING

Cue in beginnings and endings of separate melodic lines.

Develop basic beat patterns for 4 and 3 beat measures.

Translative

Notate and read phrasings and slurrings.

Notate and read bar-lines.

Achieve vertical alignment in scoring rhythmically independent parts.

Vocabulary

Slur	Polyphony	Enharmonic spelling:
Phrase	Articulation	C♯ = D♭
Measure	Beat pattern	D♯ = E♭
Bar-line	Accompaniment	F♯ = G♭
Flat		G♯ = A♭
		A♯ = B♭

Cycle 7—Sample Strategy

Two or more different melodies may occur at the same time.

Select five or six pitches to be used as a basis for melodic improvisation. A pentatonic or whole tone scale could be used for early explorations in combining two or more melodies.

Prior to any group work each student should write a melody using the pitches designated by the teacher. Pitched instruments should be available in the room for individual exploration and testing of ideas.

Divide the class into groups of 4 or 5 students. Each group will plan an improvisation using the melodies composed earlier. It should be suggested that the students experiment with their melodic material in the steps listed below so that they can evaluate the effect of their musical judgments.

The following format might be suggested to assist students in group work.

1. Listen to all the melodies available. How do they differ in length? Experiment by combining melodies of different lengths and similar lengths.
2. Listen to the melodies and analyze their individual directions. Do they move in an ascending direction, descending direction, or is there an equal balance of the two?
3. Identify a characteristic feature in each of the melodies. Discuss the possible uses of this feature and ways in which it might be highlighted.
4. Plan an improvisation using the melodies available in the group. A conductor may be used or signals such as head nods and facial expressions could be established by group members.

After an appropriate amount of time for experimentation, planning and rehearsing, the improvisations can be performed for the class.

TEACHING PLAN   **F**   **Mini-Course 1**
                                              BARBERSHOP QUARTETS

The quartet, male or female, presents an excellent opportunity for the young voice to become acquainted with four-part music, the skill required for holding a part alone, the ability needed for blending with other voices, and simple stage deportment which will carry over into many areas. If the male voices of the school choir are not strong, this ensemble will strengthen the male section quicker than any known procedure.

Since the voices of the group may not be developed in range or tone color, your quartets will not sing with the same maturity of sound found at the local Barbershop concerts (SPEBSQSA). If need be, the music should be adapted to fit the ranges of each quartet. This should not be difficult for most music teachers, and after some explanation, quartet members may be able to assist in preparing selections. Begin with simple quartets in chordal style, followed by rhythmic song materials and some emphasis upon humorous compositions. The old standards are still favorites with young men and women. Avoid most pop songs even though the students may know them well since much of this music is difficult to sing in four parts and often difficult to arrange in this style; singing in unison or two parts defeats the purpose of this ensemble. Stress a cappella singing, and although intonation and blending problems may occur at first, improvement will be evident within a few weeks. Esprit de corps will improve not only in the quartet but also in the choir.

Girls' barbershop quartet, Parrish Junior High School. Salem, Oregon. Charles Graber, director.

Warning: do not force the girl voice down to cover the low part of commercial arrangements. Re-pitch the songs and rewrite the parts if girl quartets are desired.

TEACHING PLAN   **F**   **Mini-Course 2**

POP VOCAL GROUPS

Popular ensemble singing requires a special approach, tone color, and blend as compared to the usual choral work found in the school music series or in junior high school octavo music. The tone production remains the same as with standard literature: basic, neither of poor quality nor artificially produced. The tone color of the group comes from a different concept of balance and part assignment; the blend results from working with close or open harmony; and the special approach demands a different kind of accompaniment, with rhythm playing a more intricate part in the total structure. Four types of popular singing predominate and warrant attention.

1. The all-male group emphasizes unison singing. Although featuring the small unit (6 to 12 voices), special effects are provided by the solo or the unison duet, all with a minimum request for part work. Harmony, when used, is more often two part, rarely three. The block harmony found in most choral literature is nonexistent. The accompaniment (bass guitar, piano, drums, assorted percussion) takes a major role in the overall effect. Although not always rock, this pop style imitates some of the characteristics from rock male groups. Because of this similarity, no example will be given.

2. The mixed quartet features close harmony. This group utilizes and relies upon four-part chords. Sometimes there may be an equal number of girls and boys, but more often the males prevail, with boys on the bottom three voices. A minimum of four persons are needed; if the parts are doubled, two girls and six males generally make up the group. Well-known tunes with a limited range adapt well to this type of singing. The following examples show three types of arranging (simple to difficult) which may be used for this ensemble, depending upon their ability, their voice blend, and their rhythmic capabilities. (See page 392.)

3. The mixed group may sing pop music, using standard choral arrangements published commercially. With these a larger group will sound better than a small one; consequently, a group of eight to fourteen is recommended, with emphasis upon balance even if an uneven number of persons are on the part due to differences in tone production. The SAB commercial arrangements work well with this age group; usually piano accompaniments are acceptable.

4. A second type of mixed group places a high priority upon unison singing, sometimes using rhythmic scat, with strong chordal accompaniments of guitar, string bass, piano, and light brushes on a snare if desired. The unique vocal color stems from the particular grouping of mixed voices and usually from the unison passages which often feature only the male or only the female voices. Any number or combination of voices may be used, so that five females and two males are possible as well as five males and two females. Rhythmic variations of a standard melody provide interesting material, with good reading ability a necessity. "Happy Birthday" is an example of one such arrangement: a standard melody for unison scat singing. (See page 393.)

These singing groups offer an interesting opportunity to the musically talented person who may not have an outstanding voice but whose adolescent voice quality will blend well with others. All of the singing may be light, placed in a range adaptable to the young adolescent, and the production can be made attractive through rhythms and accentuations which would not be possible with other literature.

Mini-Course 3
CLASS PIANO

This class uses the piano as a tool in musical learning. The student is introduced to aural imagery, visual imagery, the chording of songs, the playing of melodic lines, and elementary ensemble experiences. Afterward the student may wish to proceed to standard piano literature, but the class will be successful if a basic group of chords are learned and bass notes are played with the chords in correct rhythmic patterns, along with learning some elementary musical concepts.

The following outline will serve as an introductory procedure.

I.   Establish high and low; that high or low may also be fast, slow, soft, or loud. Sounds may be imitated at the keyboard: elephants, birds, sirens, raindrops, wind, thunder, going up stairs, monsters. Clap rhythm patterns with emphasis upon two and three pulsations per unit; then play on one pitch; on several pitches.

II. The eye can most easily locate the white key "D" between two black keys. Accompany songs with one repeated note, using the correct accented rhythm ("Row Your Boat" in D, "Old MacDonald" in D, "Dear Lisa" in D, "Whistle, Daughter, Whistle" in D. Change these to a different key: C, A, G). This may be expanded with songs involving a two-note accompaniment (D and A, C and G, G and D, A and E).

III. Aural melodic patterns may be dictated and duplicated at the keyboard: three notes by step; four notes by step; three notes with one skip. The rhythmic pulse may be tapped, conducted, then played at the keyboard with pitches on D, D and A, D G and A. Later, students may notate these rhythms and pitches on staff paper, placing one or two notes to the measure, using dotted halves, halves, and quarter notes with the appropriate duple or triple rhythm. Explain three-note values in relation to the pulsations learned earlier. From the note of "D" on the keyboard, other note names may be found and used, progressing to the right and to the left. All names should be learned easily. Associate this with accompanying notes as well as simple melodic patterns.

IV. Students should progress from melodic patterns to simple melodic tunes. "Hot Cross Buns," "Hey, Betty Martin," and "Aunt Rhody" are excellent examples of tunes to be learned after melodic patterns. The Doolin Bell charts also could be of assistance, and will aid the learning of note names. Play these tunes in several locations on the keyboard to assist the student in understanding change of home tone and relating tonal imagery to the keyboard. Tunes should be played from memory as well as read.

V. I chords, I and V chords, then I, V, and IV chords in simple keys should be learned first by position at the keyboard, then by sound, and finally by notation. They should be used to accompany a tune first by ear, then by sight. Again use one-chord tunes, followed by two-chord tunes. Chords should be played in both G- and F-clefs. As one student plays the chords at the keyboard, part of the class should sing the roots of the chords, while the remainder of the class sings the melodic line. Eighth notes should be introduced as melodic material.

VI. Chord names and symbols should be introduced so that a student will be able to play them at sight. Rhythmic patterns for chords should be practiced enabling the student to organize accompaniments in common meters. Chords should be taught in positions which require as little hand movement as possible. Contracts for melodic material should be introduced. Ensemble material should be introduced.

The following lesson material comes at the end of the work just outlined. The student is being introduced to two new chords: A-minor and E-major. These come in a logical sequence when used in the hand position as given below. The lesson includes harmonic material, melodic material, and a student contract. The contract is by courtesy of Wurlitzer Company, DeKalb, Illinois.

Harmonic Material

A. Play the new chords several times each.
B. Play the new chords in relation to D, in relation to F, to G, and to C. This reviews the old chords which have been learned before and constantly plays the new chords which are being learned.
C. Practice the chords in duple meter in the sequence given below.
D. Practice the chords in triple meter in the sequence given below.
E. Create and sing a melodic line as the chords are being played (both meters).

F. Use the following sequence to practice the new chords. Also create a melodic line above this sequence.

a	D	G	C
a	F	G	C
a	D	G	C
a	F	E	a

G. Create other sequences from the chords above which are attractive to you.

Melodic Material

A. Play the following melody:
   1. Hands separately.
   2. Hands together.
   3. Define the chords which fit the melody.
   4. Play both chords and melody.

Student Contract

A. Includes individual and ensemble work
B. Includes right- and left-hand activities
C. Includes three review chords
D. I will complete all of the following:
   1. Play the melody (Part 1)
      a. Right hand alone;
      b. Left hand alone;
   2. Play the melody with the right hand adding the indicated chords with the left hand;
   3. Create a new melody using this chord pattern;
   4. Play all parts of the quartet with the following people,

   _____, _____, _____

   5. Listen to the fourth movement of Schubert's "Trout" and outline the instrumental activities in the different variations.

           Student's Name _____
           Completed (Teacher's Name) _____

Mini-Course 4
                                        COMPOSITION (TONAL APPROACH)
                                           INTRODUCTORY PROCESSES

A mini-course in composition would service those students who have shown a somewhat better than average interest and talent in creativity throughout the upper grades of the elementary school. Even though the student may have been involved with creativity for several years, it is best to assume that he knows little about tonal composition and begin the course with elemental procedures. With such a consideration, the course could conceivably service those students who have had little experience with creativity in the elementary school but who wish to attempt creative work. On the other hand, this procedure would not produce two levels within one class.

The following outline uses a particular approach to the area of composition, culminating in one small composition which conceivably could be performed publicly. Other approaches could be used, but the emphasis should always be upon the progression from the simple to the complex, the little known to the more advanced. The exact steps could be different with different teachers.

Little attempt is made to work with music theory; nor is this considered already a part of the musical vocabulary. Rather, the emphasis lies with other musical ideas such as phrasing, the contour of a melodic line, and the mood of the music. This seems advisable in a short course since the student needs to realize a musical product and to not become involved with the theory of music, which demands much time and could rob from the creative progress.

Outline: Composition (Tonal Approach)

I.   Creating a melody to a prepared accompaniment
     A. Use of instrument familiar to student (piano, recorder, trumpet, etc.)
     B. Emphasize the demands of the accompaniment for the melodic line

II. Study of rhythmic elements
     A. Combining rhythmic elements for a composition
     B. Combining rhythmic elements to assist a melody

III. Poetry as a guide for rhythm and phrasing
     A. Combining melody and rhythm to create a phrase
     B. Poetry assists in a search for mood

IV. Review of notation
     A. Rhythmic notation assists the establishing of a meter signature
     B. Melodic notation assists the establishing of a tonal signature
     C. Mood shown by tempo, meter, expression markings

V. Experimentation with harmony
    A. Use of keyboard, guitar, autoharp
    B. Hearing chord progressions for a prepared melody
    C. Writing chord progressions for a prepared melody

VI. Study of simple forms
    A. Motive, phrase, and period construction
    B. Similar, parallel, contrary phrases for elongation and development

VII. Composition of a fanfare for the entire school band (no orchestration)

Since the latter part of the outline is more obvious and probably more easily taught, the early portion of the plan will be described in detail.

I. Creating a melody to a prepared accompaniment
    A. On a tape recorder place a comparatively short accompaniment, using only a I V I chord sequence. The accompaniment may be on a piano, may be piano, drums, and string bass, or may be elongated chords played by members of the band or orchestra or sung on a neutral syllable by the choir.
    B. With the tape recording of this accompaniment playing and with the possibility of its repeating, the student should create a melody which fits the accompaniment, using an instrument which seems comfortable to him such as the piano (diatonic in C, pentatonic on G^b), the recorder, the trumpet (concert B^b or E^b), or song flute.
    C. A second recorder should be in operation to record the product and the attempts.
    D. The demands of the accompaniment should be stressed by using this teaching device for more than one assignment. On later assignments the students would be confronted with accompaniments using I, IV, V, and I chords as well as I, VI, IV, II, V, I series. These accompaniments could be in different meters and using different accompaniment figures.

II. Study of common rhythmic elements
    A. Using only whole, half, and quarter notes with half and quarter rests, request that the students write at least twenty-four different rhythmic arrangements of these elements using 4/4 meter. (24 measures)
    B. Number each measure and then arrange in different patterns by choosing numbers at random.
    C. Using rhythm instruments (tambourine, guiro, tone block) write a three-line score, choosing the numbered rhythmic measures at random.
    D. Choosing specific measures as a grouping, segregate those which contain

little activity, less activity, and much activity. Create a composition which arranges these ideas in phrases.

    E. Study how dynamics seem to align themselves with these measures: usually louder with much activity and softer with less activity.

III. Combining rhythmic elements with a melody

    A. Using telephone numbers, numbers from a dollar bill, or numbers chosen at random, assign pitches to these numbers and play according to assigned rhythmic measures.

    B. Ascertain the need for similarity of melodic rhythm and variety of melodic rhythm.

    C. Free creativity of pitches using the rhythm measures.

    D. Free creativity of pitches and rhythm.

IV. Poetry as a guide for rhythm and phrasing

    A. Consider the rhythm of the line in comparison to the rhythms previously studied.

    B. Using the rhythm established, create a melodic line using two pitches.

    C. Using the rhythm established, create a melodic line of three, four, and five pitches.

    D. If additional pitches are needed, these may be used.

    E. Consider the mood of each line of the poem: do the melodies transcribe the mood? Which melodic lines portray it best? Some poems should express their mood satisfactorily with a three- or four-pitch melody. For practice the teacher should seek this type of poem as a beginning exercise.

COMPOSITION (TONAL APPROACH)
INTERMEDIATE PROCESSES

A second approach to composition which probably would assist the student who is more experienced with musical fundamentals has been used at the Evanston Township School in Evanston, Illinois. This plan places considerable attention on listening, a mix of styles, as well as certain foundational concepts of creativity.

The following beginning portion of the plan services a nine-week block. Other sections of study have been defined but are not included here.

I. Practice of simple compositional devices

  Reference points: non-Western, early European, and contemporary music

    A. Background discussion, reading, and listening emphasize

      1. Very early sounds contrasted with contemporary sounds

2. Old and new notation
3. Compositional devices which use variations of sound in time, pitch, and texture
4. Religious monophony and early secular songs
5. Parallel, free, and melismatic organum
6. Motets and madrigals
7. Instrumental dances and keyboard music

B. Contemporary listening
1. *Tabu Tabuhan*—Colin McPhee
2. *Dark Star*—Grateful Dead
3. *Music of Bali*—Gamelan
4. *Masterpieces of Music*—Estampie
5. *Dance Music of the Renaissance*
6. *Mikrokosmos*—Bartok
7. Satie "Gymnopedies"—Blood, Sweat, and Tears

C. With this background of discussion and listening, the student is requested to write a composition using
1. Any pentatonic scale
2. Heterophonic texture
3. Free form

D. After completion of the first assignment, the second should use
1. Dorian mode
2. Open and closed cadences
3. Balanced phrases
4. Renaissance instrumentation

TEACHING PLAN   **F**   **Mini-Course 5**
                                                                  RECORDER

The recorder is an old instrument which dates to the Middle Ages. For many centuries it was the most popular of the woodwinds, being used by minstrels as they entertained or played by royalty for singing and dancing. About the fifteenth century the instrument became so popular even the peasants owned them. King Henry VIII, a respectable musician, is reputed to have owned seventy-five recorders, playing them for his own amusement or the entertainment of his court. At one time the recorder was a part of the orchestra, but later was replaced by the flute, the latter having a stronger and more even tone quality. During the past two decades the recorder again has become a well-known instrument and much old and new music is being played by amateurs, professionals, and students from elementary schools to colleges. The junior high student is capable of playing the recorder in unison with his singing classmates or in ensembles.

Soprano, alto, and tenor recorders. Photo courtesy Selmer, Elkhart, Indiana.

Eight different sizes of recorders have been used, but today only five are common. The instrument offers an opportunity for the student to learn not only the instrument, but music of several periods and ensemble technics. Although the tenor and bass are larger and require special care in blowing, some students in the intermediate school will handle these instruments well.

Since several excellent texts are easily obtainable, all of which carry a methodology, no outline of procedure will be presented. Rather, several suggestions will suffice.

1. When teaching the beginner—
    a. Use the song approach;
    b. Sing songs by words ("Hot Cross Buns," "Jingle Bells," "Lightly Row," "Go Tell Aunt Rhody");
    c. Sing songs by letter names after learning well with words;
    d. Sing songs with letter names while fingering recorder;
    e. Play songs on recorder.
2. The Doolin Bell Charts are adaptable to the recorder.

3. Students may create harmony parts while others play the melodic line.
4. Rounds evoke interest.
5. Two-part music may be used with soprano recorders. Use elementary music texts as one source.
6. If students have been introduced to recorder in the elementary school, an intermediate class may be organized in the junior high which features ensemble playing.

Suggested Methods

BOUCHARD, ROBERT. *Let's Play the Recorder*. Boston: Bruce Humphries Publishers, 1962.
GROSSMAN, PATTY. *Recorder Fingering Book for Beginners*. Pacific Grove, California: Boxwood Press, 1957.
JONES, ROWLAND. *Practice Book for the Treble Recorder*. New York: Oxford University Press, 1962.
THOMPSON, JOHN. *Your Book of the Recorder*. Levittown, New York: Transatlantic Arts, Inc., 1969.
WOELFLIN, LESLIE E. *Classroom Melody Instruments—A Programmed Text*. Glenview, Illinois: Scott, Foresman and Company, 1967.

Suggested Reference for the Instructor

RIGBY, F. F. *Playing the Recorder*. London: Faber and Faber, 1958.

TEACHING PLAN   **F**   **Mini-Course 6**
GUITAR

During the past decade the guitar has become a classroom instrument for thousands of young people. As a result of the instrument's wide use in the pop field, music educators, capitalizing upon this popularity, teach the instrument along with some music theory. The accompanying possibilities of this instrument and the beauty of its soloistic qualities may be demonstrated by professional and amateur alike, and these qualities are not lost upon most students.

Class teaching of guitar has replaced the general music class in some schools; more often, however, guitar is a special class for those electing it, and in some schools mini-courses I, II, and III of six to fifteen weeks each progress the student from beginner to intermediate.

The guitar may successfully be introduced in the intermediate school. Most teachers introducing the instrument in lower grades have found students' hands not large enough for the instrument. Consequently, in lower grades monolines,

Guitar class, Mehlville Junior High School. Mehlville, Missouri. Corky Funk, director. Photo courtesy Mel Bay Publications, Inc., Kirkwood, Missouri.

Guitar class, Le Mars Community School. Le Mars, Iowa. Mrs. Coleen Scholten, teacher.

Guitar class, Le Mars Community School. Le Mars, Iowa.

zithers, and mandolins have been used as introductory instruments for this family.

A large number of beginning guitar methods are on the market, a few with film strips, cassette recordings, or a record. The audiovisuals assist the class, particularly aiding the student where the teacher knows little of the instrument. Because these materials present methodical approaches for the young adolescent, no outline of suggested procedures will be given in this text. Rather, you will find a listing of some of the methods which have been helpful to teachers in the schools. In addition, a few standard strums will be described along with fourteen chords for the instrument. This is not meant to be a complete listing of strums or chords, but only an assist for the beginner.

Strums

1. The simplest strum uses the thumb across all the strings. This may be played on each beat, every other beat, or even following the rhythm of the melodic line. The choice will depend upon the nature of the song and accompaniment desired.

2. This strum is somewhat similar in that the thumb plays the bass note of the chord on the accented beats of the measure and then plays the remaining strings on the unaccented beats of the measure.

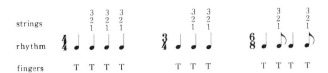

3. The thumb plays the appropriate bass note on the accented beats of the measure, while on the unaccented beats the middle three fingers of the right hand pluck the top three strings.

4. The thumb plays the appropriate bass note on the accented beats of the measure; the unaccented beats are subdivided and the finger next to the thumb brushes across strings 1, 2, and 3 followed on the next half beat by the same finger playing the top string. This is commonly called the Carter Family-style strum.

5. Every beat is subdivided and the thumb plays the appropriate bass note on each accented beat, followed on the unaccented beat on string four; the first finger (next to the thumb) alternates a chord member, first on string 2 and then on string 3. This is the Elizabeth Cotton style strum.

6. This strum works best for triple meters, although possible for duple and quadruple meters. All beats are subdivided. The thumb plays the appropriate bass note on the first beat of the measure, followed on each successive half beat by strings 3, 2, 1, 2, and 3 played by the three middle fingers of the right hand. When the meter is duple, one extra thumb and third string is used on the final portion of the measure. On this beat the thumb could play the chord member of string 4.

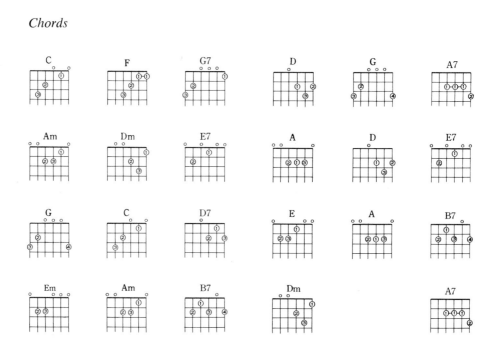

Chords

Suggested Materials

LOMAX and SEEGER. *American Folk Guitar*. New York, N.Y.: Robbins Company.
SILVERMAN. *Beginning the Folk Guitar*. New York, N.Y.: Oak Publications.
JOHN PEARSE. *First Guide to Guitar*. New York, N.Y.: Esandess, Simon and Schuster.
SILVERMAN. *Folk Singer's Guitar Guide*. New York, N.Y.: Oak Publications.
FOGLIA and GUERTIN. *Graphic Guitar*. San Antonio, Texas: Southern Music Co.
MISTAK. *Guitar Goes To School*. Cole Publishing Co.

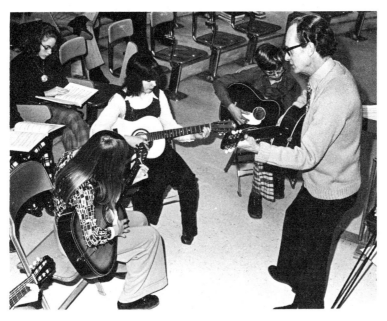

Guitar class, Wise Junior High School. Albion, New York. Earl S. Cole, teacher.

TIMMERMAN and GRIFFITH. *Guitar in the Classroom.* Dubuque, Iowa: Wm. C. Brown
    Company Publishers.
Guitar Magic. Atlanta, Ga.: Educational Productions Inc.
Mel Bay's Guitar Class Method. Kirkwood, Mo.: Bay Publications.
TONY McHOLA. *Play the Guitar in Thirty Minutes.* New York, N.Y.: Cornerstone
    Library.
HENRY EISENKRAMER. *Strum and Sing.* Chicago, Illinois: Summy.

In schools where verbal reading levels are low, a film strip–record approach
may be useful. For many young people, and particularly the beginning college
student, I recommend the Timmerman and Griffith text since it begins with simple
chords and the book contains easy song material for every step of the learning
process. The book may be used for individuals or classes.

TEACHING PLAN   **F**   **Mini-Course 7**
                                                              HANDBELL

Bells have an attraction for all persons but only simple abilities are required
for their playing. A good handbell team will vary in size, depending upon the
range of the bell set: fifteen bells require a minimum of seven ringers; a chromatic

set of two octaves requires ten ringers; while a three-octave set requires twelve ringers. Although a professional group of ringers may prefer persons who read music and have a good rhythm, the amateur may learn much of bell ringing while being introduced to notation and accurate rhythmic responses. Some bell sets using only upper pitches offer no size or weight problems for children, although sets which include some of the lower sounds involve bells which weigh five pounds or more. An intermediate student may be required to play such a bell.

Handbell Ensemble, Cockeysville School. Cockeysville, Maryland. John M. Schaffer, director.

Since an idle player becomes bored, it is best to assign two or three bells to each person. During the playing of most easy material, chromatics would not be used, resulting in each person playing but one bell; only occasionally may he be required to handle a bell in each hand. It might seem logical to arrange the bells and players in scalar order in front of the director; although possible, there is no need for this order and some directors arrange the personnel according to height of the players, or place low-pitched bells in the center, with the higher pitches to the sides in alternating order. A good assignment for a two-octave bell set follows; other sets use similar assignments.

Holding the bell upright and playing on the down stroke, the easiest for the young person to master, should be the only stroke recommended for the amateur.

In addition, however, he should practice ringing his bells at different dynamic levels.

The reading of music, not difficult since each player may be concerned with but two or three pitches, may be begun early in the learning process. Some directors use a baton to indicate the exact location on the master score which is placed so as to be seen by all players. A few groups play by memory.

The director or teacher usually arranges the music, but printed bell arrangements are available on a limited number of items, mostly hymns or carols. A student with some background could arrange music for the bell choir and add immeasurably to his understanding of harmony and its practical use.

The following outline may be of assistance for the teacher inexperienced in the use of handbells.

I.   Beginning routines
     A. Care of the instruments, proper storage
     B. Holding
     C. Playing stroke
     D. Easy material for small groups (two teams)
         1. Letter charts
         2. Six-note tunes

II. Introduction to notation
     A. Quarter-note melodies
     B. Known tunes using quarter notes, half notes, eighth notes
     C. Known tunes using dotted quarters

III. Introduction to harmony
     A. Enlarging the number of bells (one team)
     B. Use of dynamics
     C. Extending the scope of notation on one staff

IV. Introducing the F-clef

V.   Damping, rests, and rolls

Suggested References

BIGELOW, ARTHUR. *Bells and the Organ.* New York: J. Fischer, 1955.
FLETCHER, C. W. *Handbell Ringing.* Ann Arbor, Michigan: Finch Press, 1888, 1973.
PARRY, SCOTT. *The Story of Handbells.* Boston: Whitemore Associates, 1957.
TUFTS, NANCY. *The Art of Handbell Ringing.* New York: Abingdon Press, 1961.
WATSON, DORIS. *The Handbell Choir.* New York: H. W. Gray Co., 1959.

Manufacturers of Handbells

Petit and Fritsen, Aarle-Rixtel, Holland.
Schulmerich Carillons, Inc., 9893 Carillon Hill, Sellersville, Pa. 18960.
Whitechapel Foundry (Mears and Stainback) 32–34 Whitechapel Road, London E–1, England.

TEACHING PLAN F Mini-Course 8
DEVELOPING A RECORD LIBRARY

Many young people appreciate the opportunity to discuss the availability, quality, and purchase of recorded material. They wish to share their personal current likes and do not dislike hearing about those of other persons provided he appears open-minded and knowledgeable. Such a class could widen the preferences of enrolled students if they share their interests and tastes with each other.

To deepen the taste and widen the interest of each student should be the goal of such a course. By using the preferences of the students and then expanding upon the type of music which they already prefer may best accomplish the goal. The following outline will indicate how this could be accomplished. It assumes that the students in the class will have a current interest in pop music, street marches for the band, and at least one type of solo instrumental music.

I. Pop music
    A. Pop music of today which interests the student (not all students will be attracted to all kinds)
    B. Pop music of the thirties or forties (when parents were young or a current revival attached to a known TV personage)
        1. The music may sound dated; agree, but—
        2. Discuss how pop music becomes old-fashioned and why
    C. Pop music of the 1600s
        1. The madrigal
        2. Why it was popular
        3. Don't assume they should like it, but discuss it
    D. Pop music of the 1860s (use a period of history studied recently)
        1. A war song
        2. Why it was popular
        3. Compare to other types of pop music studied

II. March music
    A. Marches of the street which appeal to a large audience; why

  B. Wedding marches and why they are popular
  C. Processional marches (churches, commencement) and their popularity

III. Solo instrumental music
  A. Solo guitar music
      1. Semi-popular in nature
      2. Virtuoso standard guitar music
  B. Solo drum music
      1. Pop solo drum music of several recent eras
      2. The standard drum solo
  C. Marimba solo music
      1. Marimba solos in pop style
      2. Standard marimba solos
  D. Ask a school student to present a solo on one of these instruments

The preceding outline was developed for the class which indicates a narrow interest in music. The exact examples within each portion of the outline could be altered to fit another class. For example, instead of using a guitar and other members of the percussion section, the brass instruments may be a departure point if one member of the class plays one. March music was chosen since a member of the class might have been a band member. A number of different ideas could fit into the outline for the class. Uppermost throughout the entire mini-course is the attempt on the part of the teacher to expand the interests and tastes of the class, using their current concerns as a stepping-off point.

In addition to a presentation of different kinds of music, the teacher should discuss new releases, how to store and file recordings, care of recordings, and the stereo system. A presentation by the owner of a record shop concerning ordering, display, sales, and incidental information would prove of interest.

TEACHING PLAN   **F**   **Mini-Course 9**
                                                      MUSIC IN OUR COMMUNITY

The purpose of this mini-course is to assist the student in comprehending the universality of music, even in his own community, and to offer him an opportunity to explore with guidance the various types of music in his immediate locale.

I. Music related to the heritage of our community
  A. Music as a social force, a morale builder, a recreation, an expression of feeling, as fun
  B. Popular and folk music of earlier times
  C. Music of the national or ethnic background of the local people

II. Current music in the community
  A. Music in the churches
    1. The music
      a. Hymns, chants, chorales, folk music, gospel songs
      b. History and present use
    2. The singers
      a. Choir and its role in the mass, anthem, and chant
      b. Solo singers: chanters and cantors
    3. The accompaniment
      a. Organ and organ literature
      b. Contemporary instruments
  B. Civic organizations
    1. Symphony
    2. Vocal groups
    3. Sponsors of touring talent
    4. Music study clubs
  C. Music as a business in the community
    1. Music and record stores
    2. Instrument stores: band, orchestra, piano, and organ
    3. Stereo equipment stores
    4. Private teachers in the community
    5. Musak
  D. Music of our schools
    1. Differences in music for different levels
    2. Ensembles and concerts
    3. Contests and festivals
    4. Sports events
  E. Music and the radio
    1. Visit to a station
    2. Discussion of music played on different stations
  F. Recreation music
    1. Square dance club
      a. Discussion of music, including country-and-western
      b. Music instruments used
    2. Barbershoppers
      a. Men's group
      b. Ladies' group
    3. Pop and rock
      a. Teen dances
      b. Clubs and bars
      c. Professional musicians and their role
  G. Civic and patriotic functions

1. Music
2. Parades

Although the cataloguing of various musics in the community is informative, the class should stress the music, its variance of styles, and how the styles service different groups of people or the same persons in different ways; the form and how it differs with the function; the expressiveness and what controls are placed upon it by its function; the types of rhythm used in the various musics.

Where greater resources are available, students may become involved with more professional organizations which can bring special assets to the school or present programs for the school. These should not detract from the items listed above which help the student understand that music is more general than just the concert hall and helps him understand the forms and styles of everyday music which professional organizations rarely use.

In some large cities, programs have been organized which make use of a large number of professional organizations to service the student in the school as well as the concert hall.

In Oklahoma City the public schools are cooperating in joint programs with the following agencies:

> Oklahoma City Metropolitan Ballet Company
> Oklahoma City University Drama and Music Departments
> Oklahoma Historical Society
> National Cowboy Hall of Fame
> Oklahoma City Symphony

The cooperation between schools and community resources have produced themes which are utilized by classrooms and cooperating community agencies. This is officially known as the Opening Doors Program.

TEACHING PLAN   **F**   **Mini-Course 10**
                                                  MUSIC COMMERCIALS AND THE
                                                    SPEAKING CHORUS

This six-week mini-course could include students who participate in standard musical ensembles as well as those who have had little background or experience in music.

A. Providing the adolescent with learning activities which demonstrate music as a contemporary force in society, this course stimulates creativity and performance.

B. Exposing the student to the rhythm of words, the importance of words, it provides an opportunity for oral expression in imaginative language.
C. The musical commercial emphasizes simple creativity in a complex context.
D. The adolescent participates in a learning activity which demonstrates how music is a language, and how musical tools and knowledge manipulate the spoken word.

During the six weeks, learning activities will include listening to recordings of choral speaking, creative sing-speaking activities, defining and organizing aesthetic experiences, performances with an infinite variety of material, and composing words and music. Further, this course helps fill a creative need for those adolescents who are concerned with and concentrate mostly upon a day-to-day existence.

The following outline for the course defines its unique characteristics.

I.   Choral speaking—musical characteristics
     A. The rhythm of speech
        1. The words
        2. The phrase
        3. Extending the vowel
        4. The meaning within rhythm
     B. Pitches
        1. The vowel
        2. The phrase
        3. Contrast of vocal color, male and female, high and low, thick and thin
        4. The meaning within pitch
     C. Combining pitch and rhythm
        1. Reading of poetry
        2. Reading of prose
        3. Prose becomes poetic in sound
        4. Poetry becomes un-rhythmic, non-tonal for effect

II. A study of commercials
     A. Discussion of appealing characteristics
     B. Listen to, discuss, and sing some musical commercials
        1. Coke, Pepsi
        2. McDonald's, Kentucky Fried Chicken
        3. Others, including locals
     C. Comparison to speaking commercials in rhythm and pitch

III. Creating commercials
     A. Verbal commercials using speaking chorus

   1. Experiment with rhythmic speech
   2. Experiment with rhythmic and tonal speech
  B. Commercials using speaking with rhythmic instruments
   1. Voices in contrast to instruments
   2. Voices with instruments
  C. Melodic commercials
   1. One-part melody plus rhythm, plus speech
   2. Two-part melody plus accompaniment

IV. Commercials for performance
  A. School: classes, programs, games
  B. Community: outstanding characteristics or events

The following commercial for MUSIC may be used for speaking chorus, or parts may be sung; it adapts to polyphony, antiphony, solo lines, rhythm instruments, or chordal accompaniments. The rhythms opposite the first verse are suggestions for the words as well as fill-ins; some pitch suggestions are included.

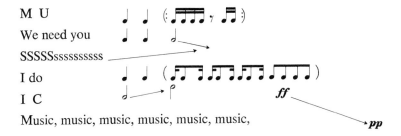

M U

We need you

SSSSSssssssssss

I do

I C

Music, music, music, music, music, music,

High, low, fast, slow
Ritard, then we go
Feel that rhythm
Hear that tune
Rhyme those words
With soon, dune, zoom!
That's music.
Beat the drum
Rum te de dum
Play the flute
Root toot toot
That's music

1: Emmm
2: Emmm

1: U
2: U
1: Esss
2: Esss
1: Eye
2. Eye
1: See
2: See
Both: Music
ALL: DO YOU?

TEACHING PLAN   **F**

Mini-Course 11
ETHNIC MUSICS

The teaching of ethnic musics has been on the increase during the past decade. Much of such teaching should be part of the approaches to junior high school music explained in Chapters 4, 5, and 6. The unit plan particularly lends itself to the explorations of ethnic musics, and the film strips, books, and recordings listed at the end of that chapter underline these possibilities.

In addition, many of the newer approaches to music teaching have stressed ethnic musics. For example, the CMP declared such emphasis an important part of the Common Elements Approach, and you will find references to it in earlier portions of this chapter; certain emphases of the study of pop and rock music lead us into ethnic musics; the subsection, Aesthetics and Culture, carries many implications for these musics in that section; and the MMCP program could make use of ethnic music as a vital part of its learning thrust.

Thus, ethnic music study stands upon its own foundation, servicing any good teaching of music, but not dependent upon a particular program. In those schools where the mini-courses are prevalent, ethnic musics can rightfully become an exciting part of the program because of the attraction young people have for the different, the interesting, the basic, and the expressive.

Because all the programs listed above offer possible approaches to the teaching of ethnic music in the mini-course, no detailed outline will be proposed. Some general suggestions will prove valuable.

I.   Many excellent books are available, discussing a wide variety of ethnic groups, their art, including music, and their culture. When their format and vocabulary are aimed at the intermediate student, their use is imperative.

II.   Excellent film strips are available through such reputable sources as Bowmar or Keyboard Publications; rare recordings may now be found through local record stores or Folkway Recordings, Inc.

III. The recent elementary series present an abundant supply of ethnic music of even remote areas. These may be adapted for the intermediate school in a number of ways. The newer junior high school music series, particularly American Book Company's *New Dimensions in Music,* recognize the value of this music.

IV. For a mini-course, develop and discuss a particularly characteristic element rather than an entire spectrum of music. For example:
   A. *Japanese Haiku.* Discuss the value of the poems to the people, their artistic qualities, their musical potentials; and set them to music, concentrating upon a few basic elements of Japanese music, their native instruments, and the unique aesthetic qualities of their art.
   B. *The Sitar of India.* Although not providing a complete picture of the music of India, this instrument, its sound, its scale, its accompanying possibilities, and its recent acceptance by Western civilization, gives an understandable picture of the music of the country for an intermediate student.
   C. *Jewish Feast Days.* By studying but one of the Jewish feast days, a student will obtain a feeling for their music, their culture, and why these have become a part of the lives of so many people.
   D. *Hawaiian standing and sitting Hula.* The teaching of this expressive movement should provide a background to the music, the culture, and the traditions of an interesting people.

V. The planning of an ethnic music mini-course should consider the locale of the school and the community it services. In a German community in Texas, the study of the heritage folk music during a mini-course provides an insight into and education for the American-born students, and culminates in a folk fair which attracts the entire community. Different related musics become a feature each year.

If possible, discuss the choice of study with students, remembering that many may not comprehend the great number of possibilities available nor the attractiveness of each. At the beginning of the school year, indicate the three or four musics to be studied. During a second year, repeat those which are requested, developing one or two new areas. A two- or three-year cycle might be feasible.

TEACHING PLAN   **F**   **Mini-Course 12**

MATCH BOX

The term "MATCH" stands for Materials and Activities for Teachers and CHildren. The BOX contains materials, equipment, supplies, and activities which work together to promote the teaching and learning of specific items or concepts at the junior high level. The BOX requires little or nothing from the teacher or school. The teacher's guide within each box serves to organize and activate the encounter between the materials, the children, and the teacher.

The BOX can be developed and circulated to schools through material resource centers, libraries, museums, or AV departments. Its purpose is to promote learnings and concepts which would be difficult or impossible without special materials and conditions.

With the prepared BOX, the teacher furthers aspects of music impossible with a limited background or training. A teacher with a musical background could add to the basic ideas of each BOX in an individualistic manner. The BOX described below was designed for exploring five basic aspects of sound.

I. Contents of the BOX
   A. Four rubber bands
   B. Unassembled violin; bow
      1. Set of strings
      2. Bridge
      3. Glue
      4. Caliper
      5. Tension scale
   C. Plastic hose of six lengths and two diameters
      1. Two plastic mouthpieces
      2. Disinfectant liquid
      3. Two funnels
   D. Thirteen metal bars of various sizes
      1. Twenty-six felt washers
      2. Twenty-six nails
      3. Two wooden rails
   E. Plastic drum with plastic head; steel drum
      1. Tuner
      2. Records of steel drum music
      3. Film on tuning steel drum
   F. Two washtub bass kits
      1. Two dowel sticks
      2. Two #3 washtubs
      3. Two four-foot pieces of nylon cord

II. Activities with the materials
   A. Rubber bands illustrate lack of control over tension and quality of sound.
   B. Assemble the violin
      1. Caliper for measuring the size of strings
      2. Tension scale to measure pounds tension on each string at correct pitch and to change pitch one-half step
   C. Assemble the hoses
      1. Play with mouthpieces and funnels as bells.

2. Cut and play again; measure the tonal difference.
3. Note differences of pitch due to length, diameter, and funnel.
D. Construct a marimba
   1. Arrange metal bars to accommodate pitch.
   2. Define the effect of size upon pitch.
E. Tuning of drums
   1. Tune a plastic drum head.
   2. Tune a steel drum.
   3. Define the effect of tension upon pitch.
F. Build washtub basses
   1. Define the effect of a resonator upon loudness.
   2. Define the effect of tension upon pitch.
G. Creativity
   1. Create tunes with each of the instruments.
   2. What type of melody best suits the instruments?

III. Explore the following basic rules of sound:
   A. The larger the string, the lower the pitch.
      Is there a discernible ratio of pitch to diameter?
   B. The tighter the string, the higher the pitch.
      Is there a ratio of pitch to ounces of pressure?
   C. The longer the air column, the lower the pitch.
   D. The larger the air column, the lower the pitch.
   E. The smaller the portion of metal, the higher the pitch.

There should be no time limit for the completion of any one step; the desire to learn should determine the progress. Students familiar with music will still learn and may become more creative with a BOX as a base.

Two major activities stem from the BOX: (1) Explore the BOX, discern the rules, build and use the instruments, create musical compositions; (2) devise and assemble a BOX for the next group registering for a MATCH BOX mini-course.

ADDITIONAL READINGS AND BIBLIOGRAPHY

Periodicals

ALEXANDER, A. H. "Electronic Manipulation Effect on Aesthetics of Music." *School Musician* 42 (December 1970 and February 1971): 30 and 18.
BOTTJE, W. G. "Electronic Music; Creative Tool in the Classroom." *School Musician* 42 (August 1970): 62–3; (October 1970): 58–9.
DANZIGER, H. "Popular Music in the Schools." *Music Journal* 29 (November 1971): 16–17.
———. "Does Rock Music Belong in the School Curriculum?" *School Musician* 42 (August 1970): 60–61.

FOWLER, C. B. "Case Against Rock." *Music Educators Journal* 57 (September 1970): 38–42.

FOX, SIDNEY. "From Rock to Bach (Youth Music on Our Terms)." *Music Educators Journal* 56 (May 1970): 52–55.

GONZO, CAROL. "Aesthetic Experience: A Coming of Age in Music Education." *Music Educators Journal* 58 (December 1971): 34–7.

GRAHAM, J. P. "Nurture the Feeling Response in Music." *Music Educators Journal* 58 (November 1971): 81.

HAGEMANN, V. S. "Are Junior High Students Ready for Electronic Music?" *Music Educators Journal* 56 (December 1969): 35–7.

HOUSEWRIGHT, WILEY. "Youth Music Symposium." *Music Educators Journal* 56 (November 1969): 43–74.

———. "Innovative and Exemplary Programs in Music Teacher Education." *Music Educators Journal* 58 (October 1971): 43.

KUCHLER, A. F. "Musique Concrete and Aleatory: Two Ways to Recapture Interest." *Music Educators Journal* 59 (February 1973): 42–4.

LEAHY, S. "Upbeat Music Curriculum." *American Education* 7 (June 1971): back cover.

LORENTZEN, B. "Electronic Music Means Switched on Creativity." *Music Educators Journal* 57 (November 1970): 56–7.

MODUGNO, A. D. "Electronic Composition." *Delta Kappa Gamma Bulletin* 36 (Summer 1970): 50–3.

———. "Electronic Creativity in the Elementary Classroom." *Today's Education* 60 (March 1971): 62–4.

MOSES, H. E. "Relevance Starts with Human Involvement." *Music Educators Journal* 58 (September 1971): 24–7.

———. "Material for Listening and Analysis; A Piece for Tape Recorder by Vladimer Ussachevsky." *Music Educators Journal* 56 (February 1970): 74–5.

NOLIN, W. H. "Patterns of Teacher-Student Interaction in Selected Junior High School General Music Classes." *Journal of Research in Music Education* 19 (Fall 1971): 314–25.

SCHWADRON, A. A. "Some Thoughts on Aesthetic Education." *Music Educators Journal* 56 (October 1969): 35–6.

———. "Youth Music's Educational Issues." *Music Journal* 28 (June 1970): 44–5.

SHERRER, M. "Jazz Deserves More Attention." *Music Journal* 30 (May 1972): 16–17.

SILLIMAN, A. C. "Aesthetics in the Training of Musicians." *American Music Teacher* 21 (January 1972): 28.

SONENFIELD, I. "Bird's Eye View of Musical Aesthetics." *Music Educators Journal* 56 (March 1970): 75–83.

———. "Sound of a Revolution: Manhattanville Music Curriculum Program." *Catholic School Journal* 70 (April 1970): 14–18.

STAUB, C. M. "Electronic Music in the Classroom." *Music Journal* 28 (June 1970): 62.

SZABO, H. "Improvisation Stimulates Development." *Music Journal* 30 (October 1972): 30.

THOMAS, RONALD B. "Rethinking the Curriculum: Manhattanville Music Curriculum Program." *Music Educators Journal* 56 (February 1970): 68–70.

———. "Where Does Rock Music Belong in the Schools?" *Today's Education* 59 (May 1970): 34–6.

WILLIS, T. "Youth Music on Their Terms." *Music Educators Journal* 56 (May 1970): 56–9.

Overview
and
Summary

18

The Complete Music Program

In preceding chapters we have examined the young adolescent as a personality, the school and its organization for this young person, and the music program which might service him. Most of our discussion has centered upon the person who does not consider music a major educational interest. This emphasis is justified for several reasons.

These students are by far the larger number in every school, sometimes totaling eighty percent of the student body.

In many schools, the seventh grade becomes the final one in which a music requirement is to be met.

The music training which this young person receives during this crucial year will probably be his last exposure to formal music teaching in the field.

The general music class presents musical information which will be helpful and informative to all students of the school and forms a core upon which other learnings and future learnings could be built.

We owe it to the student, but we also owe it to the educational institution and to society, to present him with the broadest and highest quality musical experiences possible.

Despite these responsibilities and challenges, music teachers have taught most poorly where good teaching was required to bring lasting results. In contrast, other facets of the music program, particularly the performing organizations of choir and band, have been well taught for years, and they service well those limited numbers of students who perform within them. This does not say that the preparation or organization of performing groups in the junior high school is easy. It merely states that this facet of the program has had a more continued success in a larger number of school situations.

The diagram (p. 424) places the general music class at the center of the musical learning circle, with ensembles and special classes stemming from it. Without a

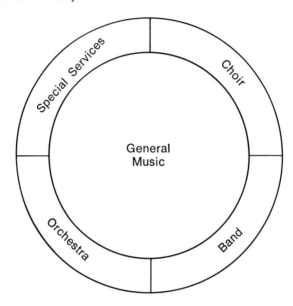

strong general music program, the average student enters adult life with little basis for an intelligent musical consumership; without a strong general music program, the student who participates in musical ensembles or activities relies upon that ensemble to provide a broad understanding and knowledge of music, its artistry, its relationships within history, as well as an aesthetic understanding of many musics which will remain with him into adult life and the twenty-first century.

All intermediate students, trying to find themselves in a complex world of personal, home, school, and community relationships, need the approach to an art provided by a general music class. Vocal and instrumental ensembles and special music classes should provide additional experiences in music for those who desire them.

In previous chapters this text has discussed approaches to junior high vocal ensembles. In keeping with a complete music program and the diagram above, it is appropriate that some observations be given concerning instrumental ensembles. There are many good texts which describe the details of organizational and pedagogical technics for beginning or intermediate instrumental ensembles. Consequently, this discussion will emphasize their role in the total program for the intermediate school.

Instrumental Ensembles

Instrumental ensembles should be a regular part of every adolescent school. The young person who has the talent and the interest should have the opportunity to play with a school band or orchestra. Such participation not only satisfies the musical development of the student but also provides the school with a means of spirit and pride. In addition, it acts as a training ground for the young instrumentalist as he looks toward high school ensembles.

Some teachers believe that instrumental music should begin with the move from the elementary school to the adolescent school. Muscular coordination, physical growth, and mental development studies lead to this decision. Other music teachers have been successful in persuading their schools to begin instrumental classes as early as the fourth grade on the premise that the child needs instruction in instrumental music at this earlier age if he is to better take his rightful place in the ensembles of the upper schools.

Recent studies of learning indicate that the student is best suited physically and mentally for beginning instruction during the junior high age. Students who participate in beginning classes during the seventh year of school are usually ready for beginning ensemble work during the next year. Little or no loss of technic is found with students who begin later as compared to those beginning at an earlier year; later beginners progress much more rapidly and remain in the program longer.

Students who begin during the fourth or fifth grade usually advance much more slowly. This slow progress often is a handicap to interest. Some directors argue, however, that the student learns the basics more securely at the slower speed. Statistics have not proved this to be the case. Schools which offer beginning classes during the junior high years also find that they can control instrumentation much more significantly, and that students can be placed upon larger instruments almost immediately without beginning instruments being involved.

Schools which adhere to the plan of working with the younger child often consider three instruments as best for beginners: the clarinet, the cornet or trumpet, and the violin. Beginning on either a basic brass, reed, or string instrument, a child should move from these to other members of the same family to satisfy the interests of the child, the instrumentation of the organization, and/or the physical needs of the student. Some directors have stretched this theory to include drum, saxophone, flute, or possibly a few others, thus weakening the concept, somewhat.

With string instruments, Suzuki's methods for the preschool child has furthered the string teacher's belief that one should begin strings at an early age on the premise that it takes much longer to develop a good string performer. Several factors seem to be operating at this point.

1. The quality of the instruction is important in any learning. If a string player is to be developed in a short time, it becomes necessary for him to have good instruction. Too often the teacher of strings is not well qualified.
2. Disregarding the experienced understandings of the class lesson approach,

string teachers often are not as well prepared to enter public schools as their wind counterparts. Good class teaching at the college level has become a pride with wind teachers who are preparing students for the band ensemble.

3. String teachers often are less well trained to teach young people. The concert string artist employed by colleges often has little sympathy for the study of strings by the class method, and many do not understand recent pedagogical approaches in relation to the child. Consequently, string education in the public schools has not yet reached the ordered success which is witnessed in the wind field.

String teachers are apt to blame their deficiencies upon the glamour of the band attracting the best talents; the lack of appeal of string instruments during the learning stage, thus negating practice; and the difficulty of the instruments. All of these are true in part, but the overwhelming problem is the lack of understanding by string teachers of the psychology of the learning child in relation to the instrument. Where good string programs exist, the teacher has mastered this problem.

Suzuki has developed a psychology of string teaching, and though he has proven his point by working with the young child, the process is also successful with the young adolescent and will produce string players at virtually the same

String orchestra, Wooddale Junior High School. Memphis, Tennessee. Charles Clark, conductor.

rate of speed as the wind teacher produces performers for his organizations. At this time in our schools, we have many teachers using the Suzuki method who have not mastered thoroughly the technic but have adopted some of the emphases after attending short summer workshops in this country. Other string methods, although successful with some students or successful with college beginners, do not make the same impact with the young student.

When instrumental instruction is begun in the elementary school, students of seventh grade participate in the ensembles immediately. When the student is a beginner during his first year of adolescent school, ensemble participation is delayed until the second year. Some teachers circumvent the latter problem by operating beginning classes through the summer months for longer blocks of time than possible during the school day.

Some large schools schedule ensembles for the second- and third-year student based upon grade segregation. Other schools, following a more contemporary approach to grade line, segregate the students into ensembles according to ability. Smaller schools, or schools with modest instrumental programs, maintain but one ensemble which services all talents and grades.

Classes for the beginner should be open to any person in the adolescent school. Too many schools operate a cutoff point for the beginner so that if he does not become involved with an instrument during the elementary years, it is all but impossible to begin later. Although school officials and music teachers will not readily admit this procedure, in fact, many systems operate in this manner.

Quality ensembles should exist in every school, but beginning classes in any instrument should be available for any student in any grade level. Child-concerned schools operate in this fashion.

A Sample Approach

Marjorie Skinner Hemphill, well-known director of junior high school bands in Oklahoma and Texas, spoke recently at an MENC convention concerning the development of her ensembles. Four basic rules apply to herself and her students:

> If it works—use it.
> Never laugh at a student or another person.
> Never say can't—just try.
> Come early and stay late.

In the summer after their sixth grade, she introduces her students to four beginning instruments: flute, clarinet, cornet, and trombone. Using no entrance tests, she assigns instruments according to the physical characteristics of the young people. Grouping the students heterogeneously, she keeps her students on mouthpieces from two to three weeks. For a student to play in the junior honor band the student must attain the goal of seven accurate scales, learn chromatics, and play thirty rhythms correctly. Her rhythmic teaching includes the physical down-up foot motions which correlate with a one-te-two-te rhythm of compositions and the "ready-breathe" statements at the beginning of each exercise. No private lessons are given, but through a buddy system, students assist each other with a problem analysis sheet as well as a student report card.

Cadet band, Le Mars Community Junior High School. Le Mars, Iowa. Dean Pelz, director.

The summer program becomes most important as she takes the students through the beginning steps at that time. In the fall, the student joins the marching band and plays scales on the field as he marches eight-to-five with eight counts to the single pitch of each scale, to develop breath support and tone. By the time the student reaches Christmas vacation, he is urged to prepare an easy solo which he must play before the entire band as an elimination prelude for later competition. Concert music for the group should demand more than two weeks work or it could contain too few challenges; if it requires longer than six weeks to prepare, it is too difficult, considering the musical ability of the ensemble.

In this description one can read evidences of good, specific teaching skills:

1. Physical development precedes the request to approach mature musical skills.
2. Physical development assists the teacher in assigning a proper instrument.
3. Basic steps are well learned before a student moves to new material.
4. Attention spans are considered along with ability levels.
5. Rhythm is understood to be a physical response.
6. The adolescent student enjoys physical movement, and the marching band satisfies this demand.
7. Marching band can be an assist to musicianship.
8. Solo and ensemble skills are developed early along with other musical learnings.
9. Student evaluations are learning assignments.
10. Students learn from one another.
11. Basic ideas may be taught on specific beginning instruments more quickly and with better results than a complete instrumentation. The instrument is not difficult—music is.

One can understand that such a program will bring results which are musically sound, consistent from student to student, and attractive to the young adolescent.

Vocal Ensembles

Adolescent schools have moved through two phases concerning the vocal ensemble. Some years ago, all schools offered the student opportunity to sing with a boys' chorus or a girls' glee club. This division and separation of the voices was deemed beneficial since the boy voice, offering certain problems, could best be handled musically and psychologically in an all-male group. In addition, it was reasoned that this age group actually preferred to be separated socially and such a division promoted musical growth and learning. Some directors still believe this to be the best musical arrangement, and all-boy or all-girl groups exist in many schools.

Recently, however, the mixed group prevails. To service the changing boy voice with its limited range, the mixed ensemble offers more musical possibilities. In other words, the girls' voices assist the boy voice with its range limitations during uncertain times. When the boy range is limited, the girl voice can provide melodic and harmonic possibilities to assist the boy and consequently his interest in music. Those teachers who explain well the changing voice to the boy find that he has few problems in accepting his role in the mixed group whether it be with girls on a soprano or second part, or with other boys in a changing voice part. In addition, some directors believe the mixed group provides a variation of tonal color so greatly needed since the adolescent voice has definite limitations as to color and loudness in both girls and boys.

Although the general music class includes singing, each school should offer the specialized vocal group to afford an opportunity for personal growth and expression, part-reading experience, and a wider exposure to literature. As with the instrumental ensembles, vocal groups offer an opportunity for psychological and social growth.

Voice Class ·

Throughout the adolescent years the child voice develops toward maturity. During this time it could be beneficial for the student to be a part of a voice class. If taught correctly, this class would assist the young person in proper voice development through concentrated study of vocal production, breathing, enunciation, and an introduction to simple vocal solo literature. Voice classes are not vocal ensembles, but they do involve a number of students singing simultaneously. Some solo singing could be a part of the class, but this is not a major emphasis. Its main thrust is the development of the voice, and this class could be an interesting way of aiding and working with the changing boy voice and the maturing girl voice.

Music for the Exceptional Child

Although our classes are filled with children who deviate from a norm, those on the outer fringes of the masses often need specific assistance. This group includes the exceptionally intelligent child who finds difficulty in school because nothing challenges him; to him school is a waste of time. The child with low intelligence also is exceptional. The most recent trend to place these children in as many regular classes as possible might be only partially developmental. The child with psychological disorders, although not damaged deeply enough to be institutionalized, as well as the child with physical disabilities, often require special consideration.

Music can speak to and can offer unusual opportunities to all of these young people. At this most precarious age of beginning adolescence, music can find an important place with such young people which is not possible with other subject areas.

Our junior high schools or adolescent schools should have available a person trained in special education and music. Such a teacher could work with the exceptional child and through music, aid the development of his understandings, his skills, his psychological growth, and his personal adjustment toward regular school life. For these children, the general music class or the special ensembles are not enough. A complete music program assists these children, specifically. It has been estimated that by the year 1985 70 percent of the children in our schools will be involved with psychological problems, mostly due to a family and home life which leads to personality instabilities. A complete music program will involve these young people through special classes and, hopefully, through well-trained personnel.

Summary

This text attempts to prepare the young teacher for work in the school servicing the young adolescent. It has emphasized the importance of a complete music program and discussed numerous methods of achieving this goal under various teaching situations.

Most of the text has involved the backgrounds necessary for the successful teaching of the general music class. This most important music offering, often a required class, services the large group of students who are often neglected by special music classes and ensembles during the later years of schooling. General music classes should be a bridge between the elementary school and the high school or adult life. It should awaken, continue, broaden, and service. Too often it has been the sole responsibility of the vocal teacher. In the future, a person trained especially in general music for junior high school should be in charge of these classes, using vocal and instrumental personnel as assistants.

But the adolescent school should not only emphasize general music. The large ensembles, the small ensembles, and the special music classes—all warrant considered attention. A complete, well-taught offering for all young boys and girls costs very little more than a poor program.

The aim of this text has been to better enable you to take your place in the teaching profession in full knowledge that you are equipped to do the required tasks, that you understand the administrative structures in which you could find yourself, that you have studied the personality of the young adolescent, and that you realize that good teaching should fit the child and the school.

ADDITIONAL READINGS AND BIBLIOGRAPHY

BOSWELL, JACQUELYN. *An Application of Bruner's Theory of Mental Growth to the Teaching of Musical Concepts in Beginning Instrumental Music.* Ph.D. dissertation, University of Illinois, 1969. (chaps. 3 & 4)

COLWELL, RICHARD J. *The Teaching of Instrumental Music.* New York: Appleton-Century-Crofts, 1969.

CRAMER, WILLIAM F. *The Relation of Maturation and Other Factors to Achievement in Beginning Instrumental Music Performance at 4th through 8th Grade Levels.* Ph.D. dissertation, Florida State University, 1958. (chaps. 3 & 5)

————. *How to Promote Your Band.* Elkhart, Indiana: H. and A. Selmer, 1957. (all)

HOLTZ, EMIL A., and JACOBI, ROGER. *Teaching Band Instruments to Beginners.* Englewood Cliffs, New Jersey: Prentice-Hall, Inc., 1966. (all)

HOUSE, ROBERT WILLIAM. *Instrumental Music in Today's Schools.* Englewood Cliffs, New Jersey: Prentice-Hall, Inc., 1965.

KAPLAN, LIONEL. *The Relationship between Certain Personality Characteristics and Achievement in Instrumental Music.* Ph.D dissertation, New York University, 1961. (chaps. 4 & 6)

KOHUT, DANIEL. *Instrumental Music Pedagogy; Teaching Technics for School Bands and Orchestra Directors.* Englewood Cliffs, New Jersey: Prentice-Hall, Inc., 1973.

KUHN, WOLFGANG. *Instrumental Music, Principles and Methods of Instruction.* Boston: Allyn & Bacon, Inc., 1970. (chaps. 3, 5 & 6)

LACY, GENE. *Organizing and Developing the High School Orchestra.* West Nyack, New York: Parker Publishing Company, 1971. (chaps. 1, 2 & 11)

LEE, RONALD THOMAS. *A Study of Teacher Training Experiences for Prospective Inner City Instrumental Music Teachers.* Ph.D. dissertation, University of Michigan, 1970. (chaps. 4 & 5)

NORMANN, THEODORE F. *Instrumental Music in the Public Schools.* Philadelphia: Oliver Ditson Co., 1941. (chaps. 4, 6 & 9)

PRESCOTT, GERALD, and CHIDESTER, LAWRENCE. *Getting Results with School Bands.* Minneapolis: Schmitt Music Co., 1938. (Part II)

RIGHTER, CHARLES B. *Success in Teaching School Orchestras and Bands.* Minneapolis: Schmitt, Hall and McCreary, 1945. (chaps. 3, 6, 8–11, 13–15)

SAWHILL, CLARENCE E., and MATTHEWS, GLENN. *Intonation Manual for Instruments.* Bryon-Douglas Publications, 1969.

VANDERCOOK, H. A. *Teaching the High School Band.* Chicago: Rubank, Inc., 1926.

WARD, SYLVAN DONALD. *The Instrumental Director's Handbook.* Chicago: Rubank, Inc., 1940. (all)

Appendices

APPENDIX A

Tweener Charts

The study procedure for Chapter 9 included tweener charts for completion. The following suggestions offer one set of influences and needs in the area of music. Compare your conclusions made on the Tweener Charts in Chapter 9 to those found on the following pages.

TWEENER CHART 1

The Tweener Wants Sufficient Knowledge and Skills Which Permit Him to Proceed on His Own

These Traits of the Tweener	Influence the School Program	Indicating a Musical Need For
An interest and an enthusiasm in gathering information and developing skills which will give meaning to him.	More reading and search activities about new fields and areas of interest.	The promotion of instruction in the basic skills of music reading, singing, rhythm, creativity, and listening.
	Provide required courses for a broad exposure and elective courses for varied talents. Provide honor courses to develop abilities to the fullest.	Special projects to help student search and organize studies. Ex: Indian music, jazz, etc.
		General music classes, elective ensembles, specialty courses.
A better understanding of his own ability.	Offer a program of testing to help Tweeners find where their greatest talents and abilities lie; then be placed in situations where they could experience some degree of success. Deficiencies are painful to accept at this age.	The music teacher could provide tests in singing, theory, etc., to help the student evaluate how much he knows about various phases of music. Study groups enable him to share knowledge with other students.

Characteristic	Provisions	Musical provisions
A concern about wanting to be accepted by the group.	Provide individual and group guidance to help the Tweeners learn more about themselves. Organize special activities which will help young people overcome handicaps and deficiencies not cared for in the regular classroom.	Varied elective subjects. Mini-courses requested by students. Offer various ensembles; for example, keyboard, recorder, percussion, as well as large group activities.
A wide range in his skills, knowledge, physical growth, and emotional maturity.	Promote school and class groupings which will enable Tweeners to receive adequate instruction and yet not be separated permanently from the large group. Offer a wide range of subjects from which he can choose. Adequate facilities. Use many types of materials in a wide range of learning situations.	Wide variety in class activities and repertoire to account for non-homogeneity of group. Wide range of musical opportunities.
A hesitation in participating in activities that point out his deficiencies.	Avoid singling out students because of their failures.	Self-study and individual progress situations.
An enthusiastic and persistent reader.	Assignments in relation to the subject matter which "explore" ideas. Good libraries.	The provision for reading assignments in music literature and an understanding and knowledge of composers, periods, and forms, relating these to other art forms.

TWEENER CHART 2

The Tweener Desires Many Outlets for Expressing His Ideas and Feelings

These Traits of the Tweener	Influence the School Program	Indicating a Musical Need For
An intense interest in practical manipulative arts.	Provide classes in which *all* the students can participate—general, not specialized courses. Provide opportunities for Tweeners to explore and develop skills in the areas of art, music, speech, dramatics, and handicraft.	Each student to express himself through music—singing, writing lyrics, composition; students perform pieces that will allow them to express the way they feel—concert, rock, or electronic.
A longing to participate in creative activities which give pleasure and relieve tension.	Plan creative activities in the classroom which involve each student. Set up centers where Tweeners may pursue special interests, such as creativity in the arts, reading, handiwork, dramatics, photography.	Musical interest centers in school library and music room. A music class centered around creativity.
A desire to argue with others—giving him an opportunity to clarify his own thinking and to hear the sound of his own voice.	Use more dialogue situations in classroom teaching. Set up problem-solving situations allowing open class discussion or group work activities.	Special planning sessions in which students can air their own creative ideas.

Promote club work and activities that encourage an exchange of ideas: open forums, panels, public assemblies.	A music club.
The copying of speech patterns similar to those of his own age group or the personality he is idolizing at the time.	
Courses where role-playing would assist learning. Teachers who are tolerant of peer influence.	A teacher who understands pop music and can use it as a departure point for other learning.
The determination to try out his own ideas.	
Encourage a creative classroom environment which provides Tweeners the opportunity to express themselves in many activities and to receive thoughtful adult reactions to their ideas.	Allow students to write original compositions, individually or as a whole class.

TWEENER CHART 3

The Tweener Is Concerned About His Relationships With Other People

These Traits of the Tweener	Influence the School Program	Indicating a Musical Need For
A desire to become useful and of value through affiliations with service organizations and welfare movements.	Opportunities for volunteer work within the school. Assist with civic and service programs through school clubs, home room, or special service groups.	Musical programs for shut-ins, welfare centers, etc. Performing for or work with underprivileged children. Tutoring small children in music. Helping with community music programs—handing out programs, setting up chairs, etc.
A feeling of inadequacy toward many of the new demands of growing up.	Teachers and administrators need be aware of teenage problems. Give consideration to the feelings of each person.	Avoiding elementary sounding music. Encouragement toward adult, musical behavior.
A difficulty in getting along with people and a tendency to blame conditions that are not the cause.	Employ teachers who are mature enough to cope with adjustment problems of this age without being personally threatened themselves. Encourage the use of self-evalua-	Evaluate progress in the music classes. Let each student evaluate himself from a prepared set of evaluation criteria.

An indifference that sometimes takes the form of cruelty toward those not in his group.	Employ teachers who can accept people of all types without judgment or discrimination. Promote many small group activities, making a conscious effort to change the membership frequently.	Seating students to avoid cliques. Small music ensembles whose membership is determined by ability rather than friendship.
A tendency to be stubborn at home, resisting family authority.	Sponsor discussion groups of school and community affairs which include both Tweeners and parents.	Social get-togethers where students, parents, and teachers can become acquainted. Inviting parents to an open rehearsal.
An inclination to question the manners, morals, and ethical standards of adults.	Provide problem-solving situations in which young people are put in the position of the decision-making adults.	An exposure to the music of other cultures, correlated with a study of the world's people.

TWEENER CHART 4

The Tweener Shows Increased Interest About Himself and His Environment

These Traits of the Tweener	Influence the School Program	Indicating a Musical Need For
A desire to learn about his special abilities, strengths, endurance, and stage of growth.	Provide programs which allow him to develop and see progress within himself.	Study of his physical self and how he uses his body as and with an instrument.
	Provide a setting which will give young people an opportunity to explore special interests and be creative.	Beginning and advanced level music offerings.
A concern about acquiring skills, knowledge, and hobbies that will make him valuable to others.	Offer a variety of electives which cover many areas.	Provide a variety of courses and activities in music so each student will be able to find some area in which he does well. General music teacher should relate music to today's life.
A shifting between feelings of superiority and feelings of inferiority.	Faculty should be understanding of adolescent development.	Examples of how students his age obtain success.
	Provide opportunities for self-evaluation in skill development, aptitudes, interests, and physical growth.	Encouragement and recognition of achievement by adults and teachers.
		Self-evaluation of progress in musical skills.

A desire to reconcile the realities of life with idealistic teaching.	A good counseling program should be in effect. Classes should be taught with objectivity, so that the student can see both sides.	Individual conferences with students.
A tendency to overreact to his successes and failures.	Stable and understanding faculty.	Constructive teacher evaluation of progress in musical skills. The opportunity for the Tweener to be creative in his musical interests, encouraged by adequate facilities and equipment in the music room.
An urge to improve upon the realities of his environment.	Courses which study local and national problems. A beginning sociology class.	Music to be understood as an art form, an expression of man in society.

TWEENER CHART 5 — The Tweener Has to Adjust to Rapid and Profound Body Changes

These Traits of the Tweener	Influence the School Program	Indicating a Musical Need For
A concern about his personal appearance.	Physical education and home ec programs should include a unit on grooming. Provide reading and audiovisual materials which stress ways to improve personal appearances, grooming habits, cleanliness.	Showing student that personal appearance counts in making the total appearance of the music group.
An awareness of strange feelings that he does not understand.	Plan activities which will permit young people to express feelings and make interpretations: creative writing, sociodrama, informal speech and music experiences, role playing.	Opportunities for expression of feeling through music (creativity). Discuss emotional content of art works. Writing a musical or creative work involving role-playing, singing, costumes.
A boundless amount of energy or sudden fatiguing.	Activities to use his energies in an educational direction.	Provide work in numerous small groups. A marching band. Music which could involve body movement.

An interest in and concern about his changing body contours.	Explanations concerning body development.	Showing him that weight or growth change does not always affect the performing ability. A study of voice change to help boys and girls realize their problem and not to be ashamed or overly concerned.
A nervous or emotional reaction to the awkwardness that results from weight and growth changes.	Physical education courses for boys and girls where they can better understand these body changes.	The organization of health studies as they relate to music production, vocal or instrumental (might include mouth positions, body positions for good sounds, breath control studies, etc.) Never placing the student in situations where his awkwardness or nervousness will embarrass him.
An increasing amount of skill in use of large and small muscles.	Provide physical activities involving individual and group work, organized sports, coeducational games, contests, and social events.	Music activities involving hand-eye coordination. An increase in technical demands in music production.
An uncertain and confused feeling about sex.	Sex education can be included in curriculum including doctors as guest speakers.	Coeducational music organizations offering rehearsal, performance, and social situations at school and in the community

TWEENER CHART 6

The Tweener Tries to Achieve Independence and at the Same Time Maintain Security

These Traits of the Tweener	Influence the School Program	Indicating a Musical Need For
A willingness to work hard to gain recognition through accomplishment.	Offer schoolwork responsibilities such as librarian, office assistant, teacher's aid. Honor courses to provide an outlet and competitive opportunities.	Student responsibility—music librarian, section leaders, etc. Recognition of students who have striven for accomplishment; awards for outstanding music students.
An insistence on having his own way and making his own plans.	Offer creative activities regularly. Class opportunities where independence can be learned.	Conductor of the day. Have sectionals and section leaders to develop responsibility.
A tendency to regress to childish behavior to regain or insure security.	Promote activities in which the need for conventional and formal ways of doing things is stressed.	Teacher to evaluate his own actions in class to see if they encourage childish behavior. Patience with childishness, but urge more adult behavior.
A desire to be allowed to choose his own friends, clothes, hours.	Provide a variety of interesting and challenging social, recreational, and educational activities.	Project in music class which offers a choice of opportunities.

Characteristic		
An emerging interest in vocations.	Explore vocations through interest tests, units of work, reading, field trips, and guest speakers.	Professional performers, composers, or teacher requested to speak to class or club about music as a vocation. Interest tests, music aptitude tests, field trips related to music activities.
A desire for job experience.	Work with parents in developing a spare-time job placement center. Participate in the distributive education program.	Recommendations for jobs, and a respect for jobs when calling extra rehearsals. Distributive education program in music.
A tendency to transfer from family to peer authority.	Use "peer authority" as a means of self-governing student body under the guidance, but not domination, of faculty. Establish a self-directed study program.	Use of advanced students to assist younger students as teaching aids in instrumental program.
A desire to be grown-up—attaching undue importance to what he thinks are signs of being a mature individual: smoking, bragging, swearing.	Quality of teacher personality can influence what the student considers adult. Provide clubs, student activities, and community contacts which give needed training and experience in assuming responsibilities. Plan faculty study groups which will help teachers to understand the childish behavior of Tweeners.	Never treating the student as a child, but as an adult. Visits to opera, symphony, and concerts to teach customary audience etiquette. Teacher examples of grown-up behavior that does not hinge on smoking, bragging, or swearing.

TWEENER CHART 7 The Tweener Strives for Personal Values in His Social Setting

These Traits of the Tweener	Influence the School Program	Indicating a Musical Need For
A desire to have adults think through the problem with him.	Well-trained guidance counselors. Opportunity for teachers to relate to students and discuss problems.	Good teacher-student relations. Teachers who understand students as well as music.
A willingness to accept explanations that are reached through reasoning with him.	To set up situations involving the use of problem-solving procedures.	Directing students into behavior that all will respect and follow.
A desire to understand the purpose of life.	To provide opportunities for Tweeners to read and discuss biographies, novels, a poem, historical materials.	Discuss purpose of music in life—past and present. Opportunities for Tweeners to read about and discuss composers' lives and other historic materials related to music literature.
A concern about right and wrong and a strict adherence to his code of behavior.	To include Tweeners in the planning and evaluating of school activities and projects.	Teachers whose actions at all times represent the highest goals of musical and personal behavior.
A tendency to imitate the person he most admires at the moment.	Teachers with good characters, but many types of teachers.	Teachers who are consistent and honest. A good example of adult behavior.

A keen sense of loyalty.	Plan activities of a religious and patriotic nature, encouraging club and class groups to have some formal ceremonies for groups and public participation. Organizations which promote strong school spirit.	A "Music Week" at school, with organization and planning by music classes. Inspiration of loyalty to organization, school.
A desire to reconcile the everyday happenings he observes with idealistic teaching.	Give perspective to daily events through classroom, educational procedures.	Discussion with interested students about certain philosophies of music education.

TWEENER CHART 8

The Tweener Wants to Participate as a Responsible Member of Larger Social Groups

These Traits of the Tweener	Influence the School Program	Indicating a Musical Need For
A desire to be a member of many social groups in and out of school.	Provide many activities of a social, recreational, and special interest nature, thus providing Tweeners an opportunity to be good members of social groups.	Opportunities to be a member of choir, band, orchestra, and other musical groups.
A concern about being socially accepted.	Classes of all sizes using varied technics to ensure interaction.	Classes and ensembles of various levels, sizes, interests, offering response opportunities and responsibilities.
An interest in serving school, community, and other groups.	Plan for cooperative participation of Tweeners in all phases of the learning process: planning, discussing, interviewing, reporting, evaluating.	Incorporating such activities in the music program if at all possible.
An urge to be a full-fledged citizen.	Offer some means of organizing and channeling students in service projects for the community.	Students to help service music department, organizations, or facilities.
		Have members of the class interview professional musicians (performers, educators) and report to class.

Perform for old-folks home, in-valids, etc.—a social gathering plus a community service.

Ensemble officers.

Encourage Tweeners to take pride in a clean, well-organized music environment.

Opportunity for membership in a music club or small ensembles, with a variety of experiences such as field trips, speakers, etc., stressing loyalty to school through ensembles.

Classes which require decisions in musical matters.

Concern and tolerance of the musical ability, skills, and preference of all students.

School student council.

Encourage Tweeners to take pride in keeping clean, neat, well-organized school environment.

Offer a large number of social or educational activities.

Programs that help students in making plans and decisions but do not demand their acceptance as the only right answer.

Teachers who have time to help students in their plans and decisions.

Stress fairness and concern in all areas, as well as sports.

A longing to be a member of one or more closely-knit groups.

A desire for direction and help in making plans and decisions, with the privilege of rejecting or accepting suggestions.

An ardent admiration for sports-manlike behavior.

APPENDIX B

National Association of Secondary School Principals' Statement Concerning Music in Upper Schools

At the 1962 meeting of the National Association of Secondary School Principals, an organization which includes administrators for junior and senior high schools, the following statement was adopted concerning their expectations for music programs in relation to each student[1] Note the wide diversity of considerations and the implications for a total music program. It becomes the responsibility of each junior high music teacher to assist his administrator in interpreting these goals and in explaining this interpretation to parents, students, and citizenry.

Each student, according to his abilities and interests, should have the opportunity to:

1. Develop skills in music so he may:
    a. participate in some kind of musical performance either as an individual or as a member of a group;
    b. listen to music with understanding and enjoyment;
    c. associate the musical score with what is heard or performed;
    d. improvise and create music of his own.
2. Become an intelligent critic of jazz, folk music, popular music, parade music, and major types of serious music.
3. Develop a sense of responsibility for exercising his critical judgment for the improvement of the musical environment of his community, including offerings on radio and television as well as live performances.
4. Recognize music as an international language and a vehicle of international goodwill.
5. Acquire such knowledge about music as: history of music, form and design of music, symbolism of music score, the quality of tone and other characteristics of the various musical instruments and the ranges of the human voice, the combinations of instruments and voices, the role of composers in various historical periods, and the relation of music to such other disciplines as science, mathematics, and literature.
6. Understand how emotional expression as a part of normal, healthy, happy living can be enhanced by music.

7. Desire to continue some form of musical experience both in school and following graduation; for example, select and use recordings and tapes, engage in small vocal and instrumental ensemble work, and participate as performers and listeners in community musical activities.[1]

1. "The Arts in the Comprehensive Secondary School," *Bulletin of the National Association of Secondary School Principals,* XLVI, no. 275, Washington, D.C., National Association of Secondary School Principals, September, 1962, p. 6.

APPENDIX C

Contest and Adjudication Forms

Prospective teachers should have experience in using and studying various adjudication forms before entering the professional field. The Solo and Ensemble Adjudication form which follows—a local adoption form—offers additional experience from the forms which were prepared by NIMAC, the National Interscholastic Music Adjudication Committee. The latter are more often used throughout our country, but forms similar to the following may be found in many local situations.

Local Solo and Ensemble Adjudication

EVENT _____ Class (I, II, III) _____

SCHOOL REPRESENTED _____ CITY _____

TITLE OF SELECTION _____ COMPOSER _____

INSTRUCTION TO JUDGE: Listed below are some of the factors which should receive your attention as this solo performs. Make no attempt to grade each factor objectively. Your written comments will indicate both strength and weakness.

Tone:
   Quality   Quantity
   Intonation   Blend
   Control   Balance
   Naturalness

Interpretation:
   Dynamics   Style
   Tempo   Accompaniment
   Phrasing   Rhythm

Technic:
   Attack   Diction
   Rhythm Accuracy Release
   Pitch Accuracy   Breathing
   Smoothness   Tonguing
   Fingering   Pedal
   Embouchure   Articulation
   Bowing

Selection:
   Suitability to capacity of performer(s)

General Effect
   Stage Presence Artistry
   Memorization   Posture

CONSTRUCTIVE COMMENTS

RATING: (circle one. Do NOT add minus or plus)

I   II   III   IV   V

Write in rating here _____   _____
                                    Signature of Official

Percussion Solo and Ensemble

PSEBO-10, Official Adjudication Form. Copyright 1958 by National Interscholastic Music Activities Commission, 1201 Sixteenth Street, Washington, D.C. 20006. Must not be reprinted without written permission.

RATING

Use no plus or minus signs in final rating

Order or time of appearance_____ Event No._____ Class_____ Date_____ 19_____

Name of Ensemble _____

Kind of Solo or Ensemble _____

School _____ City _____ State _____ District _____

Selection _____

Performers' Names _____

Adjudicator will grade principal items, A, B, C, D, or E, or numerals, in the respective squares. Comments must deal with fundamental principles and be constructive. Minor details may be marked on music furnished to adjudicator.

TONE _____ ☐

_____

_____

RUDIMENTS—TECHNIQUE _____ ☐

_____

_____

POSITION (body, hand, instrument) _____ ☐

_____

_____

INTERPRETATION (balance, dynamics, expression, phrasing, rhythm, tempo) _____ ☐

_____

_____

SIGHT READING (accuracy, dynamics, tempo) _____ ☐

_____

_____

MUSICAL AND GENERAL EFFECT (artistry, stage presence and appearance) _____ ☐

_____

_____

MEMORIZING (when required) _____ ☐

_____

_____

* May be continued on other side.   Signature of Adjudicator _____

Vocal Solo

Order or time
of appearance_____

Event
No._____

Class_____

Date_____ _____19____

RATING

Use no plus or minus
signs in final rating

Name _____ Voice Classification_____

School_____

City_____State_____District._____

Selection _____

Adjudicator will grade principal items, A, B, C, D, or E, or numerals, in the respective squares. Comments must deal with fundamental principles and be constructive. Minor details may be marked on music furnished to adjudicator.

TONE (beauty, control)_____ ☐

INTONATION_____ ☐

DICTION (clarity of consonants, naturalness, purity of vowels)_____ ☐

TECHNIQUE (accuracy of notes, breathing, posture, rhythm)_____ ☐

INTERPRETATION (expression, phrasing, style, tempo)_____ ☐

MUSICAL EFFECT (artistry, fluency, vitality)_____ ☐

OTHER FACTORS (choice of music, stage presence and appearance)_____ ☐

*May be continued
on other side.

Signature of Adjudicator_____

455

Choral—Small Ensemble

RATING

Use no plus or minus signs in final rating

Order or time of appearance_____ Event No._____ Class_____ Date_____ 19_____

Name of Organization _____

School _____ Number of singers_____

City _____ State _____ District _____ School Enrollment_____

Selections _____

Adjudicator will grade principal items, A, B, C, D, or E, or numerals, in the respective squares. Comments must deal with fundamental principles and be constructive. Minor details may be marked on music furnished to adjudicator.

TONE (beauty, blend, control) _____ ☐

INTONATION _____ ☐

DICTION (clarity of consonants, naturalness, purity of vowels) _____ ☐

TECHNIQUE (breathing and posture, precision, rhythm) _____ ☐

BALANCE _____ ☐

INTERPRETATION (expression, phrasing, style, tempo) _____ ☐

MUSICAL EFFECT (artistry, feeling of ensemble, fluency, vitality) _____ ☐

OTHER FACTORS (chocie of music, discipline, stage presence and appearance) _____ ☐

Signature of Adjudicator _____

Used with permission of Music Educators National Conference.

Instrumental Ensemble—String

Order or time
of appearance _____

Event
No. _____ Class _____ Date _____ 19 _____

Name of Ensemble _____

School _____ City _____ State _____ District _____

Selection _____

Instrumentation _____

Performers' Names _____

SIE-15, Official Adjudication Form. Copyright 1958 by National Interscholastic Music Activities Commission, 1201 Sixteenth Street, Washington, D.C. 20006. Must not be reprinted without written permission.

Adjudicator will grade principal items, A, B, C, D, or E, or numerals, in the respective squares. Comments must deal with fundamental principles and be constructive. Minor details may be marked on music furnished to adjudicator.

TONE (beauty, blend, control) _____ ☐

_____

INTONATION (harmonic parts, melodic line, tuning) _____ ☐

_____

TECHNIQUE (bowing—choice and execution, fingering, precision, rhythm) _____ ☐

_____

BALANCE _____ ☐

_____

INTERPRETATION (expression, phrasing, style, tempo) _____ ☐

_____

MUSICAL EFFECT (artistry, fluency) _____ ☐

_____

OTHER FACTORS (choice of music, stage presence and appearance) _____ ☐

_____

*** May be continued
on other side.**

Signature of Adjudicator _____

Sight Reading—Choral

RATING

Use no plus or minus
signs in final rating

Order or time
of appearance _____

Event
No._____

Class _____

Date_____ _____19___

Name of Organization _____

School_____ Number of Singers_____

City_____ State _____ District_____ School Enrollment_____

Selections _____

_____

Adjudicator will grade principal items, A, B, C, D, or E, or numerals, in the respective squares. Comments must deal
with fundamental principles and be constructive.   Minor details may be marked on music furnished to adjudicator.

TECHNICAL ACCURACY (correct intervals, feeling of tonality, note values, rhythm figures)_____ ☐

FLEXIBILITY (balance, precision, response to director)_____ ☐

INTERPRETATION (expression, phrasing, style, tempo)_____ ☐

MUSICAL EFFECT (confidence, fluency, intonation, tone)_____ ☐

GENERAL COMMENTS_____ ☐

*May be continued
on other side.

Signature of Adjudicator_____

Used with permission of Music Educators National Conference.

Choral—Large Group

RATING

Order or time
of appearance_____

Event
No._____

Class_____

Date_____19____

Use no plus or minus
signs in final rating

Name of Organization _____

School_____ Number of Singers_____

City_____State_____District_____School Enrollment_____

Selections _____
_____
_____

Adjudicator will grade principal items, A, B, C, D, or E, or numerals, in the respective squares. Comments must deal with fundamental principles and be constructive. Minor details may be marked on music furnished to adjudicator.

TONE (beauty, blend, control) _____ ☐

INTONATION_____ ☐

DICTION (clarity of consonants, naturalness, purity of vowels) _____ ☐

TECHNIQUE (breathing and posture, precision, rhythm)_____ ☐

BALANCE_____ ☐

INTERPRETATION (expression, phrasing, style, tempo)_____ ☐

MUSICAL EFFECT (artistry, feeling of ensemble, fluency, vitality)_____ ☐

OTHER FACTORS (choice of music, discipline, stage presence and appearance)_____ ☐

*May be continued
on other side.

Signature of Adjudicator_____

Adjudicator's private comments for_____, to be detached by *adjudicator*
(Name of Director)
and sealed in attached envelope furnished by Festival Chairman.

Use reverse side for additional comments

459

Visitation Assignment

This form has been used to provide information for students visiting a junior high school. It gives pertinent details and reminds them of their responsibility to the school and the teacher visited. The student signs the form and leaves it with the teacher to prove attendance.

Place: Atkins Junior High School

Location: Avenue U at 53rd Street

Teacher: Mrs. Carol Boland

Transportation: Individual

Routine: 1. BE SURE TO ARRIVE BEFORE CLASS BEGINS
2. CHECK INTO THE PRINCIPAL'S OFFICE
3. PRESENT THIS SHEET TO THE PRINCIPAL OR HIS SECRETARY
4. PRESENT THIS SHEET WITH YOUR NAME TO MRS. BOLAND UPON ENTERING THE ROOM
5. YOU MUST ARRIVE BEFORE CLASS BEGINS AND REMAIN FOR THE ENTIRE PERIOD

Class Times: 8:45 A.M.
9:45 A.M.
10:45 A.M.

Dates for visitation: November 13, Thursday
November 18, Tuesday

Class Background: General Music
Seventh Grade
Unit Plans
First Unit: Instruments of the Orchestra
Second Unit: Broadway Musicals
Present Unit: Electronic Music

November 13—second day of unit
November 18—third day of unit

Class meets twice weekly and alternate Fridays

Your signature _____

Student Teacher Rating

This form has been used in class when all students rate a fellow member who has taught a junior high lesson for part of a period. The grading required on this form by the college students is based upon a five-point range for each part, with thirty possible points. After collection of the forms, grading of each paper by the college teacher is based upon an honest evaluation of strong and weak areas and the recognition and discussion of these by the student. Some appropriate comments are typed anonymously onto a separate sheet and shared with the student teacher. This form is returned to the writer.

NAME OF STUDENT TEACHER _____ YOUR NAME _____

1. Classroom effectiveness

Grade _____

2. Clarity of presentation

Grade _____

3. Student contact and/or involvement

Grade _____

4. Time judgment (Pacing and time use)

Grade _____

5. Planning (Was it evident and purposeful?)

Grade _____

6. Additional Comments

Total Grade _____

Vocal Lesson Evaluation

Students in a junior high music class who are not vocal majors can benefit from some private vocal instruction; vocal majors can benefit by teaching these students. This form has been used to assist the student in summarizing his instruction and in analyzing his own vocal problems in an attempt to increase the impact of the work completed.

STUDENT EVALUATION BLANK

Your name _____ Name of your student voice teacher_____

1. How many times did you meet with your teacher? _____
   Would you say that the person most responsible for not meeting more often was

   you or your teacher? (not both) _____ Why? _____

2. What do you consider your primary or most obvious vocal problems?
   _____
   _____
   _____

3. What did your teacher do to assist you with these problems?
   _____
   _____
   _____

4. What did you learn from this experience which you believe could be used in a future teaching situation?
   _____
   _____
   _____

5. What do you believe hindered your teacher from being more effective?
   _____
   _____
   _____

6. What do you believe to be your teacher's best assets?
   _____
   _____
   _____

7. What letter grade would you give your teacher? _____ yourself? _____

Peer Evaluation of Teaching and Conducting

A large variety of teaching projects are a part of the college junior high school music class. Each student who assumes responsibility for teaching and/or conducting knows he will be judged by his peers and that some of the comments will come back to him anonymously via the teacher. This form has been used to evaluate student-directed special projects near the end of the semester or term.

EVALUATION OF SPECIFIC PROJECTS

Your name _____ Date _____

1. You have seen the following teach and conduct in class:

   Margaret Cavenagh
   Kelly Ewen
   Ellen Field
   Diane Kesey
   Ray Owens
   Eluid Rios
   Tim Holder

   List the two teacher/conductors you believe were most effective. Tell why.

2. You were a member of a small ensemble which rehearsed and sang in class. These were conducted by Tim King, Steve Davis, David Murphy, and Jedda Jones. Evaluate your teacher as to effectiveness with a group and to rehearsal procedures.

APPENDIX D
_____

Sample Tests

The following sample tests have been given to classes in the development of this text.

Chapters one through six cover the early portion of the text, while Chapters seven through fourteen deal with the central portion.

Chapters One Through Six

USE A BLUEBOOK FOR YOUR ANSWERS.
DO NOT PUT YOUR NAME ON THE BLUEBOOK—USE ONLY THE NUMBER WHICH YOU CHOSE WHEN YOU ENTERED THE ROOM.

The points assigned to the questions should provide some indication of the time you should use to answer them. Do not use a long time answering questions of few points. This is a 75-point quiz for our 75-minute period.

1. *a.* Define general music. (5 Points)
   b. What educational assets does such a program have for the junior high school? (10 Points)

2. *a.* List three approaches to teaching general music. Describe each. (6 Points)
   b. State advantages and disadvantages for each of the three approaches, explaining each of your points in some detail if you believe this necessary for clarity or emphasis. (24 Points)

3. *a.* Each of the above three plans include singing. Describe the problems in the teaching of singing in the junior high school. (12 Points)
   b. Define range and tessitura. Give the ranges of the junior high school voice; the tessitura. (10 Points)
   c. In selecting music for the young adolescent, what are the basic criteria? (8 Points)

Chapters One Through Six

USE A BLUEBOOK FOR YOUR ANSWERS.
DO NOT PUT YOUR NAME ON THE BLUEBOOK—
USE ONLY THE NUMBER WHICH YOU CHOSE WHEN YOU ENTERED
THE ROOM.

1. Discuss the general music class: (20 Points)
   a. Define it.
   b. What should it provide the student?
   c. What advantages does it offer to the school and/or curriculum?
   d. What benefit does it offer the music program?
   (This question submitted by Andy Davidson)

2. Discuss three standard teaching plans for general music: (18 Points)
   a. Name the three plans.
   b. Define each.
   c. List three advantages and three disadvantages for each plan.
   (This question submitted by Mike Murphy)

3. Rethink lesson plans: (8 Points)
   a. What are first considerations before solidifying a lesson plan?
   b. What should a lesson plan contain? Why?
   (This question submitted by Rita Reinsch)

4. Consider level and sequence: (8 Points)
   a. Give a definition of each, placing emphasis upon their differences.
   b. What advantages do they offer to the knowledgable teacher?
   c. How does the student stand to benefit?
   (This question submitted by Elicia Keele)

5. On the right below, you will find statements from our sequence and level charts. On the left, you will find grade areas. Each of the statements fits one particular grade level. Circle the appropriate grade level for each statement. (16 Points)

SKILL: HAVE A FAMILIARITY WITH
FOLK DANCES OF VARIOUS
COUNTRIES.

1–2 3–4 5–6 Junior High *a.* Folk dances assist in the understanding of social studies.

1–2 3–4 5–6 Junior High *b.* Folk songs sung as rote songs.

1–2 3–4 5–6 Junior High *c.* Introduction of simple folk dances.

1–2 3–4 5–6 Junior High *d.* Folk dances assist with an understanding of history and the role of folk music in history.

SKILL: PLAY THE BELLS OR OTHER
SIMPLE INSTRUMENTS

1–2 3–4 5–6 Junior High *a.* Create phrases on bells.

1–2 3–4 5–6 Junior High *b.* Use bells and recorder as an expression of musical and artistic values.

1–2 3–4 5–6 Junior High *c.* Use recorder and bells for music reading and creativity.

1–2 3–4 5–6 Junior High *d.* Simple reading of melodies and rhythms on bells; introduce the recorder.

SKILL: READING OF RHYTHMS

1–2 3–4 5–6 Junior High *a.* Reading of simple rhythms from musical notation; introduction of rhythm syllables (One-te, two-te).

1–2 3–4 5–6 Junior High *b.* Rhythmic reading to increase skill and strengthen understanding of irregular rhythms.

1–2 3–4 5–6 Junior High *c.* Long and short dashes distinguish rhythmic sounds.

1–2 3–4 5–6 Junior High *d.* Read compound rhythms and dotted eighth and sixteenth patterns.

SKILL: SING AND RECOGNIZE MOST
MELODIC INTERVALS

1–2 3–4 5–6 Junior High *a.* Sing chromatics with accuracy and name standard intervals.

1–2 3–4 5–6 Junior High *b.* Sing diatonic intervals by rote.

1–2 3–4 5–6 Junior High *c.* Sing chromatic intervals and simple modulations.

1–2 3–4 5–6 Junior High *d.* Singing and reading simple diatonic intervals.

Chapters Seven Through Fourteen

USE A BLUEBOOK FOR YOUR ANSWERS.
DO NOT PUT YOUR NAME ON THE BLUEBOOK—
USE ONLY THE NUMBER WHICH YOU CHOSE WHEN YOU ENTERED THE ROOM.

1. Discipline is one of the major problems in the school for the young adolescent.
   a. List three considerations dealing with the physical condition of the music room which affect discipline. Write one or two sentences which explain why you listed each item. (3 Points)
   b. Self-confidence of the teacher is important in discipline. List two items which deal with self-confidence which you believe important. Write two or three sentences for each item to explain why it is important. (4 Points)
   c. List five practical suggestions which could aid in classroom control. (5 Points)
   d. If punishment becomes necessary, it should follow certain guidelines. List three of these suggestions. (3 Points)
   (This question submitted by Richard Edwards and Christina Lemke)

2. The changing voice is another of the major problems for the teacher of the young adolescent.
   a. List the four methods of handling the changing voice in the adolescent school. (4 Points)
   b. Briefly describe each method. (4 Points)
   c. List four factors to consider in choosing singing material for young adolescent voices. (4 Points)
   (This question submitted by Christina Lemke and Alfred Klaerner)

3. A third problem in considering education for the young person is the school itself. Discuss five organizational plans for schools for the early adolescent.
   a. Identify and describe each plan. (10 Points)
   b. List two advantages and two disadvantages of each plan. (10 Points)
   (This question submitted by Alfred Klaerner and Karen Rozell)

4. Our fourth problem deals with the maturity development and growth. In class, we discussed several methods of describing and studying the personality of the young person. Three of these were examined in detail: Havighurst, Strang, and Tryon. Compare the three. (9 Points)
   Consider: *a.* What is different about each?
   b. How do they approach personality definition?
   c. What is the main emphasis of each?
   (This question submitted by Martha Anthis, Cindy Clifford, Rita Riensch, and Bob Daniel)

5. Match the following general terms with the descriptive phrases. Each of the terms may be used only once. Be sure that each descriptive phrase is matched once and only once.

   _____*a.* Psychoanalytic theory

   1. There are four lags between society and the adolescent.

   _____*b.* Psychological theory

   2. Just as any teacher, he would be faced with large group lectures, small group discussions or explanations, and individual assistance times.

   _____*c.* Psychological-sociological theory (Havighurst)

   3. Two basic yearnings during adolescence are mourning and love.

   _____*d.* Sociological theory

   4. The environment is controlled so that certain learnings will take place.

   _____*e.* Biological theory

   5. Answers provided for the administration, the parent, and the taxpayer.

   _____*f.* Expanded-period day

   6. Membership in ensembles would depend only upon talent or scheduling.

   _____*g.* Module

   7. During adolescence a value set evolves.

   _____*h.* Team teaching

   8. Music stands to lose considerably in a school organized by the six-period day.

_____*i.* The core

9. Society expects young people to acquire certain knowledge, attitudes, and skills at certain points in growth.

_____*j.* Non-graded schools

10. Both vertical and horizontal approaches are possible.

_____*k.* Accountability

11. The preparation of the child for musical learnings has been little considered. It is possible children react negatively to music because they are not in the proper stage as the demands of the material.

_____*l.* Behavioral objectives

12. There is a direct relationship between the personality and brain growth and stratification.

_____*m.* Ontogenetic concepts

13. The music teacher must have a background of some breadth as well as an interest in other humanities.

APPENDIX E

Audiovisual Aids

Films and Video Tapes

The following recent list of music films and video tapes are appropriate for the young adolescent. This list will not include items in recent collections usually found in libraries and audiovisual centers.

A Band Is . . .	Coca-Cola Bottling Co. (your local company)	14 min.
American Art Song	U of M	30 min.
A Musical Marriage, Composer and Wife	U of M	30 min.
The Art of Ornamentation	U of M	30 min.
The Automated Instruments	U of M	30 min.
The Beats Go On: Percussion from Pleistocene to Paradiddle	Xerox	13 min.
Bernstein on Beethoven (Ode to Joy)	BFA	27 min.
Bernstein on Beethoven (A Tribute)	BFA	14 min.
Bolero	National Endowment for the Arts	28 min.
The Chamber Choir	U of M	30 min.
The Classical Clarinet	U of M	30 min.
Concert with the Courtes, Viola and Pianist	U of M	30 min.
Discovering Jazz	BFA	22 min.
Discovering the Music of Africa	BFA	22 min.
Discovering the Music of India	BFA	22 min.
Discovering the Music of Japan	BFA	22 min.
Discovering the Music of the Middle Ages	BFA	22 min.
Discovering the Music of the Middle East	BFA	20 min.
Duo, Piano and Flute	U of M	30 min.
French Art Song	U of M	30 min.
Grieg—the Man and His Music	AIMS	17 min.
Guitar—from Stone Age to Modern Rock	Xerox	14 min.
Harp and Violin	U of M	30 min.
House of Music, the Musical Stout Family	U of M	30 min.
The Horn	BFA	21 min.
In Our Time, Ross Lee Finney, twentieth-century composer	U of M	30 min.

The Keyboards, Piano, Organ and Harpsichord	U of M	30 min.
Music Speaks, When and Where Tunes Are Written	U of M	30 min.
The Musician as Craftsman, the Piano Tuner	U of M	30 min.
The Musicianly Singer, the Solo Voice	U of M	30 min.
Music's Generation	Audiovisual Services NEA	18 min.
New Sounds in Music	Churchill	22 min.
New Wine in New Bottles, Music of the Early Twentieth Century	U of M	30 min.
The Noble Brasses	U of M	30 min.
Of Periwigs and Genius, Haydn and Mozart	U of M	30 min.
Of Romance and Revolution, Music and World of Beethoven	U of M	30 min.
On American Music	U of M	30 min.
On Composing	U of M	30 min.
On Humor in Music	U of M	30 min.
On Jazz	U of M	30 min.
On New Directions	U of M	30 min.
On Persuasion in Music	U of M	30 min.
On Pleasure with Music	U of M	30 min.
On Rock	U of M	30 min.
On Soul Music	U of M	30 min.
On This Music Business	U of M	30 min.
On Upward Paths, Church Music of the Middle Ages	U of M	30 min.
The Oratorio Soloist	U of M	30 min.
O Widening World, the Krummhorne and the Serpent	U of M	30 min.
P is for Percussion	U of M	30 min.
Percussion Sounds	Churchill	16 min.
Pixillation, UFO's, Olympiad, Enigma	Bell Laboratory	15 min.
Quintet, Woodwind Quintet	U of M	30 min.
A Reign of Emotion, Romantic Music of the 19th Century	U of M	30 min.
Search for New Sounds	U of M	30 min.
The Singers, Chants, Troubadors and Madrigals	U of M	30 min.
The Singer's Goal	U of M	30 min.
The Solo Cantata	U of M	30 min.

The Solo Ensemble	U of M	30 min.
The Son of Getron, Medieval Music Drama	U of M	30 min.
The Song Recital	U of M	30 min.
Soul, Clap Hands and Sing, Initial Development of Songs	U of M	30 min.
Sounds and the Composer	U of M	30 min.
Sounds of Brass	U of M	30 min.
Sounds of Percussion	U of M	30 min.
Sounds of Saxophones	U of M	30 min.
Sounds of Singing, a Voice Lesson	U of M	30 min.
Sounds of Strings	U of M	30 min.
Sounds of Woodwinds	U of M	30 min.
Strings and Their Sounds	U of M	30 min.
String Sounds	Churchill	16 min.
Student Glee Club	U of M	30 min.
Taste of an Age, Musical Taste	U of M	30 min.
To Be a Composer	Churchill	25 min.
To Be a Conductor	Churchill	25 min.
To Be a Performer	Churchill	25 min.
Trio, Violin, Viola, and Cello	U of M	30 min.
What Is Music?	Contemporary Music Project	20 min.
What Is Music?	Churchill	16 min.
Wind Sounds	Churchill	16 min.
World of the Baroque	U of M	30 min.
World of Sound	U of M	30 min.

AIMS Instructional Media Service
c/o Crowell-Collier Macmillan Inc.
866-Third Avenue
New York, New York 10022

BFA Instructional Media
2211 Michigan Avenue
Santa Monica, California 90404

Churchill Films
662 N. Robertson Blvd.
Los Angeles, California 90069

U of M = University of Michigan,
310 Maynard Street
Ann Arbor, Michigan 48108

Media Suggestions

A number of teaching plans offered throughout the book could make use of various media. This is particularly the case with the units described in Chapter 5 and the newer teaching procedures described in Chapter 17.

An interesting assist for the use of projects using visual media could be the adaptation of film. If the school has appropriate work facilities, the following ideas could be of interest to some students.

1. Create film strips: Film a setting in various periods, using pictures of persons, of instruments, of paintings, and scenes made from cardboard sets. A carousel slide projector will accomplish the same effect as a film strip. Record background and narration on tape.

2. Color for music themes: While listening, the teacher or student may add a bag of different-colored water onto an overhead projector to dramatize and emotionalize different themes. (Utilize Saran baggies filled with different colored water, and laminate the end with a hot iron to seal.)

3. Create films: Obtain old 16-mm film from libraries. Soak in Clorox to clear the plastic of existing pictures. Using magic marker or felt pens, draw original designs. Remember, film moves at twenty-four frames per second.

accountability—tangible proof that the amount of education received (progress of each child) is in relation to the amount of money spent.

aesthetic—mental and emotional responses to the arts.

arytenoid cartilage—one of two small cartilages in the larynx.

asthenic—slender body type.

athletic—average or medium body type.

behavioral objectives—learning steps or procedures in the education and growth of the individual, which are external and measurable.

cambiata—one of the stages of vocal development between the child voice and the mature voice.

Carnegie unit—the credit or unit earned from a course taught five days a week for one year, usually in senior and junior high schools.

cerebellum—a portion of the brain, located below and behind the cerebrum, which acts as a center for the control of voluntary movements, posture, and equilibrium.

cerebrum—a portion of the brain, located above the cerebellum, which acts as a control for the conscious processes.

CMP—Contemporary Music Project.

core—combining of two or more subject matter areas in some way.

corporal—pertaining to the body; physical.

cricoid cartilage—a ring-like cartilage at the base of the larynx.

cycloid—a fluctuating personality, moving from gaiety to depression.

developmental process—the permitting of the boy voice to mature without the aid of phases, stages, or suggested ranges.

diphase school—(6–2–4) organizational plan for the adolescent school containing grades seven and eight.

double school—(6–6) plan for school organization using two equally divided units.

dual progress—school organization built simultaneously upon formal classes and elective, non-graded classes.

endothermic—to absorb heat, to deflect intensity of feeling, anger, irritation.

esophagus—tube through which food passes from the mouth to the stomach.

exceptional child—noticeably above or below the norm.

expanded-period day—a greater number of class periods than the conventional six.

exploration—to examine unfamiliar or previously unknown areas.

fad—novel approach to a common item.

glottis—division between the vocal cords, particularly on the upper side of the larynx.

heterosexual—pertaining to the opposite sex.

horizontal team—teachers of different disciplines teaching together.

intermediate school—(4–4–4) organizational plan for an adolescent school, one part of three equally divided units.

junior high school—(6–3–3) the most common method or organization for an adolescent school.

larynx—an organ of the respiratory tract containing the vocal cords.

level—degree of ability or development of musical learning.

·macro—large or long in duration, usually applied to rhythms or phrasing.

metropolitan area—geographic region functionally tied to a city of fifty thousand or more.

metropolitanism—social and educational problems resulting from inner city deterioration and suburban growth.

micro—small units or divisions, usually applied to rhythms or phrasing.

middle school—(5–3–4) organizational plan for an adolescent school including sixth grade, but omitting ninth.

module—unit of time, usually twenty minutes, used as a base of scheduling.

MQ—musical quotient, similar in scope and meaning to an IQ.

multiphase process—definite stages of vocal growth leading toward maturity.

non-graded—elimination of grade levels.

ontogenetic—a learning process considering the background of the individual and his particular needs at any given time.

pentad—consisting of five parts.

physiological—the manner in which plants or animals function under differing conditions.

planned gradualism—process to aid the child with increasing independence within the school organization.

psychoanalytic—one consideration of the developing adolescent which involves the interpretation of mental states and conflicting drives, usually stemming from the unconscious.

psycholinguistics—a theory of learning where language becomes the key or the enabler.

psychological—mental phenomena, especially those associated with the conscious.

puberty—the growth period during which an individual becomes physiologically capable of reproduction.

pyknic—short, squat body type, usually with a large abdomen.

review—a retrospective survey.

schizoid—shy and withdrawn personality.

school-within-a-school—small complete units of a large school.

sequence—the order of succession of musical ideas for efficient learning.

synthesis—combining of separate elements into a whole.

team teaching—use of more than one teacher for a subject or subject matter area.

tessitura—that portion of the vocal range most easily and effectively produced.

thyroarytenoid muscle—attached at one end to the arytenoid cartilage and the other to the vocal cords, this muscle aids in the movement of the cords.

thyroid cartilage—the large cartilage of the larynx which, when coming together at the front, forms the Adam's apple.

trachea—tube through which air passes from the larynx to the lungs.

tweener—the young adolescent, usually from ages twelve through fifteen.

unit—a quantity of scholastic work, usually one part of the whole, and having a special function.

vertical team—teachers of the same discipline teaching together.

vocal cords—two membranous bands of the larynx stretching across the trachea.

Index

Index of Music and Musicians

The following names and titles appear in the text, lesson plans, or study materials. Additional composers, titles, albums, and single recordings are found in Suggested Materials lists at the end of chapters or in the Appendices.

Abbey Road, The Beatles, 362
Abravanel, Maurice, 317
"Adoration of the Earth" from *Rite of Spring,* Igor Stravinsky, 104
African folk songs, 108, 327
  "Ghana Game Song," 360, 365, 367
  "Jikel Emaweni," 327
"Ah, No My Dear Mama," German folk song, 96
Aida, Giuseppe Verdi, 320, 321
"All Who Sing," T. Goodban, 69, 71
"America," Henry Carey, 108
"America the Beautiful," Samuel A. Ward, 108
"America, Variation on," Charles Ives, 59, 60, 61
American folk songs, 75–76, 77–78, 108, 110, 393, 394
  "Dear Lisa," 393
  "Hey, Betty Martin," 394
  "It'll Be Comin' Round," 75–76
  "Old MacDonald," 393
  "Workin' on the Railway," 77–78
American Indian music, 97, 98, 99, 100
  "Corn Song," *Songs from the*

Iroquois Longhouse, 99
"Hopi Version of Dixie," *Songs of the Pueblo, Toas, San Ildefonso, Zuni, Hopi,* 100
"I am Going Away," *Songs of the Chippewa,* 99
"Iroquois War Dance," *Songs from the Iroquois Longhouse,* 99
"Love Song," 97, 99, 100
"Omaha Tribal Prayer," 97, 99, 100
"Song of the Indian Coquet," 97, 99, 100
"Song of the Wren," 97, 99, 100
Songs of the Chippewa, 97
Songs from the Iroquois Longhouse, 99
Songs of the Pueblo, Toas, San Ildefonso, Zuni, Hopi, 98
"Toas War Dance," *Songs of the Pueblo, Toas, San Ildefonso, Zuni, Hopi,* 99
"Zuni Rain Dance," *Songs of the Pueblo, Toas, San Ildefonso, Zuni, Hopi,* 100
American mountain song, 70, 79–80
  "He's Going Away," 70, 79–80
American Pie, Don McLean, 360
"American Tune," Paul Simon, 352, 356
"A Mighty Fortress is Our God," Martin Luther, 141, 142, 143
"Anchors Aweigh," Alfred

Miles and Charles Zimmerman, 108
Antheil, George, 380
  Ballet Mecanique, 380
"Appalachian Spring," Aaron Copland, 141
Arab world folk songs, 108
"Army Goes Rolling Along," E. L. Gruber, 108
"Aunt Rhody," traditional, 394, 401

Bach, Johann Sebastian, 122 123, 135–39, 141, 142, 143, 352, 353, 357
  Christmas Oratorio, 353, 357
  "Jesu, Joy of Man's Desiring," 122, 123, 135–39
  "O, Sacred Head," 352
  "Thee With Tender Care," 353, 357
Ballet Mecanique, George Antheil, 380
"Ballet of Unhatched Chicks," from *Pictures at an Exhibition,* Modeste Moussorgsky, 386
Barber of Seville, Gioacchino Rossini, 321
  "Largo al factotum" from, 321
Bartered Bride, Friedrich Smetana, 95, 97
  "Polka" from, 95, 97
Bartok, Bela, 313, 400
  Mikrokosmos, 400
  "New Hungarian Folk Song," 313
Beatles, The, 362, 370
  Abbey Road, 362